Charlotte Mason
COMPANION

Personal Reflections on
The Gentle Art of Learning

KAREN ANDREOLA

CHARLOTTE MASON
RESEARCH & SUPPLY

A Charlotte Mason Companion
Personal Reflections on The Gentle Art of Learning
by Karen Andreola

ISBN 1-889209-02-3

Copyright ©1998 by Karen Andreola
Published by Charlotte Mason Research and Supply Company

Cover illustration by Runcie Tatnall
Cover & Book Design by Mark Dinsmore
Editing by Nancy Drazga

Printed in the United States of America

To my family

Table of Contents

Foreword to the
Original Home Schooling Series

CHARLOTTE MASON founded her "House of Education" in Ambleside, in the heart of the English Lake District, in 1892. "It is far from London," she wrote at the time, "but in view of that fact there is much to be said in its favour. Students will be impressed with the great natural beauty around them, will find a country rich in flowers, mosses and ferns. They will learn to know and love the individuality of great natural features mountain pass, valley, lake and waterfall." The "House of Education" is now the principal's house, "Springfield," and I am writing this foreword in the room that was Charlotte Mason's own living room. I look out of the window and can confirm all its attractions.

Charlotte Mason came to Ambleside when she was nearly fifty, and the college was to be the main focus of her life's work from then until her death in 1923. Hers was no simple success story. Her early childhood is obscure, and she seems never to have wished to elucidate it. She was probably brought up by her father, a Liverpool merchant who, it seems, went bankrupt and then died when Charlotte was still in her teens. Aided by friends of her family, Charlotte became a pupil teacher in Birkenhead and then attended a training college for teachers in London from 1860 to 1861. After qualifying, she taught in an infant school in Worthing, Sussex, until 1873. She then obtained a post on the staff off Bishop Otter Teacher Training College, Chichester, where she lectured in elementary school teaching method. The college was in the forefront of educational thinking in its dedication to the principle of education for all— including girls. W. E. Forster's Education Act of 1870, which provided for elementary schools to be set up across the country, was still fresh and needed trained teachers to implement the promises. The Bishop Otter College certainly influenced Charlotte Mason's thinking, but, for reasons that are difficult now to disentangle, in 1878 Charlotte felt dissatisfied with her work, left the college, and went to live with friends in Bradford in Yorkshire.

Apparently with financial help from these friends (she was certainly never rich), Charlotte began to write. In 1880 she published a series of books on the geography of England, which were well received. But it was her book *Home Education*, published in 1886, that sparked off the most interest. In it one can certainly see the influence of other educational thinkers of the nineteenth century, particularly the child-centered views of Pestalozzi and the artistic ideas of John Ruskin. What Charlotte Mason added was a practical, down-to-earth perspective that showed how one could actually set about and do it. Her style and her exposition were homely, both in the sense that she wrote in an easy, intelligible way, and in the sense that she stressed the influence and responsibility of the home. She also wrote from a firmly held evangelical perspective.

The book turned out to be a kind of educational "Dr. Spock" avidly bought by women anxious to ensure the best possible upbringing for their offspring. The need was real, especially among middle-class women of modest means. Education was a subject of much debate and discussion, which had led to the Education Act of 1870, though the reality of primary education all to often was but the palest reflection of Pestalozzi, Ruskin, or even W. E. Forster. Many concerned parents, perhaps more particularly concerned mothers, were looking for something better. Charlotte Mason's *Home Education* offered it. It explained how parents could—and should—provide their children with a broad, stimulating, even exciting education, far removed from the common diet of so many elementary schools of the day.

The book sold well and in influential circles. Very soon the Parents National Education Union (PNEU) was established, with the bishop of London as its first president. Miss Beale, a formidable protagonist in the fight for women's education, was an early member of the organization, as was Anne Cough, the founder of Newnham College, Cambridge. Branches were set up in many major towns and cities, and by 1890 the organization had its own monthly magazine, "The Parents Review," edited by Charlotte Mason herself. Charlotte had quickly become a leading authority on early childhood.

In 1891 Charlotte came to live in Ambleside. A friend of her student days, Selina Healey, had lived in Ambleside, and Charlotte had visited her and had gotten to know the Lake District well. She loved the area, particularly the quiet town of Ambleside. When she moved into Springfield, she was sure she had found the ideal place to train governesses for young children.

So, in January 1892, the House of Education was established. There were four students. Two years later, with thirteen students, the college moved into Scale How, a beautiful Georgian house across the main road from Springfield on a hill amid the trees with fine views of the town and of Loughrigg across the Rothay valley.

Charlotte saw children as thinking, feeling human beings, as spirits to be kindled and not as vessels to be filled. And she demonstrated how it could be done. She believed all children were entitled to a liberal education based upon good literature and the arts. These were in her own day radical thoughts and practices, certainly not just confined to Charlotte Mason, but few of her contemporaries had the sheer practicality that she displayed. The practicing school attached to the House of Education took in local children with no payment; Charlotte firmly believed that her liberal education ideas were applicable to all children regardless of class, status, or ability, and she put her ideas into practice, as she always did.

The college flourished, never larger than fifty students in Charlotte's own lifetime, but with a reputation out of proportion to its size. By the 1920s the PNEU had established several schools as well as a correspondence school, run from Ambleside, which sent out lesson notes and advice on educational matters to parents and governesses.

Charlotte died on January 16, 1923; by then she was the object of deep veneration within the movement. She was buried in the churchyard at Ambleside, close to the graves of W. E. Forster and the Arnold family. Educationists flourished—and died—in Ambleside.

— *John Thorley, Principal*
Charlotte Mason College, 1989

Preface

· · · · · · · · · · · · · · · · · · ·

MY PRAYER is that this book will provide the encouragement and information that mothers need who wish to give their children a Charlotte Mason-style education. I've tried to provide a broad range of Charlotte Mason's philosophical and practical ideas. However, to more fully comprehend her working philosophy of education, I invite you to seize the odd and quiet moment to read Charlotte's own writing. *Companion* is not meant to replace the reading of *Home Education,* or any of her other volumes. I do not claim to condense Charlotte's wonderful work into my own writing, making it a "C. M. in a nutshell." My heroine does not fit into a nutshell any more than she fits into the pages of this book. Instead, I welcome you to consider Charlotte's principles of education—what I call her "gentle art of learning"—as you read my humble opinions and examples of those principles.

Perhaps, like myself, you don't always read books neatly from beginning to end, but sometimes (in a less patient mood) are drawn to thumb through and follow the dictates of your fancy. That's OK. In fact, feel free to do so, because the most important concepts are repeated (similar ingredients in a different dish). So much of what Charlotte proposed interrelates and works well together, supporting the central theme of living an educational life.

I was excited about commissioning a professional artist to do a portrait of Charlotte for this book. I think such a colorful one as this has been needed for some time. The background depicts the Lake District in Ambleside, England, where Charlotte spent so many of her days teaching teachers, answering letters, walking the hills, and reading Sir Walter Scott (all of his novels, on a rotating basis). The original oil painting is hanging in our house.

Much of my work for Charlotte Mason Research & Supply Company is in opening, sorting, and answering hundreds of pieces of mail. In answering this mail, I try to promote the wonderful words of Charlotte and minister with encouragement. However, due to the

9

amount I receive, I have found it impossible to answer these queries in adequate detail. In this book I have attempted to answer the questions I am most frequently asked—hopefully in much greater detail than my handwritten letters permit.

Although I strongly believe Charlotte's philosophy and method work well in the high school years, this book introduces you to them within the context of the elementary school years. I have finished laying a Charlotte Mason foundation during the elementary years of my eldest daughter and have begun to see the fruit of it in our high school experience. With a little modification, Charlotte's philosophy and method can carry over to high school work. Perhaps this will be the theme of *A Charlotte Mason Companion, Volume Two.*

A Charlotte Mason Kit for Each Grade Level

The most frequently-asked question is whether there exists a full curriculum course based on the Charlotte Mason method that would carry a parent through all the subjects that Charlotte advocated in a manner that holds true to her method. Ahhh . . . wouldn't this be a dream come true? But from Charlotte's writings I sense that she believed a PNEU education really doesn't boil down to one particular set of books, set of pictures, set of music tapes, etc. It has to do with students forming relationships with these things, whether they are part of a curriculum or not. Somehow her ideal dwindles just a little when we confine it to a set course.

Many of you already know that Charlotte adjusted and adapted her course from year to year. But a course must be obtained by each Charlotte Mason-minded person. Some of us piece together a course of our own choosing. Others follow an established course and tailor it to suit more of a Charlotte Mason philosophy. However a curriculum is chosen, it is undertaking it with Charlotte's philosophy as a foundation that somehow imbues the books, the pictures, the music, the mathematics, the science and nature study, with a certain brightness.

I feel that those of you who have written me are going forth toward an ideal, unsure of all the turns and twists in the road, but sure of the kind of education you wish to give your children. And your personal ideal is what I have tried to help you achieve. Thank you for supporting and complimenting my work. It has been encouraging—and the best part of all—to meet you through the mail over the years. ➤⊢

Chapter One

·······································

What Drew Me to
A Charlotte Mason Education

IT HAS BEEN SOME YEARS since I first read Susan Schaeffer Macaulay's book, *For the Children's Sake*. It has been the most helpful book in forming my own philosophy of education of all those I have read, and I have referred to it often since that first reading. What intrigued me from the first was Mrs. Macaulay's repeated mention of the work of Charlotte Mason, a 19th-century British educator who was instrumental in founding a chain of parent–controlled schools, called the Parents' National Education Union (PNEU). I learned that she had also positively influenced many families to employ her early education and child training methods in their own homes. I wanted to know more about this amazing woman and her work with children.

Consequently (and not a little, no doubt, as a result of my oft-voiced yearning to learn more about Charlotte), my husband, Dean, acquired copies of Charlotte's original writings. Believing they should be made available to the Christian world, in 1989 he asked Tyndale House to publish them. They did, and the result is the six-volume set entitled *The Original Home Schooling Series*. Since that time I have been trying my best to put into practice with my own children all the wonderful things I've read about. And I've been enthusiastically sharing what I've been learning with other mothers who have also been drawn to Charlotte's philosophy and method. I am thankful to Susan Macaulay for putting me in touch with Charlotte's sound, sensible, and wholesome educational philosophy.

This book is the result of nearly ten years of experimenting, sharing, and writing. If you have read all the issues of my *Parents' Review* magazine "for home training and culture," you will already be familiar with many of the ideas in this book. Perhaps you have read my column in Mary Pride's magazine, where I have had the opportunity to share Charlotte's findings with a wider audience. Maybe you've read some of my product reviews and endorsements in the Great Christian Books catalog. On the other hand, everything in this book may be completely new to you. Whatever your prior acquaintance with me or with Charlotte Mason's ideas, I'd like to share with you what drew me to a Charlotte Mason education.

Living Books

One of the first things that impressed me about Charlotte was her method of using whole books and first-hand sources. At the time, my first two children were young, and we were already in the habit of taking the bus or walking to the local library, with our youngest in the stroller. (We were living in England, where walking is a normal everyday activity.) Along with illustrated story books, I also read aloud from nonfiction picture books. Therefore it wasn't difficult to carry this concept over into homeschooling in the early elementary years—those years when "whole" books normally begin to disappear to make room for authoritative textbooks.

Textbooks compiled by a committee tend to be crammed with facts and information. This dryness is deadening to the imagi-nation of the child. Charlotte advocated what she called "living" books. Whole books are living in the sense that they are written by a single author who shares personally his favorite subject with us, and we pick up his enthusiasm. Textbooks written by one author—usually these are ones written some time ago—might make this claim, too.

Charlotte noted that very few real books were ever put into the hands of children in school. This, she thought, was a shame, since England is a land so known for its literary genius.

Narration

With living books a child gains knowl-edge through his own effort. He digs out facts and information, and he expresses what he has learned by clothing it in liter-ary (conversational) language—in short, by telling it back to you in his own words. The simplicity and thoroughness of this method of having a child narrate intrigued me. I became convinced that Charlotte was correct in her claim that narration is the best way to acquire knowledge from books. Narration also provides opportunities for a child to form an opinion or make a judgment, no matter how crude. Because narration takes the place of fill-in-the-blank and multiple-choice tests, it enables the child to bring all his mental faculties into play. The child learns to call on the vocabulary and descriptive power of good writers as he "tells" his own version of the passage or chapter. My experience with using narration over the years is shared with you in later chapters.

No Homework

Another attraction of Charlotte's philosophy is that her schools never gave homework to students under the age of thirteen. When a child follows her method, there is no need for homework in the elementary years, because the child immediately deals with the literature at hand and proves his mastery by narrating at the time of the reading. Studies have proved homework to be less effective than this form of immediate reinforcement.

Instead of homework, my children enjoy cozy evenings with good books and parental attention.

No Grades–Short Lessons

Charlotte was an idealist who created an opportunity for putting her ideas into practice. She wanted children to be motivated by admiration, faith, and love, instead of artificial stimulants such as prizes (stickers, candy, or money), competition, and grades.

As a result of Charlotte's methods, her students retained their inborn curiosity and developed a love of knowledge that they

maintained all through their lives. The children took examinations, narrating orally or on paper from "those lovely books" that they had read during the semester. Each child learned first to acquire the habit of attention by listening to and narrating short stories, and by completing short lessons in the drills and skills. Short lessons discouraged dawdling and they encouraged the child to concentrate and make his best effort. Because the Charlotte Mason method employs whole books, narration, and short lessons, a child taught this way will try his best even though he will not be graded.

My own children love reading. "Ma, guess what?" can be heard in our house when one of the children enters the room to tell me about something new she has read silently on her own. Now—years after we began using this method—my older children are disciplined enough to do much longer lessons in subjects that they do not "take to" naturally, such as mathematics and grammar. I owe this success to Charlotte Mason, who has taught me the gentle art of teaching.

Free Afternoons

Formal lessons in the Charlotte Mason scheme of things end at one P.M. or earlier, if the children are quite young. High school students will probably need some afternoon study time, but overall the afternoon is free for leisure. This is another aspect of Charlotte's philosophy that so easily finds its way into the modern homeschool.

Leisure for children usually means running, climbing, yelling, and so forth—all out of doors. It has been observed that boys particularly cannot flourish without this opportunity for physical activity. Handicrafts, practicing an instrument, chores, cooking, gardening, visiting lonely neighbors, observing and recording the wonders of nature may also be enjoyed during this time.

Sadly, public school children (young

and old) must endure such long lessons and long hours that they are frequently tranquilized with drugs in order to pass through the system. They ride the bus home just in time to see the sun set and do homework.

Charlotte placed an emphasis on being outdoors to observe nature. Her students kept a Nature Notebook of drawings and descriptions of their many "finds." Noble thoughts and expressions of appreciation for God's creation found in poetry, hymns, and mottoes also decorated these notebooks. I include a chapter on nature study because I consider it to be the foundation of all the sciences. Because I spent most of my summers outdoors in field and wood, I wanted to give my children the opportunity to enjoy and learn about the wonders of nature, too. I share in this book Charlotte's concern for learning in the fresh air and hope to provide some ideas that will strenthen limb, lung, and intellect.

Few Lectures

I was also drawn to Charlotte's philosophy because it doesn't require me to give lectures. Charlotte pointed out that I need not be a certified teacher trained in the skill of giving lectures in order for my children to learn. This was a relief to me.

I have never had a formal swimming lesson, but I spent many of my childhood summers in the water without any fear of it. That thought occurred to me *this* summer as I was on my back, floating, trusting the buoyancy of salt sea water, at rest over the rolling waves of the Atlantic ocean, while my children battled the breakers and rode them into shore. I must have educated myself by watching others and doing what they did. Likewise I have never had a formal teaching lesson—neither do I have a state certification—but I find myself at rest in my teaching nonetheless. How did this come about? By trusting in the buoyancy of Charlotte's wisdom and direction and then jumping into the water.

Through Charlotte's method, we need not do very much teaching. Children gain the ability to educate themselves. They do not depend upon notes they have taken from a teacher's lecture—where most of the information has been pre-digested by the teacher. With Charlotte's superior method of narration from books, the child, at age six or seven, comments on the carefully chosen words of an author in essay form, either oral or written. Too much explaining by the teacher can be a detriment to self-education, a concept that is addressed in a later chapter.

Girls & Boys

Ideas and Culture

Children's love of knowledge is dependent upon how clearly ideas are presented to them. The mind feeds upon ideas. To quote Charlotte, "Ideas must reach us directly from the mind of the thinker, and it is chiefly by the means of the books they have written that we get in touch with the best minds."

This includes all forms of human expression, including paintings, poetry, music, dance, etc. This is why Charlotte said that the Bible and "varied human reading as well as the appreciation of the humanities (culture) is not a luxury, a tidbit, to be given to children now and then, but their very bread of life."

Charlotte's curriculum enabled children of all classes to experience books and culture in abundance, in contrast to the typical Victorian mind-set that the arts and humanities belonged only to the "well-to-do" classes.

Today, with so many pictures and art print books available, children can observe museum pieces and learn to recognize the works of dozens of artists over time just by changing what goes under the thumb tack once every two weeks or so. Our children can easily become familiar with the music of great composers by listening to cassettes and CDs, when years ago it would have been necessary for them to visit a concert hall. The chapters on music and art explain more about introducing art and music into the homeschool.

Charlotte wished to prevent dryness in her teachers and so she reminded them never to be without a good book at hand. She understood the necessity to keep reading, to keep growing in the spiritual and intellectual life. She wanted teachers to pursue cultural activities, too. I bid you do the same—to take part in Mother Culture.

Education is a Discipline

One of the challenges of homeschooling is that it is simply a new thing to think about and to do. I wanted to teach and train my children, but because I was taught and trained by institutions, teaching this new way felt rather awkward at first. Feelings of insecurity and inadequacy make for a distraught mother.

Happily, Charlotte's definition of education most surely includes a large dose of discipline. This helps the anxious mother get everything under control. What Charlotte meant by "discipline," in Victorian-day terms, is that proper education must be supported by good habits. Charlotte said,

> The mother needs to acquire her own habit of training her children so that, by and by, it is not troublesome to her, but a pleasure, She devotes herself to the formation of one habit in her children at a time, doing no more than watch over those already formed.

For more of the "hows and whys" of instilling good habits, I invite you to read the chapter on habit.

Sane Education

If the above ideas sound as sane and sensible to you as they do to me, perhaps it is because Charlotte Mason hasn't been the only one sharing these "open secrets." Others are now voicing conclusions similar to those that Charlotte Mason advocated so many years ago. It is said that great minds think alike. Whatever the case, these newer voices are confirming Charlotte's ideas about what makes a well-brought-up person. ⇥

Chapter Two

·······································

A Living God for
a Living Education

–by Dean Andreola

CHARLOTTE MASON was a pioneer in the field of education and educational reform. Her significant contribution helped mold turn-of-the-century Great Britain. With the passing of years her methods were widely assimilated into the (secular) British educational system, yet the Christian principles upon which they were established were for the most part eliminated. As a result, her writings became less popular, went out of print and were hard to find. She remained generally unknown in the United States. Then in 1984, Susan Schaeffer Macaulay, in her book *For the Children's Sake,* introduced Miss Mason to modern readers hungry for Christian-based alternatives in education, child raising, and character development. Four years later, while working for a literature mission in England, I searched for and found Charlotte Mason's complete works in six volumes, which were reprinted in the United States under the name *The Original Home Schooling Series.*

In order to more fully appreciate Charlotte Mason and her Christian-based method of education, I feel it is necessary to describe more fully the times in which she lived, and share with you from some of her own writings so that you will more fully understand the passion, the high esteem, and the reverence that she had for Jesus Christ her Savior.

In England, during the late 1800's, children were not treated as whole persons. They had no rights to speak of. Poor children of the lower classes were labeled by the well-to-do as "bad" and were considered of little use to society. They received little or no education, and were required to work many long hours in harsh and unsafe conditions—if they were "fortunate" enough to find work. On the other hand, children from wealthy families were labeled "good" and received the best education money could buy. But even wealthy parents spent little time directly raising and educating their own children. This task was left to nurses, governesses, and tutors. Overall, many people were indifferent to the spiritual, emotional, and intellectual needs of children.

About this time, Dickens and others began to bring the plight of children to public attention, and the national conscience began to change. By the turn of the century, Charlotte Mason had become one of the key figures in the battle for better education for children of all classes and the restoration of the family. She took as one of her mottoes, "For the Children's Sake." She even started a retreat center for parents to teach them the fundamentals of parenting. Those who attended nicknamed the retreat "The House of the Holy Spirit," because here they were learning to draw closer to God as well as to their children.

In the preface to all her books Charlotte reminds us that "children are born persons" (full of human potential). "They are not born either 'good' or 'bad'" (in relation to their family's blood line, wealth or social rank), "but with possibilities for good and evil" —(not in regard to their eternal or spiritual condition, but rather in regard to their potential for good or bad behavior and character). And it is most definitely the role of parents to shape children for the better.

Throughout her writings she addresses the spiritual condition of children at great length, and very clearly explains the parents' responsibility for the child's spiritual as well as intellectual upbringing. In *Home Education* she said:

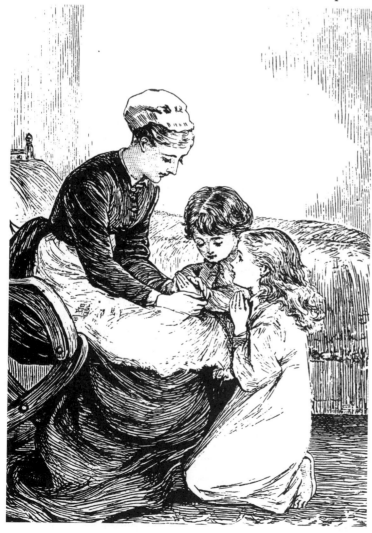

The Essence of Christianity is Loyalty to a Person— Christ, our King. Here is a thought to unseal the fountains of love and loyalty, the treasures of faith and imagination, bound up in the child. The very essence of Christianity is personal loyalty, passionate loyalty to our adorable Chief. We have laid other foundations— regeneration, sacraments, justification, works, faith, the Bible—any of which, however necessary to salvation in its due place and proportion, may become a religion about Christ and without Christ. And now a time of sifting has come upon us, and thoughtful people decline to know anything about our religious systems, they write down all our orthodox beliefs as things not knowable. Perhaps this may be because, in thinking much of our salvation, we have put out of sight our King . . . Let us save Christianity for our children by bringing them into allegiance to Christ the King. How? How did the old Cavaliers bring up sons and daughters, in passionate loyalty and reverence for not too worthy princes? Their own hearts were full of it; their lips spake it; their acts proclaimed it; their style of clothes, all was one proclamation of the boundless devotion to their king and his cause. That civil war, whatever else it did, or missed doing, left a parable for Christian people. If a Stuart prince could command such measure of loyalty, what shall we say of "the Chief amongst ten thousand, the altogether lovely?"

Again she writes about the Savior:

Here is a thought to be brought tenderly before the child in the moments of misery that follow wrong-doing. "My poor little boy, you have been very naughty today! Could you not help it?" "No, mother," with sobs. "No, I suppose not; but there is a way of help." And then the mother tells her child how the Lord Jesus is our Saviour, because He saves us from our sins . . .The indwelling of Christ is a thought particularly fit for the children, because their large faith does not stumble at the mystery, their imagination leaps readily to the marvel, that the King Himself should inhabit a little child's heart.

Regarding our parental responsibility in religious training, in *Parents and Children* Charlotte writes,

To bring the human race, family by family, child by child, out of the savage and inhuman desolation where He is not, into the light and warmth and comfort of the presence of God, is no doubt, the chief thing we have to do in the world. And this individual work

with each child, being the most momentous work in the world, is put into the hands of the wisest, most loving, disciplined and divinely instructed of human beings. Be ye perfect as your Father is perfect, is the perfection of parenthood, perhaps to be attained in its fullness only through parenthood. There are a few mistaken parents, ignorant parents, a few indifferent parents, even one in a thousand, callous parents; but the good that is done upon the earth is done, under God, by parents, whether directly or indirectly . . . The highest duty imposed upon him, it is also the most delicate; and he will have infinite humility, gentleness, love, and sound judgment, if he would present his child to God and the thought of God to the soul of his child.

Although Charlotte Mason wrote chiefly about education, child training, and parenting, she would never stray far from spiritual matters, as this was the driving force behind her method. It is what gave her method life and hope. She once said that "such a recognition of the work of the Holy Spirit as the Educator of mankind, in things intellectual as well as in things moral and spiritual, gives us 'new thoughts of God, new hopes of Heaven,' a sense of harmony in our efforts and of acceptance of all that we are." She taught that we, as educators of our children, must strive to work in co-operation with the Holy Spirit. As I read through *The Original Homeschooling Series*, I am surprised and grateful for Charlotte Mason's unashamed love for the Savior, and for the beautiful and inspiring verse she employed to communicate her brilliant and living ideas. She wrote a section in *Parents and Children* called "Parents as Inspirers." For me, Charlotte has been, and continues to be, fuel for the fire of ideas—a true Inspirer of Parents! ⇥

Be sure that your children each day have:

 SOMETHING OR SOMEONE TO LOVE

SOMETHING TO DO

SOMETHING TO THINK ABOUT

Chapter Three

·····················

What Is Education?

"The finest of all the fine arts is the art of doing good and yet it is the least cultivated." —T. DeWitt Talmage

HOW DO YOU PICTURE EDUCATION? A schoolroom crammed with bored children? A teacher idly lecturing about things that the children will soon forget? Education is thought of as an affair for teachers, something to major in in college, something that requires a large amount of brains and has very little to do with ordinary people.

Charlotte Mason had a different concept of education. If Charlotte were with us today, she would use the old Saxon phrase "bringing up" to express her educational ideas.

We all wish our children to be well brought up, and when we have come to understand what that means, we know that we need to go beyond simply fitting the child with the basic skills to make a living. Making lots of money is not identical with success, and a person who succeeds at making lots of money but has not the moral attributes, cultural niceties, educational background, or self-knowledge to use his wealth wisely will find his life empty indeed. Every person must achieve his own kind of success, and such success is far more important than how much money he makes.

First and foremost in importance is the power to live the life God has given in the way God intended. In order to have this power, a person must be at his best in his heart, mind, and soul. He must know how to choose good and how to refuse evil.

We, as persons, are not enlightened by means of multiple-choice tests or grades, but rather by the other people in our lives that we come to know, admire, and love. We are educated by our friendships and by our intimacies. For instance, think how the actions of someone you admire influence your behavior. Similarly, think also of how a boy's interest is sparked by a hobby he loves, and to which he devotes all his time and trouble. Whether it be gardening, keeping house, or governing a state, love of work—like love of people—teaches things that no school, no system, can.

Children are inspired by relationships, and this helps form their personalities. And so, throughout their educational life, we put them in touch with persons, places, and things.

Providing Opportunities

What is the best curriculum for a well-brought-up person? Whatever the specifics of the curriculum used in your home, be sure that your children each day have:

- Something or someone to love
- Something to do
- Something to think about

Something to Love

Whether it be parents, brothers, sisters, friends, a cat, dog, rabbit, or hamster (in some homeschooling circles it seems that sheep, goats, chickens, and pigs are also coming back in style), everybody needs someone and some thing to love. There are

opportunities for love in every home. There are also many ways to provide services (labors of love) to others if you look for them.

Something to Do

By "something to do," I mean of course something *worthwhile* to do. A child staring passively at a television screen is not really doing anything worthwhile.

When our children complain, "There is nothing to do!" they really mean, "Please amuse me." Amusing oneself with idle pastimes all day is not really doing anything. A little amusement is fine, but boredom will be transformed into real interest when your children are given meaningful tasks of recreation or of service. They like to see and measure results of their activities. A frequent request at our house is "Mom, look what I made!".

Such "things to do" could be:

- Sewing doll clothes, quilting, learning to make a mitten
- Planning or tending a garden
- Helping stamp and stuff the support group newsletter
- Peeling vegetables for soup or salad
- Learning ten new French words from a French song
- Listening to little sister read aloud
- or teaching her how to "jump in" at jump rope
- or pitch a stone at hopscotch
- Putting together a model Roman villa, a pyramid, a castle
- Writing a play to put on with family members
- or recording a radio play with sound effects
- or making puppets for a puppet show.

Something to Think About

"Something to think about" gets left out in so many homes, yet it is one of the most important parts of living. Thinking is quite impossible without *something to think about.* It is enjoying other peoples' ideas and thoughts and jokes . . . noticing beauty in music and pictures . . . enjoying country sights and sounds, birds and flowers. Children's horizons of thought need to be wider than their workbooks. Children who are not given something to think about grow up at best with two ideas: to work hard and to amuse themselves when they are not working.

Everyone needs a certain amount of amusement, but amusement is not an adequate substitute for something to think about. People who enjoy using their minds do not rush off to every kind of amusement or get hooked on routine visits to the video store.

When you give your children a Charlotte Mason-style education, you will be endowing them with the substantial things of our culture, and their interest in these things will naturally spill out, like a cup running over, into their leisure activities, even as they enter adulthood. When children are guided to seek after something to think about during their home life, they will continue this habit throughout their lives.

25

So where do we find something to think about? Charlotte Mason often said that ideas to grow on are present in books—real, "living" books. And it is we as parents who are responsible for giving our children a taste of the finest, so that they will acquire a taste for the best our civilization has to offer. The power of finding joy and refreshment in reading is an incredible resource! Charlotte wished every child to be equipped with this power, a power that was more than just finding out the sense of printed words, a power that included making the written thoughts and experiences of great men and women his own. This is why she required narration from quality books. The child learned to dig out the ideas by relating a passage in their *own* words.

Whatever curriculum you use, remember to give yourself and your children three things: something to love, something to do, and something to think about. Accomplish this and your goal of having well brought up children will be much advanced, and you will be experiencing, as well, the educational life of which Charlotte Mason spoke.[1]

Questions for Personal Reflection or Support Group Discussion

1. *When you hear the word "education," what is the first impression that comes to mind?*

2. *What is meant by "We are educated by our intimacies"?*

3. *What opportunities for loving can your home provide?*

4. *Name some worthwhile things to do at home or for others outside the home.*

5. *Have you heard it wisely put, "You are what you eat?" In what way do we become what we read (with discernment and discretion)?*

6. *What are three simple things to remember about educating—whatever curriculum you choose?*

Your Own Personal Reflections

Chapter Four

....

Education is a Science of Relations

WE PARENTS CAN BECOME QUITE ANXIOUS about covering and completing all the requirements for a particular grade level, and seeing that our children excel in the skills demanded of that grade level. It's a woeful business when parents look toward doing what the grand system of education says is right for a child within their little homeschool. But when parents pursue knowledge for its own sake they need not be subservient to this grand system. Many young children hunger for knowledge. Yet they dutifully serve the system of textbook overview with never-ending worksheets and, under a system that does not feed their hunger for vibrant, vital knowledge, they begin to pine away. It is then that Mother loses confidence and feels discouraged and unqualified to teach. The children, for their part, find it harder and harder to obey. Parents and children alike are stuck in a system that stifles curiosity and initiative, and makes learning uninteresting.

Charlotte Mason understood this predicament. More than one hundred years ago she was at work making changes. She had a strikingly different and refreshing view of education. Charlotte resisted systems. Her focus was on developing a philosophy and method of education. She said,

> The idea that vivifies teaching . . . is that 'Education is a Science of Relations;' by which phrase we mean that children come into the world with a natural [appetite] for, and affinity with, all the material of knowledge; for interest in the heroic past and in the age of myths; for a desire to know about everything that moves and lives, about strange places and strange peoples; for a wish to handle material and to make; a desire to run and ride and row and do whatever the law of gravitation permits. Therefore . . . we endeavor that he shall have relations of pleasure and intimacy established with as many as possible of the interests proper to him; not learning a slight or incomplete smattering about this or that subject, but plunging into vital knowledge, with a great field before him which in all his life he will not be able to explore. In this conception we get that 'touch of emotion' which vivifies knowledge, for it is probable that we *feel* only as we are brought into our proper vital relations.

Doesn't the above passage sound like a person who knew children? Charlotte reached these conclusions as a result of spending her days with children. Generations of children were brought up on her principles. In her later years, she started a training college in the beautiful country of the Lake District to train young women to teach children by her practical and beneficial principles. She set up a little community school for children on the premises. For almost all of the ten years I have spent teaching my own children, I have tried to follow Charlotte's freeing advice and put my children directly in touch with knowledge. My training college has been Charlotte's original writings. My homeschool has been the training ground. Acquiring math and language skills are important "have to's," but we have also studied the *"want* to's."

Only during moments of worrying—when I compare our little homeschool to a grand system—have I felt on my shoulders a burden hard to bear. My children have learned much of what others say they are supposed to know, but more importantly, they have been learning what I wanted them to know and they have explored on their own within my safe hedge of guidance. I have learned to understand the balance of keeping to a schedule and holding to a structure while allowing for all the wonderful "unscheduled" learning experiences that can feasibly be accomplished. Charlotte's yoke is easy.

It was Charlotte's desire that all children gain knowledge about—and establish relations with—God, man, and the universe.

God

Home is the place to learn about God. The Amish learn the three "R's" in their one-room schoolhouses. At home they have a different set of three "R's" —religion, respect, and responsibility.

The desire for children to know God personally is in the heart of every Christian educator. Children learn truths about God and his attributes through the Old Testament Bible stories, the life of Christ, the catechism, prayer, and our example of living the Christian life.

Like theologians before and after her, Charlotte held to the fact that all truth is divine, that "every good gift of knowledge and insight comes from above, that the Lord the Holy Spirit is the supreme educator of mankind, and that the culmination of all education is that personal knowledge of, and intimacy with, God, in which our being finds its fullest perfections."

I think the following poem by the Quaker poet John Greenleaf Whittier, which is one of my favorites, highlights very well Charlotte's sentiments:

We search the world for truth. We cull
The good, the true, the beautiful,
From graven stone and written scroll,
And all old flower-fields of the soul;
And when seekers of the best,
We come back laden from our quest,
To find that all the sages said
Is in the Book our mothers read.

Man

Relationships are an important part of the human experience. Through homeschooling I have felt I could more effectively develop and retain a close relationship with my children. I wouldn't want to turn into the lady who quietly and complacently stirs the gravy on the stove in the evenings, ignorant of how her children spent the last six hours of their day, or be the lady who waits in the hot parking lot to taxi her children somewhere different each afternoon, or the woman who sees to it that the homework is done even though she is exhausted from her career outside the home, her children exhausted from their schedules as well. And I would *dread* becoming the mother whose words and precepts, in the eyes of her worldly children, are less relevant than those of their peers or their youth

group leader. I agree with Queen Victoria's assertion that "The greatest maxim of all is that children should be brought up as simply and in as domestic a way as possible, and that (not interfering with their lessons) they should be as much as possible with their parents, and learn to place the greatest confidence in them in all things."[1]

My husband and I did whatever we could to allow me to stay at home. It wasn't easy. We have had to move dozens of times, from rented place to rented place, from job to job, from state to state. We started a small home business. We even lived with relatives on four separate occasions. But I wouldn't trade our life for the life of any of the ladies above. Though it is an awesome responsibility, I am so thankful that I can be with my children and be the greatest influence in their lives.

As William Ross Wallace says in his 1865 poem, "What Rules the World:"

They say a man is mighty,
He governs land and sea,
He wields a mighty scepter
O'er lesser powers that be;
But a mightier power and stronger
Man from his throne has hurled,
For the hand that rocks the cradle
Is the hand that rules the world.

Next to God and the family, Charlotte Mason thought the main part of a child's education should be concerned with "the great human relationships, relationships of love and service, of authority and obedience, of reverence and pity and neighborly kindness; relationships with [extended family], friend and neighbor, to 'cause' and country, . . . to the past and the present.

31

History, literature, archaeology, art, languages, whether ancient or modern, travel and tales of travel; all of these are in one way or other the record or the expression of persons."

Looking with eyes accustomed to seeing things in terms of subjects, we can accommodate our record-keeping responsibilities and employ such subject headings as history, literature, or science, for example. But all the while we can be happy to know that we are taking advantage of the freedom and opportunity to put our children and ourselves in touch with the study of persons and God's dealings with persons. What a joy it is to see various homeschool catalogs filled with biographies, historical fiction, legend, myth, and delightful picture books—all written by authors who love their subjects. Within our grasp there is a wealth of information in the form of literary language. Charlotte would be pleased to see that so many children have escaped the bounds of dry textbooks that present the dry facts of history stripped bare of any life—stripped of the emotions, the struggles, the ideas, and the religious faith of the men and women of whose lives history is comprised. "What is all history," said Emerson, "but the work of ideas, a record of the incomparable energy which his infinite aspirations infuse into man? In its pages it is always persons we see more than principles. Historical events are interesting to us mainly in connection with feelings, the sufferings, and interests of those by whom they are accomplished. In history we are surrounded by men long dead, but whose speech and whose deeds survive . . ."[2]

Ourselves

In Shakespeare's *Hamlet,* the character Laertes is given some wise advice as he leaves the safety of the castle walls to make his way in the world. His loving father, the Lord Chamberlain, making his appeal to his son, ends with these words:

This above all, to thine own self be true,
And it must follow, as the night the day,
Thou canst not then be false to any man.
Farewell; my blessing season this in thee!

— Hamlet, Act I Scene iii

Like the Lord Chamberlain, Charlotte thought one of the relations proper to a child is to know himself. (Self-examination is different from introspection.) A child should be true to himself, aware of his weaknesses of character, admit when he is cross, selfish, clumsy, lacking self-control, etc. But also he should understand that because he is a child of God, his soul is precious and he can attempt great things for God because so many beautiful possibilities are available to him. Charlotte could think of no book to recommend to parents to teach their children what it means to be a human being, so she wrote *Ourselves* and suggested it be read little by little, given by means of Sunday talks.

Universe

"The child who learns his science from a textbook has no chance of forming relations with things as they are because his kindly obtrusive teacher makes him believe that to know *about* things is the same thing as knowing them personally," said Charlotte.

At a recent meeting at my house, the topic was "Education is the Science of Relations." I gave a ten-minute talk on how we can look at education as "getting children in touch with things." I asked the mothers seated comfortably around my living room to share what relations their children had formed.

"My little boy is very interested in ants. He watches them so attentively," said one mother. She smiled while she shared.

Another mother said, "I gave my

daughter *Little Women* by Louisa May Alcott and she has been reading Louisa's other books on her own."

"My daughter showed particular interest in anything to do with American Indians, so we made leather moccasins, read Longfellow's "Hiawatha," and spent more time reading about different tribes than I'd done with my eldest child," said another.

It was my turn. "My son likes anything to do with space," I chimed in as I held up one of the books I had taken out of the local library.

Grandpa Takes Me to the Moon by Timothy R. Gaffney had lain around the house for a day. "Nigel, would you like me to read this to you?" I asked my son.

"I've already read it," he answered plainly.

"Oh," I said simply.

During the previous month—in February or March of 1997—I had pointed out from which part of the sky the Hale-Bopp comet might possibly be seen. I had read aloud from a library book on comets that traced the history of who had spotted Haley's comet and when. Nigel showed no special response but was interested in the idea of such a thing existing. Later that same week he screamed for me from the upstairs bathroom where he was

supposed to be undressing for his bath. I thought there was something dreadfully wrong, so, trying to remain calm, I rushed to him. As soon as I entered the bathroom he pointed out the dark window to the night sky and said excitedly, "There's the Hale-Bopp comet!"

Dad was skeptical but came bounding in with his binoculars.

"You're right, that's it!" he agreed.

"Wow, cool!" Nigel hooted.

It might be that he never took a bath that night, I can't remember. But I will always remember that he made a relation with something in the universe. It contributed to his curiosity to learn more about anything out in space.

A Special Day

One of my friends who couldn't come to the meeting told me about her family's walk by a lake. Her husband is fond of the countryside near the Chesapeake Bay. He works late but since in the summer the sun sets later in the day, after supper one summer evening he drove his family to his favorite park. One by one he pointed out the ducks and told his children the names of the four different kinds of ducks they were seeing. Then they just relaxed by the water's edge and watched them. Their five-year-old son, who has Down's syndrome, came closer and closer to one duck who couldn't walk away as fast as the others. It was handicapped. When the boy caught up with it he fed it some bread crusts. His mother noticed how her son was drawn to this duck and how he gently spoke to it. It occurred to her that her son instinctively knew that this duck had something different about it. Perhaps he knew that it was handicapped like himself. Charlotte taught that "the first step in intimacy is recognition. We don't measure a child's education solely by his progress in the three "R's," but by the number of living and growing things he knows by look, name, and habitat." I think my friend's evening provided a gentle way of seizing the opportunities God provides for making relations with the things of his creation.

Signs of Forming a Relation

When a child shows interest that he wants to know more about something, that is one sign that he is forming a relation with it. He cares about it. Compare this with the familiar question, "Do we have to know this for the test?" In other words, the student will read and try to remember this bit or that if he is going to be graded on it, but there is no real interest in learning about it. Charlotte said that unless our method of education allows children the opportunity to establish relations with many different things, a gallon of teaching will result in only an ounce of learning. As Essex Cholmondely—a teacher from Charlotte's training college—wrote in an article that appeared in the *Parents' Review:* "We never know just where a child's talents lie, until we give him a variety of opportunities and a wide curriculum. The child is eclectic; he may choose this or that; 'therefore, in the morning sow thy seed, and in the evening withhold not thy hand, for thou knowest not which shall prosper.'"

Friendship with Knowledge

Charlotte urges us to establish a relationship with Knowledge. A relationship with Knowledge is like a friendship. When you are introduced to someone, you are courteous and friendly, but you don't have a meaningful relationship. To establish one often requires patience and perseverance. Unfortunately, many lessons—such as those in many textbooks—are only introductory. "It is nice to meet you," we say, nodding to Knowledge. But we need to go about after introductions are made and work toward establishing a relationship if we are really going to "know."

Ancient Mr. Smith has been shoeing horses in Vermont for fifty-five years. His least favorite horse to shoe is the Morgan and he tells young James why. Wow! What knowledge can be had through James' direct contact with one who really knows his trade and enthusiastically shares his knowledge. Mr. Smith even lets James find things out for himself by allowing James to do for himself and learn from (not too dangerous) mistakes.

Firsthand experience is not always available or convenient. Our children may not be able to hold a conversation or be personally in touch with a deep sea diver, a geologist, or a person from ancient times, but they can come to know any of these people through the books they have written. A single author does a wonderful job of helping form relations. How do I develop the art of standing aside to let my children develop relations with things, be they paintings, poems, bees, bears, or biographies? Through the use of narration and real books, observation, and experience. Not all of my instruction has allowed for these relations, but in the past some relation was made each season with a subject or two (mainly history, science and literature), and I believe this has kept my children fond of knowledge, questioning and wanting to know more. I do not believe that the modest amount of morning structure required by the Charlotte Mason method robs the educational life of its vitality. It is whatever interferes with the forming of relations that does this. (See *Philosophy of Education* pp. 302–303.)

My eldest daughter, Sophia, is too young to have experienced World War II (firsthand knowledge), but recently she has gotten to know someone who did—Corrie ten Boom. Corrie shared her experiences with Sophia in her book, *The Hiding Place.* Our history textbook may make its introductions, its outlines, its overviews, to a time in history. But it can never do what Corrie can do (what all real books can do): help form a relation. My younger daughter, Yolanda, has never ridden a horse, yet she gains a certain knowledge and enjoyment of horses through the stories of others that have. *Black Beauty, Misty of Chincoteague, Stormy,* and *The Black Stallion* are some of the horse books she has read. I have found little information on horses in school textbooks. Have you?

The Teacher's Business

Charlotte said, "Let them learn from first-hand sources of information—really good books, the best going, on the subject they are engaged upon. Let them get at the books themselves, and do not let them be flooded with [diluted talk from] the lips of their teacher. The teacher's business is to indicate, stimulate, direct, and constrain to the acquirement of knowledge. The less the parents and teachers 'talk-in' and expound their rations of knowledge and thought to the children they are educating, the better for the children . . . Children must be allowed to ruminate, must be left alone with their own thoughts." I give a student what I call "narration requests" after some reading on a subject. Then I let him

describe the selection with the details that have impressed him—retell it from his own point of view. This is one way for a student to be put in contact with ideas from books and then be left to think them through and do the telling himself.

Perhaps fresher terminology, in place of the word "education," should be "applied wisdom."

Filling in the Holes

The conventional system of education prides itself in what it covers. "It will all be covered on the test," says the classroom teacher. Confused and concerned mothers have written me saying that they believe in what Charlotte says, but are worried they won't be covering everything the schools cover. "Calm yourself," the system tells them, "we will cover everything. It's all right here in the outlined chapters of these textbooks, see?" What can be seen is a little information here on this, a smattering of information there on that, with what Charlotte called an "infestation of testing." The goal of covering material for tests should not be allowed to get in the way of relations being made with God, man, and the universe during the early years of school life. Rather than feeling it is our duty to pass children through a sys-

tem, it should be our duty to ask ourselves how our children can acquire knowledge. If we desire our children to acquire personal knowledge of God, other people and themselves, and things, we accomplish this by letting the *children* fill in the "holes." We *can't* teach them everything. What *can* we do? We can expand their horizons with a wide range of interests and then practice the fine art of education—that art of standing aside to let a child develop the relations proper to him. It is needless to worry about the "holes" if we believe that "education consists in the establishment of relations."

Structure and Support

Our knitting the net of subjects makes a sort of hammock: though it has holes, it will uplift and support its owner. While we knit, the children fill in the holes. By means of self-education they acquire genuine, long-lasting knowledge—the real stuff. Why be unequally yoked and overburdened by continually serving a system that works for very few children? With all the standardizing, evaluating, consolidating, synchronizing, and the rest, education has become, as Headmaster Gibbon bluntly put it, in a letter to the *Parents' Review,* "a gigantic sausage machine—the pig going in

at one end and coming out educated pork at the other." Are we all to learn a little about all the same things, for example, and express the same opinion of them?

Culture Versus Cram

We owe it to our children to stimulate in them a wide range of interests in their elementary years. Wherever we go, whomever we talk to, whatever we see can be of some interest to children if we stand aside and let them question and consider or examine and research. It should not be "How much has our child covered?" but "How much does he *care?*" and "About how many things does he care?" Charlotte's method of education that teaches children to care supports culture. The children go beyond just becoming *interested* in someone or something. They develop a deeper *understanding*—a greater appreciation—when relations are formed. They become cultured. A system primarily supports cram. Make your choice—culture versus cram. Others may feed the sausage machine. I would like to remain outside the factory and, like Mr. Gibbon suggested, "look on education as something between the child's soul and God." As he says, "Modern education tends to look on it as something between the child's brain and the standardized test, . . . There is an issue at stake. It is part of the whole modern policy of quick returns, of the substitution of immediate and temporary values for ultimate and absolute ones."

In upcoming chapters we will look at some things with which relations can be formed, and how to gain knowledge of them through observation, experience, or the use of narration. ➤

Questions for Personal Reflection or Support Group Discussion

1. *Do you feel you have submitted yourself to a system of education that is designed predominately to test and evaluate?*

2. *Are your children hungering for knowledge in literary form (living books), yet yoked with the system's textbooks and workbooks?*

3. *Are your children finding it more and more difficult to obey?*

4. *Could it be you are stuck in a system—and feeling discouraged and unqualified to teach? Charlotte understood this predicament, which does not serve the teacher or those taught.*

5. *What is Charlotte's remedy? Explain the principle "Education is a Science of Relations." Share a personal experience.*

6. *There are three areas of knowledge. What is the first? What are your goals for teaching the first? Give a personal interpretation of Whittier's poem.*

7. *Relationships are important. Would you like to improve relations with your children?*

8. *What materials can help us present a study of man?*

9. *What does Shakespeare's character Laertes mean when he says, "to thine own self be true?"*

10. *Tell what sign or signs give evidence a child is forming a relation. "We don't measure a child's education solely by his progress in the three R's," said Charlotte. What is the measure we use?*

11. *How is knowledge like a friendship? How can we use whole books to our advantage without ridding ourselves of all textbooks?*

12. *What is one thing a mother might worry about when she leaves the system to follow Charlotte's philosophy and method?*

13. *We expand a child's horizons. We knit the net. How are the hammock's holes filled in? Give some practical examples.*

14. Why does Mr. Gibbon compare the modern system of state education with a giant sausage machine?

15. Between what two principles is our educational choice to be made?

Chapter Five

Self-Education

MISCONCEPTIONS about Charlotte Mason's philosophy and method are floating around everywhere—perhaps because her method of education relies less on textbooks and workbooks and more on a variety of real books and narration. I've been hearing that Charlotte Mason's philosophy reflects a style of education so loosely structured that activities or subjects are entirely directed by a child's or a mother's whim. This is not the case, and those who are interested in this style of education will not find it promoted in Charlotte's writings. What *is* found there, however, is a wonderful balance between what Charlotte termed "masterly inactivity" and direct teaching.

"Masterly inactivity" gives a child space to independently explore, ruminate and reflect in his educational life. The authority of the parent is *felt* by the child within the atmosphere of the home. This is balanced with regular times of structured learning when a child follows assignments or interacts with the teacher directly.

How is this balance accomplished? Charlotte uses a child's curiosity and trains him to develop good habits. She sets before the child the kinds of activities and books he will readily "take to," the kinds of things he needs to grow in character and intellect. And then she guides him to work like a busy beaver to acquire knowledge from these things and make it his personal possession. What she *does* promote is self-education.

Ideas for a Living Education

Aren't life and growth miraculous? A plant grows from within. When the environment is right the plant flourishes because it is *living*. Christ's parable of the sower gives us insight into the true spiritual life. The seed that falls on good soil hears the Word and understands it. This is the seed that grows. It produces many more times what was sown. We cannot do the growing, understanding, or learning for a child, but we can provide what he needs for growth: *ideas*.

Charlotte wrote, "A person is not built up from without but from within, that is, he is living, and all external educational appliances and activities which are intended to mold his character are decorative and not vital." According to Charlotte, the more we do for a child the less he will do for himself. If we give him watered-down material, many explanations, much questioning, if we over-moralize, depend on the workbook to work the mind, what thinking is left for the child to do? How is his mind to grow from within if what we are doing is only superficial—like applying lotion to the skin rather than eating a wholesome diet that would provide the entire body as well as our skin with the proper nutrients?

Children are "Idea Picker-Uppers"

"The life of the mind is sustained upon ideas," said Charlotte. "There is no intellectual vitality in the mind to which ideas are not presented several times, say, every day. . . Every child gets many of these ideas by word of mouth, by way of family traditions; in fact, by what we might call a kind of oral literature. . ." Numbers were the first "schoolish" thing my son, Nigel, cared about. He picked up the idea of a numeral representing dots in a particular formation on a cube as a result of playing a simple board game with his sister Yolanda when he was quite young. I discovered this one afternoon when, having spent the afternoon cleaning the kitchen from top to bottom—and I must have been in there for a long while—I escaped into the living room to find him reading a die with deep concentration. He barely knew I was standing there, watching, as he read one face of the die after another.

"When did he learn this?" I asked Yolanda in delighted surprise.

"Today," was the answer of his not-much-older sister.

Although children will pick up ideas, they will also run out of them unless they are given a regular supply. Charlotte said that most schools graduate many clever young persons who are lacking initiative, the power of recollection, and the sort of moral imagination that would enable them to put themselves in another's place. These qualities can only flourish with a proper diet. And sadly, this diet is not well provided by the ordinary school book, or in sufficient quantity by the ordinary lesson.

He Hates School

There are so many children in schools who become frustrated, despondent, or hopelessly bored. Last summer our family was enjoying a picnic lunch at a park. Our picnic table was very close to two mothers who were having an intense conversation. One mother had a very loud voice and very definite opinions. I couldn't help overhearing, and when I realized their conversation was about school, I guess I lazily resisted any effort to turn my attention elsewhere.

"But he hates school," said the quiet mother, with anxiety in her tone. "He doesn't get along with his teacher and he's not motivated to keep up with his classmates." Sitting alone at a different table nearby was a boy about nine years of age, who must have been her son. He had his head in his hands, his elbows pressed into his knees, and he was staring at the ground. He wasn't playing with the other children. I had never seen a child so downcast.

"He'll outgrow it, honey," said the loud one. "All kids get used to school eventually. Just give him time and he'll realize that everyone has to go to school. It's just part of life!"

An emotion swept over me that was difficult to contain. I crossed my arms tightly, because I was shaking. How I wanted to impose upon them, to interrupt their conversation to give them the good news! But I hesitated. Later I learned that the loud mother knew about homeschooling but was of the opinion that her friend's son most certainly would display more unsociable behavior if he were homeschooled. That conversation still plagues me. I had a pearl to share (Charlotte's discoveries), but I didn't share it. To this day, whenever I remember that despairing young boy, I wonder if I should have *not* "minded my own business."

Hungry for Food for Thought

Charlotte realized that a child's mind feeds on ideas. We give him food for thought and expect him to do the thinking. She provided children with opportunities to establish relationships with real books, books written primarily by single authors on a variety of topics. She called these "living books" because they enlivened the child's mind. Through them knowledge is passed from mind to mind, from person to person. It is knowledge with a human touch.

Writing about knowledge, she says, "We feed upon the thoughts of other minds, and thought applied to thought generates more thoughtfulness. No one need invite us to reason, compare, imagine. Like the body, the mind digests its proper food; it must have the labor of digestion or it ceases to function."

What Charlotte terms narration, in which a child tells back what he has learned from the passage just read, gives a child the opportunity to digest this mind-food. Reading the right books and using the method of narration, he develops a taste for knowledge and comes to enjoy satisfying that very personal thing: curiosity. He becomes a thinker. He grows from within. His concern need not be for "keeping up with his classmates" because his narration (the measure of what he knows of a passage), though it be presented somewhat differently than another's, is just as valid.

God Made Us His "People"

Children are persons, Charlotte reminds us. They are human beings. A true intellectual life is not achieved by exercising children's minds as if they were nothing but memory machines. This is where Charlotte's method is in disagreement with Dorothy Sayers' strong emphasis on memory work in the early grades. Unlike Dorothy

Sayers, Charlotte spent all her grown life with children, observing them and teaching them, always refining and reforming education for the children's sake. She writes, "'Education,' said Lord Haldane, some time ago, 'is a matter of the spirit.' No wiser word has been said on the subject, and yet we persist in applying education from without. . ." She began to see the truth of this while working closely with children. "No one knoweth the things of man except the spirit of man which is in him; therefore, there is no education but self-education, and as soon as a young child begins his education, he does so as a student. Our business is to give him mind stuff. Both quantity and quality are essential."

Naturally, we mothers who have embarked upon this career of teaching our own children "everything" have only a limited knowledge of "everything" up our

sleeves. But we know where to procure it, for the best thought of the best minds the world possesses is stored in books. All we have to do is open to children real books—the best books—our only concern being that of "abundant provision and orderly serving." This is not teaching by whim but with a definite plan toward self-education.

Education Is a Way of Life

Self-education by means of real books, narration, first-hand experience, and observation is such a very satisfying and rewarding process that it naturally continues throughout life. Self-education is not dependent on a system of artificial rewards, prizes, and grade scores, because it is not bound to a *system* of education, but a

method of learning. A system and a method are two different things. A system depends on a cycle of tedium: read the textbook chapter, find the facts and record them as answers to the chapter's list of questions, take the test, get the grade, get it over with. A system makes the process more important than either the information or the learner. On the other hand, a method emphasizes the process by which the goal is attained. If the goal is an educated child, a variety of means will best achieve it.

The Key of Self-Education

Charlotte discovered a key that opens the doors to what should belong to every well-educated child. This key was self-education. Self-education in Charlotte's

schools was achieved by a regular and steady diet of the best books combined with the use of narration to develop retention and understanding of what was read. This approach maintained students' interest and helped them develop the habit of attention, as well as a literary style, a readiness in speaking, a wide vocabulary, and a love of books. This is self-education, because ultimately it is the child who is doing the work. And self-education may be the kind of education that is begun in the classroom, but a child continues it (the key is in his pocket) throughout life.

An Invitation with Warm Wishes

I invite you to give Charlotte's approach a try. If you are already using a full curriculum course with which you are relatively happy, you can still add your own choice of real books. There is a bountiful selection of historical fiction and biography that will work well with any curriculum program. In so many schools real books are nowhere to be found.

Incorporate narration into what your students are reading. This will be more easily accomplished when you use books of real literary vitality, but even having a child simply tell about or write about what he has learned from a chapter in a science book can be a nice change—for both teacher and student—from just following a list of questions or filling in the blanks.

Every year I scan the catalogs I receive. Over the years I have purchased a lot of good books through them. Once I came across a description of a study guide to a book I particularly liked. It said that the guide provided lots and lots of good fill-in-the-blanks for digging into the text. But I knew that with narration my child would do his own digging, so no sale was made. A few "how or why" questions can be asked by the teacher, but while narrating, the child's mind poses questions that he

answers for himself. Not every detail will be brought forth. We cannot expect any narration to be "word-for-word perfect," and we don't *want* it to be. We want a child's own mind to act on the text so that he *knows* it—it becomes his own possession. The child who dutifully studies his lessons over and over again, artificially motivated by grades and prizes might do well on the test, but does he *know*? Is he *knowledgeable*?

What is Knowledge?

What is knowledge? Charlotte had no pat, neatly framed answer to give. But I learned from her that "this only can we assert: knowledge is that which we know, and the learner knows only by a definite act of knowing which he performs by himself." And the means by which this "knowing" is accomplished I have discussed above.

A Relief to the Teacher

Charlotte concludes her chapter on self-education in her book, *Philosophy of Education*, in this way:

> In urging a method of self-education for children in lieu of the vicarious education which prevails, I should like to dwell on the enormous relief to teachers, a self-sacrificing and greatly overburdened class; the difference is just that between driving a horse that is light and a horse that is heavy in hand; the former covers the ground of his own happy will and the driver goes merrily. The teacher who allows his scholars the freedom of the city of books is at liberty to be their guide, philosopher and friend; and is no longer the mere instrument of forcible intellectual feeding.

Wherever my husband Dean and I have spoken on Charlotte's principles, there always seems to be some overburdened mother (or father) who comes up to us afterwards and says, "Can I really do the things that you have talked about?" It has been her heart's desire all along but she has been hesitant to let go of old notions of what school is supposed to be—an idea that school is based on a system, not a method. Such parents give a sigh of great relief after deciding to rest on the truths of Charlotte's philosophy. They have new-found courage and are ready to take the plunge from the dreaded textbook/workbook grind to real books and narration— even though it may feel like diving into cool water on a warm day.

One father from New York, a pastor, admitted that he and his wife had had a very difficult year. They had lost hope at times and after they resorted to placing one of their daughters back in school, they felt this was even less workable for their family.

"Thank you for coming," he said. "I liked what you said at the very end of your talk so much that I wrote it down."

"What was it we said that gave you so much hope?" I asked.

"Let me see . . . Oh, here it is," he answered as he leafed through a notebook. "When you said that homeschooling is really all about living the educational life with our children. Now I understand!" he smiled.

Strange, it was something we hadn't written on our note cards, and I had only thought of adding it at the last minute in conclusion. I'm so glad I did.

Note: I am not against using workbooks or textbooks for mathematics and some language skills. However, for the more literary subjects, real books are not a luxury, but a necessity. ⇥

Your Own Personal Reflections

....

....

....

....

....

....

....

....

....

....

....

....

....

....

....

Chapter Six

The Atmosphere of Home

WHEN A FRIEND TOLD ME that she fed her large family on ten dollars a day, I was impressed. She bought food in bulk, she told me, looked for deals on dented and expired cans, and she stored lots of turkey in her freezer—turkey her family received in exchange for working well into the night on a turkey farm a few days before Thanksgiving. As a consequence, I began paying closer attention to what I was buying at the grocery store. Wishing to better economize (in an attempt to emulate my thrifty friend), I started to notice how "dressed up" the food was that I bought. My grocery cart held Grandma's molasses, Aunt M's spaghetti sauce, "home-style" this and that, bread with a farm on the label, and strawberry jam that had the lids covered with pretty red and white check cloth. The packaging gave the impression that the food was homemade, although it was prepared and processed in a factory. Food manufacturers emphasize the "home atmosphere" of their products because it is so appealing.

One Third of Education is Atmosphere

Charlotte Mason believed that as much as one third of education is atmosphere. There is, of course, more to atmosphere than fresh bread baking in the oven, white ruffled curtains fluttering in a sunny breeze, and red geraniums on the window sill. These cozy types of things do make for a pleasant setting in a home, but they are only the beginning.

It is the life-supporting atmosphere of home working in a child's life that is such an important element of his education. Atmosphere is one of only a few instruments the educator has at her disposal to encourage the work of thinking in the student and to stimulate his healthy mental, emotional, spiritual, and physical growth. M.F. Jerrold, in an article in the *Parents' Review,* said that "there are many important aspects of home-life from a child's first training to his highest education, but there is nothing in the way of direct teaching that will ever have so wide and lasting effect as the atmosphere of home."

An idea may exist in a clear, distinct, definite form as that of a circle in the mind of a geometrician or it may be a mere instinct, a vague [association] towards something . . . like the impulse which fills the young poet's eyes with tears, though he knows not why. To excite this relationship or appetite toward things lovely, honest, and of good report is the earliest and most important ministry of the educator.

How are we to impart ideas to our children? Do we spoon-feed them ideas the way we give them medicine? "For good ideas. Take two spoonfuls upon rising or at bedtime." Even Mary Poppins would find ridiculous the notion of spoon-feeding our children ideas, because this is not how we absorb ideas. Ideas are of spiritual origin. God has made us spiritual people. Therefore, ideas are passed on from person to person—through conversation or books written by those who love their subject matter.

Charlotte urges us to give children a regular feeding of ideas through sweeping tales of history, wonderful inventions and discoveries in science, lives of great men and women, stories that radiate the moral life as well as paintings, plays, Psalms, poems, symphonies—and everything else wonderful we can think of. She says these ideas are the children's very bread of life.

Ideas

What are some elements of the home atmosphere that are conducive to the education of children? One element is that of the absorption of ideas from the "thought environment" we provide them. Ideas are food for the mind. A child's mind automatically grows as he considers ideas.

What is an idea? Charlotte Mason tells us this:

Thus she taught by way of the humanities. But Charlotte also says,

> Ideas are held in that thought environment which surrounds the child as an atmosphere, in which he breathes in unconscious ideas of right living emanating from his parents. Every look of gentleness and tone of reverence, every word of kindness and act of help, passes into the thought-environment, the very atmosphere which the child breathes; he does not think of these things, may never think of them, but all his life long they excite that vague appetency [relationship] towards something out of which most of his actions spring.

She goes on to tell us that "a child draws inspiration from the casual life around him. The thought of any of our poor words and ways being a daily influence on a child should make the best of us want to hold our breath."

There is no way of escape. We are inspirers, whether we feel confident or not because, as Charlotte says, "about the child hangs, as the atmosphere around a planet, the thought-environment he lives in. And here he derives those enduring ideas which express themselves as a life-long kinship towards sordid or things lovely, things earthly or divine."

Wanted—Homemaker

We've learned that our children will pick up many kinds of ideas from the atmosphere we provide in the home. What do we need to insure that this atmosphere inspires them on to the kinds of things we want them to learn? First, someone loving needs to be home to make it a home. We are living in a career-minded, materialistic culture that depreciates the role of the mother. But the fact is that a mother is the irreplaceable foundation of a home.

During World War II, when America was imprisoning Japanese families in camps, a reporter stepped up to a little Japanese-American girl waiting at a train platform. "How does it feel to be without a home?" the reporter asked. "Oh," replied the little girl, "we have a home, we just don't have a house to put it in."

Protecting Wings

A Christian home provides the protecting wings of a religious atmosphere. A catechism is essential teaching for children to understand what and why we believe as we do, but as absolutely necessary as such teaching is, it will not in itself create a religious atmosphere. In her article on atmosphere in *Parents' Review,* M. F. Jerrold stated:

> The test will be whether religion is the center of our life—our joy of our joy, the consolation of our sorrow, the one eminently important thing for which all others have to give way; whether we view the things of daily life primarily with reference to it, and whether all else is felt to be relatively devoid of interest and value . . . As love and faith are the two wings of the Divine, so they are of natural religion, and it is their strong protecting wings that our children must ever feel around them.

I like what Charles Spurgeon said about the religious atmosphere of home: "When home is ruled according to God's word, angels might be asked to stay with us, and they would not find themselves out of their element." Isn't this a high ideal? Don't be discouraged, dear parent, with the heavenly command, "Be ye perfect." We may not reach our ideals, but it is our fervent, faithful reaching towards them that matters greatly.

Open Communication

Another essential ingredient in the home atmosphere is open communication. By that I mean the freedom to express opinions in an atmosphere in which discussion is open and far-reaching. In Charlotte Mason's philosophy of education it is an excellent thing to have an opinion of your own, provided you are not bent on sticking to it. We preserve the natural candor of children by listening with a patient and sympathetic ear. And we can expect attentive listening from children if we do not scold them. A helpful book to read for those desiring gentle encouragement to improve the atmosphere of their homes is Henry Clay Trumbull's book *Hints on Child Training*. I particularly like this paragraph from the chapter on sympathy:

A parent loses his opportunity for good to his child, if he fails to have sympathy with this child in that child's weakness and follies and misdoings. It is in every child's nature to long for sympathy at the point where he needs it most; and when he has done wrong, or has indulged evil thoughts, or is feeling the force of temptation, he is glad to turn to some one stronger and better than himself, and make confession of his faults and failures. If as he comes to his parents at such a time, he is met with manifest sympathy, he is drawn to his parents with new confidence and new trust.[1]

Physical closeness is, perhaps, an uncomfortable topic for some to consider. Too many of us who were cuddled as babies cannot remember being hugged in after years by our parents. Therefore it is one kind of communication worth mentioning here. Human beings bestow hugs and kisses to show nonverbal love and care. Our children are not our pets, but should our pets receive more physical attention from us than do our own children? Girls like to have their hair combed and arranged. Boys like a pat on the back or a handshake. We can "greet each other with a holy kiss," and bestow the same when saying goodnight or good-bye. If hugs weren't prevalent in your childhood, start a new custom with your family. What may seem uncomfortable at first will become a comfort in time.

Manners—More Than Meets the Eye

Courtesy towards others is another important aspect of communication, for it is through the many small tendernesses that are a consequence of good manners that we demonstrate our respect and esteem for others. In the eighteenth century, etiquette was expected from all persons of "good breeding." One needs only to read one of Jane Austen's delightful novels to become acquainted with the mannerly characters of her time—for all through the nineteenth century as well, "respectable people" observed traditional decorum.

Today, any form of etiquette seems to belong only to these "prim and proper" Victorians. You will find an almost universal lack of manners everywhere on the part of people who are supposedly "educated." Perhaps having good manners is seen as infringing on one's freedom to express oneself without constraint. When manners are employed, all too often they are the hollow tactfulness and manipulating flattery some salesmen use on the selling floor. Our children can have worthier reasons for exhibiting good manners. Good manners can be another term for duty, for righteousness, for morality. True politeness simply consists of treating others just as you like to be treated yourself. This polite treatment comes from a little direct teaching but is also the result of a caring home atmosphere where a child will acquire a servant's heart like that of our Savior's.

Let Home Have the Greater Influence

As children grow older, they may become more and more fascinated with the world. When they are very young they may fill their pockets with rocks, acorns, pine cones, shells, or feathers. When they are older they will more consciously collect impressions of the ways and happenings of the world around them. The pull of the world, and their curiosity about it, seems to be strongest in the teen years. We grown-ups may forget what once enticed us—especially if our fascination with the world has faded. How much influence the world has over our children really depends on what standards we set at home—the standards by which the children are accustomed to measure things—and the strength of the family ties. A respect for parents, the satisfaction of learning together, a fondness for simple pleasures, good humor amidst hard work, sympathy in sorrow, and the joy of worshipping together are a part of the atmosphere of a close family. Such families give the gift of unworldliness. May we all be enabled to provide our children with such an atmosphere.[2]

Questions for Personal Reflection or Support Group Discussion

1. *What do you envision a pleasant atmosphere of the home to be like?*

2. *What changes can you put into effect to create this type of atmosphere in your home?*

3. *Are you running about town every day with your children, hardly spending time at home? Has this been a detriment to your home atmosphere?*

4. *Morning chores get the blood circulating and make the house pretty so that when students sit down to lessons mother isn't disturbed and distracted by the crumbs, clothes, and clutter. Do you feel uncomfortable when your house is messy? How does this affect your home teaching?*

5. *Atmosphere is one third of education, and when a good home atmosphere is wanting, it seems to be a crucial factor for parents when deciding whether or not to give up on home educating. Those who are discouraged may have become so because they haven't understood the importance of making the home atmosphere a priority. How will creating (and maintaining) a more pleasant atmosphere make a difference in your homeschool?*

Your Own Personal Reflections

....

....

....

....

....

Chapter Seven

....

Bickerings

"You did, I tell you!"
"I say I didn't!"
"Didn't you say I could take this fossil collection into my room?"
"No, I didn't!"
"You did, you just don't remember."
"Put them back right now!"
"Why should I? You're rude."
"Then I'll take them back!"

WITH THIS, the speaker, an angry little girl—hair awry, cheeks flushed, and eyes flashing—rushes at the younger child and snatches the shoe box of fossils from his hand.

The little brother cries out with a dismal howl, and while trying in vain to recover the box from his sister's sturdy clutch, it drops onto the tile floor with a crash. Little brother whimpers, "You are *so* selfish, and I am going to tell Mom!" and runs out of the kitchen, slamming the door behind him.

As the door slams, the sister sobs as if her brother were still in the room, "Now look what you've done!" She stares down at the shattered pieces of her cherished rock collection.

Mother enters, sweeps up the ruins, and then tells the two they will have no cake for dessert that night. She goes off to ponder sadly on the quarrelsome nature of children, while the culprits are left glaring sulkily at each other.

This is only one of many similar scenes that take place not only in this sunny kitchen but in many others. And every childish quarrel loosens a little bit the family bond of esteem or love, till it eventually grows too slack to hold the members together. The big brother who tyrannizes over his younger sisters will not prove a trustworthy guardian of their rights in after years, and such early intolerance one for the other is the cause of the inheritance lawsuits in our day. Sisters who never give in to each other when it comes to sharing playthings or sweets are likely to become jealous rivals of each other in later years. When they are grown up they will have no sympathy for the home circle.

"Can't you keep the children from quarreling so much?" said a perplexed father one day to his wife.

She responded anxiously, "What can I do? They are all born with tempers."

"There must be something wrong with their training," he sighed.

He was right, but few are the parents who recognize this or know what is wrong. They accept their parental duties; they fulfill them according to their own good sense and conscience. They wash, clothe, and feed a child, and even punish him when he's naughty. But do they know how a child's soul grows?

A Two-Sided Character

There was a little girl who had a little curl
Right in the middle of her forehead.
When she was good she was very very good.
When she was bad she was horrid.

—Nursery Rhyme

Charlotte knew that a child's character is complex and contains all the possibilities for good or evil. A child will show generosity, pride, ambition, love, and enmity, all in early stages of growth. His character is two-sided and, according to his training, his character qualities are either nurtured into virtues or allowed to degenerate into vices. Pity is a virtue if it cares for another. Idle pity just says, "Too bad." Pity can turn into self-pity, which is not a virtue. Truth-telling is a virtue, but if it is blunt and tactless— spoken without love—it is not a virtue.

The only way to make the virtues grow is to train the child's conscience and instill in him a love for others. To breed vices, the most powerful agent is love of self, and this begins almost in the cradle. The toddler who cries, screams, whines, or whimpers for his own way (and continually gets it) can become the youth or an adult who terrorizes his family with his fits of rage.

Main Causes for Bickering

But about family bickerings. The two main causes of them are selfishness and harsh judgment of others. No punishment is of the smallest use to combat these. In fact, punishment may awaken resentment and arouse greater spite against the person on whose account it is incurred. It will never diminish the selfishness. Penalties will suffice for the moment, but another kind of correction is needed.

Virtues, like flowers, grow in the sunshine. You can cultivate them or draw them out with love and reason, but you can neither force nor whip them into existence. Try to do so and the virtue you want will come forth in the guise of its corresponding vice. Instead of truth-speaking courage, you will get a lying cowardice; instead of obedience, obstinacy.

Of course the best way to prevent bickering is never to allow it from infancy, to train the child to find its happiness in giving others pleasure, to show him always how good and kind others are to him; in fact, to let the names of mother, father, sister, and brother stand for love and lovingkindness to him.

If, unhappily, this has not been begun from the cradle, then an entire change of treatment will be required. Never be angry when the children are cross, and never add a harsh word of reproof when a child is still sore under what it feels to be an injustice. This is often difficult to do because it is our natural response to control his temper with a stronger one of our own. Yet I recommend you work against any tendency to overpower the child in this instance. Gently draw the belligerent's mind to the fact that he is feeling very unhappy, that this is merely the natural result of saying unkind things; and that, as it would not be fair to make everyone else unhappy too, he must for other people's sakes go away from the room, or leave the game till he can be pleasant.

If you have seen the beginnings of a quarrel, try to get the children to talk it over with you when they are cooler, and suggest to Katie that if she had answered softly when Tom was first angry, all the tears and misery would have been avoided. Put it to Tom that if he would only remember in time that it is the man's privilege to protect the woman, and learn to be generous and gentle to Katie, she would always look up to him and try to please him.

The Value of Stories

You may have tangible wealth untold;
Caskets of jewels and coffers of gold.
Richer than I you can never be—
I had a mother who read to me.

—from "Reading Mother"
by S. Gaillilan

Bedtime story hour is a fine time for cultivating the child virtues and discouraging bickering. When the boys and girls sit round the fire with mother or father, a series of stories might be told, evening after evening, bearing on instances of love and self-denial. Then you have the opportunity to ask, "Wouldn't you like the chance to do such a caring thing for another person?"

Rarely read stories where wrong actions are the theme, unless they are actions the children have already committed, and you want to show the natural consequences of them. Sadly, though, modern children's stories don't show just consequences. There are a few we have read that do, however. E. Nesbit's *Five Children and It* is a kind of fairy tale. The sand fairy, a funny looking "It," provides each of the children in turn with his wish. However, the fulfillment of the wishes proves to be very unsatisfying. The "It" demonstrates how each made a selfish choice. Happily, the children recover when the wishes are undone and they learn from the experi-ence. *Charlie in the Chocolate Factory* is another good example. It is silly and ridiculous in one way and condemning of selfishness in children in another. The spoiled children who visit the tempting chocolate factory meet with nasty consequences when they disregard the factory safety rules. Charlie, however, discovers that his patience and a lack of greed do him a good turn in the end. On the other hand, the character Pinocchio, in the original Italian fairy tale, has good intentions but a weak will. He justly suffers the consequences of his foolish choices, but eventually is able to follow the right path. Even so, suggestions of good and virtuous actions are much more likely to lead young minds upwards towards virtue than the constant suggestions of evil, even in the form of warning.

For instance, Johanna Spyri's *Heidi* is a story of reconciliation. Heidi's love melts the hard heart of her grandfather. In *The Little Princess*, by Frances Hodgson Burnett, Sarah shows kindness, courage, generosity, and hope after her father dies—even though she is mistreated by the school headmistress. Hans Brinker, the main character in *The Silver Skates*, by Mary Mapes Dodge, exhibits faith, honor, diligence, loyalty, and patience as he tries to procure a doctor for his disabled father. A compassionate family is displayed in the very different characters of *Little Women*, by Louisa M. Alcott. *Swiss Family Robinson*, by Johann Wyss, entertains us with the strange adventures of the family while they are deserted on a South Sea island. They pray together, work together, and play together. We have enjoyed all of these bedtime books in our family.

Build upon an Idea

Charlotte always thought it best to start with an initial idea before a sequence of actions are encouraged, because it provides direction, motivation, and inspiration to the child. Then, one might proceed to put these newly awakened ideas into action. One day, for instance, you might say to Katie, "I am going to drive to the store but I can only take one of you. As you are the eldest, it has been your opportunity to come with me most often. I know there is something in particular you have been waiting to buy, but I think it would be good of you if you passed on the opportunity to Darla. It would be a chance for you to be kind to her, especially since she was laid up all week with a cold." Katie would probably

give up going with Mother and would stand at the door watching Darla's happy face with satisfaction. Only, make sure Darla thanks Katie for it on her return, for children are exacting in the way of justice, and recognize gratitude when they see it.

Never force a child to sacrifice for another family member, but merely suggest to the child that here is a way to give up self, and do a kind and lovely action. At times the suggestion will be refused, because virtues are not so easy to train. That is the time to draw the child's attention to any suffering or discomfort that may be occasioned by his selfishness: "Imagine the pleasure you could have brought to your little brother had you built that sand castle with him this afternoon, and had not sulked in your room bored because Sarah could not come over to play after all." This is making a mental picture for the child of what could have been.

When an unselfish action has been performed, give the child the full benefit of the happiness it brings, remark on the other's enjoyment, and show the light of a mother's smile and approval.

Yesterday, it gave me such joy to hear my daughter Yolanda figuring out how to play "Happy Birthday" on her cello, though she had only several lessons behind her. She was also rehearsing her brother Nigel, giving him direction on how to sing along loudly—like an opera singer. They also spent time in secret, getting little presents ready, while I picked daisies and lilies from our yard for a table bouquet. Everyone laughed at the opera performance and we were impressed with the cello playing, too. "Wasn't it a lovely birthday, Sophia?" I asked. She made a sly comment that told me she was pleased.

It also gives me joy to hear one sibling praying for another. The prayer could be for a recital to go well, for a cough (or bad attitude) to "go away," or a thank you for something another has received.

Help from the Word of God

If causes of bickering have been around for a long while, we must fight back with religion and reason. I have had talks with my children about their power to render others either good and happy, or naughty and miserable, and the great responsibility this power brings us. Just as they dislike critical and accusing remarks made to them, so they must refrain from criticizing the behavior of others. If my children begin to nit-pick each other, I tell them that the right to criticize is only mine and their father's. If you thus cut off the family thorns of criticism, you stop more than half the bickerings. It is when older children jeer at little brother because he is "so stupid" or such a "cry-baby," and when children make fun of each other's personal struggles, that anger and resentment are aroused. It is much better to show sympathy as sister tries to play as beautifully on piano as big brother does. I do think a little harmless teasing is OK. It is far better for a family to rub away the corners of one another's personalities and reveal little failings than for children to discover what they are by the comments of someone outside the family.

No Bickering

I once read about a large family in which bickering was unknown, though at one time there were signs of great friction among the members. The mother weeded out the thorns of family upsets by working with each child's imagination. She set them up to fight giants. Her lessons began with a parable, for there is no moral teacher better than the parable. The mother, apropos of Jack the Giant-killer, gave a sketch of the giants that beset young people, and morally devour them, such as Self-love, Vanity, Obstinacy, and Falsehood, and she excited their interest by telling them that these giants were so curiously huddled together that if one were conquered the others would probably flee.

As the Advent season was upon them, she told them that it would be good to think of giving secret gifts of abstaining from personal faults that rubbed the other family members the wrong way—and to do something good in place of displaying that fault. She told her children that in order to do this, they would have to fight a battle with a personal giant—a spiritual enemy. Each child was to keep his own secret, and whisper into Mother's ear the especial giant he wanted to fight, and she would give him the right weapons for it.

One by one the whispers came to her. Cubby Susie said she thought she was "dreadfully greedy for sweets," and she would fight that ogre. Mother would do her best not to have so many Christmas delicacies around the house, but keep to the traditional Christmas pudding only. A more nervous member whispered that she did not want to "feel so cross at Johnny," whose teasing jokes always seem to bother her. A third confessed that her enemy was "Vanity." She did not "want anybody to do things" as well as herself. And a fourth sighed that it was "very hard to keep one's temper" when everybody seemed so aggravating. That evening Mother came up with her weapons: seven Bible texts, one for each day.

"If by Christmas the giants are not dead at least they will certainly be wounded, and have less power," promised Mother.

As a sample from the King James, I list here those given to the child who could not hold her temper:

Sunday. "Pleasant words are as a honeycomb, sweet to the soul." Prov. 16:24.

Monday. "He that is slow to anger is better than the mighty; and he that ruleth his spirit than he that taketh a city." Prov. 16: 32.

Tuesday. "Love as brethren, be pitiful, be courteous; not rendering evil for evil, or railing for railing, but contrariwise bless-

ing." I Peter 3:8.

Wednesday. "If we love one another God dwelleth in us, and his love is perfected in us." I John 4:12.

Thursday. "Withhold not good from them to whom it is due, when it is in the power of thine hand to do it." Prov. 3:27.

Friday. "The servant of the Lord must not strive; but be gentle unto all men, apt to teach, patient." 2 Tim. 2:24.

Saturday. "If it be possible, as much as lieth in you, live peaceably with all men." Rom. 12:18.

On Sunday, all the children were given a promise:

"Him that overcometh, will I grant to sit with me in my throne." Rev. 3:21.

The little girl who did not want "to feel cross" had the attributes of charity spread, verse by verse, through the week.

The child who wanted to fight her vanity had such texts as: Charity envieth not, vaunteth not herself, is not puffed up;" "Be kindly affectioned one to another with brotherly love, in honour preferring one another;" "Be not wise in your own conceits," etc.

The children kept their own part of the bargain as seriously as they kept their secrets, and the result, if not quite perfect after the Advent season, was a complete victory after the next season. In overcoming greediness, Susie lost all that self-seeking manner that rubbed her sister the wrong way. In fighting down her pride, Jessica began to find all kinds of talents in others' good points, and learned to take as much pleasure in their successes as she took in her own. She no longer pushed to the front, and consequently aroused no feeling of jealousy nor made quarrels.

In this sunny atmosphere, the young people developed any amount of talents that that deadening family criticism had kept down, and have now so many real occupations that they never find time to waste on bickering.[1] ➤

A few household rules for a better atmosphere in the home

1. *Brothers and Sister are comrades and shall not be permitted to give constant critic.*

2. *Parents are the tutors and rulers that will judge with Christian kindness.*

3. *When one deems another person in the wrong, try to find out how he feels himself in the right, before you show anger towards him.*

4. *If you find the subject has two sides to it, then you shall agree to differ but not attempt to make differences agree.*

5. *To steal another's credit or praise shall be dealt with as stealing.*

6. *Never let an opportunity pass of doing a kind action, or saying a kind word.*

7. *Charity or love begins at home, and is the key to household peace.*

Your Own Personal Reflections

....

....

....

....

....

....

....

Chapter Eight

·····································

A Page From My Journal

EARLY ONE SUMMER MORNING, I crept downstairs in my nightgown to a corner in our library. I needed to spend some moments alone in prayer and preparation for the coming season. I jotted down some notes in an effort to make personal applications of Charlotte Mason's philosophy. I think the following notes can be used as a small example of the thoughts of one mother, at dawn—with a large purring black and white cat on her lap.

Notes on Fall Atmosphere

Prepare. Plan. Resist rushing about the day: hurry has ill-effects. I desire to be peacefully going about doing the "next thing."

Habit of Attention: Continue to establish the habit of attention in my youngest student. Encourage greater concentrated effort by the older students. Less interesting lessons should not drag on but be completed in due time, so that a wide variety of interesting subjects can be accomplished throughout the week. I desire a busy, happy, humming homeschool thriving in an atmosphere of ideas from living books. (See *Philosophy of Education,* pp. 97–98)

Words Spoken: A home atmosphere is pleasant when words are gracious. Nit-picking, grumbling, bickering, etc. should be far from our lips. Pray and seek God's guidance for encouragement. Let requests be made with thankfulness. Give older children opportunities to argue points of view in history, science, literature, etc. during school time or table talk.

I Can: Helping one another patiently to work through difficult lessons allows us to say, I AM, I CAN, I OUGHT, I WILL in our home schoolroom. Also let the children alone to work out problems I know they can do independently (masterly inactivity).

Literature Choice: Select literature that is refreshing, inspiring, and morally challenging for leisure reading and evening read-aloud times. Let such writings contribute to our spirits as we ponder, contemplate, consider, and relate to what the author has shared with us.

Admonishment: If admonishment be needed for rules broken, let it be with hope and positive correction. Plan ahead to determine what natural consequence will be given as penalty for certain rules broken.

Recreation and Rest: Don't over-schedule outside activities. Do not feel guilty when I need to say "No." Give the gift of time for imagining.

Fall crafts: 1) make corn husk dolls for the fourth year in a row—a family tradition I'd like to continue; 2) do candle dipping this November and use the candles during dark winter evenings; 3) Take up that home-spun wool I was given (in exchange for a subscription last year) and make a set of mittens. Along with fall nature walks, bicycling, and quiet times, these activities should insure a healthy nervous system and renew intellectual vigor.

Determination: I must be resolved to manage the home well this fall and seek wisdom to do things better—or differently. Improvement or change doesn't happen by itself. They may not need to be bold changes. Subtle changes will bring about improvements by degrees. It is the cooperation of their wills that I desire from the children, not just control on the surface. Make needed changes with courage.

Promotion: Children like "promotion," asserted Charlotte Mason. I've discovered that she is right. When children experience the joy of success they are motivated to progress. Promotion is different than competition. "Now you are on *what* song in your music book? Wow, you're coming along, aren't you?" Mother confirms. Daughter smiles.

"Mom, Yolanda measured my head. Do you know how tall I am now?" Brother asks excitedly. Mother chuckles.

"You moved up to Level Five in our math drill book today. You no longer need to do Level Four." A "Hooray!" is heard.

"Ma, I'm finished with the *Lord of the Rings* trilogy," the older student says with satisfaction—and a little disappointment that the adventure has come to an end.

"This linguine, olive bread and salad is delicious, Sophia. Your meal is a success," declares Dad. Sophia is glad, confident, and encouraged to cook a whole meal again.

Recognize promotion of character, too, having a mind to developing virtues. "You have a more sunny disposition today, Yolanda. You must be working on being more patient and less cross with your little brother, as we discussed earlier this week in *Beautiful Girlhood,* says Mother.

"Nigel, thanks for raking the leaves from the walk. I think your helpfulness without my asking shows you are maturing, don't you?"

Mom's Character: Promote my own character development this fall. Be calm without being complacent, show emotion without being emotional (mood swings). Be anxious in nothing.

Time with Husband: Take autumn walks with Dean.

Privacy: Remember to give my older children hugs. Casually spend time alone with each child in turn—whether it is a walk, a drive to the grocers, or a garden chore. May this one-on-one time of personal closeness allow my children to share without an audience of listening ears. May we pray our way through our struggles and fears and count our blessings.

Notes on Fall Discipline

In early spring we long to escape the bounds of accumulated structure and indoor restrictions. The monotony of yet another week of routine before we can dig in the garden or venture to the beach is hard to bear. After a time of long sunlight leisure—perspiring, swimming, digging in the dirt or sand, hiking up hills in the humidity, eating too many cucumber salads, shopping, visiting, entertaining—the word "routine" becomes a cozy word that invites us to gather round the dining room table for regular lessons again. We are ready for a more disciplined educational life even though we do academics sparsely and read interesting books all summer.

Orderliness: Order presupposes priorities. One priority is to complete most of our academics in the morning hours. Expect interruptions and intrusions—those things that throw us off schedule or prevent us from reaching a goal. This is "real life" education. It could be that Mother has another miscarriage, Brother gets chicken pox, the family car dies, the water heater malfunctions, another appliance catches fire, the house needs major repair, Father loses his job or changes jobs, and it becomes necessary to start packing boxes in preparation to move to a different town or state yet again. All of the above and more have occurred during our homeschooling years—experiences probably shared by many of you, too. Habit and order preserve weary homeschooling parents so they can keep to their original priorities and get back on track again. Getting off track wasn't a "bad" thing, it was a "real life" thing that God will work out for good if we are truly His children. Old faithful habits make order out of disorder and leave space for both practice and play. We can be content

to be God's children through life's challenges.

Healthy Cooking: Set fall recipes in motion—hot oatmeal, luscious late summer fruits and vegetables, soups and salads.

Healthy Living: Keep regular hours for meals, school work, chores, and bedtimes, for the health of the entire family. Allow time for pursuing personal interests.

Notes on Fall Educational Life

Charlotte Mason says that "education is the science of relations." The trick is not how well we make "subjects" relate to each other but rather how well a child relates to the subjects. I desire my children to form relations with what they study—not to know meagerly "about" something but to really *know* something by establishing a relationship with it.

Most of the topics on my "list" are addressed in greater detail in various other chapters of this book. I hope this sample of my notes (to myself and my readers) will help you to organize your own thoughts in preparation for your next teaching season! ⊷

"The only way to make the virtues grow is to train the child's conscience."

Chapter Nine

The Happiness of Habit

"Good habits are the best magistrates."

WE ARE, EACH ONE OF US, a bundle of habits. How easy it is to brush our teeth, comb our hair, or wash our faces. How effortlessly we drive a car or wash a pile of dishes while holding a conversation with a friend. You may not have noticed that you use the same series of movements each and every time you brush, wash, or drive. This is because much attention need not be given to these actions—they have become habits. These habits are actions that you have repeated and repeated. Some habits you have had for as long as you can remember.

Schedule—Routine

New thoughts and new actions are not done out of habit. They are in formation. We must give them lots of attention and care if we wish them to become habits. When my children were very young, I would occasionally use my weak hand—my left—to brush my teeth or hold a crayon. This enabled me to sympathize with my little ones as they were learning new skills—forming good habits. I can also sympathize with you who wish to learn more about the discipline of habit.

As a new mother I understood that children do better on a schedule. My days with babies and toddlers went pretty simply. Our occupations were naturally scheduled around dressing, meals, indoor play, outdoor play, story time, and bedtime. But when several of my children became school age, I became aware of the need for new habits. My days did not go nearly as smoothly as I would have liked. Although homeschooling was an attractive idea to me, it was a new experience.

Reading *Home Education* by Charlotte Mason was the encouragement I needed. In that book, Charlotte advises the mother to first acquire her own habit of training her children so that having children in the house with her all day is not a problem, but a pleasure. When it came to acquiring the skill of training my children to form good habits, although I sometimes felt as awkward at it as using my weak hand, the initial work it took to form even one helpful habit was not work in vain. The reward of the established habit was a great help to the homeschool day.

The Bad Telephone Call

During the first years of my home-schooling experience—while I was daily striving to establish orderliness in our homeschool morning—a neighbor called me up to chatter about her morning. I was soon sorry I had picked up the phone. She complained about all the fuss and attention it took to get her three children up and dressed, make their bag lunches, feed them breakfast, and make sure they got to the bus on time. When it was all over, she said, she was relieved to finally get some peace, to sit down to a cup of tea and watch what was going on in the real world through her morning news/talk show.

I tried very hard not to let her complaining get me down. She had only one morning hour to oversee her children, while my task was to organize an entire day of home activity. And not all our days went smoothly. I began to have doubts after hearing her complain, and asked myself, "Can I really do this?" But I was determined to keep trying.

I discovered Charlotte Mason was right in declaring that working daily to create habits—whether intellectual habits or ones of etiquette—depended on the energy of the students as much as the teacher. I trusted her when she also declared that children need a regular sprinkling (or sparking) of inspiring ideas of righteousness to evoke their cooperation. The discipline of habit and the help of inspiring ideas strengthen a child's will to obey. He can then take an active part in his learning. What a great opportunity home education has to promote that wonderful ability to be self-disciplined (self-governed), self-motivated, self-educated.

New Homeschooler—New Habits

As a first or second year homeschooler, it is normal to feel somewhat awkward, because both mother and child are in need of acquiring new habits. A mother's sweet present of love, dedication, enthusiasm, and desire to educate her own children may be wrapped in the brown paper of apprehension, insecurity, and dismay. A homeschooling mother's opinions on education and her daily responsibility will most likely be very different than those of her neighbors. The educational life that it is her heart-felt desire to live with her children will most likely be different than the routine life she experienced growing up. And she *wants* it to be different. The contrast in lifestyle will be even greater if she is determined to have a Christian atmosphere in the home even though she was not raised in one.

I still have occasional bouts—or should I say "pouts"—of apprehension when difficulties arise. I've seen that living the educational life with children involves much more thoughtfulness than opening up the box of curriculum the UPS man dumps at the door. Reading Charlotte's books convinced me that it is best to have a philosophy and method that backs up how we live out the educational life. In our rising up, our sitting down, and in any other wayside moments of the day, children pick up knowledge from our lips, our attitudes, our example—not just during those few sacred scheduled hours. But scheduled lessons we must have. And this is where Charlotte Mason's method should not be confused with those who have no schedule. "There is a time for everything under heaven."

Distractions—Interruptions

I remember the frazzled years, when in order to keep up with the needs of the children, my focus of attention was constantly redirected. One true scenario: Two little girls are seated at the kitchen table with heads bent over their penmanship books. Mother suddenly notices and appreciates the quietness of the moment. She begins to experience the peace and satisfaction of one habit formed. One child asks, "Mom, where's Nigel?" The restful moment all too quickly disappears as Mom searches the house, only to find the basement door open and a red tricycle missing. Standing at the end of the driveway, she squints and spots Nigel at the edge of the horizon (the end of a long suburban block). While she is running down hill to retrieve him—her haste and the incline conspiring to make her a truly comic figure—the girls look for Mother and begin to meander toward her. Making regular rounds, a police car slowly patrols the neighborhood, passing a mother with a dangling two-year-old boy over one elbow and a tricycle over the other. She trudges up the hill back home, almost out of breath. "Get in the house, girls," Mother says with a perspiring brow, noticing with relief that the police car is disappearing out of sight. "You're supposed to be in school," she nervously thinks to herself. "Phew! Now . . . where were we?" Although today I smile at the memory of that morning, I wasn't smiling then.

Laying Down Tracks for the Good Life

When there are lots of little ones in the house, the day naturally has its distractions and interruptions—which can contribute to a little frazzling—but habit can get lessons placed back on track. When the rails of habit are laid down, like the tracks set out for a locomotive train, lessons can go along easily and smoothly. The train moves easily, but the laying down of the rails has taken a lot of effort. Imagine yourself as John Henry, the steel-driving man who, with determination and perspiration, hammered those rails, laying miles of track across America.

I remember days of exhaustion. I'd flop face down on my bed at the end of a humbling day, almost too tired to untie my shoes or change into my bedclothes. But my prayers and supplications were heard by God. And because I heeded Charlotte's direction to underline the day with habit formation, I also have a mother's keepsake of *fond* memories, not just unhappy ones.

The Habit of Observation

I remember holding chubby hands on nature walks. "Look at the color of this leaf, Mommy!"

"That's a maple leaf, darling. Shall we iron this one between wax paper, too?"

"Oh, yes, and this one and this one."

My children have retained their wonder of nature over the years. We have made it our habit to notice and observe nature in the changing seasons of our neighborhood. Drawing and writing about our "finds"—Nature Notebook-style—has made science an intimate part of our educational life. This is just one of the many happy memories I have as a result of Charlotte's sound advice—the result of her teachings on the happiness of habit.

One Third of Education is Discipline

Charlotte claimed that as much as one third of education is the discipline of habit.

That's a pretty big chunk, isn't it? She emplored, "The mother who takes pains to endow her children with good habits secures for herself smooth and easy days; on the other hand she who lets habits take care of themselves has a weary life of endless friction." The latter will come about because, she says, if we "fail to ease life by laying down habits of right thinking and right doing, habits of wrong thinking and wrong doing fix themselves of their own accord." We begin with an awareness of any repeated action becoming either a bad habit or a good one. The actions a mother wishes repeated (the good ones) become her endowment.

A frustrated homeschooling mother may relieve some of the friction in her day by deciding what it is that bothers her most. It might be loose papers cluttering all available counter or table space. (I keep at least one two-foot-square of counter space available at all times, for the sake of my sanity.) It could be an unnecessary heap of towels piled outside the bathroom door (each used once). It might be children who dawdle, daydream, or "forget" to do something. Have they picked up any subtlely rude remarks lately? "Where did you hear that *outlandish* phrase?" I asked one day. (I really do talk to my children this way at times. Weird vocabulary does wonders to secure their attention.) "We heard it in the song that was playing at the orthodontist's," one confessed. I decided to nip that radio phrase in the bud at once, before it became a habit of rhyme with no reason. I had read "The phrases that men hear or repeat continually, end by becoming convictions."

Try This Simple Recipe—With Prayer and Supplication

To remedy friction, here is a recipe for the formation of a habit: Let a mother discipline herself to establish a particular habit in her children that would be to her favor and theirs. With devotion she focuses on forming one habit at a time, doing no more than watch over those already formed. She strives to be faithfully consistent. Tact, watchfulness, and perseverance are needed, especially during the first week or so, but when the habit is formed, there is not much fear of its being broken. Patience does its perfect work too, for it may take several months for even one small habit to stick. This is when many a mother makes it her supplication to ask for more patience, as she may sense it running out. She prays she will not fall into the temptation to be discouraged, inconsistent, or complacent. The dangerous time to run out of determination is just before the habit is formed. For instance she may think, "Becky has remembered so well up to now that I won't bother to call her back to put away her things this time."

"A place for everything and everything in its place. I always put my things away, That I might find them another day."

—Victorian verse

Be Faithful

Years ago, I made the mistake of allowing my young children time off from certain good actions on the weekend before certain habits were solidly formed. My failing became apparent to me when I discovered that—like the month of March—Monday morning came in like a lion! To insure that Monday comes in like a lamb, those weekday actions of neatness, politeness, obedience, must be employed on the weekend, too. A new goal for me was: Let good actions not become relaxed on the week-ends. Only then would these good actions become good habits.

Brain Shaping

In Charlotte's book, *Parents and Children,* she tells us that our intangible thoughts leave their mark upon the tangible substance of the brain. These thoughts, she said, set up connections between the nerve cells of which the brain is composed. In short, the cerebrum grows to the uses it is most constantly put to. How interesting it was for me to read how much of our modern research on brain shaping, such as is published in the book *Endangered Minds* by Dr. Jane Healy, simply confirms what was known in the nineteenth century by Charlotte and other educators of her day, who understood children and the way they learn.

Charlotte tells us that "one of the great functions of the educator is to secure that actions will be so regularly, purposefully, and methodically sown (in the brain) that the child will reap the habits of the good life, in thinking and doing, with a minimum of conscious effort." To quote an old saying attributed to Thomas à Kempis:

Sow an act, reap a habit,
sow a habit, reap a character,
sow a character, reap a destiny.

Some Habits to Develop:

- The Habit of Attention
- The Habit of Obedience ("Let thy child's first lesson be obedience, and the second will be what thou wilt." —Poor Richard's Almanac)
- The Habit of Manners
- The Habit of Truthfulness
- Habits of Thoroughness, Punctuality, Taking Turns, Doing Our Best, Prayer, Gratitude.

Charlotte said a child should enter his adult life with about twenty of these sorts of good habits. She labeled them the "minor moralities." By "minor" I think she meant that they are the least we can do for our children (in the minor leagues of life). "Educate the child in right habits and the man's life will run in them, without the constant wear and tear of moral effort of decision," she told us. Does this remind you of a scripture verse we so often hear in homeschooling circles? "Train up a child in the way he should go and when he is older he will not depart from it."

A child with his conscience in training may need to remind himself, when he is with other children, "Now I will be truthful; now I will take turns; now I will be gentle with the younger ones." But by the time he is mature, all the minor moralities of life will have become habitual to him. He has been brought up to be courteous, prompt, neat, considerate, thankful, and helpful, and he practices righteousness without much conscious effort. It is much easier to behave in the way he is accustomed than to originate a new line of behavior. His mind is running in a rut, so to speak. The ruts made in the mud by the first wagon in a wagon train of American pioneers heading westward made it easy for the next and the next wagon to follow. Likewise, ruts (fibrous connections) are found in dissected brain tissue. Both Charlotte and Dr. Jane Healey agree that this adaptation of brain tissue is the result of our educational efforts, wherein habits are graciously and mercifully ordered in the brain. Wow, everything we do leaves its mark? What a responsibility!

Charlotte assured us that when we train our children in virtues while they are young, the enormous strain of moral decision will come upon them only occasionally. Can you see how habit (training in self-government) plays a big part in the character development of our children? As goes another old saying: "He is ill clothed that is bare of virtue."

Discipline Requires More Than Spanking

When I was a new mother I was led to believe, in a book about child training, that training children is as simple as knowing when to spank or when not to spank. Spanking is not of relevance here except to say that I have learned from Charlotte (whom I recently began calling my adopted grandmother) and Henry Clay Trumbull, author of *Hints on Child Training,* that there is much more to child training than spanking. The spiritual force of an *idea* has its part to play, too. I introduced the concept of "idea" in an earlier chapter. Let's look more closely at this "accomplished friend." A habit is set up by carrying out an initial idea through a long sequence of corresponding acts. We know how the Biblical cloud of witnesses in Hebrews spurs us on to live by faith. In the same way, we can draw a child forward with an inspiring idea, instead of using an endless string of nagging

or threatening do's and don'ts. Idea is the motivating power of life. It is the friend of those who make it their aim to be disciplined from within, rather than from without. Charlotte said, "It is because we recognize the spiritual potency of the idea that we are able to bow reverently before the fact that God the Holy Spirit, is Himself the Supreme Educator, dealing with each of us in the things we call sacred and those secular. We lay ourselves open to the spiritual ideas, whether these be conveyed by the printed page, the human voice, or whether they reach us without visible sign."

Example is the Best Sermon

Here is Charlotte's example of using an idea to begin a series of acts. You can tell a child that the Great General slept in so narrow a bed that he could not turn over because, said he, "when you want to turn over it's time to get up." The boy does not wish to get up in the morning, but he does wish to be like the hero in his history book. Stimulate him to act upon this idea (invoke his cooperation) day after day for a month or so, and getting up promptly becomes just as easy as not getting up, because the habit is formed.

When one of my daughters was about four years old, we used to watch a certain chipmunk from her bedroom window while I nursed her baby brother. I told her a story about how a chipmunk keeps its underground home tidy. I explained how it had different rooms, one for its bed, one for its food, one with a back door to escape in case of danger, and one as the toilet. All the rooms were kept clean. Dry leaves and dry grass, which lined the rooms, were replaced daily. "See how busy he is," I pointed out to her. She was entertained and, I think, inspired. The idea of the neat and tidy chipmunk was very helpful to me when reminding her to pick up her toys and hang her change of clothes on her row of pegs.

For those who decide to embark upon the career of habit formation, remember:

- one habit at a time
- one day at a time
- practice good actions weekends, too
- nip the weed in the bud because formation is more efficiently accomplished than reformation.

But be encouraged with this wise old saying, "One habit overcometh another." You may not be able to teach old *dogs* new tricks, but God is able to make all things new again. Isn't this a great blessing?

For developing the habit of attention, a very useful educational habit, see the chapter on Inconstant Kitty.

Questions for Personal Reflection or Support Group Discussion

1. *The time for laying down the train tracks of habit come when we begin a new task. Why is it helpful when good actions become good habits?*

2. *What is meant by laying down the rails of habit?*

3. *If good habits are not established in the home, what kinds of habits will fix themselves on their own accord? Are there any bad habits that interfere with the smoothness of your day? What contrary habit can you begin to set in motion to replace the bad one?*

4. *Laying down the rails of habit in a child's day takes watchfulness, care and consistent correction on the part of the mother. Why is this initial care worthwhile in the long run?*

5. *What are some rewards of an established habit within a homeschool day?*

6. *When is the most dangerous time to run out of determination while working to establish a habit?*

7. *What does habit formation do to brain tissue?*

8. *Explain how providing children with an idea through a story provides inspiration and motivation?*

9. *List some good habits with which you would like to equip your children. Why is it good to focus on one at a time?*

10. *When we train our children to be faithful in little things, we make them ready to be faithful in bigger things for God. Isn't this exciting?*

Your Own Personal Reflections

Chapter Ten

························

The Way of the Will

THE CONCEPT OF "THE WAY OF THE WILL" is not an easy one. I read Charlotte's passages over a number of times before I understood it, I admit. I read it over yet again to decide if it was important enough to be rewritten into this book . . . and again to form the questions . . . and again to remind myself what my aims are, as I try to put Charlotte's principles into action in my own home (the hardest part). I hope you will not get discouraged if you don't quite "get it" with one reading. Some of the concepts Charlotte took hold of in order to insure an adequate education seem so new to us. Give them time. They can't be rushed. The pieces will come together with time.

Henry C. Trumbull has an easy-to-read, enlightening chapter on the Will in *Hints on Child Training* called "Will-Training Rather than Will-Breaking." I highly recommend it.

I had heard the term "will power" used in reference to diet and exercise, but never applied to anything else until I considered Charlotte Mason's writings. Then the bumper sticker, "Just say No," came to mind. And with my new knowledge about the Will, I realized that saying "No" in the midst of many others who are not, may not be as easy as the phrase suggests. It requires a strong Will.

Children have a Will that is underdeveloped. I was curious when Charlotte spoke of the importance of developing and training the Will of the child. What did this have to do with upbringing and education? First of all, what is the Will? The great things of life—and life itself—are not easy to define. The Will is part of the soul of every man. But can we define it? If the Will is such an intrinsic part, how is it that so many people go through life without a single definite act of "willing?" Doing what everybody else seems to be doing (convention), fitting in with the crowd (custom), seem to steer the course of the average man. He may get up, dress, breakfast, follow his morning's occupations, eat his fast food for lunch, and relax in the evening with his television without any act of choice.

What we do know about the Will is its function to choose, to decide. And you may have noticed that the more difficult the decision—and the weaker we may sense our will power to be—the more strenuous an effort it takes to decide. All around us opinions are provided for us. Advertisements bombard our senses until we gravitate toward convenience, convention, and covetousness. To follow the crowd and the way of least resistance seems to be all we need to get through the day.

But what is necessary of every man is character, and character is as Charlotte speaks of it—finely wrought metal beaten into shape and beauty by the repeated action of Will. We who teach should make it clear to ourselves that our aim in education is less good conduct than good character. We may mold good conduct in our children, but it is of value to the world only as it has its source in character. To have a strong, virtuous character, we need a strong, vigorous Will.

Each Right Choice Creates Greater Will-Power

Every assault upon the flesh and spirit of man is an attack, however insidious, upon his personality—his Will. In *Screwtape Letters,* C. S. Lewis lets us follow the course of action and point of view of a few of the devil's demons. The letters, written from one inexperienced demon to his uncle, are in one sense humorous, and in another, frighteningly accurate in their depiction of the average man. The uncle, in his letters, gives his nephew advice on how to instigate trouble by influencing ordinary upstanding humans like ourselves. The subtle attacks made by the demons are aimed directly at the Will. The initial aim is to promote petty squabbles and a growing dislike for the ones we live with ("the wicked plot . . . " Psalm 37:12).

It is discouraging how crime and promiscuity have risen, but there will always be persons of good Will among us—God's remnant—who resist the general trend. Our duty as parents and teachers is to turn out into the world persons of good Will.

Parents keep a child's Will weak by constant suggestion. By suggestion Charlotte means deciding everything for our children—with nagging reminders—instead of giving them little bits of responsibility, room to fail, and consequences to face.

Someone once called it "feeling the pain of [one's] decision." At first, I was puzzled at this because I knew we should not give our young ones too many choices. When they are young they cannot make wise decisions. But as our children mature and learn to recognize what would be the right thing to do, there should be a time when we give them the opportunity to exercise their Wills, so that through exercise, they can gain in strength, and learn to become reliable. A reliable person needs no constant reminder, no constant suggestion to do right.

What we do with the Will is voluntary. What we do without the conscious action of the Will is involuntary (habit). The Will's function is to "choose," and with every choice we make, we grow strength of character.

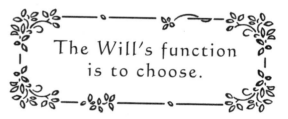

The Will's function is to choose.

Each Individual Must Build His Own Will-Power

I remember the old cartoons where the main character was shown with a red devil on his left shoulder whispering in one ear and a white angel on his right doing the same. Such whispers will reach us all through our lives. Part of our education is learning to choose between them. We know how important it is for a child to learn the habit of obedience. But this is the curious thing. Charlotte Mason says that "obedience is valuable only insofar as it helps the child towards making himself do that which he knows he ought to do. Every effort of obedience which does not give him a sense of conquest over his own inclinations, helps enslave him." He will resent the loss of his freedom by getting his own way whenever he can. "But invite his cooperation," says Charlotte, "let him heartily intend and purpose to do the thing he is bidden, and then it is his own Will that is compelling him, and not yours; and he has begun the greatest effort, the highest accomplishment of human life—the making, the compelling of himself . . . Let him enjoy a sense of triumph and of your congratulation, whenever he fetches his thoughts back to his tiresome [math page], whenever he makes his hands finish what they have begun."

A child can learn this secret of Willing. By an effort of Will, he can turn his thoughts to the thing he wants to think of—to his lessons, his prayers, his chores, and away from distracting thoughts and wishes to be doing something else. If he can get to the "shoulds" and fix his mind upon them, do them well and in good time, he will have the approval of his mother and time for the leisure and pleasure that should naturally follow.

Charlotte says,

It is something to know what to do with ourselves when we are beset, and the knowledge of this *way of the will* is so far the secret of a happy life, that it is well worth imparting to the children. Are you cross? Change your thoughts. Are you tired of trying? Change your thoughts. Are you craving for things you are not to have? Change your thoughts; there is a power within you, your own Will, which will enable you to turn your attention from thoughts that make you unhappy and wrong, to thoughts that make you happy and right. And this is the exceedingly simple way in which the Will acts.

But to change or fix the thoughts, a child must have had

trained in him the power of paying attention. If he has never been trained to apply his whole mind to a given subject, then no energy of Will can make him think steadily on the thoughts of his choosing—or of anyone else's, for that matter. So before he can strengthen his Will—by changing his thoughts—he needs to have developed the power to fix them.

A bad habit can grasp firmly to the rope on one side of the tug-of-war with the Will. Because Habit's muscles have been exercised so regularly, he may prove too strong for feeble Will. When a child's thoughts or actions (like throwing a fit) have become habitual, it will be a struggle, but exercising the muscles of Habit less and practicing efforts of Will more can help Will become the victor.

The teacher's part is to provide children with a wellspring of right thought to draw from. Right thought flows upon the stimulus of an idea, and ideas are stored—as we have seen—in books and pictures and the lives of men and nations. These instruct the conscience and stimulate the Will, and man or child "chooses."

Fortifying the Will

There is no occasion for panic if you haven't considered the Will up till now. It is time, however, that we realize that to fortify the Will is one of the great purposes of education. An understanding of human nature would help. Children should learn what it means to be human, to know of the wonderful goodness that humans are capable of, and an idea of the damages of sin. Everyone may be of service to mankind, everyone may climb those delectable mountains, like Christian in *Pilgrim's Progress*—from whence he gets the vision of the Celestial City. He must know something of his body—with its senses and its appetites, of his intellect, imagination and aesthetic sense, of his moral nature, which is ordered by love and justice.

Realizing how much good mankind is capable of through God's grace, as well as the perils that may assail his soul, he should know that the duty of self-government belongs to him. The governing powers are the Conscience and the Will. The whole ordering of education with its history, poetry, art, and arithmetic, is based on the assumption that Conscience is incapable of righteousness without regular and progressive instruction.

Ruled by Will Versus Impulse

A child also needs instruction concerning the Will. To "commit your way to the Lord," is an act of the Will. Our more mature children should clearly understand the possibility of drifting into an easy life led by appetite or desire in which the Will plays no part. To become a person of good Will, a young person must always rely on his will-power to do the responsible thing. The power to Will is a slow growth, but it grows stronger as it is put to use. Charlotte tells us that the Will is the controller of the passions and emotions, the director of the desires, the ruler of the appetites. The Will builds its muscles as it is exercised. Every time a child represses the urge to have a fit, to hang his head in self-pity, or snatch something he wants away from another child, his Will is exercised and grows stronger. But the Will also needs nourishment to grow strong, and so we feed it with ideas. With noble ideas of the Christian life we train a child's conscience to do what is right, to *Will* and to do for His good pleasure.

It should be pointed out that a turbulent (impatient, fitful) person is not ruled by Will at all, but by impulse, passion, and desire. To lose control is a sign of a feeble Will. And if a new word could be made to suit this state, it would be Willessness.

It is possible to have a steady, strong Will with unworthy or evil intent. Professor Moriarity from *The Adventures of Sherlock Holmes* comes to mind. Even before meeting him, Detective Holmes deducted that the professor was intelligent, diabolical, and had a strong Will to stay on his evil track in anticipation of reaching his goal. This Holmes knew by examining the clues made by the professor's criminal tracks.

It is also possible to have a strong Will towards a good end but to come to it by unworthy, unrighteous means. I think of the death of Julius Caesar by the conspirators. It wasn't an easy thing for Brutus to do—to stab someone he loved and admired—but he cared more for his ideals for Rome and the safeguarding of the republican form of government. Therefore, he believed it was an honorable (politically

IF

·······

by Rudyard Kipling

If you can keep your head when all about you
   Are losing theirs and blaming it on you;
If you can trust yourself when all men doubt you,
   But make allowance for their doubting too:
If you can wait and not be tired by waiting,
   Or, being lied about, don't deal in lies,
   Or being hated don't give way to hating,
   And yet don't look too good, nor talk too wise;

If you can dream—and not make dreams your master;
If you can think—and not make thoughts your aim,
If you can meet with Triumph and Disaster
   And treat those two impostors just the same:
If you bear to hear the truth you've spoken
   Twisted by knaves to make a trap for fools,
   Or watch the things you gave your life to, broken,
   And stoop and build 'em up with worn-out tools;

If you can make one heap of all your winnings
   And risk it on one turn of pitch-and-toss,
   And lose, and start again at your beginnings,
   And never breathe a word about your loss:
If you can force your heart and nerve and sinew
   To serve your turn long after they are gone,
   And so hold on when there is nothing in you
   Except the Will which says to them: "Hold on!"

If you can talk with crowds and keep your virtue,
   Or walk with Kings—nor lose the common touch,
If either foes nor loving friends can hurt you,
If all men count with you, but none too much:
If you can fill the unforgiving minute
   With sixty seconds' worth of distance run,
   Yours is the Earth and everything that's in it,
   And—which is more—you'll be a Man, my son!

correct) thing to do—to "sacrifice" Caesar's life and end any threat to tyranny. This story of good intentions is a tragedy-because the end result was more bloodshed.

The simple Will, what our Lord calls "the single eye," would appear to be the one thing needful for straight living and serviceableness. But always the first condition of Will, for good or ill, is an object outside of self. By degrees we may come to realize that just as "to reign" is the distinctive function of a king, so "to Will" is the function of a man. A king is not a king unless he reigns, and a man is less than a man unless he Wills.

Another thing to be observed is that even a strong Will needs times of diversion and recreation so that it may return to its post with freshness and readiness.

Resisting Temptation

The child must learn, too, that the will is subject to solicitations all round, from the lust of the flesh and the lust of the eye and the pride of life. He must also learn that Will does not act alone, that it takes the whole man to Will, to "just say no." And a man Wills wisely, justly and strongly, in proportion to his instruction and training. We must understand in order to will to do the right thing. "How is that ye will not understand?" said our Lord to the Jews. This *way of the Will* is the secret of self-government, which children should acquire. Decisiveness is a practical virtue that offers peace of mind and well-being, and enables us to live a righteous life for Christ.

"Choose ye this day" applies to the thoughts that we allow ourselves to receive and accept or reject. There have been many times when my husband and I have had to pray, "Lord, what would you have us do in this sticky situation?" To seek the Lord's Will, to wait on the Lord, to use whatever knowledge we have to solve a complicated problem, and then to live by faith, has at

times been very difficult. This is why the concept of "the way of the Will" is so intriguing to me. I want to make it less confusing and less strenuous for my children. It has been said that the instructed conscience and the trained reason support the Will in those little or great things by which men live. If a good conscience, reason, and a strong Will are what we need to commit our ways unto the Lord and align our Will with his, let us then acquire them and train our children in them.

Educating the Will

Will power is the outcome of a slow and ordered education in which precept and example flow in from the lives and thoughts of other men. This is yet another purpose for Charlotte's emphasis on the Bible and the humanities. All the historic heroism, the moral vision within the verses of poetry, the moral value within simple stories, and great literature, art, and music, will spontaneously help train the conscience. To form opinions on these, to evaluate these with scripture, is to begin to reason. And Charlotte hoped that all this would become as regular and natural as the air we breathe. But the moment of choice is immediate, and the act of the Will voluntary. Thus the object of education is to prepare us to make instantaneous choices and voluntary actions each day.

We should beware of too much of a "self-centered" focus when teaching "self-knowledge, self-reverence, and self-control." It has been said that those who are wrapped up in themselves make small packages. We want children to grow to be magnanimous. Education must mostly be outward bound, and the mind that is concentrated upon self-emolument, even though it be the emolument of all the virtues, misses the higher and the simpler secrets of life. Duty and service are sufficient motives for the arduous training of the Will that a child goes through with little consciousness. The gradual fortifying of the Will must have an object outside of self to become large-hearted. A poet has said the last word about will so far as we yet know:

Our wills are ours we know not how;
Our wills are ours to make them Thine.

Letter from Amy on the Will

Some years ago, I received a letter from a subscriber of the *Parents' Review* asking for clarification on certain matters relating to Will. I share it with you here because I think Amy's question is a good one.

Dear Karen,

The more I read Miss Mason, the more I praise God for giving such insight and wisdom into bringing up children. However, I have a question. What does Miss Mason mean when she talks about training children by "suggestion?" I have looked up the word in the dictionary but I'm still a little confused. Would using rewards, incentives, and punishments in training a new habit be considered using suggestion? If so, I have found no other way to make sure that certain actions are repeated enough times in order to form a habit or to deter certain undesirable actions from occurring. For example, the children learned the habit of making their beds because I kept a chart. If the bed was made six days out of seven, my sons (who, by the way, are ages five and eight) enjoyed a trip to Sonic for a milkshake. After the habit had been formed they were informed that any time they "forgot" to make their beds from now on, they would be reminded by having to do an extra chore. This worked. One concern about this system, however, is that I am possibly training my children to love milkshakes more than chores. I really want them to learn to enjoy helping out and keeping things in order. I want them enjoy a clean bedroom. Any thoughts on this subject in future issues would be much appreciated.

Thank you a million times for bringing the ideas, philosophy, and advice of Miss Mason into our lives.

Sincerely yours,
Amy

Dear Amy,

I think Charlotte Mason is using the term "suggestion" in place of our term "nagging." The word nagging never appears in her writings. With regard to forming habits and strengthening the will, the old meaning of the word nagging really may be too harsh a word. King Solomon warns his son against the nagging woman. Her nagging seems to have at its heart a detestable attitude. But I think most of us would be guilty of one failing in our child training—that of "always telling," which is most often done with good intentions rather than nagging (a nasty word derived from the verb "to gnaw"). Let's look in Charlotte's book, *Parents and Children*, under "Discipline," Chapter 16. There is a section with the subtitle, "Always Telling." You may wonder why I am so familiar with this portion of her writings that it immediately comes to mind. Mine is highlighted. Yes, I find myself needing to be reminded periodically of Charlotte's admonishments about "always telling," especially just before and after we experience a household move. To quote Charlotte:

"'I'm sure I am always telling her to keep her drawers neat, or to hold up her head and speak nicely, or to be quick and careful about an errand,' says the poor mother, with tears in her eyes, and indeed this habit of 'always telling' him or her is a weary process for the mother; dull, because hopeless. She goes on 'telling' to deliver her own soul, for she has long since ceased to expect any result: and we know how dreary is work without hope. But, perhaps, even this mother does not know how unutterably dreary is the 'always telling,' which produces nothing, to the child. At first he is fretful and impatient under the pitter patter of idle words; then he puts up with the inevitable; and comes at last hardly to be aware that the thing is being said. As for any impression on his character, any habit really formed, all this labor is without result; the child does the thing when he cannot help it, and evades as often as he can. And the poor disappointed mother says, 'I'm sure I've tried as much as any mother to train my children in good habits, but I have failed.' She is not altogether dispirited, however. The children have not the habits she wished to train them in; but they grow up warmhearted, good-natured, bright young people, by no means children to be ashamed of. All the same, the mother's sense of failure is a monition (caution, warning) to be trusted."

What is wanting here is the need for natural consequences in training. If you read from the beginning of the chapter on discipline, you see that punishment is necessary but is only effective if it is a natural consequence. We cannot really allow our children to experience the direct consequences of their dangerous activity (falling from heights, tasting poison, etc.). We can make up something that is near to that action, as you have done. "If the bed isn't made you will need to do an additional chore." You're right, Amy, it works. The action of doing an additional chore may be experienced more than once, but it is a more impressionable reminder.

Years ago, when my children were very small, a more experienced mother told me that when it was discovered that her one son didn't make his bed before breakfast, he was told he would have to make his brother's bed, too, the next morning. After her son's experience of having to make both beds one morning she never again needed to interrupt her breakfast preparation by calling at the foot of the stairway with her suggestion, "Did you make your bed, Johnny?"

An atmosphere of authority should take the place of "always telling," or shows of exasperation on our part. The child can know we are disappointed with him without our wearing our emotions on our sleeves, even if this is the fourth time William needed to experience the same natural consequence.

It is frustrating when some children seem to need to experience failure more than others before they are thoroughly corrected. But let William alone to feel the pang of regret without being distracted by how much we are affected by his failure. In other words, keep your cool.

Compliments and other demonstrations of pleasure over a chore well done, or a behavior lovingly manifested, are deserved treats. An occasional edible treat is fine, but I wouldn't make it a regular thing. There are also pleasing natural consequences to consider such as, "We all have done our chores so diligently that there is time for us to go cycling together around the neighborhood." My children enjoy this very much. Perhaps you can think of a pleasing activity you may enjoy doing together as a reward for a chore well done or a child's attitude changed for the better.

My mother used to say, "sweets are for the sweet" because she wanted her children not to name-call, criticize, or speak unkindly to each other. I have proclaimed this motto in our home. One of my children gets in more trouble by her mouth than her siblings. Her natural consequence is to be left out when cookies are passed out or the apple pie is cut. It is not what you put in your mouth that makes you sweet but what comes out.

"Always warning" is another form of always telling. We warn our children too many times in a row and thus do not allow them to experience a natural consequence. This might be your tendency if you can hear yourself saying, "I thought I told you . . . ," or "Didn't I warn you . . . ?" and it is left at that with no penalty carried through. Give fewer warnings. Your child may act surprised when she hears you say, "Lucy, you will not listen to any cassettes (of music or stories) today or tomorrow." You had warned her not to leave loose cassettes about the house—between couch cushions, by the dog's dish, on a dining room chair. She cries or is cross when the privilege is taken away. Do not let your heart sink for her crying. She needs to be responsible with cassettes at her mature age of eight when you are not always beside her to remind her (suggestion) to put one cassette back before she takes another out. Your previous constant reminding only got you frustrated, and didn't really affect Lucy.

These are my thoughts, Amy. I hope they have been helpful.

Sincerely,
Karen

Questions for Personal Reflection or Support Group Discussion

1. *"Our aim in education is less conduct than character," says Charlotte. How much more valuable is a child's conduct that is rooted in his character? Give examples. We do not give our youngest children many choices, but train them first to obey. However, when a child begins to reason and his Will has been instructed with noble stories from the Bible and literature, why is it good to let him make "nickel and dime" mistakes and experience consequences?*

2. *"What we do with the Will we describe as voluntary. What we do without the conscious action of will is involuntary. The job of the Will is to choose." How do we grow in character with every choice we make? Explain.*

3. *In place of constant suggestion, what is it that we should present to children (and ourselves) to instruct the conscience and stimulate the Will?*

4. *What kind of character does a chivalrous person have? What part does the Will have in it? Name some chivalrous persons in history. How were they willful?*

5. *What part does recreation play in the preservation of Will power?*

6. *Gradual fortifying of the Will needs to be done without too much focus on "self." What other focus is preferred?*

Chapter Eleven

··

Inconstant Kitty

BEFORE THE ADVENT OF THE TELEPHONE, in the days when written correspondence was more frequent, a letter was sent by two homeschooling parents to their aunt, in which they shared their concern for the character development of Kitty, their six-year-old daughter. As many of the same concerns are experienced by homeschooling parents in modern times, perhaps you will find this peek into their letter—and their aunt's response—useful in your endeavors with your own children.

A Plea for Help

But for now the real purpose of this letter, Auntie—does it take your breath away to get four pages? We want you to help us with Kitty. My husband and I are at our wits' end, and would most thankfully take your wise head and kind heart into counsel. I'm afraid we have been laying up trouble for ourselves and for our little girl. The ways of nature are very attractive in all young creatures, and it is so delightful to see a child do as " 'tis its nature to," that you forget that Nature, left to herself, produces a waste. Our little Kitty's might so easily become a wasted life.

Let me tell you the history of Kitty's yesterday—one of her days is like the rest, and you will be able to see where we need your help.

Picture the three little heads bent over "copy books" in our cheery home school-room. Before a line is done, up starts Kitty.

"Mother, may I write the next copy 'shell?' 'Shell' is so much nicer than—'know,' and I'm so tired of it."

"How much have you done?"

"I have written it three whole times, Mother, and I really can't do it anymore! I think shell is so pretty!"

By and by we read, but Kitty cannot read—can't even "sound out" words because all the time her eyes are on a sparrow on the topmost twig of the cherry tree; so she reads "With birdie!" We do sums; a short line of addition is to poor Kitty a hopeless and an endless task. "Five plus three equals nine" is her last effort, though she knows quite well how to add her figures under ten.

Half a scale on the piano, and then—eyes and ears for everybody's business but her own. Three stitches of hemming, and the idle fingers play with the hem or fold the dusting cloth in a dozen shapes. I am in the middle of a thrilling history talk: ". . . So Christopher Columbus—"

"Oh, Mother, do you think we shall go to the sea this year? My pail is quite ready, all but the handle, but I can't find my spade anywhere!"

And thus we go on, pulling Kitty through her lessons somehow, but it is a weariness to herself and to all of us, and I doubt if the child learns anything except by quick flashes. But you have no idea how clever the little girl is. After idling through a lesson, she will overtake us at a bound at the last moment with a clever comment, and thus escape the wholesome guilt of being shown up as the dunce of our little party.

Kitty's dawdling ways, her restless desire for change of occupation, her always wandering thoughts, lead to a good deal of friction, and spoil our schoolroom party, which is a pity, because I want the children to enjoy their lessons from the very first. What do you think my darling child said to me yesterday in the most coaxing pretty way?

"There are so many things nicer than lessons! Don't you think so, Mother?"

Yes, dear aunt, I can see you put your finger on those unlucky words, "Coaxing, pretty way," and hear you say to yourself that awful sentence of yours about sin being bred of allowance. Isn't that it? It is quite true; we are at fault. Those butterfly ways of Kitty's were so enjoyable to behold until we thought it time to set her to work, and then we found that we should have been training her from her babyhood. Well,

If you break your plaything yourself, dear,
Don't you cry for it all the same?
I don't think it is such a comfort
To have only oneself to blame.

So, like a dear, kind aunt, don't scold us, but help us to do better. Is Kitty constant at anything? you ask. Does she stick to any of the "many things so much nicer than lessons?" I am afraid our little girl is "unstable as water." And the worse of it is, she shows eager excitement to be at a thing, and then, when you think she has settled down for a half an hour of pleasant play, off she is like a butterfly. She recites her little poem about the busy bee dutifully, but when I tell her she is not a bit like a busy bee, but rather like a foolish, flitting butterfly, I'm afraid she rather likes it, and makes up to the butterflies as if they were akin to her, and were having just the good time she would prefer. But you must come and see the child to understand how volatile she is.

"Oh, Mother, please let me have a doll's wash this afternoon! I'm quite unhappy about poor Peggy! I really think she likes to be dirty!"

Great preparations follow in the way of tub and soap and apron. The little laundress sits down, greatly pleased with herself, to undress her dirty Peggy, but hardly is the second arm out of its sleeve, than, presto! a new idea presents itself, and off goes Kitty to clean out her doll house, deaf to all of my remonstrances about "nice hot water," and "poor dirty Peggy."

If the chief business of parents is to train character in their children, we have done nothing for Kitty. At six years old the child has no more power of application, no more habit of attention, is no more able to make herself do the thing she ought to do—indeed, has no more desire to do the right thing than she had at six months old. We are getting very unhappy about it. My husband feels strongly that parents should labor at character as the Hindu gold-beater labors at his vase, that character is the one thing we are called upon to effect. And what have we done for Kitty? We have turned out a "fine animal," and are glad and thankful for that, but that is all: the child is as wayward, as unsteady, as a young colt. Do help us, dear Auntie. Think our little girl's case over. If you can get to the source of the mischief, send us a few hints for our guidance, and we shall be yours gratefully evermore."

Sincerely anticipating your response,
Estelle.

My Dear Estelle,

And now for my poor little great-niece! Her mother piles up charges against her, but how interesting and amusing and like the free world of fairy-land it would all be were it not for the tendencies which, in these days, we talk much about and watch little against. We bring up our children in the easiest, happy-go-lucky way, and all the time talk solemnly in big words about the momentous importance of every influence brought to bear upon them. But it is true: these naughty, winsome ways of Kitty's will end in her growing up like half the "girls"—that is, young women—one meets. They talk glibly on many subjects, but test them, and they know nothing of any. They are ready to undertake anything, but they carry nothing through. This week So-and-so is their particular friend, next week, another. Even their amusements, their "one real interest," comes and goes. And, all the time, there is no denying, as you say, that this very fickleness has a charm, so long as the glamour of youth lasts, and the wayward girl has bright smiles and winning, graceful ways to disarm you with. But youth does not last, and the poor girl who began as a butterfly ends as a grub, tied to the earth by the duties she never learned how to fulfill—that is supposing she is a girl with a conscience. Wanting that, she dances through life whatever befalls: children, husband, home, must take their chance.

Kitty has been on my mind all the time, and it is quite true, you must take her at hand.

First, as to her lessons: you must help her to gain the power of attention. That should have been done long ago, but better late than never, and an aunt who has given her mind to these matters blames herself for not having noticed the need sooner. But I can guess you are saying, "If the child has no faculty of attention, how can we give it to her? It's just a natural defect." Not a bit! Attention is not a faculty at all, though I believe it is worth more than all the so-called faculties put together. This, at any rate, is true, that no talent, no genius, is worth much without the power of attention—and this is the power that makes men or women successful in life. (I talk like a book because I've been reading up on this lately.)

Attention is no more than this: the power of giving your mind to what you are about—the bigger the better so far as the mind goes. Kitty must get this power of attention—to be able to give her mind to a task at will. Kitty must be taught to give her mind to sums and reading, and even to dusting. Go slowly—a little today and a little more tomorrow.

In the first place, her lessons must be made interesting. Do not let the whole of the reading lesson be the tedious task of "sounding out" every word. Give her some interesting, easily recognizable sight words from the nursery rhymes she likes best.

The chances are great that she will be learning much of the most commonly used words in our English language by practicing these rhymes. Children's poems and nursery rhymes are enjoyable because they are short and easy to master. Let every day bring the complete mastery of a new word to recognize by sight, as well as the keeping up with the old ones and practice in "sounding out."

But do not let the lesson last more than ten minutes, and insist, with brisk, bright determination, on the child's full concentrated attention of eye and mind for the whole ten minutes. Do not allow a moment's dawdling at lessons. Complete and entire attention is a natural function which requires no effort and causes no fatigue; the anxious labor of mind of which we are at times aware comes when attention wanders and has again to be brought to the point.

I should not give her rows of figures to add yet; use dominoes or the domino cards, the point being to add or subtract the dots on the two halves in a twinkling. You will find the three can work together at this, and will find it as delightful as any table game. Kitty will be all alive here, and will take her share of the work merrily, and this is a point gained. Do not, if you can help it, single the little maid out from the rest and throw her on her own responsibility. It is a heavy and a weary weight for the bravest of us, and the little back will feel the burden of bending under life if you do not train her to carry it lightly, as an Eastern woman her pitcher.

Then, vary the lessons: now head, and now hands, now tripping feet and tuneful tongue—but in every lesson let Kitty and the other two carry away the joyous sense of "something attempted, something done."

Children are only happy with a lesson if they have a sense of accomplishment. Give her the opportunity to say to herself, "I did it!"

Allow no weary sense of monotony over the old stale work—which must be

kept up all the time, it is true—but rather review by way of a game that lesson of the day, which should always be a distinct step that the children can recognize. Let her see a light at the end of a dark tunnel by way of a small incentive, "When you have finished your row of penmanship, could you draw in the rest of the rabbit I've started for you at the end of your row?"

When a child is not interested in certain monotonous practice, her tendency is to drag the occupation out further. You do not realize until you try, how the "now or never" feeling about a lesson quickens the attention of even the most volatile child. What you are allowed to meander through all day, you will; what must be done, is done. Then there is the by-the-by gain besides that of quickened attention. I once heard a wise man say that, if he must choose between the two, he would rather his child should learn the meaning of "must" than inherit a fortune. And here you will be able to bring moral force to bear on wayward Kitty. Every lesson must have its own time, and no other time in this world is there for it. The sense of the preciousness of time, of the irreparable loss when a ten minutes' lesson is thrown away, must be brought home.

Let your disappointment and hidden distress at the loss of "golden minutes" be felt by the children, and also be visited upon them by the loss of some small childish pleasure which the day should have held. It is a sad thing to let a child dawdle through a day and be let off scot-free. You see, I am talking of the children, and not of Kitty alone, because it is so much easier to be good in company, and what is good for her will be good for the trio.

But there are other charges: poor Kitty is neither steady in play nor steadfast in love! May not the habit of attending to her lessons help her to stick to her play? Then encourage her: "What! The doll's tea-party over? That's not the way grown-up ladies have tea! They sit and talk for a long time. See if you can make your tea-party last twenty minutes by my watch." This failing of Kitty's is just a case where a little gentle jest might do a great deal of good. It is a weapon to be handled carefully, for one child may resent, and another take pleasure in being laughed at, but managed with tact I do believe it's good for children and grown-ups to see the comic side of their doings.

I think we make a mistake in not holding up often enough certain virtues for our children's admiration. Put a premium of praise on every finished thing, if it be only a house of cards. Steadiness in work is also a step on the way towards steadfastness in love. Let Kitty and all your children grow up to glory in their constancy to every friend.

There, I am sending a notable sermon instead of the few delicate hints I meant to offer, but never mount a woman on her hobby—who knows when she will get off again!

With Love,
Auntie Laura[1]

Questions for Support Group Discussion or Personal Reflection

1. *Do you have a student who could use improvement in his power to apply himself?*

2. *Why is it so important to develop the habit and power of attention in a young student? How can this be achieved?*

3. *How can we hold a student's attention during a review lesson?*

4. *The loss of "golden minutes" should be felt by the student. What natural consequence should be the result of dilly-dallying?*

5. *What words of encouragement could you give the student to demonstrate you are pleased with his efforts toward constancy?*

Chapter Twelve

....

Living Books

"THE AUTHOR, who has been interested in American Indians since his child-hood, is indebted to many people for the stories and facts in this book."[1] This is the first sentence of a little paragraph of acknowledgments written opposite the title page of the book *The First Book of Indians* by Benjamin Brewster. I picked up this small hardcover for one dollar at a used curriculum sale held in the parking lot of a church. I recognized it as a "living book"—a term originated by Charlotte Mason. How could I tell it was a living book? First, it was written by an author who took special interest in his subject. Secondly, the facts were presented in story form. The illustrator aimed at accuracy in depicting headdresses, canoes, totem poles, and other aspects of Indian life, but also depicted action. The different tribes of American Indians were busy fishing, dancing, grinding corn, and hunting deer. I am sure there are other living books on Indians. It is not this particular introduction to American Indians that I am recommending, rather, I am recommending the kind of book in which such an introduction would be found. Such a book is the kind of book that ministers to children.

A rather warm and personal forward, preface, introduction, or acknowledgment is something many living books have in common. In them we read why or how the author came to write his book. The acknowledgment pages in Holling Clancy Holling's books, for instance, highlight the fact that his books are living books. In *Pagoo* he writes: "This book provides only a peek into tide-pool life. If it awakens some young reader to further interest in the world under water, Pagoo will have done his bit." He tells us he picked a hermit crab (Pagoo) as the main character "because these clownish creatures are found along the beaches of many seas."[2] Pagoo may be "clownish," but his story is told against a factual, detailed background. The story is based on personal observation and the author acknowledges the scientists for their helpfulness and advice. Sadly, we would not find *Pagoo*—or any of Holling's other wonderful books—used in the typical classroom. Should we let this bias lead us to think that such a delightful combination of story, fact, and accurate illustration is not educational enough for our young children? On the contrary, such a book is very educational because **it reaches children in ways most typical school books cannot.**

If we want the mind of a child to come alive, we feed him living ideas. Ideas reside in living books, which I think has something to do with the intermingling of story, fact, and author's opinion or viewpoint. I find one of the most important aspects of Charlotte's method of education is her use of *real* books. It was evident to her, over one hundred years ago, that children have a natural aptitude for literature, and she firmly believed that this should determine the kind of instruction we give them.

While Charlotte was alive, hundreds of teachers following her principles wrote to her describing the experience of watching children pick up ideas from well-written books. Charlotte said, "The finding of this power which is described as 'sensing a passage,' is as the striking of a vein of gold in that fabulously rich country, human nature." Those teachers found that "children have a natural aptitude for literary expression which they enjoy in hearing and reading and employ in telling [narration] or writing."

With books of literary character, that is, books that Charlotte said have the "terseness and vividness proper to a literary work," we put children directly in touch with the mind of the author. This is one reason, in Charlotte's method of teaching, that the teacher's talk is passed by in favor of reading these kinds of books. Thoughts that are "fresh and finely expressed" are written by those who love their subjects. In other words, an author takes much care in choosing his words so that he conveys the precise message he wishes his readers to receive. Through his carefully chosen words we sense his intimacy with, and his enthusiasm and fondness for his subject. Literature gives us a little peek at the per-

sonality of the author because it has emotion. Living books, unlike the compressed compilations of textbooks, are laced with emotion, saturated with ideas, and they convey information as well. Whenever possible, it is well to use living books for instruction. Use them in place of the stolidly presented information of the textbook—especially during the elementary years. Books of pure fact and information do have a place in education. We do not need to exclude them entirely (my son likes how directly textbooks answer his questions), but they cannot be called literature, and therefore would not be considered living books by Charlotte.

The One-Page Test

Here is another way to recognize a living book. First examine the book to see if it promotes noble thoughts rather than a jaded or misleading outlook on life. If the book captures your interest it very well may capture that of your children's. Once you have determined its general suitability, simply give the book—whether fiction or non-fiction—the one-page test. Start reading it aloud to your children and look for signs that it is opening the doors of their minds. Stop at the end of the first or second page. You will know you have found a living book if you hear them plead, "Read me more!"

What is Literature?

Writing in which no human feeling enters is not literature. So a report of pure scientific fact is not literature. (However, some people consider the works of Newton or Euclid, for example, to be literature. These classic writings on science and mathematics are read in colleges where great books are studied.) Neither is mere historical record literature, as for example, the news in the newspaper. What Charlotte called "journalese" is the dry style of writing given to school children in most textbooks. Sherwin Cody said in his book, *The Art of Writing and Speaking the English Language,* (written in 1906):

All histories, treatises, philosophical works, and textbooks and handbooks are literature only in such cases as an appeal is made to the universal heart or the emotions common to mankind. . . The mind has three aspects: the intellectual, which gives us truth; the ethical, which gives us nobility; and the aesthetic, which gives us beauty. It is really impossible to separate one of these things from the other entirely; but we may say that in science we have nothing but the intellectual, or truth; in religion nothing but the ethical, or nobility; and in art nothing but the aesthetic, or beauty. But as a religion without truth or beauty would be a very poor affair, so art without truth or nobility would be almost inconceivable.[3]

The test of literature is that it must be all three; it must bring us truth, nobility, and beauty. Literature must be somewhat intellectual and give us truth. It must be ethical so that we are well-nourished with noble ideas. It must also be artistic and make its appeal through the emotions. Why ought our school books be living books—books written in literary language? Because as Charlotte reminds us, children are born persons—they are human beings—and the style of writing that appeals to them is that which includes the human touch. So we look for books with that touch of originality—books that warm the imagination.

I am happy that there are a host of nonfiction picture books in our local library. I like to borrow those with the uncluttered look—those that have one simple photograph or drawing every page, or every other page. I read a few paragraphs and if the flavor of the writing sounds as friendly as it is informative, I take it home and pile it in our (laundry size) library basket.

Work and Play with Living Books

Living books have a certain amount of "play" in them. And just as "all work and no play make Jack a dull boy," all textbooks and no living books will make Jack and Jill dull children. Their minds might have retained a few facts, but

will their minds be livened-up, their imaginations warmed up, and their curiosity stirred up, to want to know more?

To narrate from living books requires both work and play. The play is the enjoyment experienced in the literary aspect of a book that provokes thought. The work is putting the thoughts into one's own words, borrowing phrases, vocabulary, and facts, using a train of thought to sequence events or processes, and generally making sense out of the reading. This is accomplished without interruptions by the teacher and without relying on her ever-ready explanations. My eldest child, Sophia, has read many living books over the past ten years. This morning she and I took a bicycle tour around our neighborhood together. We like to talk as we ride. It was as we were discussing what I was writing in this chapter, that she told me she doesn't think too much whether a book is going to be easy or difficult to read. She just reads it. Some books will be naturally more work to read than others. But she has come to expect that all living books—all literature, whether easy or hard—will bring an experience somewhat new and different from the last.

When reading is approached in this way, it is looked at as an adventure. It doesn't quite matter whether the trip is on a rocky cliff, across a sandy beach, or down a shaded wooded path; the mind likes to travel across whatever terrain is presented. The quickened mind is curious. And though one road may bring more challenging travel than another, nevertheless, each road is leading somewhere new, providing new knowledge along the way.

The Textbook as a Secondary Tool

We have used several textbooks over the years. They are usually used as an outline to which we tack on living books and experiences. There is a chapter on birds in our fourth grade science textbook, for instance. The information is helpful, but it doesn't stand on its own. In 1991, in my first issue of the *Parents Review*, I told about one way we use textbooks and living books in our educational life:

This winter we set up a nature feeding station ten feet opposite the our kitchen's picture window. On frosty December mornings while the other children of the neighborhood were huddled together waiting for the school bus, we were gathered in comfort at the picture window, spying on birds—some of which we'd never seen before. We passed around binoculars for a closer look at little detailed markings on feathers. Our field guide was at hand to differentiate between male and female. We referred to our science textbook chapter on birds to learn about their migration, hollow bones, differing uses of beaks and talons, and how the air flow over a wing provides lift. We enjoyed drawing a bird in our Nature Notebooks and picking out a poem.

I read aloud from the writings of Ernest Seton Thompson—a naturalist that Charlotte recommended. In his book *Wild Animals I Have Known* is a true tale of a crow he named Silverspot. Because of its tiny spot of silver-colored feathers, Mr. Thompson was able to follow and observe this one crow's activities over a period of years and learn of its particular habits, as well as its place within the social structure of the crow community. As I read the story aloud during our week of lessons, we found ourselves not only learning interesting details about crows, but growing quite fond of this Silverspot. We were sad to come to the end of the story and hear, in Seaton's gentle style, of Silverspot's death.

A few months after our study of birds, in a shopping center parking lot near an open field, we met up with a big black crow. It was perched very close to our car, and as we approached it gave out a loud abrupt caw-caw rather than a longer c-a-a-w. (Thanks to Silverspot, we knew that there is a big difference between one kind of caw and another in crow language.) Just as it flew over our heads I was struck with how, because of our new knowledge and a feeling of intimacy with this particular one of God's creatures, we were now more attentive to this commonplace bird that we would not have previously noticed.

Can you see how textbooks used alone fall short of inspiring the student, especially when compared to a curriculum incorporating living books?

An Owl in the House is a naturalist's diary. In it we read entries made by zoologist Bernd Heinrich as he raises Bubo from a chick. His photographs and drawings of Bubo around the woods of his cabin in Maine help us appreciate his experience. Books like these do science justice.

Living books on a number of subjects add long-lasting value to any educational program. Children will gain a richer memory from what is taught in literary language. And when they tell it back in their own words (narration) it becomes their own possession. Charlotte wished the reading of living books to be part of every child's inheritance.

Geography

Learning geography (and/or social studies) through living books may take a little longer (it is impossible to cram a living book) but the impression it leaves makes the invested time worthwhile. Wherever the setting of your story, find it on the globe and look up facts about that country or place (its hillsides, lakes, deserts, food, costume, music, art, etc.). Draw a map and tell how you would get there, if you were to travel to that place. I'm somewhat sure my children could point out the country of India on our globe. But I don't think they know much about the people and their ways. This year my eldest is mature enough to read *My India,* one of my husband's books that I read some years ago. The author, Jim Corbett was an Englishman—raised in India and educated in the 1880's and 1890's in an English school in the Kumaon hills—who wrote a number of books about his life among the people of India. His stories are both grim and fascinating. He worked on the railways and hunted huge man-eating tigers of the jungles. His service to the Indian people and the high adventure he relates plant in the reader a sympathetic picture of his adopted country that leaves an impression deep and long-lasting. The knowledge acquired through this kind of literature is more substantial than the bland information supplied in an average geography or social studies textbook. Therefore, whatever the subject, whenever you can, learn about God, man, and the world through the Bible and living books. ⇥

Questions for Support Group Discussion or Personal Reflection

1. *From what kinds of books have you and your children enjoyed and gained the most helpful insight?*

2. *List them. What quality do these books possess that enables them to hold our interest and help teach us what we don't already know?*

3. *Define the term "living book."*

4. *What kind of book did Charlotte Mason determine would make a good schoolbook?*

5. *How do living books stir up the mind, warm up the imagination, and liven-up the curiosity in ways textbooks do not?*

6. *Give an example of a book that has a flavor of writing that is friendly to children but not twaddly.*

7. *What is gained when we read books by a single author? Name a biography, a non-fiction title, or a piece of literature that taught you substantially more than a textbook would have.*

8. *How can living books be used for science, geography, history, or literature?*

Your Own Personal Reflections

Chapter Thirteen

How We Use Whole Books

RECEIVING HUNDREDS and hundreds of letters over the years helped me determine to publish this *Companion*. I, too, have asked the questions my readers ask. Although I've basically worked out much of what I've read in Charlotte Mason's original writings, there are areas I am still working out. Therefore you'll find me making such general statements as: "However you can, whenever you can, use whole books and narration and you'll do well. Things will begin looking up for you in your homeschool."

I have received literally dozens of letters asking the same questions asked by Donna, a subscriber to the *Parents' Review,* who wrote me as follows:

Dear Karen,

I would be interested in knowing about your family reading of real "whole" books (or living books). Do you read on themes or by authors or do you choose books at random? Is there a guide you use for choosing books? Do you have perhaps a list of "Books I Want Us to Read Before the Children Leave Home?"

Sincerely,
Donna

This chapter is an attempt to respond to that question for Donna, as well as for the many others who share her question about how to choose living books.

Sequential Versus Random Selection of Science Books

Several years ago I visited the local library to borrow whole books on science topics that matched those in our science textbook. I eventually discovered that textbooks used by both the public school and the homeschool have sequentially the same topics from chapter to chapter. Thus, when I searched for books on the planets, for instance, they were all checked out. A month after I wanted to study the sun, the moon, and the solar system, I found the book trolley full of interesting selections ready "to be shelved." After I caught on to this "topic competing," I arranged our homeschool schedule so we were either several chapters behind or ahead of the other borrowers, so we would be able to find books we needed.

The next year, when we moved to a house several blocks from the local library, we didn't refer to any textbook for science, but instead randomly borrowed whole books from the library on whatever science topic was available at the time of our visit. We also used some books I had purchased. This was a freedom we enjoyed very much. Therefore I offer you this advice: keep a textbook if you must, but do not ignore the joy that can be experienced by using whole books—ones that you and your children choose. I know our reading would not be lively enough without them. For most of our elementary years of science study we mainly read about science in living books and pursued nature observation.

When I borrow books randomly, I choose one or two topics each visit. It could be ecology, pond animals, desert plants, the human digestive system, weather, or electricity. There is no need to empty the shelf of a topic. We try to take out only what we can read in two weeks. Whole books for the early elementary grades often go into more detail than do chapters in science textbooks for those grades. Young children can learn quite a bit from whole books—and remember much of what is learned when they narrate from them. This is good to keep in mind if you begin to feel any insecurity about straying from the textbook. My enthusiastic science-minded son pulled more books off the science shelf during his year of first grade than we could get to. Dad sometimes reads a science chapter from one of these "extra" books at bedtime.

An older student will need to rely more on a textbook, but for the early ele-

mentary years a student can get through science exclusively with whole books, a few experiments, and nature study. This is best accomplished when curiosity is mixed with discipline.

Obstacles to My Structure

One April afternoon I was priding myself for thinking a little ahead while I casually perused the shelves at our local library, looking for supplementary books on the American Civil War in preparation for—and in anticipation of—our next month's history studies. I needed one book to provide an outline (or concise explanation of the War) to complement the biographies I had purchased. A few picture books on the Civil War would have been nice, too. But I found that every Civil War book had been borrowed. The shelves were empty on the subject. There was not one Civil War-related book in sight! I was perplexed. Then, one evening in May, after a month of feeling my powers of patience dwindle, I chanced upon a pile of Civil War books in an out-of-the-way "to be shelved" area. I must have made some sort of joyous outburst that was heard by the librarian because she quickly came over to see if I needed assistance. When I explained my joy she explained the mystery behind the previous absence of the books. She said there was a homeschool co-op that had been enthusiastically studying the Civil War for a couple of months. They had visited Gettysburg, PA, and were chosen over other "schools" to partake in the re-enactment there.

The moral of the story is: If there are many whole-book homeschooling families in your area, be prepared to purchase more books on a subject, or be less casual than I was, and research farther ahead.

This past summer I planned well in advance: I did my research and made a list of almost every book title I would need for the coming year. I then placed onto their own shelf the titles I had purchased, dug out of old boxes stored in the basement, or found scattered on various shelves of our bookcases. I arranged the history titles in sequential order.

An Abundance of History

Real books are a pleasure for me to add to our history curriculum. It is easy for me to get excited about this subject. I like that so many catalogs have made it easy to choose historical fiction, biography, and also history texts by arranging titles by time periods. My eldest has read so many real books on her own that relate to history that I have lost count.

Picture books on historical themes are so easy to use and are a delight to the youngest students. I've spent a pretty penny on these. However, an overabundance of history need not be read aloud to the youngest students.

Time lines and teacher's guides for using whole books in the study of history can be found in various catalogs. My students are creating their own history notebooks. Captions to pictures are written by my young student. Written narrations are recorded in the older students' notebooks.

Parts of Whole Books

A word to prevent burn-out: Living books have very much made our homeschool a happy place. Charlotte Mason advised us to use quality books in quantity. Yet, we don't have to read all the books a thick catalog sells, or all that sit on the library shelves. Sometimes even just a chapter or two out of a certain book will give you the information you need to complement other material you are reading on the same subject. Let books be your servants, and not the other way around.

My children listen to biographies and literature on cassette and see an occasional video for geography, science, or history. We visit historical sites and museums when we can, but most of their knowledge does come from books (or parts of books).

How We've Used Whole Books for Science

Several years ago we moved to Maryland, where the school authorities require a portfolio rather than an achievement test. I wanted my children's portfolios to look impressive. So I was happy when my children latched onto my idea to accurately draw what they see in books about science. When studying the human body we took turns reading aloud from a library book, *The Story of Blood,* by Edith Lucie Weart. At the end of our study my students drew a diagram of the human heart and labeled its chambers and other parts. The book's diagram is black and white, so I advised them to define the chambers with the appropriate blue and red coding.

When studying ocean life, an array of undersea creatures were drawn,

influenced by Pagoo's adventures in a book by Holling Clancy Holling, and a book by Jacques Cousteau. A diagram of the tides was copied out of our textbook showing the bulging effect of moon and sun on the waters of our blue planet.

One week, I asked the children to record Newton's three laws of motion, using a picture book called *Eureka! It's an Airplane* by Jeanne Bendick. (I had originally taken this book out of the library to satisfy my young son's large appetite for airplane knowledge.) The girls drew an airplane and diagrammed the flow of air over the wing, labeling the difference in air pressure from below and above the wing. A short oral narration was given by one of them describing why the wing is shaped the way it is and how this provides lift. This little picture book went into more detail than did our textbook's chapter on machines and motion (upper elementary material).

Still on the subject of motion, my eldest daughter decided to use water-color paints and a fine brush on her drawing of the four stages of a cylinder in a combustion engine. Although not exactly the kind of water-color drawing one would find on a greeting card, I noticed it did add a subtle feminine touch to a somewhat masculine subject.

Because we had been trying to follow Charlotte's method of narration and living books, apart from lots of math pages there were few tests and workbook pages in our portfolios. (I sprinkled in some workbook pages to satisfy expectations of the examiner.) I was anxious about how impressive (and somewhat schoolish) we could make our portfolios appear and yet still be in keeping with Charlotte's philosophy. But my anxiety was alleviated when the examiner leafed through our pages with praise on his lips for the "wonderful pictures." He didn't take much time to read our carefully done writing. I suppose he was thinking that since it was there in quantity and neatly done, it must mean the children were doing what was required. He particularly liked my daughter's cylinder diagram.

Instead of coloring birds, flowers, insects, animals, etc., in sophisticated coloring books, over the years my children have drawn freehand what they have found in nature. This is preferred in the Charlotte Mason method. (See the chapter on nature study). Since I wanted to include these nature drawings in our portfolios, the children no longer drew all their nature drawings in a bound Nature Notebook, but on loose paper. These Nature Notebook-style pages were more easily included in the three-ring portfolio binder.

I remember the morning we discovered a gold and mauve moth by the back porch light. It lay still long enough for the children to draw it as accurately as they could, color it, and mark the date and time it was found. Just after it was measured (more like tickled) with a centimeter ruler, it flew away.

I've found drawings of life cycles to be very useful demonstrations. These personally-drawn diagrams have a way of sticking in the memory. I can still remember drawing the life cycle of a mosquito in third grade. Which one did you draw—the toad, the butterfly, or the ladybug? The cycle of water is another possibility. It really should not be surprising that science and drawing go well together. Leonardo Da Vinci thought the pair made congenial companions. Drawing—besides speaking and writing—is another form of Charlotte's important use of narration. Would your children welcome an opportunity to draw and label what they see or what they are reading about out of a living book or textbook? How can formal drawing accompany a subject in your home schoolroom? I've provided these suggestions in hopes that similar drawing projects will suggest themselves to you.

Here is one project that recently suggested itself to my younger daughter. Having researched facts on the ways of the manatee from several sources in the local library, Yolanda decided to make a picture book about a manatee's birth and its relationship with its mother. Together they escape red tide, migrate to warmer waters, and do a lot of eating and snuggling. In one episode the mother (cow) has her back cut by the propeller of a boat. It heals and becomes one of other scars. In another episode the calf is freed by the cow when he gets caught in some plastic garbage. He rises to the surface just in time for a breath of air. Her drawings of the manatees are quite accurate, as are her drawings of sea weed and coral. Students who follow Charlotte's living book regimen are used to extracting facts from stories. This time Yolanda took facts and placed them into the context of her own story. Either way we have found facts within stories a delightful way to learn and remember.

Evening Reading

For bedtime read-alouds I choose fiction. *Twenty-One Balloons* was read last year, which is a compromise for my scientific-minded son, as it could be called science fiction and is funny, too. *Miss Hickory* was read aloud some years ago, but I liked it so much that I read it aloud again this year. Its main character is a forgotten wooden doll who has a series of harrowing experiences with nature's woodland creatures. Clumsy, yet good-natured *Paddington Bear* has a particular fondness for marmalade—as does Dad in our house. Reading aloud *Chitty, Chitty, Bang Bang* was an auditory delight, as it's important to perform the necessary mouth noises when reading it aloud. Since *Cricket in Times Square* was read last spring, my son wishes us not to harm any of the many crickets that inhabit our damp basement every autumn. I read it aloud six years ago to one of my daughters so she could narrate back to me during school mornings. I remember it was a hit with both reader and

listener. I don't ask my children to narrate their bedtime stories although children's literature is excellent material for narration for the younger students during morning school hours.

Always a Read-Aloud Started

There is always a read-aloud started in our house. Library books—because they must be returned—are worked more tightly into our morning schedule. I don't plan to finish an "evening" book in any particular time period. Therefore we use as bedtime read-alouds books we have purchased, so I can read at a comfortable pace.

A Christian biography makes a good "Sunday book." It is so inspiring to follow the course of one who has purposed to live for Christ.

Some evenings, my daughters like me to read and discuss chapters from *Beautiful Girlhood* with them in the privacy of their bedroom.

I would like to get back into reading more poetry aloud. We somehow drifted away from it some months ago. When my girls were very young we did more memorization of poetry than we have done lately.

Books of Quality

My eldest students always keep a "morning book" and their Bible beside their beds. They wake just after dawn in late spring and all during summer (the sun is bright nice and early), to read before chores and breakfast. They have read a selection of children's classics in this manner. What a pleasure it is to see my eldest reading high school/college level classic literature that she has chosen herself. Their younger brother has caught on to this habit of morning reading initiated by the girls. In his own bedroom across the hall, he settles down with an easy reading book after being expelled from the bedroom of his elder sisters. Meanwhile I am having my own "quiet time"—the earlier I arise the more quiet it is, naturally. During the dark winter (holiday and flu season) we are not consistent with mornings (although it is our goal to be), therefore literature is read during the day or evening.

The morning books are sometimes narrated and discussed while I prepare breakfast and as we eat together. I may ask questions about what they are reading. If the breakfast discussion goes well, I encourage them to incorporate their talk into a writing assignment. I've learned that when the children have a lot to say about something, this "talk" becomes good material to write down (and then polish).

Vocabulary

My children past fourth grade are supposed to jot down new vocabulary from their reading, guess the meaning from the context, and then match their guess with the dictionary meaning. They were consistently lax about it this last year, claiming from week to week few new words. Finally, at the end of the school year, I told them, with hands on hips, that this couldn't possibly be true. This fall, I've decided to be insistent about my vocabulary plans, especially since they will be reading harder books. Perhaps I'll purchase attractive notebooks for this purpose.

I have not followed teacher's guides for teaching literature in the elementary years. I am happy that in our house the reading of good literature is done without my prodding, because there are other aspects of school (and other subjects) that are more of a struggle. I've always been careful not to "over-work" literature by picking it apart or by scheduling in very many suggested activities listed in those expensive study guides. One or two related activities, at most, have worked fine for us. And these usually have been ones invented by the children themselves, during play. I remember the time they cut holes out of a brown paper bag to make Roman armor. It was a perfect fit. Charlotte Mason advised teachers to allow literature to stand on its own. For young students she strongly believed that simply reading a book with some narrating is sufficient for "studying" it. The smaller the study guide, for me, the better, because these seem to be the more pertinent. I prefer guides with a Christian perspective—ones that provide a little helpful insight for the teacher who hasn't read the book. Consider them for older students. Since you have already done the work of choosing good books, let the younger children just enjoy them. They will pick up from their "lovely books" whatever vocabulary or ideas impress them.

Bible

For Bible study I sometimes preview portions of Matthew Henry's *Commentary* on a given Bible passage and read this aloud with some discussion. I may paraphrase the things I am learning in my own study, yet try to heed the advice that Charlotte Mason gave of not mediating between children and author. Therefore I also invite them to offer explanations. I find the writings of R.C. Sproul insightful. Dad teaches from a catechism.

So much material for older children is designed for the youth group. The tone of the writing encourages the teen or pre-teen to live for Jesus despite his heathen parents or wayward peers. The main Biblical message is very good, but being a caring parent who prefers not to be categorized as a dud, I wish the material could be rewritten. Since my children aren't allowed to loiter on the streets or go to teen parties, the examples described in these books for living for Jesus are not fitting ones. In them the suggestion is made to share closest feelings and problems with a buddy. What about a parent?

Use Your Own Style

Include real books, whole books, living books, whatever you wish to call them, in your homeschool however you can. Then your little school will liven up. Once you learn to live with the occasional uneasy feeling of insecurity—which is a normal symptom experienced from time to time by many home teachers because we are doing things differently than the grand (intimidating) institutional style of teaching—you will be free. With whole books you are free to create an opportunity for you and your children to pursue the love of knowledge together. What wonderful freedom! It doesn't have to be done in the same manner as our family (a manner which has evolved). You don't even have to follow the same manner or schedule as your best homeschooling friend. I encourage you to try whatever method most suits your interests and energy level. One mother wrote me that she does an hour of reading aloud from various books (with narration) with her children directly after breakfast. Then they do their separate studies. Another mother has her children accomplish their skill subjects first. She waits until her baby and toddlers are asleep in the afternoon before she does any reading aloud and narration. She stretches out on her couch for a rest while doing so. Any written narration is brought to her for correction. Another mother reads aloud during lunch while her children are quietly eating. In midwinter I like to bring to the table a pot of tea and "elevenishes." This light refreshment with my reading aloud tides us over until half-past-one on days when Dad plans to join us for a hot lunch.

Childhood is too precious to waste on television. That is why instead of giving the television a prominent place in our living room, we have lined it with bookshelves. Our large library basket rests on the floor between our fireplace and the fish aquarium. I stand a different array of books up in the basket each month. Our television/VCR is used sparingly, is kept out of the way, and is not the focal point of leisure.

Book Lists

There are books I want my children to read before they leave home. As yet I haven't prepared a complete list. Choosing semester by semester as we go along has worked fine over the years. However, now that my eldest is doing high school and reads through books rapidly, I am preparing a list to go along with our American literature course. Two years will be spent doing a history of English literature course. As she also studies twentieth century history this year, there are some more mature titles that will complement her history very well, such as *To Kill a Mockingbird* , *Around the World in Eighty Days*, *Goodbye Mr. Chips*, and *Lost Horizon*.

There are descriptive lists in books compiled by Christians. Our eager young readers have benefited from *Honey for a Child's Heart, Books Children Love,* and also some Newbery Award winners. Terry Glaspey's *Great Books of the Christian Tradition* has little description of individual titles, but will advise you which authors' works are worth making part of your "mental furniture" and why. Pastor James Stobaugh has a three-page list of recommended secular reading in his *SAT and College Preparation Course for the Christian Student*, a course designed to strengthen the student's Christian worldview and refute wrong secular thinking—a feature that prepares the student for life, not just for the test.

The literature textbooks published for Christian high school students primarily contain excerpts from various works. Though not required by the course, taking time to read the whole book (or more stories) by writers introduced in the text makes good Charlotte Mason sense, doesn't it? I was delighted to discover my high school student doing this very thing during our visits to the local library. Curious to read more, on her own initiative, she is borrowing books by authors profiled in her literature textbook. She then writes papers about selected authors and their works.

Thematic Reading

One thing I don't attempt to do is center all our literature, history, and science reading around a particular theme. I find it works well in our home to allow the children to make their own associations. We find that subjects overlap more often than expected, without any particular effort on our part. As an example, last year for science we read about the digestive system in a library book titled, *When Hunger Calls*. The first chapter contained a short story of a French Canadian man who received a gunshot wound from an accidental firing at a trading post in 1822. Dr. Beaumont was able to observe a large part of the man's stomach while it was healing, and to undertake experiments without harming the injured man. We were studying wilderness and pioneer families for American history at the time. The two subjects—science and history—overlapped, but quite by accident.

I do match up literature with history, however, as was done in Charlotte Mason's

schools. Some large families find the thematic approach very helpful in organizing their school work. They have a lot of fun together. For others—judging by the letters I've received—this approach is too much work for the teacher. According to Charlotte Mason, all-encompassing themes are not necessary for learning to take place. She discovered that the minds of children naturally make their own associations.

What We Don't Read

Donna didn't ask about what we *don't* read, but someone else recently did. And to answer that letter: My daughters do not read fiction series for girls. I have encouraged them to read a variety of books instead of being immersed in all of *The Boxcar Children,* for example. Many children happily develop reading fluency with these. For this reason "series books" are quite helpful. But I'd like to emphasize that there are so many delightfully different kinds of stories. We are responsible as parents and teachers to develop a taste for reading the best. As soon as a student is fluent, we should challenge him with progressively harder and harder books—books of real quality. Simple stories and leisure reading have a place in any repertoire, but to allow a child a series of a dozen books of effortless reading, once is he is quite fluent, would limit him (even in the summer). Provide older children with three or four longer, challenging books a semester. These are to be preferred over dozens of easy stories—no matter how much the student seems to enjoy them. I say this with concern and, I hope, enough politeness, because Charlotte Mason would not have children fall into a habit of what she called "desultory reading."

Practice Purity

The passion novel, sometimes disguised as a "romance" novel, is to be avoided. Racks of these paperbacks are positioned at the very entrance of our local library. The best books are way in the back. Sadly, I have seen mothers with their daughters approach the library check-out counter with a stack that reaches just under the chin. These books arouse sensuality sometimes in subtle ways, but more often with quite obviously erotic plots. Teen-age romance and horror stories, though prominently displayed in libraries, should not become the thoughts that feed minds. (See *Home Education,* pp. 128-129)

Love poetry is of a different nature. The love poems of Byron and Shelley, for example, are gentle, peaceful, contemplative, and appreciative. They relate much sweeter emotions and endearing sentiments in eloquent phrases. This can be contrasted to the lustful yearnings exemplified by the passion novel. For romance, the novels of Jane Austen and the Brontë sisters teach lessons of purity, patience, and perseverance.

> *See how she leans her cheek upon her hand!*
> *O that I were a glove upon that hand*
> *That I might touch that cheek."*

—Romeo and Juliet, Act II, scene 1

These are some of my favorite lines of Shakespeare. But even with Romeo and Juliet, Shakespeare makes a point that their love is not the best of examples. At the start of the play we learn that Romeo loves being "in love." He turns his gaze easily from the girl that he loved with great longing onto another girl he has just met (Juliet). But it is a definite improvement on the subject, wouldn't you say? (See *Ourselves,* pp. 22–23.) Praise of another's character makes for some of the best love poetry.

No Prizes

We do not participate in any "read such-and-such number of books this summer for a prize" type of activity. I also do not pay my children money to read a book or give them points that they can "cash in." The reward for reading is experienced in the reading itself, and this is what Charlotte Mason would wish for every child. Your reading and also that of your children can be one such rewarding experience. When the best books are a part of the educational life, they have the power to satisfy the hungry, growing soul in a way that inferior books cannot. The rewards are in the reading: the treasure lies in wait for those who do the digging. ➤

Chapter Fourteen

....

Narration: The Art of Knowing

TWO SISTERS STAND SIDE BY SIDE at the bathroom sink peacefully brushing their teeth. Their four-year-old brother bounds into the room. Using much force, he lifts the heavy stepping stool and squeezes it between them. Standing on his soapbox, now eye-level with his sisters, he states, "I want to brush my teeth."

One annoyed sister, mouth full of foaming toothpaste, replies, "Can't you wait your turn?"

Her brother eloquently argues, "Haven't you ever heard the story of the little boy who couldn't get any water to brush his teeth so da-seeds grew in his mouth?"

"No, what seeds?" chuckles the sister, rinsing her mouth.

"Don't you know about da-seeds?"

"I think he is referring to gum disease," I say, coming to his rescue, wondering when he heard us talking about this topic.

The girls leave the room with clean teeth and I decide to fight "da-seeds" in my own mouth and keep a little boy company at the same time.

As you can see from this past experience of ours, children learn to express themselves with an ever-increasing vocabulary long before they begin their first language arts lesson. My son's little speech was a peek into that "art of telling" which is in every child's mind, waiting to be discovered.

As a parent you probably know how much young children delight in "telling." When they are very young we encourage them to walk and talk. Sadly, when school begins, they are told to sit down and be quiet. Children are born with the instinct of curiosity, which motivates them to discover all they can about the world around them. As they acquire their wonderful new knowledge they are motivated to tell everyone around them all about it. But all too often this ability and desire to tell is "schooled out" of children.

One of the reasons Charlotte Mason's work is enjoying a renaissance among modern home educators is that she made children's desire to tell what they know one of the building blocks of her philosophy of education. Unlike other educators of her day, Charlotte believed strongly that this "amazing gift with which children are born should not lie fallow in their education." Recognizing that narration (retelling what has just been read) is the best and most natural way for a young child to organize and demonstrate the knowledge he gains from books, she incorporated this natural gift into her school lessons and correspondence courses.

This is the method of learning we have chosen for our children. But how does it work? First, Charlotte required her teachers to read aloud to the children from the best age-appropriate literature she could find. This was all-important, both in retaining a child's interest and in giving his mind solid food for thought. As many of us have found, all children respond naturally to a good story! Then, since knowledge is not assimilated until it is reproduced, she felt children should tell back, after a single reading, what they had just heard. She called this process narration.

Information or Knowledge?

We are living in an information age. Today's children are exposed to much information, but they come away with little knowledge. Why? First, most schools use books that are purely factual. Such books can actually be an obstacle to acquiring knowledge because they are not the kind of book children naturally "take to," or can narrate from. Children need books written in literary language to narrate from. Secondly, children are persons, not parrots. Workbooks obligate children to parrot back information. Knowledge is not attained through these means because the child really hasn't narrated (or thought the ideas through and made them his own). Narrating invites children to meditate, that is, to think ideas through to their conclusion. Charlotte Mason observed that what the child digs for himself becomes his own possession. Narration develops the power of self-expression and forces the child to use his own mind and form his own judgment.

Today, this simple and delightful way of learning is too often replaced with the use of those oh-so-convenient workbooks. In so many schools—and some home-schools!—children are faced with pages of multiple-choice, true and false, fill-in-the-blanks, and long lists of questions. They wearily try to remember fragments (isolated tidbits) of information. But when children relate back a literary passage of a living book in their own words, they follow a train of thought. They pick up the "whys and hows" within the stories in science, history, and other studies. In their knowledge of it they find delight.

Beautiful Thoughts

A child who has developed and attained the power of narrating from living books tells his version of the story, using attractive vocabulary as it appeals to him. He does not merely parrot information. As one of Charlotte's teachers said, "He absorbs into himself the beautiful thought from the book, making it his own, and then gives it forth again with just that little touch that comes from his own mind." With narration, the answers given are those the child has asked himself as he was narrating. Therefore, his version of an episode might bring forth a different narration than that given by a brother, sister, or classmate. Each narration may come with a slightly different twist or point of view. Yet each can be correct, valid, and true. Isn't it interesting how the Word of God includes four Gospel accounts, each narrated from a special point of view? All are true, all minister to us, yet each is unique.

Narration Helps Retention

Charlotte found that if you use narration consistently, review is unnecessary. Narration is not merely an effort of memory, yet it increases the mind's ability to remember. Whatever a child gleans from the passage and narrates back he will remember months later, simply because it was his own narration/train of thought.

Narration of Living Books Inspires Love of Knowledge

Certainly we should drill children on the simple facts they need to memorize—arithmetic facts, important dates in history, Bible verses, scientific terminology. Short daily drills will not dampen the children's school day. However, narration should be our main learning tool. When narration from real books is practiced not as "a nice thing to do from time to time," but as a fundamental way to acquire knowledge, your children will be happy with and fulfilled by their school lessons. True personal knowledge is satisfying, and children will hold onto their favorite ideas for a lifetime, not just for a test.

Compare this important principle of education with that of the cramming of information for tests. In most schools children cram to pass, but fail to know. What does cramming do for a child's mind? Have we allowed the goal of making the grade become the ideal? Miss Mason has taught us that the love of knowledge and the desire to continue learning for a lifetime is a higher goal. It is a nobler ideal.

Narration Strengthens Mental Powers

There is more to narration than meets the eye—or shall we say meets the ear? We can see how narration invites the child's individual personality to become part of the learning process. What we may not see is how narration strengthens and challenges all the powers of mind. Attending, remember-

ing, visualizing, comprehending, synthesizing (seeing the whole from the parts), and articulating are the result of placing our trust in this method. All a parent need do is to set the table with a varied diet of true and noble ideas for the child to feast upon, and his mind does for itself the sorting, arranging, correlating, selecting, rejecting, classifying, for which textbook committees and the writers of intricately detailed unit studies think they are responsible.

Narration is Evaluation

For the literary subjects, narration is the best way to find out what a child knows. But what about other subjects? How can we call it school if we don't have multiple-choice tests resulting in statistics and percentages to point to?

Insecurity lurks to trap those of us who have put all our eggs in this one basket of

evaluation. It is so simple and enjoyable that we may feel we're cheating. As one Charlotte Mason fan wrote me,

> Americans are into insurance. We want proof of excellence, measurements of progress, and guarantees of success . . . We test for IQ, readiness, learning disabilities, learning aptitude, creativity, achievement, development, brain hemisphere dominance, perception, and on and on and on. We have placed our hopes in what can be seen, measured, graphed, reported, and compared. We want visible signs of an infinitely complex, invisible reality. As educators we have listened to our fears and have sacrificed education to the god of security. Charlotte Mason can inspire us, but cannot give us what we must become ourselves—people of faith.

Narration: How To Do It

Read aloud to your children when they are young to accustom them to words. Nursery rhymes are fabulous. They teach that words can cleverly come in interesting patterns (rhythms). The ear is thus trained to anticipate rhyme. Children also learn that words carry meaning. They describe what people do and how they feel or react. "Little Miss Muffet" is one such simple example. Also, conversation is extremely beneficial. Talking to little ones throughout their day helps them to think. When children are talking they are usually thinking—unlike adults, who may occasionally do one without the other. We can guide their thoughts to anticipate and prepare. "Daddy will be home any minute! Have you put the plates on the table?" "What else do we need for the table to be set? Let's pick some zinnias and daisies from the garden. Would you like to put them in some water?" We also listen and respond to their comments and questions. When Daddy comes home, his little daughter will probably like to tell

him what she did. "I set the table, Daddy. I know where the forks go. I picked those flowers, Daddy. Mommy likes the yellow ones, but I like the pink ones. Which ones do you like, Daddy?"

All of this language is very important, and it is a great sadness that so little of it is provided to young children today. The day care and television set stunt children's intelligence. According to Jane Healy, in her book *Endangered Minds,* oral language actually changes the shape of a child's brain, empowering it for reading. When this oral language is absent, and as a result of the over-stimulation of day care and television, the child's brain takes on a different shape. Fast-paced programs such as *Sesame Street,* which claim to prepare children for school, in reality act as devices that diminish stick-to-it-ive-ness. Instead of daily putting effort into attending (developing attention powers), the child is induced to be passive.

Therefore, giving children the gift of language is not a trivial thing at all. When you are at home talking with them, reading to them, examining a flower or an insect, you are shaping their brains, helping them to follow a train of thought, and requiring their minds to be attentive. And this, my fellow home educator, is very, very valuable. And even more valuable than these mental powers is the spiritual relationship you are building with one another.

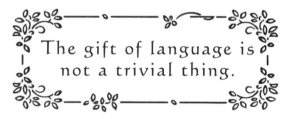

The gift of language is not a trivial thing.

Charlotte understood this "modern brain research" one hundred years ago. This is why she said that formal telling should be required of children only after the age of six. All kindergarten narrations should be spontaneous. Young students (first through third grade) should begin by narrating paragraphs. Aesop's *Fables* are handy for developing the power of narration because they are short and non-twaddly. Drawing a picture of what has been read aloud is a legitimate form of narration, too. This also develops a child's imagination, a foundational part of his intellect. Older students do not mind breaking into the narration habit with Aesop's *Fables*. Let them provide the moral of the story before it is read at the end. Children of all ages enjoy narrating fairy tales and Greek myths, and can easily tell the difference between the stories of fanciful gods and goddesses and the Bible stories they will also be narrating.

By age eight or nine, part or all of a short chapter can be narrated (about seven minutes' worth of a teacher's reading aloud). The student will then be narrating an entire episode.

At the age of nine or ten, children who have been used to the effort of narrating stories can easily go on to narrate whole chapters of history—historical fiction, biography, myths and legends—as well as science and nature investigation, and Bible. As an alternative to telling, you can give a child the opportunity to ask you questions from what he has read. His mind will work through the matter to pick out the main points as well as some subtle details that might stump you. He has already been putting questions to his mind when he narrates. "What next?" he asks as he follows the sequence. It is usually the story's action and the characters' reactions that impress him. This year I oftentimes ask my high school student to write out a set of six to ten questions on a chapter she has read for history or biology. In choosing what questions to ask, her mind scans the chapter and summarizes the main events, main ideas and the most important information from it.

For evaluation, in Miss Mason's schools and homeschools, children were asked essay questions and their oral or written narrations determined what they knew. These examinations at the end of each term, were never preceded with review. The children spoke or wrote with fluency because they knew what they had previously narrated even months before.

I've familiarized my children with typical worksheets so that they are prepared to take a state-required year-end test, but narration is basic in our homeschool. Each child narrates according to her own ability and each child loves her books.

Sunday School Founder Champions Narration

Charlotte Mason wasn't the only one who believed narration to be the best method of learning, remembering, and evaluating. H. Clay Trumbull, a founder of the American Sunday school movement and author of many books, believed narration to be an invaluable method for teaching the Word of God in Sunday schools.

Trumbull quoted pages of what great men have said about narration in his book *Teachers and Teaching* (now, sadly, out of print). One individual Professor Trumbull quoted suggested that the mind of a child is best opened by way of his mouth. "You cannot fill a bottle with the cork in," he said. Counting every passive hearer as a corked bottle, he adds: "You may pour your stream of knowledge upon them till you drown them, and not get a drop of it into them because their mouths are shut."[1]

Trumbull said that there is no mental getting and holding except through, or in conjunction with, some mental giving or doing. He looked back into the pages of history and discovered "telling" was greatly used by the ancients. Socrates, the great Greek teacher, always began his teaching by asking his students questions, in order to open their minds, and to secure their cooperation with him in the teaching process.

He insisted that he who would be a learner must not merely be a listener and a reciter, but must also be "one who searches out for himself." Trumbull urged this method be used in Sunday schools.

I hope this chapter has given you increased confidence to set in motion in your homeschool this beneficial and enjoyable use of narration. What may seem awkward at first, with time and use will become a great enrichment to your child's education. With the frequent use of narration, your children will become learned and literate young scholars. ⸺

Questions for Personal Reflection or Support Group Discussion

1. *What does a child do when he narrates?*

2. *Children are persons, not parrots. How should this fact affect how we teach them? How does parroting back information differ from telling back in a child's own words?*

3. *What kinds of books do children readily "take to?" What kinds of books can be easily narrated?*

4. *Talking with our young children and being available to hear their "spontaneous narrations" develops their brains. At what age does more formal narration begin? Why are these lessons kept short?*

5. *How can narration be used to gain knowledge from the various subjects? What are the three forms of narrating?*

6. *Regularly scheduled narration can take the place of what other devices?*

7. *Years ago, when I tried to keep an open mind about sending my young student to a school around the corner from me, my first objection was, "But she wouldn't ever get to narrate! And how would she have time to narrate at home if she had homework?" I think it is important for each child to develop the power to narrate. Are you grateful for the opportunity for the free use of narration in your homeschool?*

Your Own Personal Reflections

Chapter Fifteen

Tips on Narration

Dear Karen,

I am so sorry for imposing on you with a question, but I haven't been able to find the answer in Charlotte Mason's books. When doing narration, should the child be corrected if some of the "telling" is inaccurate? I've had my eight-year-old do a few narrations (her one of *Romeo and Juliet* ran to six pages, so it was quite a success) but when narrating her history, she tends to make up things as she imagines them. Should I break the flow of the narration to correct factual errors? Do I correct them when she is finished? She must take the narrations seriously, because she is intensely crushed when I've corrected factual errors. I believe the act of narrating does leave a strong impression on the mind, and I didn't think it should be a factually wrong impression, but I also intuit that stopping the flow of the narration may be counter-productive. Do you have any suggestions or comments?

A delighted reader,
Dianna

Dear Dianna,

I've taken care to answer questions like yours that I have received in the mail this year because I think narration is important and I think certain obstacles can be overcome with understanding.

I am happy to hear how your daughter has taken to narration. It doesn't come as easily to some children. You are right about not interrupting her narration with corrections. However, the teacher or the other children in Charlotte's schools sometimes corrected the narrator for content at the conclusion of a narration. This was seen not as a critical analysis of one child's "telling," but as open participation. It probably kept the narrator on his toes, too. I'm also guessing that the teacher made sure the corrections were not unnecessarily overdone. I have a daughter who at one time was insulted by corrections. I tried to tell her what I liked about her narration first, and only if necessary tack on a briefly stated amendment. This softened the critique somewhat.

Charlotte's students were never corrected for their grammar during or directly after a narration. Special care would be taken to see that certain noun-verb agreements, for example, were covered and reviewed, as needed. As an ounce of prevention is worth a pound of cure, a teacher helped the children give a more accurate historical narration by displaying important names, dates, and places on the chalk board. Science terminology would also be displayed on the board before the teacher read the passage aloud. You may try this technique at home with your daughter. Let me give you an example from pages 46–48 of *George Washington,* a picture book by D'Aulaire. Before I read these pages aloud to my eight-year-old, some years ago, I wrote out on paper and then read aloud the following list, telling her she would be hearing about these things in the story:

- common (park)
- Cambridge
- Boston
- New York
- Liberty Bell
- July 1776
- Delaware River

Before her narration, I said, "Please feel free to check this list for any words you decide you'll need in your narration."

The D'Aulaire books actually make good "readers" for a third grader. Remember, it is best for a child to narrate only one to several pages in the early years until his powers are developed. This helps keep narrations accurate. Gradually a child will be able to digest a greater amount of factual material. On the brink of narrating the pages mentioned above, my eight-year-old daughter sighed, "This is going to be a hard narration." There were more names than she was used to attending to, among the two pages I chose. She narrated slowly, pausing with every sentence, and referred

to the list little. But neither did she misinterpret the passage as she sometimes had in the past. Her version showed a basic understanding. She also asked a question about the Declaration of Independence, which I later attempted to answer with other material. Here is her narration of one page:

> George Washington had soldiers, but they weren't really soldiers yet. They were really just farmers so George Washington taught them how to be real soldiers. The King sent more and more of the Redcoats and George Washington and his men were going to fight for freedom. That's when the Liberty Bell rang. Sometimes the Redcoats won and sometimes George Washington won.

I was more happy with this little oral composition than I would have been if she had been able to answer the typical questions found in history textbooks, such as: "Where did George Washington win a battle?" "What river did he cross?" I was using this picture book simply as an enjoyable introduction to the character of George Washington and his place in American history. An older student should be expected to include more factual references in his narration. If he jots down names and dates while he reads, they will be handy for his narration.

The following passage from Charlotte's *Philosophy of Education,* illustrates well her concept of the interaction of narrator and teacher:

> The child of six [or seven] has . . .a definite quantity of consecutive reading, say, forty pages in a term, from a well-written, well considered, large volume which is also well-illustrated. Children can not of course read themselves a book which is by no means written down to the child's level so the teacher reads and the children 'tell' paragraph by paragraph, passage by passage. The

teacher does not talk much and is careful never to interrupt a child who is called upon to 'tell.' The first efforts may be stumbling but presently the children get into their 'stride' and 'tell' a passage at length with surprising fluency. The teacher probably allows other children to correct any faults in the telling when it is over. The teacher's own really difficult part is to keep up sympathetic interest by look and occasional word, by remarks upon a passage that has been narrated, by occasionally showing pictures, and so on. But she will bear in mind that the child of six [or seven] has begun the serious business of his education, it does not matter much whether he understands this word or that, but it matters a great deal that he should learn to deal directly with books. Whatever a child or grown-up person can tell, that we may be sure he knows, and what he cannot tell, he does not know.

Experiment with Narration

Let us give our children a variety books to narrate. Some books I have actually had to put aside as they did not foster any narration. Some books can be read just for fun and enjoyment. Some stories naturally lend themselves to a retelling. You will probably find that these are the same stories that have been passed on orally for ages. Not every book needs to be narrated. From what I've read in the old *Parents' Reviews,* opinions of PNEU teachers on this matter varied. Yet generally it seems that every chapter of certain "school" books was narrated in turn. Dianna, you sound like a concerned mother who is trying to do her best. Charlotte Mason

impressed upon us that methods of teaching may need to be tailored to the individual child. We may be apprehensive at first, but eventually through trial and error, and love, tact, and the help of the Holy Spirit, we can figure it out. Take heart Dianna, "for God has not given us a spirit of fear, but of power and of love and of a sound mind." (2 Tim 1:7) I've needed to remind myself of this many times.

Personal Reflections on Narration

A number of you wrote me expressing the need for encouragement in beginning the use of narration. Obviously, you are not going to feel comfortable or confident about something with which you are unfamiliar or inexperienced. The first attempts at incor-

porating narration will feel like the first day of gymnastics class—or any new experience, for that matter. It takes practice before one grows accustomed to doing a cartwheel. It takes practice before narration "feels right."

I realized the importance of narration by degrees. The more I read Charlotte's writings, the more apparent it became that narration was essential to the process of a child acquiring knowledge from books. When I started using narration, we had just relocated our household—again. I felt alone because the children and I were off in the Tennessee woods without a car and without any friends. I was expecting a child and was queasy in the stomach for months, so staying home felt better (and safer). I had always read aloud to the children from many different sorts of library books—fiction and non-fiction. I also enjoyed teaching my little girls to read and write and memorize sums daily. Then the conviction that I should begin using narration as a teaching tool crept up on me. Feeling unsure of myself, I started asking my seven-year-old to tell back to me the portion I had just read aloud. The books I read from were not easy books—*Robinson Crusoe* and *Heidi* unabridged, and *Pilgrim's Progress* in the original language. I hadn't yet seen a homeschool catalog (there were so few of them in 1988), nor did I remember many "special" books from my childhood, so I took hold of the book suggestions in *For the Children's Sake* and mentioned by Charlotte Mason.

Fortunately, my eldest child, Sophia, was a talker. (She still is.) Rarely did her mouth cease to express her thoughts, except when fishing out crayfish from the creek. Still, narrating required effort. She narrated these classics dutifully, sometimes while flipping around the room to act out scenes of *Heidi* that affected her in a physical fashion. I let her be, wondering all the while if this was typical or if it should even be allowed. I had no one with whom to discuss the details of narration—nor anything else having to do with Charlotte Mason, for that matter. Looking back now, I would have started out with easier books, perhaps even books with pictures, as I have done with my second daughter, Yolanda (a sight learner). Eventually narration felt normal and it took its place as an important part of our homeschool experience.

Whole Books Around the Place

Narration will come together for you and your children. Think of the wonderful living books awaiting them. There are now more books available for children than ever before. There were fewer books for children in the days when Charlotte began her educational reforms. There were basically Bible stories, fairy tales, Greek myths, *Robinson Crusoe,* and innumerable Victorian goody-goody stories. Therefore she had the children narrate from all but the goody-goody stories. *Pilgrim's Progress* in its original language was not thought of as a book for children, but Charlotte discovered that children absorbed its ideas readily and enjoyed narrating the story.

Today there are so many picture books, biographies, and historical novels that it seems there are decisions to be made weekly. Well-written fiction abounds and homeschooling catalogs get bigger and bigger. Some books are enjoyed and attended to with more vigor than others. Some make you feel that you've struck it rich, and they are the books that when you read them aloud all the children are magically quiet enough to let you read on and on. Some start off slowly, making you wait patiently for details to be in place, but after the stage is set, the children are locked into the story—formulating a more vivid imagination with each new episode. Sadly there comes along a book that seems to be a waste of money, or library searching time, but their death should not be grieved. Just put them aside and see what else awaits.

If At First You Don't Succeed...

Some books may be introduced too soon. This is sometimes the case with children's classics. I tried to read *Black Beauty* aloud to Yolanda when she was just turning eight, but she couldn't latch onto the language. I tried *Bambi* but that didn't do either. Both books were very much enjoyed in silent reading by my first child. A year later I tried again.

This is our story: now that my girls have grown up some, and we've all settled into our homeschool experience, I've seen that a bit of "wise letting alone," as Charlotte called it, has been beneficial, allowing them to experience their own enthusiasm. Also, it has given them the opportunity to experience that satisfying feeling best described by Charlotte's maxim: "What a child digs for becomes his own possession."

Yolanda, at one time, found narrating to be a large effort, but after two years of somewhat strained and brief narrations, I was listening to longer, more detailed, lighthearted ones. It was worth the wait. I guess I was conditioned by her elder, more talkative sister. Anyway, I began reading *Bambi* aloud again about a year after my first attempt. The first chapter was read in several sittings. No narration was requested. The next chapter was done in episodes by shared reading— we took turns reading it aloud. I asked her to narrate a page or two and with a quiet smile she asked, "Do I have to?" My heart sank, but I tried to remain calm and positive. "Just tell me a little of what we've just read together," I said. *Bambi* is one of those stories that has an interest level for a young elementary child but a vocabulary for one somewhat older, which makes it very useful for increasing a child's vocabulary naturally. She narrated briefly, pausing between sentences. But a day or two later, upon narrating the second episode of that chapter—Bambi's first visit to the meadow—she picked up the spirit of his rejoicing. She even used two new words.

By the third chapter she asked, "Should I read my book now, Ma?" and off she ran, disappearing down the hall. When she reappeared from her bedroom, I asked about the happenings of the story. My hands were immersed in dishwater and there were noisy sloshings about, so I told her I would hear her narration in a few moments. But I guess she couldn't wait because she let slip out a few particulars about Bambi. As a trickle can grow into a tributary, she continued to share the entire episode informally with me.

In our home not all narrations are performed in a formal seated position. Not all narrations are recorded in a narration notebook. I have found that informal narrations such as those that are preceded with a "Guess what happened in this chapter, Ma!" have a sort of spontaneous power to them. These spontaneous narrations are just as valid in the early narrating years. A homeschool can take advantage of any spontaneous narrations. This is especially true when you require the child to then write this "wonderful" narration in his composition book. By the fourth chapter Yolanda was up with the sun reading *Bambi* "by the dawn's early light." At breakfast she volunteered narrations, eager to share the story she saw in her "mind's eye."

Take Courage

The Courage of Sarah Noble is a very good book for a second or third grader to narrate. Listeners can take turns narrating the appropriately short chapters of this book. I read Yolanda the first chapter as a "freebie" (no narration was required). The following day we shared the reading and I asked her to narrate the entire chapter. All the other chapters were read silently on her own and each was narrated formally in turn. One of her narrations was recorded neatly by me, and she later copied it into her composition book over a period of three days. This was our narration style for those years.

Narration Fits All

You will work out similar things with the personalities of your children when the time comes for them to narrate. If you trust in the method, give it time to develop. I learned the things about which I am writing inch by inch, month by month, year by year. Keep the ideal before you, take heart, and you'll do well.

Narration works wonderfully with both the bright, talkative child as well as the slower or more quiet child. In learning to narrate, each child will adjust, progress, and accomplish according to his own ability in a most natural, gradual manner. Some children cannot be lured to learn by the proposed plan, that is, learning evenly and steadily all subjects and skills across the board. There will be times of seeming stagnation, when they will need to be refreshed with some diversion or play. There will be obvious learning explosions (growth spurts) when all of a sudden their interest is piqued and their understanding quick. In a homeschool it is easy to sense fluctuations. Keeping to a daily schedule is the best discipline, yet we can still be sympathetic to bumps and necessary detours in the road.

Narration Requests

Here are examples of specific narration requests. I hope they give you an idea of the kinds of specifics to ask for.

- Tell me all you know about (this was a favorite of Charlotte's): 1. the habits of the squirrel. 2. Columbus' first voyage

We proceeded differently as her abilities developed. We used more elaborate books and more factual ones. But at the time it was so pleasing to have a style with this child that felt just right. Like trying on shoes, it sometimes takes time to "find a fit."

With Yolanda I discovered it worked best to give her at least one "freebie" chapter, maybe more, before asking her to narrate. She needed to begin to formulate the story in her imagination, to "set the stage," before she could narrate. I also needed to give her the challenge of reading certain books herself, easing her into the story by first reading aloud to her a chapter or two. This was an obvious step in our goal toward self-effort and self-education; when she was younger, all of the books I chose for narration had to be read to her.

across the Atlantic. 3. the last plague on Egypt and the first Passover. 4. Heidi's visit with Peter's grandmother.

- Explain how . . . 1. a polliwog turns into a frog. 2. a rose is pollinated. 3. sedimentary rock is formed. 4. Pocahontas saved the life of John Smith. 5. Jesus healed the blind man. 6. the Magna Carta came to be written. 7. bread is made.

- Describe our: 1. trip to the shore. 2. nature walk. 3. visit to the fire station. 4. planetarium experience.

- Describe anything new you just learned from this chapter.

- Tell me five things you learned about...

- Tell back the story (passage, episode, chapter) in your own words.

- Ask or write six questions covering the material of this chapter (good for an older student).

- Draw a picture, map or likeness of . . .

- What did you learn about . . . in this chapter? (The Wright Brothers, Sarah Noble, Abigail Adams, Martin Luther, Queen Elizabeth I, Captain Ahab(from *Moby Dick*), Pinocchio. This is a quick mix of main characters to give you an idea of what a friend narration is to main characters, whether fictional or real).

Narration Is As Old As the Hills

Just as the American Indians retold tales around the fire, and Viking children learned to retell a saga, your children can pass on what they know by telling. Going back farther, the Old Testament Hebrews tenaciously held onto their religion through many travels and many years by retelling the old, old stories of God's faithfulness. Charlotte Mason says,

> Possibly the practice of telling was more used in the sixteenth and seventeenth centuries than it is now. We remember how three gentlemen meet in Shakespeare's *Henry VIII,* and one who has just come out of the Abbey witnessing the coronation of Anne Boleyn is asked to tell the others about it, which he does with the vividness and accuracy we obtain from children. In this case no doubt the telling was a stage device, but would it have been adopted if such narration were not commonly practiced? Even in our own day a good raconteur is a welcome guest, and a generation or two ago the art was studied as a part of gentlemanly equipment.

Independence

The day a child begins using narration is the day he begins to become an independent learner. With narration the mind poses questions to itself. It is independent of the questionnaire. I could have asked my nine-year-old daughter to answer the following questions about Chapter Eight of *The Courage of Sarah Noble:* "Was Sarah uncomfortable about eating Indian food?" "What did the Indians think Sarah's hair looked like?" "Why was Sarah so sad?" "What did she pray?"

Or she could have answered a list of multiple choice questions such as: Sarah was sad because: A) the Indians hurt her feelings, B) she missed her family, C) her cloak was lost. Or she could have been asked to put a list of happenings from the chapter in proper sequence. But instead she answered the questions her own mind put to itself, fitting the happenings naturally into their proper sequence. Here is her narration without correction.

The first day in Tall John's house was strange. The Indian children and Sarah played a lot together. It seemed like they understood each other. Sometimes they didn't but it didn't seem to matter. The Indians ate meat with their hands. Sarah was not used to eating this kind of food but ate it anyway and enjoyed herself. Before it was time to go to bed Sarah took out a bag. It came all the way from her old home. The Indian children watched her to see what magic she would take out of the bag but it really wasn't magic. It was her night gown and a brush and a few other things. The children watched her comb out her long brown hair. It was like corn silk in summer. Then she knelt down to say her prayers like she did when Father was there to listen. Then some tears came. And this is what she prayed: "I pray for my mother and my brothers and sisters and for our baby to get strong. I pray Father will come to me safely." Then she stopped for a minute. She was thinking whether one should pray for horses. And then she said, "And I pray for Thomas [the horse] to be coming here safely, too." Then she thought, "Does God care for Indians?" Then she said, "I pray for Tall John and his wife and for Little John and Mary." When the Indian children heard their names they looked up at their father. Sarah went to sleep.

I had to wait patiently for her powers of narration to develop. But do you see how much more is brought forth by a narration than a questionnaire? A few specific points may be illuminated by the teacher about the literature passage beforehand. Some questioning after a child narrates is acceptable.

But the narration is essential at this young age and should not be overshadowed by the talk of the teacher. With literature Charlotte Mason thought it best to allow the child the opportunity to be in direct contact with the author's writing. We should not stand in the way of this contact.

Testing

I've mentioned that answers to the questions posed by the teacher or text are not to predominate, because the mind of the child poses questions to itself. Therefore, how can there be answers to questions set for memorization for a test? How is a child to learn if he is not memorizing? Charlotte thought that grasping a concept of the whole is better than memorizing a list of irrelevant details. For their end-of-term test, the young children dictated what they knew and received a satisfactory or unsatisfactory mark. With Charlotte's method, the unsatisfactory mark was given infrequently. Individual children brought forth, in their individual narrations, their individual impressions. There is no temptation to cheat, and no means to, if each version is valid.

Charlotte writes:

A passage to be memorized requires much conning, much repetition, [much review] and meanwhile the learners are 'thinking' about other matters, that is, the [whole] mind is not at work in the act of memorizing. To read a passage with full attention and to tell it afterwards has a curiously different effect. M. Bergson makes the happy distinction between word memory and mind memory, which, once the force of it is realized, should bring about sweeping changes in our methods of education. Trusting to mind memory we visualize the scene, are convinced by the arguments, take pleasure in the turn of the sentences and frame our own upon them; in fact that particular passage or chapter has been received into us and becomes a part of us just as literally as yesterday's dinner; nay, more so, for yesterday's dinner is of little account tomorrow; but several months, perhaps years hence, we shall be able to narrate the passage we had, so to say, consumed and grown upon with all the vividness, detail and accuracy of the first telling. All those powers of the mind which we call faculties have been brought into play in dealing with the intellectual matter thus afforded; so we may not ask questions to help the child to reason, point to fancy pictures to help him to imagine, draw out moral lessons to quicken his conscience. These things take place as involuntarily as processes of digestion.

Dear reader, when we trust in a child's ability to become self-educated with the use of narration and whole books, we are not expecting them to "go it alone." We have great expectations that they will go it *along* with the help of the Holy Spirit and our direction. Children willingly and faithfully begin their voyage of absorbing "mind stuff" as soon as they are born. From the very first moment they are placed into our arms at birth and gaze into our eyes, they are learning—learning that they are loved. If we do not trip up these little ones they will retain their natural trusting curiosity. We can't do the learning for them. But we are responsible to see that they keep on learning and that what they learn is pure, lovely, true, and worthwhile. I believe nothing can do more for the homeschool than the love (guidance and discipline) of parents, the human touch of whole books with their accompanying ideas, and the independent and individual use of narration. This is education "for the children's sake." What do you believe? ⊷

Questions for Personal Reflection or Support Group Discussion:

1. *Are you using narration "now and again" but would like to become more consistent? Simply begin using it whenever you read literature aloud in the mornings. To start, no more than seven minutes read-aloud time is necessary for a narration from an eight- to ten-year-old student who is new to narration. Even less reading aloud time is necessary for six- to seven-year-olds. Is there a book you are reading aloud presently that could be used for narration?*

2. *What is the one-page test? How can you tell whether a book is useful for narration? Open to the first page of a book. Read it aloud and see if it opens the doors of the child's mind. You will usually hear "Read more!" if it sparks interest. The first chapter or part of the first chapter could be read aloud on this day. The next day, request the child to narrate an episode from the day's reading—now that he has been given a chance to "get into" the story.*

3. *If you are using a full-curriculum course, chances are there will be little direction to use narration. Why and how could you easily incorporate some consistent narration into the course?*

4. *If you don't like the idea of "calling it quits" entirely during the summer, narration from whole books can leisurely supply any bored child with new ideas on long summer days. How could you keep it casual and informal, paying heed to any spontaneous narrations? Can you think of any fun books you'd like to introduce to the children this summer?*

5. *How can we encourage self-effort or self-education in a child?*

6. *Why might narration be interpreted as a "take it or leave it" nicety? In what ways is it a strength for acquiring knowledge from books?*

7. *Older children unfamiliar with narration may be shy of hearing their own voice "tell." What other forms of narration might be more comfortable to these students? What kinds of material could you suggest an older student narrate? Is it advisable for these older students to begin with shorter passages? Why?*

8. *Preschoolers and kindergartners will like to retell familiar stories that they have heard over and over, for instance, "The Three Bears." Our girls enjoyed the challenge of retelling "The Three Bears" in their own words during a drive in the car or a quiet time indoors. Occasionally retelling familiar stories from picture books is fun. Did Charlotte Mason require children younger than the age of six to narrate from new stories regularly? Why are spontaneous narrations sufficient and valid at this young age?*

9. *Have you ever tried narrating a Sunday sermon to yourself silently on a lazy Sunday afternoon? It is a good challenge for older students and grownups. A sermon well-prepared and well spoken provides food for thought worth considering after we've left the doors of the church. How many portions of sermons do you remember? How does narration aid in comprehension and memory?*

Answers to some of these questions may not be found in the chapter "Tips for Teachers on Narration," but in *Home Education* and *Philosophy of Education* by Charlotte Mason.

Your Own Personal Reflections

....

....

....

....

....

....

....

....

....

Chapter Sixteen

More Queries About Narration

Dear Karen,

Narration takes up so much time. We have much to accomplish in our schedule. How do we fit in narration, too? Wouldn't a list of questions do the trick to go over more quickly what was just studied.

Signed,
Hurried Mom

Dear H.M.,

In the Charlotte Mason scheme, narration is not added "on top of everything else." It is used in place of many (not all) questionnaires and workbook pages. For the youngest students, narration does not really take up that much time if these substitutions are made. "Mother would like to hear you tell me about what you read today, Joseph." She doesn't give him the fill-in-the-blank page each time the teacher's guide instructs. She learns to think of narration as intrinsic to the curriculum.

Start Small

Passages read aloud for narration are kept short in the beginning. Much later, a whole chapter will be narrated. It is a gradual work, this digestion in the young narrator of text and the development of fluency in speech. It may seem to be taking up too much precious time if a teacher is not used to thinking that time spent in oral feedback is time that counts. Is it just what is recorded on paper that counts?

It was mentioned in one of our first issues of the *Parents' Review* that Robert Louis Stevenson used to dictate stories. He was a sickly child but his mind was active—not doing paperwork where an outline of thinking is already prepared, needing to be filled in, but in setting up the brain work himself in his telling. His creative stories had their roots in those stories that were read aloud to him by his nanny, and were later changed around to suit his own fancy. It would seem that these hours spent narrating in his boyhood culminated in his writing of *Treasure Island, Kidnapped,* and *Dr. Jekyll and Mr. Hyde.* His poems in *A Child's Garden of Verses* prove his memory of childhood was a pleasant one despite his weak health. My point is this: small steps today contribute to big results tomorrow.

Slow and Steady

If a child first approaches narration at an older age, he may feel awkward and take quite awhile to adjust to giving his own account of the pages read. Like a train, he starts out slowly, and goes slowly for quite some time, but watch how he will gradually build up speed and become powerful. The power of being able to narrate steadily is a valuable tool. It enables a child to acquire knowledge for his present studies—thus satisfying his immediate hunger for intellectual and spiritual growth—and lays a foundational skill for dealing with more complex and lengthier reading in later years.

Time invested in acquiring the skill to narrate is time well spent. It reaps benefits that no multiple choice or fill-in-the-blank tests can give. It actually saves time in later years when more written work (composition) is expected. Narration carries over to writing beautifully.

Schedule It In

At the start, consider making room in the schedule for one child to narrate at least once or twice a week. Write it into the teacher's planner weekly—even if you are using a preprinted one. If there is one child (or two) in the home schoolroom, narration every day should not consume time excessively. In larger home schoolrooms children can be given "turns." One child may narrate the first episode, another child the second, during one lesson. Children in a large family can narrate on different days. In general, maintain a schedule in which each student narrates something at least once a week from particular books you have chosen in the curriculum.

Listening

Most young children love to have Mother's or Father's attention while they share something they have observed. A parent can use this free time outside the school schedule to be a listener. Casual narrating at the lunch or supper table makes for good table talk. "What did you read about in *Swiss Family Robinson* today, son?" Dad might ask.

The Questionnaire

The questionnaire draws forth tidbit answers to its many tidbit questions. In order to answer the detailed questions accurately, the student must move his head in ping-pong fashion to copy answers from the text into the workbook. Charlotte calls this looking-up a "device of the idle." It can be evaluated easily: it facilitates grading and that is probably the primary reason for its existence. (See *Philosophy of Education*, page 17).

Let go and let narrate. Take the time to tell and tell well. This is an age-old way of thinking and knowing. When the chapter is read once with attention and comprehension, the telling can take less time and be a more valuable accomplishment than filling in the questionnaire.

Balking at a Narration Request

Dear Karen,

My child balks when I ask him to narrate. Should I force him?

Signed,
Disheartened

Dear D.,

This symptom may appear more with a "first" child. He hasn't grown up hearing his older brothers or sisters narrate as a matter of course. If narration was "commonplace," he wouldn't balk. One letter I received told of a child who argued, "Why should I narrate when you just read the story and we already heard it?" Well, let's look at an analogy: On the breakfast table we may observe a bowl of yellow pears. The early morning sun shines through a kitchen window in such a way that the pears appear to be in a spotlight of golden light. The pears are glowing. We may wish to remember or capture the picture, so we choose colors and brush strokes that fit our interpretation. Why paint a still life picture of pears when we can see pears at the grocery store? Precisely because our painting will make this particular bowl of pears our own. To observe, attend, comprehend, ponder, or appreciate anything and then to express it in picture, poem, story, essay, song, dance, or oral narration, is to take part in the humanities. Human expression is part of culture. This is philosophical, but children will understand that it matters what they think about something. To question, learn, and form an opinion is the opportunity of every child who is educated under the Charlotte Mason Method. An efficient way to accomplish this is through narration.

Vary the Narrating

In Charlotte's schools the children were given a variety of opportunities to narrate. For picture study they would have a turn explaining a picture painted by a great artist. An explanation is a narration. Children can draw a picture of what they hear in the music of Beethoven's "Pastoral Symphony," for instance. A drawing is an interpretation. A drawing can narrate a story or a piece of music. The writing and drawing in a child's Nature Notebook are narrations, too. When a child observes anything and then tells, writes, or draws his observation, he is narrating. Opportunities to narrate in different ways will strengthen a child's ability to narrate, and he will balk less as his ability increases.

No Balking Allowed

One child in our house has balked about narration. I simply tell my child that I will not tolerate any balking. We sit together on the sofa. I cheerfully give him my full attention and with anticipation in my tone, tell him that I'd really like to know his account of what was read—to hear it in "my very own dear child's voice" (any little honest embellishment in jest will do). I try to draw out my children with the gentle positive force of the invitation and with a pointed narration request.

One Reason for Balking

Young children of six or seven have gotten used to listening to delightful stories read aloud to them without ever being required to do the work of telling part of them back. To start a child in the work of narrating, take in hand a book he is interested in and say, "This is our book for narrating." A child will learn what is expected of him if we are consistent, and balking will subside.

Is this forcing children to learn? In a subtle way, yes, because it is something he is required to perform. But Charlotte observed that a "force" is born in children. Every normal child has it in him to tell (a curiosity to observe and express). We are simply providing his natural "force" an intelligent outlet.

Quiet Children

Have you noticed that quiet children are not usually firstborn children? These children might balk or whine quietly. Patience will be needed as younger children may compare themselves to older siblings and feel inferior. Assure the quiet child that his narrating needn't be just like Anna's or David's. With the other children set up with their occupations, go to an out-of-the way corner with the quiet one. This privacy worked with my quiet one. For the mother to be available to hear (with eye contact, too) any spontaneous narrations through the day is also a most important benefit to the quiet child.

Critique

For the quiet child it is especially important to keep the lesson positive and free of criticism. If the narrator didn't tell the sequence correctly, next time give him less text to tell back or simply remind him to go the beginning of the tale and tell this first. Children are sometimes more impressed with the outcome of a passage and tell the ending only. If you ask certain questions at the close of a child's narration, he may even correct himself. My experienced narrator is resilient enough to receive some correction, but this I do infrequently.

Tall Tales in a Narration

Dear Karen,

My child adds fantasy to all her narrations. You tell us not to correct but I do want her to keep to the truth of the story.

Signed,
Concerned

Dear C.,

I am smiling because your daughter is obviously clever and imaginative. She seems to feel there is a need to improve the story with embellishment. She has the makings of a great narrator. Use a different book, one which she will not be tempted to decorate with an added plot, one which will satisfy her intelligent cravings to use her imagination.

Just Use a Different Book

Years ago I asked my one of my daughters to narrate what I thought might make a lovely story to share together. The book was *Little House on Plum Creek*. Frankly, there is not much happening in this book, except that in one chapter, Laura almost gets swept away by the rising waters of the creek. This is exciting, but the majority of the episodes are on the ordinary side. It is basically a calm and pleasant book to read (and mothers like myself are fond of domestic scenes), but my daughter found it difficult to give a narration from it. There just wasn't enough to it. I put the book aside and found that *Farmer Boy* of the same series did a better job of feeding her imagination. Anyone who has read this book aloud can attest that the book is mouth-watering. All those delicious meals made from scratch and cooked on a wood-burning stove, minutes after the vegetables were picked from the garden, put a giggle in us both as she narrated. Our stomachs growled. Eventually I scheduled this to be our last lesson of the morning so we could make lunch directly afterward. Although *Farmer Boy* is a true story of farm life, it suplied our imaginations well.

Nourish the Imagination

Charlotte believed a daily ration of food for the imagination was the remedy for children who like to fib or stretch the truth. Most educators would do the opposite: they would restrict the child to non-fiction. Charlotte felt that the child who was embellishing the truth was doing so out of boredom with the material, and thus required more imaginative material. In her book, *Formation of Character*, she dramatizes a situation in which a child habitually fibs. In "Mrs. Sedley's Tale," she gives reasons why Fanny fibs and how to cure her. Your child's untruthfulness is probably not this extensive, dear C., but I thought we could borrow some ideas from Charlotte's remedy:

"Doesn't she delight in fairy tales?"

"Well, to tell the truth, I have thought them likely to foster her failing, and have kept her a good deal on a diet of facts."

"I shouldn't wonder if you are wrong there. An imperious imagination like Fanny's demands its proper nourishment. Let her have her daily meal: 'The Babes in the Wood,' 'The Little Match-Girl,' 'The Snow-Maiden,' tales and legends half-historic; above all, the lovely true stories of the Bible; whatever she can figure to herself and live over and over; but not twaddling tales of the daily doings of children like herself, whether funny or serious. The child wants an opening into the larger world where all things are possible and where

beautiful things are always happening. Give her in some form this necessary food, and her mind will be so full of delightful imaginings that she will be under no temptation to invent about the commonplaces of everyday life."

Next, Charlotte Mason advises us in "Mrs. Sedley's Tale" to give the fanciful mind plenty of practice in telling the truth: "Look out the window and tell me exactly what you see and only what you see, or smell or hear. I am going to close my eyes and you paint your description in my head." Since reading this tale in 1988, I've said this often to my children. I must admit to enhancing this activity once by placing a large gingerbread boy cookie on a rock by a tree in the backyard one gray winter's day. That day I heard an excited squeal from one little daughter, "Mommy, Mommy, look at the squirrel!" We gathered at the window to watch a hungry squirrel clutch the cookie in its little claws, nibble an arm of the cookie, and run up the tree with the poor gingerbread boy in its mouth. It was a funny true sight to behold. And what fun it was for the girls tell Daddy all about it when he got home. Truth does not have to be boring, and as that old British playwright said, it is often "stranger than fiction."

A Truth-Telling Game

I used to play this game with my children because it uses the faculties of the imagination and also reinforces truth telling: Put a blindfold over the eyes of the children in turn. Let them feel or smell an object from the kitchen or a toy from the bedroom. Tell them to describe it and then guess what it is.

The whole chapter of "Mrs. Sedley's Tale" might make a good one for discussion in a support group. This entertaining yet informative tale would have to be read before the date of the parley. (See page 77 of *Formation of Character*.) ⇥

Chapter Seventeen

....

Teaching Composition

*"Teaching composition Charlotte Mason's way is
so simple that I feel like I'm cheating!"*

HAVE YOU NOTICED the amount of writing curriculum available for the lower elementary grades? There are so many choices for us homeschooling mothers that it can easily put us in a tizzy.

Put your mind at rest. Charlotte Mason's method is the simplest and most natural method I've found to teach children composition. She found the clever tricks and gimmicks used in teaching composition to children of the lower elementary grades unnecessary.

With Charlotte's method, children begin to compose orally from age six, at which time the mechanical skills of writing are developing. You have already learned that Charlotte termed this oral composition "narration."

Perhaps you haven't thought of narration under the heading of "composition" or "writing" before. Look in Susan Schaeffer Macaulay's *For the Children's Sake* and you will find the subject of narration (on pp. 120–124) under the heading of Composition, just as it is in Charlotte Mason's *Philosophy of Education*. Susan shares with us how the wonderfully natural "art of telling" powerfully develops verbal skills and involves the child's thinking, which later carries over to his writing. Because "telling" was the primary way Charlotte's students gained knowledge from books, composition (first oral, later written) was an integral part of a variety of subjects—not a separate subject.

As Charlotte says in *Philosophy of Education*:

Composition in [first or second grade] is almost entirely oral and is so much associated with Bible history, English history, geography, natural history, that it hardly calls for a special place on the programme . . . . In few things do certain teachers labour in vain more than in the careful and methodical way in which they teach composition to young children. The drill that these undergo in forming sentences is unnecessary and stultifying, as much so perhaps as such drill would be in the acts of [chewing our food]. Teachers err out of their exceeding goodwill and generous zeal. They feel they cannot do too much for children and attempt to do for them those things which they are richly endowed to do for themselves. Among these is the art of composition, that art of 'telling' which culminates in a Scott or a Homer and begins with the toddling persons of two and three who talk a great deal to each other and are surely engaged in "telling" though no grown-up, not even a mother, can understand.

Do we Underestimate our Children?

How we view the power of our children's intellectual ability seems to determine what curriculum we use or, further still, how we teach it. Charlotte noticed that teachers had the tendency to underestimate children:

Even though most teachers lay down their lives for their charges with amazing devotion, we have been so long taught to regard children as products of education and environment, that we fail to realize that from the first they are persons . . . . We either reverence or despise children; and while we regard them as incomplete and undeveloped beings who will one day arrive at the completeness of man, rather than as weak and ignorant persons, whose ignorance we must inform and whose weakness we must support, but whose potentialities are as great as our own, we cannot do otherwise than despise children, however kindly and even tenderly we commit the offense.

I would particularly like to share this next quote with you:

As soon as he gets words with which to communicate with us, a child lets us know that he thinks with surprising clearness and directness, that he sees with a closeness of observation that we have long lost, that he enjoys and that he sorrows with an intensity we have ceased to experience, that he loves with an abandon and a confidence which, alas, we do not share, that he imagines with a fecundity no artist among us can approach, that he acquires intellectual knowledge and mechanical skill at a rate so amazing, that, could the infant's rate of progress be kept up to manhood, he would surely appropriate the whole field of knowledge in a single lifetime!

Charlotte Mason considered a child as he was, viewing him neither as Wordsworth did, as in the heights above, nor as the evolutionist does, in the depths below. She said, "A person is a mystery, that is, we cannot explain him or account for him, but must accept him as he is."

Less is Blessed

From Charlotte's viewpoint, we need not depend on those "How to Teach Writing" books meant for our young students. Instead, we put trust in their natural ability to communicate through the practice of narration.

"But Charlotte's method is so simple that I feel like I'm cheating," you might say. Yet, in acquiring the habit of narrating, a student gains more intellectual power than by following the step-by-step guides.

It is a pity so many educators replace the use of narration with the use of these artificial programs. If all homeschooling mothers only knew how easy it is to allow their children to tell back in their own words a story that interests them! Isn't it the most simple things in life that get overlooked?

It is never too late to narrate. Charlotte

suggests breaking into the narration method with books that are of particular interest to the student. In one informal instance, I asked my daughter to tell me what she was learning from a pet guide that explained how to care for hamsters. Her enthusiasm enabled her to "narrate" easily because the book told her more about her new pet. "What did that chapter explain about hamsters?" I asked one afternoon. She eagerly shared the information about her beloved creature. If I had had a pen in hand, I'm sure her words would have made a pleasing composition. This is an informal example for beginners.

Should We Use Any Writing Exercises?

If you and your child find some typical writing exercises an occasional pleasure, by all means do some. We do little compositions, too, from time to time. For example, *"Tell a rainy story. It may be one in your past or a made up story. Think of what wet sounding, describing words you can use; drippy, soggy, etc."*

Most of these writing exercises train the student to follow a line of questioning. Some of the topics are fun. This is good, but I've had to keep in mind that this is what Charlotte said should not, in large proportion, take the place of narrating from books.

When a child is accustomed to composing orally about what he is learning from a well-written book, or from an experience, he is so familiar with using language that writing about what he is learning comes naturally to him.

Guidelines for Oral Composition

Oral composition (narration) in grades one, two, and three lays important groundwork in the Charlotte Mason method. Formal oral narration is required of a child only after the age of six. These young children begin telling back paragraphs in their own words. After some experience older children should be in the habit of narration. I say "habit" because most children will not be accustomed to narration when it is only required once a month.

Children should take turns narrating two to three times a week. By age seven or eight they can narrate a whole chapter (equivalent to about seven minutes' worth of a teacher's reading aloud). During these years the mechanics of writing are developing. The young student copies lines of prose, poetry, or passages from the Bible into his copy book. Children can also copy portions of their (sometimes long) narrations from what they have dictated to you. Short lessons of this sort take place daily with some words to be remembered and reviewed (spelling). Very little grammar is learned. Letters to Grandmother, grocery lists, and captions to pictures drawn are typical writing experiences for every young child. Keeping his own personal notebook of experiences—things he has made, places he has visited, even if explained in just a few written words—is a better start in writing than the fill-in-the-blank, answer-a-list-of-questions technique found on writing worksheets.

Guidelines for Weathering the Transition from Oral to Written

Written narrations are expected at the age of ten or so. By this time the student would have had several years of narrating orally on a number of subjects. The amount of writing depends on the ability of the individual and the time allocated for it in Charlotte's typically short lessons. Oral narrations continue to be practiced along with the written ones.

You may discover that when you require a child to write his narration, the length of his "telling" quickly diminishes. Yet if the child is in the habit of dictating narrations to you, the content might be as long as two pages. Charlotte Mason's remedy is to allow children to write freely about what they know and not be pressed to pay attention to "starts and stops."

Imagine what it would be like if I asked you to write about a brief holiday in France. Your trip was exciting and you were quite ready to "tell." But I required you to keep these specifics in mind while you wrote:

> Put quotation marks around every occurrence of the word "and;" indent to start a new paragraph every time you use the word "that;" capitalize all words which begin with the letter "c;" and underline all words which end with "s." Every French name or place should be spelled correctly from memory, if possible, or you can stop and look it up in a French dictionary.

This split attention is what Charlotte thought should not get in the way of a child narrating on paper. A better copy can later be made from the "rough draft," but while they write, it isn't a naughty deed to give a young author the spelling of a word when he asks politely. My children are also familiar with the phrase "sound it out." This at least helps with the basic consonants while I help them fill in those fussy vowels.

At age eleven or twelve a student is ready to be more responsible for punctuation necessities. Good grammar and descriptive vocabulary have been picked up from the child's use of narrating from living books.

With this strong start in language, only short lessons are needed in grammar. These begin at the fourth grade level.

Patience Accomplishes More than Pushing

The transition from oral to written narration will not be an effortless one. Written narrations take work. I was very happy with my first child's oral narrations in her elementary years. They were detailed, thorough, rich in new vocabulary, and spoken with some enthusiasm. Yet she still struggles with spelling. Over the years she has needed daily encouragement and assistance.

Another of my daughters has always found the mechanical skills of writing, spelling, and punctuation, to be no chore. Little letters to Grandma and pen pals, and captions to drawings in a Nature Notebook have been written with ease. Our family has been quite often surprised by sentimental notes she spontaneously wrote to one or another of us. On the other hand, much effort was used to get her words out during oral narrations. During these earlier elementary years she retold Bible stories, fables, Greek myths, history stories, and nature stories with some difficulty (pauses and stuttering).

I persevered, trying not to fret, waiting for Charlotte Mason's method to take hold. Today this daughter confidently shares from what she reads silently. It is her most enjoyable part of homeschool.

Overseeing written narration is more work for the teacher. She may feel less confident about encouraging narrative writing in notebooks than handing out self-explanatory worksheets that can be checked over in minutes. Some guidelines give the student and the home teacher an idea of what to look for. Here are a few:

- Is each sentence complete?
- Do the ideas flow from one sentence to the next?
- Are the sentences varied in length and type? (In other words, don't start every sentence with the same word.)
- Are descriptive words (adjectives or adverbs) included?

I want to emphasize a point, though. If the child has been narrating from good books, he would have practiced orally a portion of the kinds of things mentioned in these guidelines years before he starts writing. Therefore, he is not writing according to the list of visible guidelines, but according to invisible composing skills which he has acquired by oral narration.

A guideline page for the eleven- or twelve-year-old could be pasted inside the front or back of his notebook, which he can use for himself as a check or reminder. Light criticism and correction will be occasionally necessary, but keep it basic, asking the child a question to draw forth improvements. Most importantly, let the child write freely for some months, or even a year or more. He needs to gain fluency. After the freedom of developing fluency, a simple writing course will help him polish the details.

The daily task to oversee the notebook style of writing is worthwhile. Children will have their strengths and weaknesses, and a wise mother/teacher knows that patience and perseverance accomplish more than pushing.

Charlotte Mason declared narration to be the most natural process for a child to learn to deal with words, with stories, and, most importantly, with knowledge from books. However, expect some months or years of adjustment as your child advances from oral to written composition, especially when you begin to give more attention to spelling, punctuation, and grammar.

Be encouraged. Wait and see, it does happen. It was this transfer of ability from one medium to another that Charlotte believed in. I've trusted the transfer, and as a result my older children's portfolios are full of written narrations that have largely taken the place of worksheets over the years.

Thus, we can say that oral narration gives impetus and form to the written narration. And, this is how Charlotte advises us to teach composition.

Narration is the Mother of Invention

"I thought the whole idea behind composition was to express something original," someone might exclaim. In a 1925

Parents' Review article on Chaucer, Essex Cholmondeley wrote:

> If the works of the great poets teach anything, it is to hold mere invention somewhat cheap. It is not the finding of a thing, but the making something out of it after it is found, that is of consequence. Accordingly, Chaucer, like Shakespeare, invented almost nothing. Whenever Shakespeare found anything directed to Geoffrey Chaucer, he took it and made the most of it. It was not the subject treated but *himself* that was the new thing. Chaucer also has something to say on mankind's power of invention in the prologue to the Parlement of Foules. He leaves us to reflect upon the great question of how far is any work or thought *original*?

> *Of usage, what for lust [pleasure] and what*
> *for lore,*
> *On bokes rede I ofte, as I you tolde.*
> *But wherfor that I speke al this? Not yore*
> *Agon, it happéd me for to be-holde*
> *Up-on a bok, was rit with lettrés olde;*
> *And ther-upon a certeyn thing to lerne,*
> *For out of oldé feldés, as men seith,*
> *Cometh al this newé corn from yere to yere;*
> *And out of olde bokes, in good feith*
> *Cometh al this newé science that men lere.*

Developing an Original Style

The power and style of writing (content) develops out of those many moments of narration. Miss Parish, a teacher in a Charlotte Mason school, said that narration is "absorbing into oneself the beautiful thought from the book, making it one's own and then giving it forth again with just that little touch that comes from one's own mind."

While taking advantage of the use of narration as a direct aid to composition, a child who is thirteen or above will have developed his own style. This is true especially since his diet of books has allowed him to feast upon living books, firsthand sources, authors with an obvious style of writing. A child who is used to doing most of his reading out of the dry writing of textbooks will not have this "style" advantage.

In *Philosophy of Education*, Charlotte reminds us that "having been brought up so far upon stylists, the pupils are almost certain to have formed a good style; because they have been thrown into the society of many great minds, they will not make a [slavish] copy of anyone but will shape an individual style out of the wealth of material they possess . . . "

Writing with the intent to copy a certain author's style with which a child is familiar will lend interest to a writing assignment. One mother inspired by Charlotte Mason's principles shared in a support group meeting that her younger student likes to narrate in the style of Thornton Burgess. After reading several of his books she can "tell" about birds as in the manner of *The Burgess Bird Book for Children*. Someday this child is sure to have her own style, but for now she enjoys playing with the style of others—an opportunity to be prized.

Be True to Your Goal

A good writing style is the result of the regular use of narration and whole books over a period of years. Reaching our goal of having our children acquire a wealth of knowledge and be able to express it in good English seems distant—on some days utterly out of reach! Yet to have an ideal, to look onward and upwards, is vital to our homeschooling endeavors.

All we need to do is to be faithful in the little-by-little, day-by-day approach of reading from great books. And when it comes to composition, we can be thankful for the humble pencil with its forgiving eraser, as well as the years of oral narration hidden within the fingers that hold it. ⇥

Questions for Personal Reflection or Support Group Discussion

1. *What are the foundational skills that enable children to compose?*

2. *Was composition taught as a separate subject in Charlotte's schools? Explain.*

3. *What kinds of things do your children like to write about?*

4. *How does "telling" transfer into writing? Why does it require patience?*

5. *Are weekly composition exercises necessary? Explain.*

6. *Do our children's compositions need to be original ones? How have other writers used their creativity, yet borrowed from other writers?*

7. *What happens when children spend years listening to "living books" read aloud and reading on their own the works of some of the best authors? How does this affect a student's writing?*

8. *Copybook/notebook-style writing requires more supervision by the teacher. How does this style of writing differ from that of the workbook? Why is the first a more worthwhile kind of writing?*

9. *What are the kinds of things Mother likes to write about?*

Chapter Eighteen

....

Kernels of Wisdom

MUCH ACTIVITY took place this fall. The squirrels made ready their treasury of nuts, the mice their store of grain. To those who are passing the winter in sleep, hunger will be their first experience when the early sunshine summons them from their nests. One mouse forgot its granary, hidden near a shrub in the garden, and when a sleepy winter has ended, up will spring a small crop of wheat. For nuts and seeds are full of vitality; they wait patiently for a long time before they spring to life.

The little hoard, laid before you in these pages, has waited many years before coming to light. It was buried in an old notebook of Charlotte Mason's, a store of ideas collected week by week during the two years' training given at the House of Education, Ambleside. The teacher trainee was discovering, during the period known as Criticism Lessons, an approach to knowledge that is direct, simple, and within reach of all.

Criticism Lessons were moments of intense effort and endurance for the teacher trainee. They were held in the room at Scale How, which had once been the drawing-room—complete with glass chandelier and French windows. Now it was a classroom. Rows of trainees were seated at the back of the room, the members of the teaching staff forming a semicircle opposite them. In the space by the windows there were desks, or a table and chairs, ready for the children who were even now walking up the drive from Fairfield School. When they had entered and taken their places before the trainee who was to give the first lesson, the door was left open. Presently Miss Mason entered, with a smile for children and students, and the session began.

The notebook records the remarks made by Miss Mason at the end of the morning when the lessons were criticized. First fellow trainees were asked to contribute, then the staff. Finally Miss Mason said a few words of comment and these words, copied verbatim into the notebook, proved to be a veritable store of nuts, a treasure of ideas that would be of life-long benefit for the students.

The notes are grouped under subject for easier reading:

The Life of Nelson. A dull lesson because of the teacher's lack of animation. She was not interested in nor proud of Nelson.

Put more of yourselves into what you can do. But don't think about yourselves.

Be on the qui vive. Listen to the narration enthusiastically. Listen actively. The PNEU has discovered the power of attention, and it is making a revolution in education.

History. Narration should not be accepted as perfect unless it really is so. "One, two, three, four things have been left out. Who can give them?" Imperfect narration means imperfect attention. Perfect attention is easier to give than imperfect.

Put the "little minds" of children out of your thoughts. Children have just as big minds as we have.

Power of attention shows an educated man.

Alert attention (animation) is the first duty of the teacher.

Where and how are we to appeal to the imagination? At the beginning of the lesson.

Teachers must teach less and scholars must learn more.

Miss X was panic-stricken because the lesson was not going well. That's the moment to rally.

Emphasize proper names. Read always as if deeply interested yourself. Read at people and meet the eyes of those to whom we read.

Lady Jane Grey. The Greek tragedies aroused the emotions of pity and fear. A historical drama should in the same way arouse emotions of pity and admiration.

Guard against inertia; be alert.

What little the teacher does must be done extremely well.

Geography. The subject was rendered commonplace.

If you do not think about the matter at hand, you think about yourself.

Conceive the whole thing. Do not interrupt narration either by questions or by any other means. This lesson was not sufficiently nutritive.

Nature Study. Narration can be helped by means of headings on the blackboard, by an interested manner, and not by questions but by remarks.

Science. There are two ways of approach: read and narrate first, then experiment; or, experiment first, then read and narrate.

You cannot tell what you don't know.

....

Clear speaking is a sign of cultivation.

....

The book, The British Museum. *Never wait too long for narration and wait expectantly.*

....

Picture Study. Let the children look again and again and again at the picture.

....

Scripture. Dull passages—sufficient animation and interest should carry the children through these and they should learn at a single reading.

....

Indian History. It is the teacher's duty to show by her attitude that, though other religions have light, our religion has the supreme light.

....

English Literature. We must pass on our feeling, but not our opinion. Feeling kindles feeling.

....

Latin. Make the children see that the book is the thing. Let them get over their own stiles. [A stile is a step or set of steps for passing over a fence or wall.]

....

English Grammar. People do not do any more than they are expected to do, or know more than they are expected to know.

....

Never lose sight of last term's work.

....

Children should have "the grand elemental principle of pleasure" in their work and the teacher must share in the pleasure.

....

Joan of Arc. [Miss Mason's notebook describes the incident fully.] The children had given good narration of the book used during this lesson. During the criticism period, a fellow trainee said that the class was "not given enough work to do." [Miss Mason asked which of those who agreed with this criticism could narrate the lesson with all dates, names etc.? No one volunteered to try.]

....

Miss Mason then showed us that the clear narration of things read or heard is true work of the mind. We must not think that because this work is done easily and invisibly that it is not true work. "Prove that it is work by doing it yourselves. It is not the question which Miss Jones asks Mary Robinson that makes Mary work, but the question which Mary asks Mary. "You must all be Mary Robinsons," she said.

Miss Mason went on to say that the best work is not visible: it does not employ the reasoning here, the imagination there. It employs the whole mind, for the mind is a whole, not a parcel of faculties. One should not think that what is not seen does not exist: when the whole mind is at work, knowledge infallibly results.

Well, there is the store of notebook-nuts. Each one has its full kernel. Happy are the teachers who can crack them and use the contents; they will find a vital approach to knowledge.[1]

Chapter Nineteen

....

Reading by Sound and Sight

We are very little creatures,
All of different voice and features:
One of us in glass is set,
One of us you'll find in jet.
T'other you may see in tin,
And the fourth a box within.
If the fifth you should pursue,
It can never fly from you.

—JONATHAN SWIFT

THE FIRST ASSOCIATION children should make with each letter of the alphabet is with its sound, not its name. Learning the names of the letters is no trouble to children. They acquire this knowledge quite easily through the alphabet song. But this song shouldn't get in the way of a young child's first association with the letters—their sounds. This was the first teaching advice I ever received and employed with my children. It was strongly advised to me by another mother in my church. We were both Sunday school teachers and I came to respect and admire her for her love of God and of children. She invited me to a little meeting at her house for people interested in home educating. The year was 1984, and although I had only one child—who was two years old at the time—I looked forward to it with anticipation. Our small church had a day school on the premises, and not wishing to be thought of as the woman who opposed it, she asked me to keep the meeting quiet.

When I arrived I met the other two mothers. They were not from our church, but I found them to be so congenial that I remember wishing they were. Our host started her talk by telling us she had a teaching degree but believed a degree was not necessary for home teaching. Helpful hints on how to teach phonics was the practical part of her talk. She recommended books by Dorothy and Raymond Moore and gave us kind words of encouragement. Her meeting dropped seeds of confidence into the hearts of three mothers who left the meeting much less apprehensive about keeping their children home. The information I picked up from that meeting was carried with me when we moved out of state and then overseas.

When it came time for kindergarten with my first child, we were living in England—eleven miles south of Tower Bridge in London. My husband, Dean, had emptied our tiny third story flat of all its dirty, "tacky" old furniture. (The love seat and chair were losing their upholstery tacks.) All we kept were three beds, two wardrobes (there were no closets), and a table and four chairs. This left an eight by eight square foot area beside the table for my two little girls to stretch their limbs. After Dad took the red double-decker bus to work at the literature mission, we walked to the playground for daily exercise. We also walked daily to the shops with our backpacks, even in the drizzle, to replenish our four-cubic-foot refrigerator. Five-year-old Sophia and two-year-old Yolanda had two cherished toys apiece, which we had brought in our suitcases along with their favorite story books. I had no curriculum with me, but the girls enjoyed hearing their story books read aloud to them over and over again. Sophia understood that the print at the bottom of the pictures somehow unlocked the

story. Although the girls were content with the same stories, one Saturday, for my sanity, Dad took us by bus to a large library in our crowded town. This familiarized me enough with the route so that I had the courage to venture there myself by bus with the girls during the week. I borrowed some of Maria Montessori's books and through them was inspired to make sandpaper letters. Montessori students trace one letter with their fingers, pronouncing its sound simultaneously. They progress letter by letter—only when the previous ones are mastered are they introduced to new letters. I was convinced this would be fine preparation for reading and writing.

Sophia was not fond of sandpaper let-

ters—like her sister was to be years later—but did them dutifully. We began with the vowels, because a vowel appears in every word. When consonants were learned she began blending sounds and then decoding three-letter words. But you couldn't fool Sophia. She knew this was not really reading because where was the so-sought-after story? She began to become impatient. After months and months of letter sounds, reviewing sounds, blending sounds, decoding three-letter words, I thought, "Enough is enough," and I began gradually to build a sight vocabulary into the lessons as well, to speed things up a bit. The most commonly used words such as "the," "and," "want," and "make" were taught by—dare I mention—the "see it and say it" method. Most likely the "sight" words I listed above fit under some phonetic classification when analyzed. But both Sophia and I were ready to pass over the nit-picking and start *reading*.

Meanwhile we had moved out of the flat and into a row house of sorts. There would be no more hiking up two flights of stairs with a stroller, groceries, and two tired children each afternoon. The narrow back garden was surrounded on all three sides by a high fence. Ferns and flowers and two very old pear trees cradled us in our own little paradise. We even had our own set of swings, and in the garden shed there was a puddle pool that could be inflated! Things were looking up.

About this time we were introduced to a British missionary family returning from Pakistan. They had several children and were planning to home educate. It was an answer to a repeated prayer of mine to find another home educating mother so that I would no longer be alone in my endeavors. She shared with me Susan Schaeffer Macaulay's book, which she had picked up when Susan spoke to missionary mothers at the Holland Conference. I stayed up part of one night reading the

first half and part of another night finishing it. Charlotte Mason, the woman spoken of by Susan, sounded so fascinating. Susan's clear and sensible description of this woman's philosophy and method put education in perspective for me. Then, through interlibrary loan, I got into my hands what I was longing for—Charlotte Mason's *Home Education*.

In Chapter Five, "Lessons as Instruments of Education," I found some good advice on teaching children to read. Here Charlotte recommends a child do some reading by sight after basic phonics is mastered. Chapter Five was my confirmation. I felt a combination of gladness and great relief. And so with renewed confidence I continued to carry out my plan of teaching Sophia to read by sound *and* by sight. Charlotte said that an exhaustive study of phonics is not especially useful to children, that it is a curious study for a philologist but inappropriate for a child. She said:

> It is time we faced the fact that the letters which compose an English word are full of philological interest, and that their study will be a valuable part of education by-and-by; *but* in the meantime, sound and letter-sign are so loosely wedded in English, that to base the teaching of reading on the sounds of the letters only, is to lay up for the child much analytic labour, much mental confusion, due to irregularities of the language."

Phonics is only one means to reading. It is not reading itself.

Charlotte believed that the child should be taught from the first to regard the printed word as he already regards the spoken word, as the symbol of fact or ideas full of interest. "How easy to read 'robin redbreast,' 'buttercups and daisies.' "The number of letters in the words is no matter; the words themselves convey such interesting ideas that the general form and look of them fixes itself on the child's brain by the same law of association of ideas which makes it easy to couple the objects with their spoken names."

I wrote out the words to the first verse of "Twinkle Twinkle, Little Star" on a chalk board easel, pointing to each word in turn as we sang it together slowly. We were choral singers as well as choral readers. Any simple nursery rhyme will supply an abundance of interesting words for sight recognition. The common sight words found in "Twinkle" will be read by a child hundreds of times, even before he is too old to outgrow the enjoyment of nursery rhymes. This is the kind of reading lesson children "take to." As Charlotte said,

> his reading lessons must advance so slowly that he may just as well learn his reading exercises, both prose and poetry, as recitation lessons. Little poems suitable to be learned in this way will suggest themselves at once; but perhaps prose is better, on the whole, as offering more of the words in everyday use of Saxon origin, and of anomalous spelling. Short fables, and graceful simple prose . . . are very suitable. Even for their earliest lessons, it is unnecessary to put twaddle into the hands of children.

I later wrote the words of the first verse of "Twinkle" on cards, scrambled them up and let Sophia piece them back in order. She was allowed to look at the easel if she needed to.

After five months with the mission, a single girl from the mission baby-sat our children for a whole day. Dean and I went into London by train. "It's about time," we sighed as we sank into the thick upholstery to watch the brick row houses whiz by us through the train window. In just thirty minutes we were in the city taking in the sights, enjoying the break from our regular

duties. We visited the Tower of London and Piccadilly Circus, after which we spent a lot of time looking in used book stores for easy books for the children to read. I had already found a few books by Ladybird, but when we sauntered into a small shop run by Oxford University Press, I was delighted to discover a scheme that fascinated me. The big glossy package of materials was for a classroom and we couldn't afford it on our missionary budget. But Dean knew an Oxford sales representative who came into his office at the literature mission who would possibly be able to get us some used samples at a discount. This was my hope and my prayer. We had supper at an Italian restaurant and ventured home satisfied that we had seen all and done all we could in one day. I don't remember if it was a week or two or three, but I do remember that it was during the time we were trying to find Charlotte Mason's original writings, which seemed to be all but scoured out of the country by Americans calling long-distance, that my miscellaneous samples arrived. Week by week the colorful books were devoured by Sophia as she learned—by sight, by picture cue, and by sound—to *read* her new little books. They had one short sentence on each page and some of the words were deliciously longer than three letters—and oh, so very interesting as they complemented the suspenseful action of the story so beautifully. There were in the kit a few objectionable stories, which I excluded.

Writing in big bold letters, I made Sophia some cards to review her sight words and keep up her practice of "sounding out." We played the Treasure Game with them. The cards were placed face up in a serpentine path on the carpet. A die was rolled, and as tiny dolls or tokens landed on the cards in sequence, green words were "sounded" and red words were "said" until the path was completed and the treasure uncovered. Sophia enjoyed the game, as did her sister and brother after her. I added a few new words each game. A small bowl of cherries was the treasure one day. For most games I would simply wrap up in a handkerchief a little object from around the house for her to uncover.

Here is an activity that was played on sunny days in our back garden. I wrote on scraps of paper phonetic words with green pen and sight words with red. All of the short phrases featured verbs, and they became secret messages for Sophia to act out. The scraps were folded up and placed in a hat (of course). She reached in and chose a message and quietly figured it out in secret. Then she acted out the suggested activity for me to guess. You'd be surprised at how many phonetic verbs can be mixed with a few sight words. For example: hop on one leg, run fast, skip in a big circle, pet the dog, clap your hands, kick the ball, pick up a stick, feel the grass, smell a flower, swing high, swing low, do a jig, climb the tree, take three steps, etc. Her actions were living proof that she understood the message, and her smile showed that she was happy that words have meaning.

Because you know which are the words your child can read easily, you can build his confidence, camouflaging an otherwise stale review of these words by adding some interesting new ones during a normal day.

Here is how I did it. (By this time we had returned to the United States and were living in Tennessee—continuing our reading progress every day while Dad was looking for a publisher to reprint Charlotte Mason's writings.) After the girls were asleep, and before I retired each evening, I would chalk a message to them on their easel. The messages came from characters out of one of their favorite stories—one of the stories I had read so many times in our English flat the year before. The characters were the elves that worked all night making shoes for the poor shoemaker and mysteriously disappeared by morning. Do you know the story? Now these elves were helping us. They had

names that were always spelled in different phonetic combinations, such as Zip, Pip, Bop, Rex, and Pix. Sight words that had been previously introduced were used in the actual messages.

The girls looked forward to—what was from Mother's point of view alone—Sophia's morning "reading review lesson." Yolanda always nudged her older sister to read it before breakfast. The elves sometimes left little things on the easel—like acorn cups, grapes, a flower from the garden, or a new magic marker. These messages didn't last forever. With my next pregnancy, I became nauseated in the evenings and found myself in bed very soon after the girls' bedtime. Thus the elves' messages became less frequent. But a surprising thing happened. Sophia started writing messages to me and her sister, signing them with the similar elfin names. If you are uncomfortable with the fantasy aspect of the game, perhaps you might try your own version with real messages from real members of the family.

I don't understand the popular warnings against sight reading except where no phonics is taught at all. I used this mixed method of teaching my girls and my son to read with success. Contrary to some people's fears and earnest pleas to avoid sight reading at all costs, my children have found it to be a refreshing change from lessons of dreary decoding. The sight reading part of their studies did not hinder their reading "properly"—as some propose it will do. Some sight reading proves that words are not nonsense exercises but that reading is pleasant and meaningful. Paying attention to vivid words is fun when they do what

... from the elves.

they are meant to do—tell a story—or simply give an idea. And those who love reading will like to write—but that's another chapter.

I can't remember when our reading *lessons* ended and their *reading* began. I do remember that I gave them as many simple books as I could get my hands on, none of which were books containing only three-letter words. I am glancing at a paragraph in my copy of *Home Education* that I had underlined seven years ago: "I should never put him into words of one syllable at all. The bigger the word, the more striking the look of it, and, therefore, the easier it is to read, provided always that the idea it conveys is interesting to a child." Charlotte goes on to say that school books graduated according to the number of letters each word contains are twaddle. A child will be lost in a hopeless fog of three-letter words which all look drearily so alike that there are no distinctive features for the eye to seize upon. Families of words, such as b-oat, fl-oat, c-oat m-oat, are good practice for "sounding out" during short lessons, but should never be so blatantly placed in their books.

Have you ever read *The Enormous Turnip?* I have seen this simple story in several versions of easy-to-read books. What a feeling of accomplishment a mother feels when she hears her child read aloud the word "enormous" on almost every page after she interprets the word for him on the first. The child reads it matter-of-factly, as it is easy to recognize among lots of shorter words.

If your child, learning to read, is finding it a wearisome chore instead of rewarding labor, why not break the current homeschool law of reading by sound only, and add some spicy sight words into his vocabulary? What a relief to instantly recognize a few sight words in a sentence rather than straining to decode every word in one's path. Here is a bland diet of phonetic practice: "The big man in a red hat sat on a log at noon soon to eat cool noodles with a spoon." As an alternative, "The big man ate red *lasagna* with a spoon at noon" will add just that right amount of zest to make the reading lesson a joy to both student and teacher. ⇥

Your Own Personal Reflections

Period One. Naming: "This is a . . ."
Period Two. Recognition: "Which one is the . . ."
Period Three. Pronunciation of the word: "What is this?"

Chapter Twenty

···

The Three Period Lesson

WHILE LIVING IN ENGLAND, I read an armful of Maria Montessori's books before being introduced to Charlotte Mason. After reading Charlotte's writings, by comparison I agreed with fewer aspects of the Montessori philosophy. But in our homeschool I used some of the practical aspects of the Montessori method—such as sandpaper letters and manipulatives. I also found the use of her Three Period Lesson to be very helpful.

When introducing young students to new colors, shapes, letters, sounds, words, objects, numbers and their properties—even a foreign language—it is handy to keep the above outline of the Three Period Lesson in the back of one's mind. Here are some examples of its use:

Color—An Example for Preschool

Period One: "This is red." "This is yellow." (yellow may be a review of a previous lesson). Period Two: "Which one is red?" "Which one is yellow?" "Well done. You chose correctly," the teacher might say when the child recognizes the color requested. Period Three: "What color is this?" The child then pronounces the name of the color. The Third Period lesson takes more mental effort than the first two.

Number—An Example for Kindergarten

Period One: "This is a set of five marbles (or pennies, or . . .)." The teacher may arrange the marbles as they appear on a die. Period One can be repeated with all kinds of different manipulatives, forks, shells, buttons, etc., before going on to Periods Two and Three.

Period Two: "Which set has five marbles?" The child is asked to recognize a set of five marbles among other sets. He may count and/or use sight recognition if he is familiar with the placement of marbles as they appear on a die. If the child is incorrect you might say, "Try again," in a positive tone. Then go back and repeat a Period One Lesson of the same number.

Period Three: "How many in this set?" or "What is the number of this set?" With this strategy a child can also learn to recognize the numerals as they are written.

Many Possible Uses

The possible uses for the Three Period Lesson in the early years are numerous. Other suggested uses with manipulatives (household stuff): Long/short, thick/narrow, heavy/light, straight/curved or crooked, light/dark, loud/quiet, fast/slow, hot/cold, smooth/rough. Many of these qualities are picked up in a general sense from a child's environment if he is in daily conversation with his parents or older siblings. However, the child may recognize that something is bigger than something else without knowing the specifics (height, width, length, etc.). Curriculum designers call the learning of these specifics "pre-math."

Cozy and Casual

The Three Period lesson can be used with any picture book of colors, shapes, numbers, or any picture book. The story is read for the First Period. Pick up the book at a later time and ask which is the square shape, or which is the tall tree, or the dark red flower—as opposed to the light red flower. This is a Second Period Lesson. Another day spent looking at the book together can provide an opportunity to ask, "What is this?" The child should say, "A square." This is a Third Period Lesson. Enjoy teaching "behind a child's back" in this casual, convenient way of sneaking in a Three Period Lesson with your young ones.

Phonics—An Example for Kindergarten/First Grade

Period One: "This letter makes the sound 'a.'" "Say 'a.'" (As I mentioned before, it is often necessary to repeat Period One lessons. It could be helpful to think of one period as one day.)

Period Two: "Which of these letters makes the sound 'a'?" As soon as he builds a repertoire of sounds, the teacher can ask many more Period Two questions in reference to other letter sounds the child has learned. "Okay, now which one says 'e'?" This makes for very good review, boosts confidence, and provides reinforcement before going on to a Period Three lesson.

Period Three: "What sound does this letter make?" Period Three uses more memory muscles. My son was saying "a" in place of "e" during some Period Three lessons, so I simply went back to doing more Period One and Two lessons for a time for the sound "e".

Sight Words—An Example for First or Second Grade and Up

Period One: "This is the word 'was.'" "Say 'was.'"

Period Two: "Find the word 'was.'" It is recommended that a child recognize the word "in context" before he is asked to recognize it alone—as on a flash card, for example. My son's little books have one sentence on a page, and each one corresponds to the action taking place in the illustration. It is easy for me to use a Period Two lesson every time he reads a book aloud to me by asking him to point out sight words like "was" in the sentence. Early in the process of learning to read I do not recommend lining up similar-looking words like "were," "was," "went," "what," to find the word "was." Reinforcement is important in the early stages. A child is more apt to choose the right word when there are some self-correcting clues to aid in thinking. This is not giving him a crutch but an opportunity—an opportunity to think by logic, or other means while his memory is developed in the process. Clues give the child the opportunity to think, "I can do it!" which strengthens his will to learn. "It was spring. The yard was muddy." "Which word is 'was'?" In both sentences "was" is the only word beginning with a "w" sound. This is one example of a clue. By pointing to the word and pronouncing the word, the child adds to his memory while his attention is fixed. After my son has read his little books aloud to me a few times, I cover up each illustration with a piece of construction paper and have him read the book again without the picture clues. By then he has become familiar with the words that he has "read" over and again with the pictures. I have allowed my children to cleverly use clues to their advantage while gaining fluency in reading. It is their most delightful "school" subject.

Period Three: "What word is this?" The teacher can point to a word in context—within a short sentence—and later in isolation by flash card. The child pronounces the word.

As you can see by the above examples, this outline of lessons can be applied to a variety of learning situations to enable the child to gain facts and information in steps. It provides the mother with suggestions for creating an atmosphere of learning that recognizes the gradual development of the child's fluency. Try it for some of your lessons. It is as easy as one, two, three! ➤

Chapter Twenty-One

....

Vocabulary

Have you heard people say: "Oh yes, I've seen the movie . . . but the book is better"? The movie industry can entertain, thrill, and rivet our attention but it cannot match the power of written words. Words can tell a story like no movie can. Words go deeper. We cannot think without them, what a book does is to get us thinking.

We watched the British video series *Pride and Prejudice,* based on Jane Austen's novel of the same name. The ladies of our household enjoyed it very much. British screenplays have a way of sticking closer to the book than do American screenplays, which is one thing I particularly appreciate about them. Nevertheless, my daughter said, "The book is better."

"In what way is it better?" I asked.

"I knew more about the characters when I read the book. I understood the story better. The movie strips away the conversation in the book and it concentrates on the plot rather than the actual lives and thoughts of the characters."

"Did you ever go back to read over certain parts of the story?" I wondered if any of the vocabulary had stumped her.

"I'd pause to re-read sentences until I understood the meaning, because when I'm into a book I tend to read fast."

I was glad to hear this, because what she was actually telling me was that she had a habit of searching out the meaning of a strange word by looking at it in context that is, by getting the larger picture. Any fuzzy word came into clearer focus this way.

Even my sight learner, who craves films about horses as main characters, still is very fond of the book versions. Children like particulars. Words have a way of describing things in a way that gives us the "inside story." Fine vocabulary lets us "zero in" on an emotion, a mannerism, a quality, or an idiosyncrasy that is lost in the movie version.

Words are a Wonder

To love reading is to be a lover of words, whether unconsciously or consciously. The Maker of Heaven and Earth chose words to make himself known to us. When a believer is "in the Word" we are closer to Him (I John 1). We worship Him with our actions, our intentions, our hearts, and with words. Words are wonderful!

"Sticks and stones can break my bones but words can never hurt me." This is a falsehood, because words penetrate the spirit of man and can represent evil thoughts and wishes. What is said—or in some cases what is not said—affects the very soul.

You have heard that the pen is mightier than the sword. Words, because they represent ideas, have the power to sway nations, touch and inspire individual lives. It seems that through the centuries, wherever Christians have lived in community, education has resided—first, to teach the Word, and secondly, to contemplate and consider the words and lives of others.

Talk Up Not Down to Children

We contribute to the maturation of our children with words. We first build a young child's vocabulary by conversation. His vocabulary increases again when we read aloud little stories.

"This one, Daddy. Mommy reads me *this* one."

"You want me to read it again?"

"Yes, Daddy, this one."

Young children not only like to hear certain words again and again but find it a satisfying comfort to repeat familiar phrases. When my children were all small, during frazzled moments I would sing or tell a nursery rhyme with which they were familiar. This distracted them from peevishness or entertained them during dull times of waiting. After one tiring Saturday of Christmas shopping, I remember telling the story "The Three Bears" as we all sat cramped together in the car with groceries and packages. This quieted and soothed the children as we journeyed home. During a subsequent car trip (another nightly return home from somewhere) Dad asked one of the children to tell the same story they were used to hearing us tell. All the travelers attentively listened to a small voice recount the familiar tale, anticipating Goldilocks' actions and each bear's response yet again.

Although "The Three Bears" is a simple story, appealing to the child mind, it is not twaddle. We want to read children "age-appropriate" stories, yet we shouldn't stag-

nate their intelligence by talking down to them with the blandest vocabulary. Rather let us awaken their intelligence with words that are new and delicious.

There exists no verbal poverty in the stories of Beatrix Potter, for example. An English teacher in a private school, author of an article in Charlotte's *Parent's Review,* wrote: "Anyone who was brought up on Beatrix Potter will remember how the uncommon words glowed in the clear setting of her style. When I first read the speech in *Jemima Puddle-duck* that begins 'Before you commence your tedious sitting, I intend to give you a treat,' I had no firm idea of the meaning of the word, 'tedious.' Indeed, the joy of it was that it was not easily capable of a firm meaning. It was a word with a tone, a style of its own, to be treasured and used exploratorily thereafter."[1] The writer went on to make his case against the "twaddle" found in so many children's books. Twaddly books would never dream of using the word "tedious." Their authors—who probably do not know what children really need—eschew such words, confining themselves to the steady useful ones with "a quickly digested significance."

Twaddle, or over-simplified vocabulary, has a deadening effect on the curious minds of children. It seems to be a human tendency to find language exciting, but this tendency will become latent and may even die if all that is given to children is "grade level" school books homogenized by editors who think it necessary to closely monitor vocabulary progress. But all that is needed is a few cues in the text to help the child figure out the strange word for himself.

Vocabulary in Context of Real Books

A child's understanding of a new word grows with each repeated meeting of the word as it appears in the context of his reading. Here is an example:

"The duckling hid in the shelter of its mother's wing."

The child *figures out* from the context that to "shelter" is to surround with protection. He will inevitably come across another example of the word in passing:

"The wind bent the branches of the trees and swirled the rain in many direction but we were sheltered by the cave."

"Now he has another example of the word "shelter," even without looking up the word in a dictionary. He may later read that God is our hiding place, our shelter in times of trouble, and apply it to his heart with a more profound understanding.

I have seen grade level vocabulary workbooks that are well-meaning but endowed with "the dullness effect." Please, let us set children free from matching one hundred identical-looking pages of "row A words with row B words" during the elementary years of learning. The time that is allocated to complete such lists can be better spent reading—or being read to. Reading itself fosters a love of language and a knowledge of words. A vocabulary workbook that includes interesting text where the meaning of a word is derived from its use in context may be helpful. But since there are so many delightful children's books available these days, wider reading is to be preferred. Older children who are good readers have become good readers not by vocabulary worksheets but by wide reading and much reading. A rule to remember is: Wide reading = Wide vocabulary.

Brush Up—Fine Tune

To "brush up" on your vocabulary is also important. Brushing up is an added touch or a refining stroke. As the experienced artist sees subtle shades of color, so an experienced reader will be able to

understand the different shades of the meaning of words. He may take an interest in how the words he has seen before relate to one another. The discovery of Latin and Greek root words with their prefixes and suffixes can help the student figure out particulars. Students will see the justice in making sense out of words with which they have some familiarity. For example, a student will read that the Latin word *vita* means "life," and *vivere* means "to live." If something is of *vital* concern it is, perhaps, a matter of *"life* and death." A doctor will check for *vital* signs. "Her *vitality* returned in the spring after she started walking again and took *vitamins."* "He is a *vivacious* expositor and I can tell the Bible is *alive* in his heart." Notice, I gave you the related words in sentences. This is the way people who write dictionaries derive a definition. They examine how a word has been used in context. By all means, look up words in the dictionary. But there is no need to be anxious about vocabulary. If books that are a

little challenging are placed in the hands of children, the children will be continually increasing their vocabulary.

The English teacher mentioned above who had a fondness for Beatrix Potter had been reading aloud to his class for some weeks from *David Copperfield,* by Charles Dickens. He shared a heartening experience:

> I remember going late once into a class that had become noisy: the door was opened for me by a boy whose self-imposed function it was to combine this politeness with a warning to the class that I'd arrived. 'Superabundant agitation this morning, sir,' he said, quoting a phrase from David Copperfield that had caught our attention the day before."[2]

This example of using vocabulary picked up from hearing good literature read aloud is one of "the best of all compliments to literature."

Narration Adheres
Vocabulary to the Mind

A wise man said, "Every reader if he has a strong mind, reads himself into the book, and amalgamates his thoughts with those of the author." Can I add that, if this be the case, he consequently shares the author's vocabulary as well?

"If you don't use it you might lose it" is the idea behind Charlotte Mason's use of narration. When a child tells back a passage of a story in his own words, there will be a lot of borrowing going on in his paraphrased version. To borrow an author's strange word is one of the best ways to learn it. The child includes the word in his narration because he considers it essential to his narration. He chooses the strange word. He uses the strange word. And he'll remember it thereafter, never as stranger, but as a friend. This completes the important cycle of impression and expression in the gaining of knowledge.

Very Remarkable Words

"Very Remarkable Words" can be the title of a student's vocabulary notebook, his personal collection of words in which he jots down any intriguing, rare vocabulary word he comes across in his reading. Let him guess the meaning from the context and, perhaps, see what a dictionary has to say about it. Word derivatives are an interesting study because they give us the history of a word. In our large dictionary not only are many words traced to the Greek or Latin origin, but a very brief example might also be given to show how and when the word was first used in the English language. This can be compared with newer uses or definitions of the word. On any occasion when words are looked up for a definition, I think attention to the short story of the word would be a kind of natural reward for the labor of looking it up.

A thesaurus is another way to compare finer shades of the meaning of words.

"Oh, I like that word," I thought to myself as I looked for any stray writing instrument with which to quickly make note of it. I've been making a collection of words that appeal to me and that I would like to make part of my vocabulary—words that I might later choose to use in my writing. I scribble them onto scraps of paper, napkins, and inside the leaves of paperback books. I jot them down on the backs of catalogs I happen to be reading, or the backs of church bulletins. My purse is crammed with old folded bulletins that haven't had their notes transcribed yet. One of these scribbled words is now printed in this chapter!

Mother's New Words

My children must listen to my voice all day. Therefore, I try to resist nagging and speak with a pleasant tone—well, *most* of the time. To ward off any tendency of theirs to turn a deaf ear to instruction, occasionally I'll attempt to tickle their ears with some extraordinary vocabulary words.

Nigel may lag a little near the end of the day. "I expected this to be executed with the utmost of swiftness," I might remind him, instead of saying, "This should've been done by now."

"Ya know mate, your recovery will strongly depend upon your ability to remain motionless, even at sea," I might say to a fretful boy who needs a tiny wound washed, instead of "Stand still!" To secure attention use less cliché.

May you and your children have a delightful time collecting vocabulary. ⵜ

Questions for Personal Reflection or Support Group Discussion

1. *Why do people who have seen a movie often say, "The book is better?"*

2. *How do words affect the spirit of man?*

3. *What is twaddle? Why do we choose books for children that have a richer vocabulary?*

4. *Why are repetitive and identically styled word lists to be eschewed?*

5. *How do children figure out the meaning of a strange word?*

6. *What title might you give a vocabulary notebook? How is it to be used? What is a word derivative?*

7. *What part does narration play in the role of vocabulary development?*

8. *A wide curriculum provides a wide vocabulary. Why should many living books take precedence over much time with vocabulary workbook pages?*

9. *How does an older child fine tune his ability to understand the meanings of words he might be already somewhat familiar with?*

10. *Words are more at home in a sentence. Why is a sentence needed to fine tune our understanding?*

Your Own Personal Reflections

Chapter Twenty-Two

···

The Servant Spelling

SPELLING IS A LOWLY SERVANT. It obediently follows on the coattails of the finer subjects. That's OK. There is no reason to make Spelling sit on a higher seat of priority. It is perfectly content to take such a humble position in the curriculum. Humble as it may be, Spelling is called for service often. Whenever written language opens its door, Spelling is willingly waiting at the threshold. Because Spelling is so needed, its services should be made available to students who will be calling on it daily for help with specific needs. Its service renders the most helpfulness when a little attention is given to it every day.

Spelling Sneaks In

The children were sitting in the living room, each waiting for his or her turn to recite a poem that had been memorized over the past week. "That was lovely, children," Mother said with true gladness, upon hearing them. "Your handwritten poems with their decorated borders are very handsome. Now I'd like you to write out your poems again, but this time from memory."

"Can we read it over closely one more time to be more sure of the spelling, Mother?"

"Yes, children, but you have only four minutes to concentrate on it."

When they were signaled to write their poems, the pencils could be heard scratching away without delay or interruption. Mother hadn't been sure of the outcome of this method of spelling, which she had heard a friend speak of just last week. When she reviewed the papers and found few errors, she was confident that this was an exercise she would assign monthly. The extra effort the children put into learning their verses by heart seemed to have some relevance to their remembering how the words of their verses were spelled. The servant Spelling had come in through a side door as the children focused their attention on reading and saying the verses over and over.

In actuality, Spelling (exact order of letters in a word) was the servant that gave them the means to read, know by heart, recite, and write something that had held a place in their pool of knowledge and ideas. Knowledge of the verses was given priority, but the servant Spelling was eager and ready to empower his master (though little credit need be given him).

A Willing Servant to a Weaker Master

"Mother, would you help me? I need to know how to spell anesthetics."

"Look in the chapter of the book you are doing your written narration from, dear."

"Oh, yes, here it is."

"How is your narration coming, by the way?"

"Oh fine, Mom. I'm telling mostly about how Dr. Long discovered the use of laughing gas. It's pretty funny," said her daughter.

"Spell the words as best you can and I'll correct your guesses."

After the rough draft was completed (about two pages), Mother corrected her daughter's writing and a short list of spelling words derived from the writing was given to her daughter to study. This older sister of the family has always struggled with spelling. She loves books and has read many. Her comprehension shines brightly in her detailed and enthusiastic oral narrations. Talking about what she learns from the books that stimulate her thinking has been a delight, but spelling it out has been another story. Phonics, spelling rules, and lists seem to swim in her mind without coming to the surface when needed. Exactly what many words look like escapes her, though she must have seen them in print hundreds of times in the books she has enjoyed reading. Mother has become worried. But she has concluded that her absent-minded speller simply needs more time and attention to assimilate and retain the spelling. Also, she needs to be doing more writing every day.

"The word togetherness has two 'esses' at the end. It is part of the 'ness' ending, or suffix. There are lots of other words that end in 'ness.' Faithfulness, kindness, forgetfulness, thankfulness are some," Mother explained. "I'd like to make these part of your personal spelling list, too."

"Ma, does the 'ful' have one 'l' in most words?"

"Mostly, yes. That's observant of you."

Her daughter would be tested on the words the next day when she began rewriting her narration neatly, and then again at the end of the week. Mother tried not to think about the label she had secretly given her daughter (poor speller). She just focused on giving her daughter more individualized spelling practice. When a word was misspelled, Mother tried to notice what it was about the word that caused the error. Then she asked her daughter questions about the word as they tried to make sense out of it together. Also, her daughter was told that she ought to study each word by seeing it in her mind's eye and by spelling it with her eyes closed.

The new (old) method her friend had introduced to her was winning with all her children. That Thanksgiving, when they copied, illustrated, memorized, and recited Psalm 100, though the dictation proved a success, the precious knowledge of the Psalm was the true aim. But Mother also decided to follow a course of study that

would take five to ten minutes daily. To be more certain her older student would learn how to spell more of the most frequently used words in the English language, she found such a "frequency" list and used it along with her daughter's personal list. For this plan she had high hopes. Perhaps her daughter indeed would spell well some day. Mother reminded herself, however, "Spelling is just a servant to higher and more important matters, so I dare not worry over it, only tailor it more to my student's specific needs."

Pre-spelling

The younger brother sat with a thick pencil in hand, copying a line from one of his favorite stories. The sentence had only four words in it, but seemed to zero in on the action of the picture that accompanied it. Copying would be a familiar exercise for him for the next few years. His writing (composition) was done orally when he was asked to retell the events of a story read aloud to him. He liked stories that gave insight into how animals really behaved, and so listened to know more about the world into which he was growing up. As a first grader he wasn't asked to spell anything, but he was getting used to the fact that each word had its definite set of letters lined up in a row. The sounds the letters made in the row gave some sense as to how the word was spoken, but not always. Copy he would do and spelling he would pick up without realizing it much.

"Mom, may I write a letter to my cousin?"

"Yes, what do you want to say?"

Mother wrote out a few sentences for her son to copy. He was happy to drop it in the mailbox. His formal spelling lessons would begin after age eight or nine, when he was reading more fluently.

A Sight-Learner Sails

A sister just several years older than the younger brother is a writing whiz. Her comprehension of what she reads needs improvement, but she can write out without much difficulty what she understands from her books. She has learned that words can be grouped according to their phonic rules, but seems not to heed that fact much. She sees most words in her head as clearly as if her imagination had taken a photograph of them. When she needs to spell a word, she simply recalls the word from her photograph-album-of-a-memory. Of course she does take into consideration the part that sounds play in the makeup of words, but how a word looks means more to her than any rule the word supposedly follows. She gets along well with her servant Spelling and he serves her avidly. When her older sister and younger brother ask for the spelling of a word, she quickly volunteers it—an ability not always to the older sister's liking.

Will My Child Ever Spell Correctly?

The above paragraphs on spelling are a description of my own experience. If your students, age twelve and up, struggle with spelling, they are not alone. This can be the age when teachers' faces flush to look upon a rough draft full of spelling errors. They may think, "Surely he should be able to spell by now." The truth is that many students still have a way to go. Spelling ability follows reading ability. For some it may follow at a greater distance, but it does follow.

Making a List and Checking it Twice

Taking steps to apply the individual spelling approach is a good plan. This method pays specific attention to words left by the wayside by the individual child.

We can customize lists for our students from the words they miss. Each writing assignment brings with it its own surprises.

Little lists are made from these surprises. Not all misspelled words need studying, only the very basic ones do. The word "anesthetics" from my daughter's written narration was not made part of her personal word list that week because she still needed to focus on more frequently used words. However, if it had been the only word she had misspelled, I would have given her the needed challenge.

Notice Characteristics

Ask your student what characterizes a word that makes it difficult for him to remember. Is there a "c" that sounds like an "s"? Should a letter be doubled? This past fall, this worried mother became more regular about making customized lists for her eldest daughter. All other spelling systems only seemed to pile up her errors, giving her too many words at one time. I became so frustrated that I focused only on her personal notebook for regular review. Phonics she knew—apparent in her written meal plan including "colyflower soop." This kind of spelling proves that the student is definitely not a poor speller, because she is thinking. Long word lists she had had one year. Taken in daily rations of a dozen, these proved disastrous upon sixth week review. More recently, with our more individual approach when she misspelled "various," I added "serious" to her personal list. When she misspelled "figure" I added "nature," "moisture," "future," and "pasture" to her list. When she spelled the word "sound" as "sownd," she made phonic sense, but I advised that she write the proper spelling of it in the contents of a funny paragraph with "found," "round" and "ground" to help her remember it.

Avoid Feeling a Slave to Any System

A little time spent each day to study the words missed on a "most frequently used word list" will be helpful if regular review is included. Going over word families—words that are grouped according to a spelling rule or phonetic rule—will be a help also. You may feel it a welcome change to veer off for a time to just study words from a personal spelling list. Every homeschool needs some regularity as well as change.

Provide the Spelling

Who wrote the rule that it is improper to give children the spelling of the words for which they are always asking? I've read that the questioning mind, in anticipation, gives ready attention to the answer given. It does not promote sloth to simply give children the spelling of words if a clever mother will make these same words become members of the student's personal spelling list. Do not grow weary of providing the spelling for the student and helping him responsibly keep these words on a list (and make sense out of them together), because the rewards of your labor will come to fruition in the years to come.

Spelling Pointers

1. Keep each daily lesson as short as five to ten minutes. Review on Friday.

2. Formulate a personal spelling list from dictation for each student who is writing, not just copying. Associate these with their word families. It is unnecessary to place every misspelled word onto this list. Focus on the frequently used words in the English language first. Add only one or two of the personal study words to the "frequently used list" daily. Chances are these will appear somewhere on that list anyway. Review words regularly. Veer off to focus on a personal list when you feel the urge for change.

3. Misspelled words from the personal spelling list become the child's study words. Four to six misspelled words a day from the list on which you have tested him are plenty. Start each new lesson with the testing of the previous day's study words. I do not let my children study these words the morning before a test. If they cannot remember what they studied the day before, it goes back on the list. Only go on to a new list when a child can spell all of those from the previous list.

4. Spelling phonetically shows your student is trying to make linguistic sense. Background knowledge of phonics is a definite help but I believe majoring in phonics will not guarantee successful spelling. Charlotte Mason taught that a child needs to "see" the words in his mind's eye. My children say each study word with correct pronunciation and spell each study word out loud with their eyes closed.

5. Get the student to talk about the words. Did he miss the silent "gh" in a word? Review certain phonics or spelling rules when needed in your discussion. For example, if he writes "mack" for "make," go over the "ck" words (crack, snack, black—short vowel sounds with "ck") and what silent "e" does for words.

6. Children can test each other unless your children giggle at this too much, as my girls sometimes do.

7. When giving a test, I use most words in a sentence. Always have students study any misspelled word by writing it in a sentence they have created. Some days my children challenge themselves by trying to use all five or six of their study words in one long silly sentence.

8. Type out repeatedly misspelled words for kinesthetic practice. Use different writing tools, such a wide point markers, crayons, paintbrushes, or chalk to "draw" the words bigger than usual.

9. An electronic pocket spell-checker facilitates rough draft writing and is especially convenient for an older student's two- to ten-page handwritten reports. Dictionary skills may be drilled on occasion after Friday's review when no new words are tested.

10. Copy, copy, copy, in the early elementary years—and thereafter—poems, captions, favorite short paragraphs from a picture book, etc.

11. Write, write, write, from the average age of nine and up—pencil and paper writing, not work page writing. Write grocery lists, recipes, written narrations of history stories, descriptions of a sporting event, a visit, or any experience, letters to pen friends, jokes, explanations of how to make something, instruction on how to grow or raise something. And again I say, write.

12. Learn to spell every word of a Bible memory verse.

I hope this gives you a look at how time spent customizing spelling instruction can be a help to any student who is giving Mother reason for concern. Expect much less of spelling in the early elementary years. Keeping the love of language alive is most important. And remember that Spelling is a servant to higher things. ⤙

Chapter Twenty-Three

Simply Grammar

*Words put together so as to make sense
form what is called a sentence, and this is Lesson One
in the study of grammar.* —Charlotte Mason

CHARLOTTE MASON tells us that because children are still hungrily learning much about "things," the study of "words" in the abstract (which is what grammar is) is in no way attractive to them. You might even go as far as to say it is a confusing distraction to them. English grammar—the significance of the position of words in a sentence and the connection of those words to one another—is a study children find peculiarly difficult to grasp.

One of the only reasons some home educators present their children with this formal study, which tends to be introduced very early, is that testing authorities put it on the year-end tests, causing us to believe it should be taught formally. This is a pity, because so much grammar is acquired by indirect teaching. When a child is surrounded with good and proper language, the direct teaching of grammar need not begin until fourth or fifth grade (at age nine or ten).

Do not underestimate the importance of all the conversations (slow and clear conversations) that a mother has throughout the day with her child. If Mother speaks clearly and decisively, she is giving the child valuable language lessons. All the reading aloud she enjoys doing every day—as her children listen attentively—is doing verbal wonders, naturally, to teach English. I trusted Charlotte and did not teach grammar directly until each young student reached the age of ten. Each always did well on the language section of the year-end test, primarily because their verb agreements were correct. They also used subject pronouns quite naturally. They rarely used an objective pronoun in the subject, as in this example of poor usage: "Them is going to play with us today." How often do your children speak this way? Probably rarely, unless they are about age two and their experience at talking has been a short one. "They" should be the "subject pronoun" and "are" is the correct verb form. Most children just need practice in hearing and speaking the English language (not television language) to get accustomed to the basic "right and wrong" of grammar. Does a child need to know the grammatical terms for the words in a sentence at such a young age? Charlotte said, "No, wait a few years."

I do correct my children. I can't resist correcting any one of them, when I hear "Me and Sophia found a baby bird," for example. I quickly respond, "You mean, 'Sophia and I . . .'" The difference between a noun in the subjective or the objective case is a rule worth understanding in the later grades, but in the younger years let them get used to what "sounds right." I've taught my children that when they hear persons talk with a dangling preposition that it is improper usage. "Where'd you leave that book at?" is now grating to them, and they know the correct way of speaking is, "Where did you leave your book?"

Learning at home provides the best opportunities for learning practical grammar, especially when children are given Charlotte's opportunity to narrate. Proper grammar is picked up from the book that is being narrated. A homeschool can provide a weighty chunk of more than twelve years of reading the best books—books which will of course be grammatically correct ones.

"One preventative or cure for falling into contemporary colloquialism and slang," said a friend of mine, "is to read an eighteenth-century novel once a month." This would certainly be a wholesome alternative to falling into the vacuities so typical of some teen-agers: " Yeah, um, it's like cool, ya know . . . awesome."

Charlotte Mason wrote *First Grammar Lessons* over one hundred years ago, and after her death teachers in the PNEU completed it. I have revised and published it for today's teachers because I am so fond of its style of presentation. It is not the tedious workbook approach to grammar. As it is an introduction to grammar, there is no diagramming. I've re-titled it *Simply Grammar* because it is an uncomplicated, lively, mind-engaging, interactive approach that introduces children to grammar concepts through the use of the spoken language. It is unique because it predominantly focuses on guided conversation between a teacher and student. Students create their own short sentences, or fit words together to tell a story—often with the help of one of the fifty large illustrations in the book. A background of experience in narration is encouraged before starting these lessons.

I have a friend who was raised in a rural town where the persons with whom she lived spoke a poor form of English. She was determined to improve herself after the birth of her daughter because she wanted to speak better English while her daughter was learning to talk. She began by reading *Simply Grammar* and has since gone on to other books. It was work, but her old habits of tongue have been replaced with new ones. When I discovered this fact, I was very impressed. There are many mothers who have been endeavoring to rise above a "less than empowering youth." In their efforts to educate their children they grasp things that had passed by them in earlier years. A love of knowledge and an enthusiasm for learning, which was once schooled out of them, is now being rediscovered and shared with their children.

Therefore, I say to you, if there is any subject—such as grammar—that baffles you, why not try a some lessons on yourself first? Whenever I have done this I have felt more at ease about our homeschool. ⇥

Your Own Personal Reflections

Chapter Twenty-Four

....

Hero-Admiration as a Factor in Education

I'VE HEARD PEOPLE SAY, "That's a good school." What is good about it, they don't say. Is it the good test scores, which in themselves are not good, just as knowledge without virtue is injurious? Goodness (righteousness) that is promoted in the school along with intellectual attainment is what should allow us to use the adjective "good." Reject religion and you reject morality, and if no absolute morality is brought into school, where is goodness to be found?

Charlotte Mason believed that a child's thinking power should be encouraged in every way. She wanted children to have the opportunity to have their imaginations quickened by awakening their creative instincts. She widened their intellectual horizons by introducing them as early as possible to the most varied works of literature. Children were urged to test and judge what they saw and heard and learned through narration. And hero-admiration was an important factor in her educational philosophy. Children had their heroes in art and fiction, history, myth, legend, and science. The heroes followed some element of truth and light. Some were Christians, some were not, but the children—through contact with those that made great contributions or who behaved with nobility—learned to admire all that was noble in them. The enthusiasm created by hero-admiration is perhaps one of its most glorious advantages. Whatever is noble, true, and pure should be considered and appreciated, because it all comes from God, whether it is delivered to us by a believer or an unbeliever. Charlotte's students had a "good" education because they were soaked in goodness through the Bible, the humanities, nature study, and hero-admiration. This soaking is what makes a school a "good" school.

The Inclination to Admire

All of us come into the world as little people who look up to bigger people. The natural inclination to admire others comes when we first become conscious of our smallness and of our dependence upon others. The mother who easily turns the door handle that the toddler has tried in vain to reach is—for the moment at least—a child's heroine. Or perhaps we bring the inclination to worship with us when we first enter the world, as Wordsworth says in "Intimations of Immortality,"

. . . trailing clouds of glory . . . from God,
Who is our home:
Heaven lies about us in our infancy!
Shades of the prison-house begin to close
Upon the growing Boy,
But He beholds the light and whence it flows,
He sees it in his joy . . .

All That is Good Reflects God's Glory

It has been said that the full joyousness of childhood can only be experienced by those who are allowed by their elders to mix heaven freely with earth, and to see angels and heroes where commonplace sinners actually stand. In order to justify this belief I will try to prove the harmlessness of a little disillusion and the beneficent influence of hero-admiration so long as it lasts. An atmosphere may be created in home life that will be conductive to the natural development of the power of hero-admiration.

It Is OK to Put People on a Pedestal

Why should children have heroes if no one is perfect and the children are bound to experience the sadness of disillusionment? Those who ask such a question seem to forget that great happiness does not exist on earth without a suggestion of pain. As the poet Shelley says to his skylark:

If we were things born not to shed a tear,
I know not how thy joy we ever should come near.

Children will suffer much disappointment when they first discover that those in whom they have placed their implicit trust have their lapses, like ordinary folk. The pain of these discoveries is sharp and the disillusions are not gotten over quickly, but the joy which preceded them certainly makes the experience of hero-admiration worthwhile. I believe that if disillusions are allowed to come naturally into a child's life, dropping gently into his mind as the coils of time unravel themselves, they will not occur before he has the strength to bear them. The moment that he allows himself to criticize his hero, he has ceased to be a whole-hearted admirer, and the readjustment of his ideas is accomplished. He has adapted to his new perspective. If he has wholesome thoughts about life in general, he will not hate the entire world just because he has ceased to adore a certain individual belonging to it. Rather, while experiencing the supreme joy of complete devotion, he has acquired a certain habit of mind. A good habit it is, too, for such a habit makes it unlikely that he will ever live without heroes. After one disillusionment, he may think twice and be more choosy about his heroes. He may never again sense that pure joy of "looking up to" a great person as when he was spontaneous about it. Nevertheless, every age has its heroes, and hero-admiration awaits to fill the heart of whomever is prepared to receive it.

The Benefits of Hero-Admiration

Any amount of admiring is beneficial for a child. Hero-admiration alleviates conceit. It motivates a child to more strenuous effort. Hero-admiration enlarges our sympathies, creates peace and joy. It is the basis of our religious and our social life.

Conceit is generally a form of self-admiration. If we care about others sufficiently to admire them, we cannot waste much time in admiring ourselves. When we admire another we tend to notice and appreciate in him those qualities in which we ourselves are somewhat deficient. Our admirable person may make us conscious of our frailties or inexperience, yet stimulate a desire in ourselves to become more like him. In so doing, we try to improve or reform ourselves. Today children are separated from adults because there is a lack of community. In days gone by, when children were able to watch adults at their professions, they had more opportunity to think, "Wow, I want to do what he's doing when I grow up," or "I want to be just like her." Children were more easily impressed with the abilities and professionalism of their elders because they witnessed their activities. And in thinking about their heroes, they unconsciously acquired high ideals, a high standard of conduct, and decreased the distance between aspiration and achievement. Children are imitators, and their heroes stimulate them to effort.

Have you heard of the American hero, Audie Murphy? He was the most decorated World War II hero. Among his many awards he received the Congressional Medal of Honor. None of it "went to his head." He was profoundly a soldier who gave his country his best. (Though he was physically a short man, this didn't stop many from looking up to him.)

True stories of self-sacrifice and devotion that are a result of responding to a nation's time of crisis rouse ordinary citizens to walk more courageously. Men and women during WW II were drawn together by common hopes and fears, regrets and apprehensions, and particularly by their appreciation for the deeds of heroism and daring like those of Audie Murphy. For a time citizens were able to distinguish between the trivialities and essentials of life around them, and they rejoiced in eagerly obeying the summons to service that in normal times most of us either fail to hear or comfortably disregard.

But children's susceptibilities are keener than those of grown-ups, and they do not require a national upheaval in order to feel the stimulus of the heroic act upon their lives. Stories of heroism—even during times of peace—will prompt them to admire. This admiration ripens their intelligence until it becomes quick to recognize noble thought and eager to receive its inspiration. With an open mind the disciple's mind grows until he can understand the conceptions of his master. On the contrary, it is a pity when a child has no one to look up to or admire. Then he suffers a great loss. He is likely to grow up with an incapacity to either respect or appreciate merit in others.

Compatible with Christianity

When we hear of lives that have been changed and blessed by Christian teaching, we mean that these people have come to obey the summons and give allegiance to the King of Kings. They have begun to follow in the footsteps of Him who is our example and to imitate the life of this King, Jesus Christ, who was crucified for the sake of the undeserving. Can anyone doubt that such hero-worship is productive of good, that it empowers unselfishness and purity of purpose and leads men to victory, inasmuch as it teaches them to obey?

Our social life, so mingled with our religious life, is based on hero-admiration. Man is born believing, and small men flutter around big men as surely as moths around a candle. It depends on the choice of our heroes and our behavior towards them whether their flame will destroy us or illuminate our paths. We cannot serve our children better than by encouraging them to seek heroes and to adhere loyally to them. We can all develop this habit of reverence. Years back we addressed people by their titles: Reverend Jones, Doctor Hastings, Professor Elliot. Today even Mr., Mrs., and Miss are seldom used. Everyone seems to be referred to by his first name, which is often itself reduced to an abbreviation. Instead of Reverend So-and-so, we talk with Jamie, Mikie, or Jake. I was standing in line at an ice-cream parlor once when something caught my ear. The young waitress addressed two elderly ladies—dressed in skirts and blouses—with, "What do you guys want?" Her tone of voice was pleasant but the "guys" was so utterly inappropriate as a form of address to these ladies that I was taken aback. We've come a long way from the days when people addressed strangers with the courteous "Sir" or "Madam," and when children addressed their elders as "Mr. Jones" or "Mrs. Brown," and in some Southern climes, as "Miss Anne" or "Mr. Tom."

I think showing appropriate respect to one's elders is the least that can be done as an outward expression of hero-admiration. It should, however, be carried further. Heroes and heroines can be found among the men and women with whom we

are acquainted. For as we learn from Carlyle, "Great men, taken up in every way, are profitable company. We cannot look however imperfectly upon a great man without gaining something by him." The little Golden Books that I used to buy at the grocery store for my little children

(the older titles like *Frosty the Snowman, Pussy Willow,* and *Scruffy the Tugboat* for instance) would show a policeman, fireman, store clerk, barber, teacher, doctor, postman, in a position that was friendly to children but also one deserving of respect. Are there any men or women in your community your children can respect or reverence?

Parents Are a Child's First Conception of Hero or Heroine

How precious it is when children respect their parents! How greatly do we as parents endeavor always to merit it. Children come into the world trusting us absolutely, yet in our weakness we may shake that heaven-given trust by an ill-chosen word or deed. Then, a stone falls out from under the pedestal on which our child has placed us. An expression of sorrow passes over a child's face when for the first time he sees the parents whom he honors with his whole heart indulge in petty arguments or cynical criticism of acquaintances of the family circle. Most little quarrels do not really affect the love which they momentarily appear to disturb. But our children do not want to hear frequent excuses for our behavior, even if we are often tired out from a very stressful or demanding job. As parents, we are our child's hero and heroine—he looks up to us, and his upward gaze is so precious to us and so immensely beneficial to him, that we strive continuously to realize the standard of conduct which our child associates with his trust in us.

Further, we should resist any urge to over-indulge our children, because excessive indulgence weakens the power of respect, and is not true love. A mother who has taken on the education of her children at home should guard against becoming a child's slave, ready to answer his questions whenever he asks them, or to play with him whenever his whim suggests some game. Let him regard your attention more or less in the light of a treat, although the gratification of his wishes may constitute the greatest joy that your life contains.

To illustrate this principle, I will relate an incident from my own life. It was two o'clock in the afternoon. I had taught all morning, made a nice hot soup for lunch, cleaned up, and was hoping to put my feet up for a half-hour when my young daughter asked, "Mom, would you play something with me?"

"You and I have done quite a lot together this morning," I answered.

"But that was school," she said plaintively.

After a morning of home teaching, I thought I had given her a lot of my attention, but she felt the schooling was my choice of activity, and now her opinion was that it was her turn to pick the activity. I was legitimately needing a break, so I let her down. She found something to keep her busy after all. A few days later I willingly participated in a game with her and it was a happy time. She savored this playtime we spent together but was not master of it.

Being aware that children like to test the strength of their growing influence upon us, we should try to live a serene life undisturbed by the variations in a child's moods. We ignore his little fit of discontent when it is unreasonable, and are unaffected by his heated remonstrances over some small rule of conduct, which it has seemed to us right to make. This serenity is essential to the proper performance of a parent's part in heroism and in doling out the appropriate penalty for his offense. For a parent ceases to be his child's hero when the child knows that at any moment he can, if he chooses, make her his victim. We are indeed his victims when we add to his fit by responding with our own.

Speak of Others' Virtues—Give Credit to Goodness Where it is Due

Where have all the heroes gone? Modern history books give little space to the life struggles and triumphs of any but a very few of those who have made an important mark in history. Biographies of noble men and women teach more than textbook history. By taking us into the lives of those who have gone before, not only do these accounts bring earlier times alive for us, but the examples set before us of devotion, ingenuity, generosity, endurance, courage, industriousness, patriotism, repentance, and selflessness convince us that these virtues are attainable. Such biographies inspire us to seize for ourselves the qualities we see exemplified in the lives portrayed.

>—┼—◆►—○—◄┼—◄

You will find it less easy to unroot faults than to choke them by gaining virtues.

>—┼—◆►—○—◄┼—◄

An easy way for me to give my children an array of heroes and to enable them to choose a favorite has been through listening to the dramatized audio cassettes of Your Story Hour. Many of these stories have been heard on radio since 1949. Because the true-to-life episodes of adventure in Your Story Hour, in some instances, do not hide the fear, pain, struggle, and even character flaws of their heroes, the triumphs are all the more inspiring, and encourage us to believe that we too can develop a more godly character and succeed in our endeavors. I am reminded of a quote by John Ruskin:

You will find it less easy to unroot faults than to choke them by gaining virtues. Do not think of your faults, still less of other's faults; in every person who comes near you look for what is good and strong; honor that; rejoice in it and as you can, try to imitate it; and your faults will drop off like dead leaves when their time comes.

Qualities not Defects

It is important that children should honor their heroes for their good qualities rather than their defects. We wouldn't want them to be intrigued by the cunning of the unrefined man because it distinguishes him. The biblical hero King David, for example, should first and foremost be known for his virtues—not his sins. Young children should not linger with ideas of coarseness and cunning. Instead, we pray that God would reveal a hero's good heart and some noble aspiration. In the home where the good, the pure, and the true are prized, I do not think that there is much danger that the children will consciously reverence the false (worldly philosophies) and the sordid. As Christians, because we are to love others and spread God's Word, we will at times relate to poorer, less-educated, less well-mannered persons. If we don't, then our children may grow up as snobs and worshipers of the "golden calf." We should not so openly and constantly "talk down" such people.

If children live in homes where heroism is held to have its roots in the Christian virtues, where children are led to revere and unconsciously imitate those men and women who live purposeful lives, and regard sincerity and purity among the highest virtues, the unmannerliness of the less-advantaged friends of the family circle will not "bring the family down." This is the advantage of a Christian education over an education whose curriculum has been stripped of Christian virtues.[1] ►

Questions for Personal Reflection or Support Group Discussion

1. *"That's what you get for putting people up on a pedestal," said the editor of one magazine in reference to the editor of another, whose behavior was letting her readers down. He went on to warn his readers not to think highly of our Christian authors and speakers. Do you agree or disagree about putting people on pedestals? Why?*

2. *How does hero-admiration benefit the child? In what way is it compatible with Christianity?*

3. *Have you ever read a biography of a Christian missionary? What effect did it have on you or your children?*

4. *Who are a child's first examples of a hero or heroine? How can this be maintained? What is a role model?*

5. *Do you ever pay attention to the good that is done by non-Christian men? How does the Christian home deter any falling into false or evil admirations?*

6. *What makes a school a "good" school?*

7. *How (and how often) did hero-admiration pop up in the various subjects taught in Charlotte Mason's curriculum?*

8. *Our children's friends—as well as our own—will not be perfect Christian examples, yet in what way should we most often speak of them?*

9. *Make a list of heroes. These can be heroes whom you have studied or would like to study.*

Chapter Twenty-Five

....

Picture Study

SOME YEARS AGO our family lived on a cul-de-sac in the suburbs of Nashville, Tennessee. The summers were exceptionally hot. Even so, the neighborhood children would congregate in the cul-de-sac most days to play stick-ball, not at all mindful of the sweat dripping down their faces. After the conclusion of one game, my eldest daughter (then age nine) said, "See you later! I'm going inside to cool off and watch a Michelangelo video."

"Oh, What Ninja turtle video is it?"

"Ninja turtle?" My daughter was taken aback.

"Yeah, you know—Michelangelo, Leonardo, Raphael . . ."

"Those are the names of the Ninja turtles?" She had seen advertisements of these turtle characters displayed at our local discount store but had never been treated to one of their films (a decision made by an authority figure—me). "Those are the names of painters," she argued.

But she found it was no use carrying on, so she came into our air-conditioned living room to watch the second half of *The Agony and the Ecstasy,* starring Charlton Heston, who plays the part of the original Michelangelo. As soon as she crossed the threshold of the front door, I heard her call out, "Ma, I learned the names of the Ninja Turtles!" And so by natural progression (the neighborhood grapevine), I too discovered the names of that militant group of green creatures—creatures that have nothing at all to do with art.

We are surrounded by just such distorted reminders of artists and magnificent works of art. What the general public sees are dim fragments of the original art because names and images are used out of context. It's commonplace to see a pair of Raphael's 500-year-old cherubs advertising coffee on a highway billboard, or Leonardo's Mona Lisa used in someone's marketing scheme. I expect most people have some vague cultural acquaintance with these great images. But for the most part our cultural heritage has been lost in the shuffle of our daily "make-a-livin'" society.

Against the rigorous demands of a full homeschool schedule that sees year-end testing in clearest view, our aims to appreciate art may drift out of sight or may even be forgotten entirely. So from time to time it is helpful to bring to mind Charlotte Mason's aim in providing certain subjects, like Picture Study, to children.

*Drawn by Sophia at age 13
from a painting by Da Vinci*

Pictures Worth Our Attention

The children in Charlotte Mason's schools had Picture Study every term from age six upwards. Between the ages of six and fifteen a child had studied reproductions of pictures by some thirty of the world's most famous artists. Why Picture Study? In order that children may be put in touch with the contribution that each famous artist has made to the world's store of all that is beautiful and worthwhile. Just as literature introduces us to the thought of the greatest writers, so Picture Study opens the gates to the ideas of the famous artists. It also provides a treasure store of images for our children that will help defend them against the commercial world's attempts to dominate their senses.

Let the Artists Speak

Picture Study yields other benefits as well. Powers of observation increase as children learn to really look at the picture. A sense of beauty will be more fully developed. But first and foremost we want our children to really "connect" with the artist's work.

Here lies the difficulty. The grown-up who arranges the lesson is an all-important middleman, but like other middlemen, must be lost in the background. Many pictures make their own independent appeal. You must judge when a helping word is needed, or when—as is especially the case with older children—too much speaking or too much enthusiasm may raise a barrier.

That same year—when Sophia was age nine—she made an interesting observation that proved to me that our time spent appreciating the gorgeous paintings of the Italian Renaissance painter Ralphael of Urbino had enabled her to make a connection. The children were playing out on that same cul-de-sac, riding their bicycles or roller skating. As usual, one child fell and scraped an elbow. It was Sophia this time who came into the house wounded, followed by the other curious and concerned siblings. The eyes of the youngest were the widest. He was particularly interested in the little emergency. As I was washing and bandaging the bright red scrape, Sophia asked, "Mom, how come every time one of us needs a Band-aid, Nigel puts on a Ralphael face?"

I was astounded. "Charlotte Mason is right," I thought. "Children *will* make their own connections."

If you have studied the paintings of Ralphael, you will understand what kind of angelic facial expression Nigel was wearing at that instant. His face is not as cubby or angelic anymore, as he is a bigger boy now. But mothers have memories.

Some Beautiful, Some Not-So-Beautiful

Children may not need to like every picture they study. We can welcome their opinions. I know a person who is fond of Picasso's controversial paintings. I was surprised when he admitted this. Not being drawn to Picasso's paintings, they were not ones I had, as yet, chosen for my children to appreciate. Our friend, however, likes the way Picasso painted people and things differently from the way they are supposed to look. It is an interest of his to try to figure out what the artist was trying to say with his awkward and most unusual portrayals. He helped me understand Picasso better and even gave us a gift of a book of Picasso's paintings.

Over time, certain pictures will become favorites to be appreciated right up into adulthood. Occasionally our children's tastes, though we try to be influential, may not be the same as ours. They may end up becoming more interested in a particular artist's paintings than we are. In other words, they may end up liking Picasso's paintings, even though we have placed our fondness elsewhere.

Determination to Draw

Since we have moved our household numerous times, our books have frequently had to be packed away. When a box is finally unpacked after many months (or a year), a child will rediscover an artist he remembers well. He will take up the book like a long-lost friend and sit cross-legged on the carpet, slowly turning the pages. At such times I sense in the child a spirit of companionship with the pictures we once studied, as if he were spending time with an old friend. On a cloudy afternoon my children might huddle around the dinning room table (without any suggestion from me) to reproduce a picture that inspires them. One of my daughters drew the Mona Lisa three times from start to finish before she was happy with her rendition. The funny thing is, with her Italian features, she looks like the Mona Lisa herself. "Is this a self-por-

The Girl with a Watering Can
by Yolanda Andreola, age 7.

yolanda
age 12

trait?" I kidded. My children have received very few formal drawing lessons but I do believe their motivation and determination to draw has come from our Picture Study. They seem to have unconsciously picked up what goes into a good picture. Could it be that the great masters have inspired them? I think so.

Charlotte Mason said in *Home Education,* "We cannot measure the influence that one or another artist has upon the child's sense of beauty, upon his power of seeing, as in a picture, the common sights of life; he is enriched more than we know in having really looked at a single picture."

About an Artist's Life

How much do our children really need to know about the artist's life? Only what is necessary to really enjoy his pictures. For example, when looking at Fra Angelica's pictures, it is helpful to know that he spent much of his life in the community of monks at San Marco. Likewise, Jean-Francois Millet's works are better appreciated by those who know that he led the hard life of a peasant.

In a very old book I found a little story of Millet's childhood and a legend of the boyhood of Raphael, both of which I read to my children. In *Linnea in Monet's Garden,* a story book by Christina Bjork and Lina Anderson, the fictional character Linnea takes a trip to France to visit Claude Monet's garden, a tourist destination for art lovers. In 1991 I published a review of the book in my *Parents' Review,* along with a review of two other art appreciation story books: *Rembrandt's Beret* by Johnny Alcorn (in which an Italian boy gets lost in the Uffizi Gallery), and *The Girl with the Watering Can* by Ewa Zadrynska (in which a little girl from one of August Renoir's paintings escapes from the painting and mischievously enters others in the National Gallery of Art).

A few years after this review, one subscriber (also a British pen friend of mine) found and read Linnea's adventures to her children and was inspired go to France to visit Monet's garden in the manner related in the story book. She shared her enjoyable experience later in an article she wrote for the *Parents' Review.* You can be sure her children will be able to recognize a Monet when they see one. What a lovely culturally enriching experience! Two illustrations of Renoir's *Girl with the Watering Can,* drawn at different ages by my daughter Yolanda, appear in this chapter.

Story books like the ones described above are delightfully instructive but need not accompany a Picture Study lesson. To attempt to interest the youngest students too much in these stories *during* a Picture Study lesson may even take away opportunities for gaining intimacy with the artist's pictures, and essentially, the pictures are what he gave to the world. The stories that have been created around them should be secondary to the pictures themselves. As Charlotte Mason said, "A child is educated by his intimacies."

Children have no need to know the lesser details of either of Fra Angelica's and Millet's fairly irreproachable lives. Nor do our young ones need to be steeped in the real or alleged moral failures of great artists such as Michelangelo and Rembrandt. This would be a distraction. The child's main occupation is getting to know art. When left alone to view the picture over a week or so, he will learn to notice how line, form, color, and shadow can be combined in so many fascinating ways.

Older children, however, *do* need to understand an artist's worldview and how it may be revealed through his paintings. However, it is best to hold off on exposing the sins of an artist until your child is able to understand that great talent does not always accompany great godliness, and vice versa.

Narrating a Work of Art

In every Picture Study lesson it is important that there is a time in which children can look quietly at the picture, uninterrupted by questions or discussion. That is when each of us will have the best chance to gain his own link with the picture and its painter's thought—in other words, to *ponder* the picture.

After a time of "looking," and while the picture is still in view, you can ask a child to describe it. This will be his narration of the picture. After children have had some practice narrating in this way, the second option can be to hide the picture from view (after a time of studying it) and ask a child to describe it. Knowing a narration may be required, the children will be encouraged to really "look" at the picture, not just glance at it vaguely.

A very young child's attention might wander, unless you give him a little help beforehand. Don't go so far as to explain the picture—that would be taking the child's part from him. Instead, provide any facts that the child might need to know in order to enjoy and properly describe the picture. For a picture like Raphael's *The Miraculous Draught of Fishes,* for example, it really helps if the child is familiar with the biblical story on which the picture is based.

With very young children it is better to tell or read the story before they have the picture, and then let them have the fun of discovering which part of the story is illustrated.

Admittedly I have asked my children some questions during a Picture Study time, but only after they have been left alone with the painting. I've done this only to encourage my less talkative student. And perhaps I've wanted to "teach" my children to become more observant. Therefore I've used the phrase, "What else . . . ?" "What else do you see in this picture?" "What else can you tell me about the background?" Or,

"Would you like to be in the picture?" "What might the characters be thinking?" Such questioning could undermine the principles of Picture Study if done regularly. We don't want children to become dependent on what, in Charlotte's words, is "a flood of talk from the teacher."

Describing the Picture

It is good to give older children a variety of ways to "narrate" the picture. They can describe it orally or in writing, or they can try to sketch it from memory. We need not expect too much from these "memory sketches." Be satisfied if your child can provide the principal lines or outlines with some shading. Only the most gifted of students will put in facial features from memory.

In Charlotte Mason's *Home Education,* she shares some descriptions children gave after concluding a study of the pastoral paintings of Jean Francois Millet. She writes:

A little boy of about nine was (with many others) given reproductions of some half-dozen of the pictures of Jean Francois Millet to study during a school term. At the end, the children were asked to describe one of the pictures which they liked best. Of course they did it, and did it well. This is what the little boy I mentioned makes of it: "I liked the Sower best. The sower is sowing seeds; the picture is all dark except high up on the right-hand side where there is a man ploughing the field. While he is ploughing the field the sower sows. The sower has got a bag in his left hand and is sowing with his right hand. He has wooden clogs on. He is sowing at about six o'clock in the morning. you can see his head better than his legs and body, because it is against the light.

A little girl of seven prefers the Angelus, and says: 'The picture is about people in the fields, a man and a woman. By the woman is a basket with something in it; behind her is a wheelbarrow. They are praying; the man has his hat off in this hand. You can tell that it is evening, because the wheelbarrow and the basket are loaded.

These children were narrating the picture they saw in their "mind's eye," as all the prints they had studied that term were hidden from view. This was an end-of-term examination. Charlotte referred to them as "memory outlines." We can see how narration was used to stimulate closer observation. Narration helps to fix the picture in the mind's eye. Narration leads a child to really *know* a picture, to recall it to his imagination. Narration aids the teacher in finding out what a child remembers—what is his own mind's possession of the picture.

Billboards and Postcards

Charlotte Mason emphasized that, in order to become well-acquainted with great artists, children should study at least six of one artist's works per semester. Studying a range of pictures is really the only way to acquire the ability to recognize an artist's particular work. This approach will allow us to distinguish a Millet from a Manet, or a Manet from a Monet.

It is difficult to find prints of a half-dozen of one artist's works. For this reason I recommend using oversize art print books—"coffee table books"—of one painter's works. Books featuring a group of painters from a similar school of art, such as the Dutch painters, the Impressionists, or the Italian Renaissance artists are also widely available. One birthday, when my children were still quite small, my husband presented me with a "coffee table" art print book of Millet's paintings entitled *Jean Francois Millet*, compiled and written by Andre Fermigier. It has afforded us many hours of pleasure.

The Charlotte Mason schools always tried to obtain good-sized pictures. When you use postcards or greeting cards to introduce children to the great art of the ages, so much of the detail is lost. Children enjoy handling postcards, and they are considerably less expensive, but whenever possible use larger reproductions. Look in your library's art section or in the art section at a new or used book shop.

Oversize art print books are a bit awkward to set up for display, but their availability and ease of selection makes them quite convenient. In our home we simply prop a book open on an end table with other heavy books laid around it for support. If the book is narrow enough, it may be opened to the appropriate page and slipped into a book stand.

When first introducing an artist's work, do not allow the children in their curiosity to thumb through the books. The intent is to allow them to focus on one painting at a time. We were given a large book of paintings by the French Impressionists as a gift some years ago. So we would not be confused by a mixture of different painters' works, I chose the paintings of one Frenchman for us to become familiar with. We would become familiar with the paintings of other Frenchmen at a later time. Any thumbing through should be done discreetly by the teacher as she lines up pictures to be studied one by one during a semester.

Americans Can Paint, Too

Our local library has an art print book describing the history of the paintings of Grandma Moses. I enjoyed previewing her famous pictures and reading about her New England country lifestyle. I plan to use her paintings in our homeschool as an example of folk art.

Last year we visited the Norman Rockwell Museum, a tiny art museum in the basement of a tall city building, around the corner from Independence Hall and the Benjamin Franklin Museum. Here are displayed the old covers of the *Saturday Evening Post*. My eldest child lingered by them and then said she had discovered a new favorite artist. All of these paintings were new to my children because we had not done any Picture Study of Norman Rockwell up to that point. This was an unplanned detour. Therefore, I cannot boast at being such a well-organized teacher. I didn't like *all* the paintings, but there were many I did like, and these made their positive emotional appeal. I particularly liked one painting whose subtitle had the word "reverence" in it—a word rarely used these days. It pictured some Boy Scouts in ironed uniforms on bended knee in a church pew.

My husband very much likes the paintings of N.C. Wyeth. His paintings are displayed in the Delaware Art Museum and The Brandywine River Museum not far from our home. Perhaps you have seen his illustrations in the children's classics *Robin Hood, Mysterious Island; Robinson Crusoe, Kidnapped , Treasure Island, The Deerslayer* and *Last of the Mohicans*. N.C. Wyeth was a student of the American artist Howard Pyle, who was known as the "Father of American Illustration."

Benjamin West and His Cat Grimalkin is a story book about an American artist by Marguerite Henry. All my children have enjoyed reading it. Young Benjamin makes a paint brush with hair from his cat in the illustration.

These are only a few suggestions of ways you can enjoy Picture Study. I enjoy the freedom to choose the painters I wish to study with my children. May you have a rewarding experience with art in your family as well.

An Outline of How to Do Picture Study

1. Choose one artist per twelve-week term.

2. Choose at least six of the artist's works.

3. Keep one picture on display for one or two weeks.

4. Give some biographical background on the painter.

5. Give a *brief* explanation of the picture (only if necessary).

6. Have the student provide a narration (oral or written) of the picture. Welcome opinions.

By following this simple method, you will enable your children to become familiar with the works of dozens of artists.

A Philosophy of Art

Once the child is about fourteen years old, Charlotte Mason's approach to Picture Study moves from simply "soaking in" everything about a picture to learning the history of the different schools of Western European painting. The young person will continue to study only one artist each semester, but he will now begin to examine the artist's relationship to the art of the past and to other members of the same school.

Senior high students will find Francis Schaeffer's *How Should We Then Live?* immensely useful. Dr. Schaeffer's book is challenging reading: not only will students learn about the influences of different worldviews upon the art of various time periods, but they will learn how different artists' philosophies reflect or differ from the Christian worldview.

Bon Voyage

Someday your family may travel to Europe, and because of your growing knowledge of the riches of Western art, instead of just asking for the directions to the restaurants and souvenir shops, you'll be asking for directions to the Louvre in Paris or the Uffizi ("U-feet-see") Gallery in Florence, in great anticipation of seeing firsthand those special paintings you have been studying at home. Don't forget to write me if you get there before I do![1]

Some Artists Worth Studying:

For young children (from age six) or just to get you started:

• Jean Francois Millet
• Mary Cassatt
• Claude Monet
• Ralphael Santi
• Grandma Moses

There are many others to get to know. Some are:

• Leonardo Da Vinci
• Michelangelo Buonarroti

(A collection of six Italian Renaissance artists can be found in *The Great Masters* with commentary by the biographer Giorgio Vasari—who lived during the Renaissance and actually was a contemporary of several of the artists.)

Some French Impressionists:

- Pierre-Auguste Renoir
- Vincent van Gogh
- Claude Monet

Artists from the Pre-Raphaelite School of painters:

- Dante Gabriel Rossetti
- William Holman Hunt
- Richard Redgrave

(I've done a mix of these from the book, *The Pre-Raphaelites,* by Christopher Wood.)

Others I recommend:

- Rembrandt van Rijn (and others of the Dutch school of art)
- Maxfield Parrish
- N. C. Wyeth

Questions for Personal Reflection or Support Group Discussion

1. *Give reasons for studying pictures.*

2. *What was Charlotte Mason's plan for Picture Study?*

3. *Do we need to "teach" art appreciation? Support your answer.*

4. *Why are larger prints preferred over postcards alone?*

5. *What advantages are there for studying at least six of one artist's works?*

6. *Can stories be helpful? Are they essential? Explain.*

7. *Must a decision be made whether or not to include certain kinds of nudes?*

8. *Schools of art and philosophies of art should be included in art appreciation at some point. How is this helpful to a student in understanding world views?*

9. *How simple it is to include art appreciation in the homeschool. Explain.*

10. *Are you interested in a particular artist's work? What is it about his paintings that impresses you?*

Chapter Twenty-Six

···

Music Appreciation

"There are things in the Christian world which cause us to be sad. One of these is that for many Christians classical music is a complete vacuum. This robs individual Christians and their children of one of the very rich areas of joy in this world."

—Dr. Francis Schaeffer

MY ELEMENTARY SCHOOL was situated in a post-World War II housing community in central New Jersey. Between rows of little Cape Cod houses stood Andrew Street School. It was a red brick building that had a ceiling so high that it appeared to be a two story building from the outside. Each classroom had several eight foot tall windows that let in enough bright light to illuminate a quantity of blackboard space. The building had great acoustics. I attended in the days when air raid drills were practiced as regularly as fire drills, when girls wore dresses with knee socks and boys wore trousers—not jeans. We all wore stiff shoes with leather soles—not sneakers. The combination of those shoes, the high ceilings, and the polished linoleum floors created an echo in the hallways that resonates in my memory to this day.

Once a week our class would crowd into a narrow room that, because it had a piano, was called the music room. The tall windows in this room provided a view of the back entrance to the cafeteria and garbage bins. Small straight back wooden chairs circled the room. Facing each other, we sang seemingly endless choruses of American folk tunes and patriotic songs. The acts of colorful characters danced in my head for repeated performances: Old Dan Tucker's face was dripping with grease from washing it in a used frying pan, verses of Liza's bucket with a hole in it began to leak onto my forehead like Chinese water torture. The outside garbage bins disappeared as I wandered out on the range where the skies were not cloudy all day and beheld purple mountains' majesty. We were a nice group of second generation immigrant children from Poland, Italy, Ireland, and the Ukraine, all singing with patriotic sentiment about our wonderful America—America the beautiful, the home of the free and the brave.

Every autumn brought harvest time songs, every December we sang Christmas carols in harmony. The higher the notes, the louder you were supposed to sing them. I remember the lively Jewish songs, too.

The teacher had a special fondness for what she called "more contemporary music." "Do Re Mi," "My Favorite Things," and "Somewhere Over the Rainbow" were three of her favorites. "Over the Rainbow" had to be sung solo by each girl. We were required to try out for the lead in the school concert. When it was my turn to stand in front of the piano, I suddenly felt the temperature of the room rise fifteen degrees. I got as far as "somewhere" but "over" never followed. It was my first experience at throat tightening. The teacher graciously played the accompaniment to my "somewhere" twice more, then called for the next girl. The two most outgoing girls—an inseparable pair whose mothers were co-owners of the town's delicatessen—were picked for the "one" part.

I experienced music at home, too. In the winter my parents brought the picnic table from outdoors into the basement. My mother purchased all the Disney story records and let me take her older record player down there. In this dark and dusty place, I would perform on top of the picnic table to what I thought was the most exciting music around.

Looking Farther Back

Now that you have had a peek into my past, let's look farther back-into the time of Charlotte Mason. Music appreciation originated in the PNEU around the 1890's. When Charlotte Mason heard that Mrs. Glover was at that time playing to her little child much of the classical music that interested her, it sparked an idea. Charlotte realized that this music might give great joy and interest to the life of all children. She felt that just as children in her home correspondence schools were given the greatest literature and art, so they should have the greatest music as well. She asked Mrs. Glover to write an article in Charlotte's *Parents' Review* on the result of her observations, and to make a program of music each term that could be played on the gramophone to the children. From that time a music program appeared with the other programs at the beginning of every term.

Classical music appreciation was not something that was part of any school at that time. But through Charlotte's insight other schools caught on to the idea. Private schools in Great Britain began incorporating music appreciation into the curriculum because of her influential idea. Sometimes attendance at these classes was voluntary, and it was encouraging to find that children came of their own accord.

I was happy to learn from Charlotte's writings that appreciation of classical music had nothing to do with playing the piano or learning any other instrument. Learning music once meant learning to play it, and it was thought that children who had no talent for playing were unmusical and would not like concerts. But Charlotte found that music appreciation has no more to do with playing an instrument than an appreciation of Shakespeare has to do with acting, or the enjoyment of pictures has to do with painting.

Classical Music & Home Atmosphere

When my children were in their early elementary years of home education, we had just returned from overseas missions. We were renting a little four-room house—which I was very happy to have. Dad drove the family car into Nashville every morning while my little girls and I remained at home in the "blue house." Lack of a second car, a piano, or money for regular lessons were three real obstacles to music lessons. I thought then that the fact that I couldn't play an instrument myself was another. But we were happy. The children were still very young and the Lord was blessing us abundantly. I had heard it jokingly said by a clever pastor that the Lord owned the cattle on a thousand hills but usually supplied one hamburger at a time.

Our accumulated "hamburger" was in the form of a few cassette tapes of folk music and hymns, a song book, and some beautiful music purchased very inexpensively. We found and unpacked our one cassette of Antonio Vivaldi's *Four Seasons,* which Dad had purchased at Woolworth's while we were living in England on a missionary's budget. We listened to it every day while I prepared meals and did the washing. We soon knew it by heart and could anticipate each measure.

Classical music was not the music I heard at home. But thanks to Antonio Vivaldi, I was inspired with the spirit of a new adventure. Thus I began our home-schooling years of classical music appreciation, adding to our collection of cassettes one at a time.

When Dad was home in the evenings, I would take the car and do the food shopping. One evening, I almost literally bumped into a spinner in our local drug store that held mostly pop and country music tapes. When I looked more closely, however, I discovered "Greatest Hits" tapes of Mozart, Beethoven, Schubert and Bach—at $3.99 each! So, I did some impulse buying—although I was supposed to be buying groceries next door. Over the months the "Greatest Hits" from this spinner became the classical music curriculum for our homeschool. I was glad the hits were picked out for me, because I wouldn't have known which pieces to look for.

You can see why I was happy to read that classical music appreciation need not be taught by a professional music teacher,

that it can be done by a parent who has no particular background or training in music. As with so many other subjects in our home education process, I have been learning along with my children, and have always found it rewarding.

Suggestions for Music Appreciation

In Charlotte's program, the music of one composer was played every week for at least half an hour. The children experienced the music of one composer per term (there were three terms a year). No piece was left for another before the children were able to recognize it and really know it.

Our house has been filled with the music of Mozart as we go about our morning chores. His trills have helped quicken our pace. The quieter pieces of Bach have been played during afternoon quiet times/nap times. Beethoven at bedtime—especially softer pieces, like his Pastoral Symphony—has helped me unwind. My personal preference is not to play music at meal times, but rather during any afternoon drawing times where the children congregate at the dining room table. Their drawing times are most often accompanied by the familiar music of one composer or another. To review pieces already introduced to them, I let my children choose what they would like to listen to. What they choose to hear over and again demonstrates what has impressed them.

Only in the last two years of my ten years of homeschooling have I had a vehicle to drive while Dad is at work. Unlike our other car, the van has a built-in cassette player. What a luxury! In earlier years we would fill the cassette player with five pounds of batteries in order to listen to the opera singer Pavarotti on the open road.

Learning an Instrument

So many of my friends' children could play an instrument at a young age. I tried not to compare the accomplishments of other children with my own, because it wasn't until my eldest child, Sophia, turned thirteen that we were able to afford lessons. Dad found a decent violin at the pawn shop and so was able to procure the instrument she had been wanting to learn how to play for some time. After a year of daily practice she became part of a small group of players. She has played at the local nursing home, a Victorian gift shop, and on "Old-fashioned Day" in the next town. I think that all the listening she did in her younger years educated her in ways that have facilitated her playing. Children who have not had a musical background may have less respect, less understanding, and less appreciation for what they are required

to learn to play on their instruments. And even if a child never learns to play an instrument well enough to be a concert performer, because he has had lessons, he can more readily appreciate those who have practiced for many years and can play very well the music he has grown to enjoy.

Recently my second child, twelve-year-old Yolanda, started cello lessons with a concert cellist (who is also a grandmother). She has learned to play harmony to some songs her sister Sophia plays on violin. Hearing my children make music together brings me a new measure of joy.

Music and Story

Our family's ability to recognize a piece of music and attribute it to a certain composer has come partly as a result of the story tapes produced by Susan Hammond that I reviewed in my *Parents' Review* in 1992. Today you can find them in many a homeschool catalog. The ones we love are: *Mr. Bach Comes to Call*, *Beethoven Lives Upstairs*, *Vivaldi's Ring of Mystery*, and *Mozart's Magic Fantasy*. The story aspect not only invokes our interest, but provides a biographical sketch of the composer. About twenty excerpts are played throughout the story, and these we readily associate with the composer after hearing the story only a few times. As with any resource that is not produced from a Christian perspective, be discerning. There may be small references in the tapes to which you object, or which you may want to discuss with your children.

Some time after we had listened to Bach's "Greatest Hits," we visited a large denominational church. As we entered the sanctuary and walked down an aisle, a prelude was being played on the organ. When we were settled in a pew, my daughter (who was quite young at the time) said excitedly, "Mommy, that's Bach!" I opened my bulletin and with a quick glance saw she was right. Normally, in church I'd nod and give my usual "Hush!" but with the kind of pride a mother is likely to fall prey to, I whispered, "Speak it a little louder, honey. What did you say?"

When young children are accustomed to listening to the music of great composers, it should be no surprise to hear them ask for Bach to be played rather than "Baa Baa, Black Sheep" or "Old MacDonald."

One Mother's Story

Let's take a peek into a homeschool in which a request for Bach from a child is quite as natural as one for a slice of apple or for permission to feed the fish. One mother tells a story of her experience in Charlotte's *Parents' Review*:

In the beginning of the school year, I choose the recordings. I play new pieces for about twenty minutes when the children are resting, drawing or playing on the floor in mid-afternoon as a sort of background music. Some of my children hardly notice it, and I always wonder if they will become enthusiastic. This year it was intriguing to watch interest grow. First, some of them asked questions about the

music. Then they began requesting music I had played, expressing their opinions. Sometimes I told my younger children the name of a piece; more often I did not. At times I just said, "Here's a piece that I like very much." I try to choose pieces that have some special characteristics such as solo instruments, an attractive and fairly obvious rhythm or a merry mood. Trumpets seem to have a special appeal. One year I introduced Jeremiah Clark's "Trumpet Voluntary." The trumpet theme is played slowly and majestically with an organ accompaniment. After the first playing of this, I told the children that trumpets were also used for such very special occasions as coronations of kings and queens. At this point Suzi told me that she would like to have trumpets played on Saturday, because it was a very special occasion—her birthday. A little later I introduced "Music of Jubilee" by Power Biggs, which has become another favorite piece. This is slightly more complicated. Another piece my children like is Enesco's "Roumanian Rhapsody No. 1." Perhaps its appeal is in the attractive rhythms and wonderful crescendos. After we played it a few times, the young ones moved around the room to the music. A few children began swooping around and whirling about. In a short time, all my little ones were dancing. They showed an amazing ability to move about gracefully in our small living room without bumping into one another. This is one reason we have no coffee table. They seemed to feel the mood of the composition, and expressed it in a freedom of movement, with complete lack of self-consciousness.

As my children mature, they are ready for more information about composers, titles, instruments, concertos and symphonies. They want to know the names of the pieces so that they can ask for those they especially like. My youngest children have not begun to read but they identify the cassettes by the pictures on the covers,

It is certainly not necessary for the teacher who introduces music to her children to be an expert herself, but it is important to have some accurate information about the music played and to know where to get further references. A good music library should be part of her equipment.

Gradually we began to have music at different times of the day, so that it became a real part of daily living. One day I was surprised to notice a sudden hush in the house. Eric was roaming around the kitchen (where the children were practicing penmanship) with the Beethoven "Pastoral Symphony" in his hand. As we had decided that music was to be played only when the room was quiet, he was busily asking all his brothers and sisters to be "extra" quiet so that he could play the cassette he wanted, and so Mother could listen too, while she was nursing the baby. As Eric used to be more of a solitary child, it was quite astonishing to see him organizing the group. The children were most cooperative, and went on with their work while they were listening. After this, special requests would arise as we were returning from a nature walk, putting away groceries, or at most any leisure time.

Some people ask whether children need a story in order to be interested in the music. When the composition is written around a story, such as "The Nutcracker Suite," "Peter and the Wolf," or "Carnival of the Animals," of course the story can be effectively introduced. However, I feel we should play most music without comment, so that children may be free to have

thoughts about it in their own way. They can have the creative experiences of discovering how it makes them feel rather than being told what they should feel. When I first played Beethoven's "Sixth Symphony," we listened to it a bit at a time. I told the children that Beethoven was a great lover of the out-of-doors, and that the title of the first movement was "Impressions on Arriving in the Country." With no more information than that, they told me that they heard birds, streams of water, and breezes rustling through the tress. They particularly liked the third and fourth movements, which are entitled "Jolly Gathering of the Country Folk" and "Thunderstorm," and soon began listening for the first crash of thunder and the downpour of the rain. They loved dancing to this part, too.

The other morning two of my children, in pajamas, came to me with the cassette of "The Birds" by Respighi and asked if they could play it while they were dressing. They began to dance gracefully and were soon joined by brother and sister. They exchanged partners and worked out a charming pattern, varying their mood with the changes in tempo. Eric, who had always found it hard to express himself in words, was one of this little quartet. Somehow, the music made it easy for him to express himself through movement. They enjoyed themselves so much that they were reluctant to eat and my children are usually very hungry when they awake. The fact is that musical expression is as real and natural a part of living as is any other aspect of home activity.

Of course quiet listening is as important an activity as participation; for before one grows up one must know that it is impossible to do a ballet up the aisles of a concert hall as the symphony plays "Swan Lake." To introduce the idea of concert listening, a talented member of the family may perform, even if perhaps he is a novice who is beginning to take piano lessons in his kindergarten days.

Titles of music are not easy to remember; hence I get some very strange requests indeed. One was for "Brown's Lullaby," and another for the "William's Hotel Overture." We had listened to William Tell the day before, and one child was intrigued with this because it is the theme song of "The Lone Ranger." He was extremely interested in hearing the rest of the music, perhaps wondering why the television show did not include the whole piece.

Toward the end of our school year I asked the children which recordings they liked best. These were the ones that made up their list:

- *Trumpet Voluntary* by Jeremiah Clark
- Music by Bach
- *Roumanian Rhapsody* by Enesco
- *The Birds* by Respighi
- *Symphonies No. 6 and No. 7*

by Beethoven
- *Piano Concerto No. 5* (The Emperor) by Beethoven
- *Concerto for Flute and Harp* by Mozart
- *Sheep May Safely Graze* by Bach
- *Jesu, Joy of Man's Desiring* (piano) by Bach
- *Nutcracker Suite* by Tschaikovsky
- Ballet music of all kinds
- *The William Tell Overture* by Rossini
- *A Midsummer Night's Dream* by Mendelssohn

I was delighted to read the above account of another mother who trusted in Charlotte Mason's plea to include classical music in a child's educational life.

Letter to the Editor

I received a letter from a discouraged mother last year:

Dear Karen,

I've tried to interest my children in classical music, poetry, picture study and some of the other lovely things that you mention in your magazine, but my children show absolutely no fondness for any of it.

Yours,
What-to-do-now

"Dear W.," I answered, "You haven't mentioned what your children have been interested in up to the time when you began introducing these "lovely" things into your home. How much television do they watch? Have they grown accustomed to hearing pop music most of the time? Are they allowed to listen to *any* radio station? Do they ever have personal quiet times or are they used to being entertained? 'Formation is easier than reformation,' says Charlotte Mason. But 'one custom overcometh another,' so don't lose hope or heart. Persevere, W. Phase out video or television watching. Phase out the popular music until it is heard only infrequently—ignoring any 'boo hoos' of the children. We don't listen to *any* popular music at home, because I know my children will hear it at shops and once a month at the orthodontist's anyway. I'd probably be surprised at the amount of background pop music we are exposed to if I added it up. Therefore I feel they haven't been deprived. If I happen to notice some particularly lustful lyrics, I cringe. Then it's time to silently pray on the spot that despite the "catchiness" of the tune and its rhyme, the lyrics will not be remembered by my children.

"We have acquired an embarrassing number of cassettes over the years," I continued. "We have cassettes of American, English, and Irish folk songs, old Disney songs, hymns, and lots of classical music. We did listen to the 'Best of John Denver,' Volumes I and II, several summers ago, and some love songs by the Beatles, such as 'Michelle' and 'Yesterday.' Dad plays the occasional Andrew Lloyd Webber or Moody Blues, both of which have orchestration. Gershwin, Rogers and Hammerstein, George M. Cohen, and Scott Joplin are definite choices for an American palate. When these are played over and over again, your children will get used to hearing great musicians and song writers.

There is no need to take a course in music appreciation or music history at this point. For now, just let music be music. It really isn't a subject, just as poetry, art and literature aren't really subjects. For now, let the music speak for itself.

"I found the motion picture *Mr. Holland's Opus* to be a good story. (It includes some bad language, though.) Near the start of the movie, Mr. Holland, the public school music teacher, tells his wife how he became hooked on so many kinds of music. In his youth a record store clerk highly recommended a certain artist so he purchased the record. With much anticipation he played it and instantly disliked it—as he was used to hearing pop and rock. He decided to play it again for whatever it was worth. Nothing. Then he played it again and the music began to speak to him. He was drawn to playing it over and over and he grew to love it. A pop song can be heard twice and we have 'picked it up.' More complex music must be heard repeatedly to bestow a familiar ring to our ears. It has to grow on us. Too many of us were not raised on classical music, but like the character in the film *My Fair Lady,* we can be tamed with some conditioning. My husband, Dean, told me that Vivaldi's 'Four Seasons' was the most popular music sold in England a few years ago. It is the truer 'pop' music that speaks to generations, so it seems. We love it because we took the time to get acquainted with this more complex music. So keep playing good music, W., keep reading aloud good poetry, keep displaying great art, and your children will be affected over time even though they might not want to admit this to you at present."

The Universal Language

I continued: "Classical music is worth pursuing even when obstacles intrude. Great music embodies man's highest experiences, his deepest emotions, and his spiritual aspirations. It has been called a universal language. When children are introduced to classical music while they are yet young, they more readily form a relation with it because it appeals to something more basic in them than their conscious intellect. They need not be aware of what the current fad says they should like or which music is in style. They simply learn to like what is good, if it is presented to them. But even children used to one style of music can be brought to an appreciation of another, so don't give up, W.

Sincerely,
Karen A.

Recent scientific studies have uncovered a startling new fact about the effect of certain types of music on a child's brain.

While children listen to music of the Baroque period in particular (Bach, Vivaldi, Handel), the brain scan reveals instant and spontaneous lengthening of fibrous brain cells. These cells quickly become amazingly active and stretch out—reaching to connect with other cells. Baroque music, unlike other styles of music, is responsible for this remarkable development. I find it interesting that so much of Baroque music was written to God's glory and that it is this music that generations find so stimulating, entertaining, and gratifying.

So of course play nursery songs, lively folk tunes, Patriotic songs, show tunes, *The Nutcracker, Peter and the Wolf,* and *William Tell's Overture,* and with these, as children enjoy and appreciate music even more, why not Bach?

Questions for personal reflection or support group discussion

1. *What music did you hear most often as a child? Do you come from a musical family?*

2. *Have you reformed or broadened your taste in music since you have become a Christian?*

3. *Why is music appreciation one of the easier subjects to teach?*

4. *Why did Charlotte recommend listening to the music of one composer at a time?*

5. *Is it necessary to be musical in order to teach musical appreciation?*

6. *What times of the day could music become a part of your life?*

7. *Do you have an opinion about pop music?*

8. *What benefits does a child derive from listening to Baroque music over pop music? In what ways is this astounding?*

Chapter Twenty-Seven

Greek Myth

FOR SOME TIME I had been curious about Greek mythology. How and why did Greek mythology become part of our Western culture, part of our English heritage? I wondered. Why did Charlotte Mason's students read the Greek myths? Is it advisable to read about Greek gods and goddesses? I found the answer to many of my questions while reading Charles Kingsley's preface to his book *The Heroes,* written in 1855. I hope it helps answer your questions, too.

I learned that during the nineteenth century children learned a lot about the Greek civilization, and were especially familiar with Greek mythology. Upper class boys who attended boarding school, preparing for the great universities, spent a great deal of time learning to read Greek and the literature of the Golden Age of Greece. Girls, though they may not have learned to read the Greek language, were sure to come across many stories taken from Greek history.

I discovered that there are a great many things we would not have if it weren't for the Greeks. We can hardly find a well-written book that hasn't got Greek names, words, or proverbs in it. We cannot walk through the streets of any city in the English-speaking world without passing a Greek building modeled after the Greek style of architecture, or go into a well-furnished hotel without seeing copies of Greek statues and ornamentation. These old Greeks left their mark upon this modern world in which we now live. As boys and girls grow up they will read more and more and find that we owe the beginnings of our mathematics and geometry to the Greeks—who taught us about the shapes of things and about the forces that make things move and stand and rest. They also gave us the beginnings of our geography and astronomy, as well as some of our concepts of law and freedom and politics. And we owe the beginnings of our logic to them, that is, the study of words and of reasoning—and of our metaphysics, and the study of our own thoughts and souls. Last of all, they made their language so beautiful that foreigners wished to speak it instead of their own. Greek became the common language of educated people all over the old world, from Persia and Egypt to Spain and Britain. And that is why the New Testament was written in Greek—so that it might be read and understood by all the nations of the Roman Empire. So next to the Jews, and the Bible, which the Jews handed down to us, we owe more to these old Greeks than to any people on earth.

"Greeks" was not their real name, however. They called themselves "Hellens," but the Romans miscalled them Greeks, and we have taken that wrong name from the Romans.

Mr. Kingsley said: "I love the old Greeks 'heartily.' I am grateful for all they have taught me. These Hellens seem to me like brothers, though they have all been dead for over a twenty-five hundred years. This is why I wrote *The Heroes*. I wish to introduce the Hellens to children. Nations begin at first by being children . . . with children's hearts; frank, and affectionate, and full of trust, and teachable, and loving to see and learn all the wonders around them; and greedy also, too often, and passionate and silly, as children are."[1]

Thus these old Greeks were teachable, and learned from all the nations around them. From the Phoenicians they learned ship-building, and some say letters beside; and from the Assyrians they learned painting, and carving, and building in wood and stone; and from the Egyptians they learned astronomy, and many things that are hard to understand. Therefore God rewarded these Greeks with wisdom as He loves to see men and children open-hearted, and willing to be taught; and to him who uses what he has got, He gives more and more day by day. So these Greeks grew wise and powerful, and wrote poems which will live till the world's end. These are the classics that so many people still read today in English, if not in Greek. They learned to carve statues, and build temples, which are still among the wonders of the world; and many other wondrous things God taught them, for which we are the wiser today.

We mustn't think that because these old Greeks were heathens, therefore God did not care for them, and taught them nothing. The Bible tells us that it was not so, that God's mercy is over all His works, and that He understands the hearts of all people, and fashions all their works. And Paul the apostle told these old Greeks later on, when they had grown wicked and fallen low, that they ought to have known better, because they were God's offspring, as their own poets had said (in whom we live and breathe and have our being) and that God had put them where they were, to seek the Lord, and feel after Him, and find Him, though He was not far from any one of them. Clement of Alexandria, a Father of the Church, said that God had sent down philosophy to the Greeks from heaven, as He sent down the Gospel to the Jews.

Jesus Christ, remember, is the Light who lights every man who comes into the world. And no one can think a right thought, or feel a right feeling, or understand the real truth of anything in earth and heaven, unless the good Lord Jesus teaches him by the Holy Spirit, who gives man understanding.

But these Greeks, as Paul told them, forgot what God had taught them, and though they were God's offspring, worshipped idols of wood and stone, and fell at last into sin and shame, and then of course, into cowardice and slavery till they perished out of that beautiful land which God had given them for so many years.

For, like all nations who have left anything behind them, besides mere mounds of earth, they believed at first in the One True God who made all heaven and earth. But after a while, like all other nations, they began to worship other gods who they fancied lived about their land: Zeus, the father of gods and men (who was some dim remembrance of the blessed true God), and Hera his wife, and Phoebus Apollo the Sun-god, and Pallas Athene, who taught men wisdom and useful arts, and Aphrodite the Queen of Beauty, and Poseidon the Ruler of the Sea, and Hephaistos the King of the Fire, who taught men to work in metals. And they honored the gods of the rivers, and the Nymph-maids, who they fancied lived in the caves, and fountains, and the glens of the forest, and all beautiful wild places. And they honored the Erinnues, the dreadful sister, who, they thought, haunted guilty men until their sins were purged away. And many other dreams they had, which parted the One God into many, and they said, too, that these gods did things which would be a shame and sin for any man to do. And when their philosophers arose, and told them that God was one, they would not listen, but loved their idols, and their wicked idol feasts, till they all came to ruin. These are, surely, sad things.

At the time when stories of the Greek heroes were recorded, they had not fallen as low as that. They worshipped no idols, and still believed in the last six of the ten commandments, and knew well what was right and what was wrong. And they believed (and that is what gave them courage) that the gods loved men, and taught them, and that without the gods men were sure to come to ruin. (But they also believed the gods could hate them, and therefore sought their favor in offerings, rather than a change of heart, and they really had no peace in their relations with the gods, because even if one god looked on them with favor, another could dislike them, and make a bargain with the other to be allowed to do something punitive.) However, this one aspect they were right about: without God we can do nothing, and all wisdom comes from Him.

When the hero stories were written, the Greeks were not very learned men yet, or living in great cities, such as they were afterwards, when they created all their works of beauty. They were country people, living in farms and walled villages, in a simple, hardworking way; so that the greatest kings and heroes cooked their own meals, and thought it no shame, and made their own ships and weapons, and fed and harnessed their own horses; and the queens worked with their maid-servants, and did all the business of the house, and spun, and wove, and embroidered, and made their husband's clothes and their own. And thus a man was honored among them not because he happened to be rich, but according to his skill, and his strength, and courage.

While these Greeks were young and simple they loved fairy tales. The old Romans had theirs, too, and they called them "Fabulae," from which our word "fable" comes; but the old Hellens called theirs "mughoi," form which our new word "myth" is taken. But next to those old Romances, which were written in the Christian middle age, there are no fairy tales like these old Greek ones, for beauty, and wisdom, and truth, and for making children love noble deeds, and trust in God to help them through.

Kingsley named his book *The Heroes,* he said, because "that was the name the Hellens gave to men who were brave and skillful, and dared do more than other men. Later it came to mean something more. It came to mean men who helped their country, men in those old times, when the country was half-wild, who killed fierce beasts and evil men, and drained swamps, and founded towns, and therefore after they were dead, were honored, because they had left their country better than they found it. We call such a man a hero in English to this day, and call it a 'heroic' thing to suffer pain and grief, that we may do good to our fellowmen."

We may one day do a heroic deed. But for today we may read how the Greek heroes worked, three thousand years ago. The stories are not all true, of course, but the meaning of them is true, and true for ever, and that is: "Do right, and God will help you."[1]

Resources for further study:

Besides Charles Kingsley's *The Heroes—Greek Fairy Tales for My Children,* I also recommend Nathaniel Hawthorne's *Tanglewood Tales* and *The Wonder Book.* Our family obtained our copies in a used book store. Modern illustrated publications can be found in catalogs. Our family has also enjoyed *Classic Myths to Read Aloud,* by William F. Russell, which offers an excellent re-telling of a wide variety of the best-known Greek and Roman myths. ⚊⚬

Questions for Personal Reflection or Support Group Discussion

1. *If the ancient Greeks are worthy of our attention, then why not look at the qualities of the Greek heroes?*

2. *Can we gain some spiritual understanding of self-sacrifice and courage through these heroes?*

3. *If truth can be found in the stories of the ancient Greeks that sheds some light on the way they thought, and what their aspirations and ideals were, can we not uncover this truth and use it for God's glory?*

4. *What did Paul preach to the Greeks who had received this knowledge? How does this let us both admire and pity the Greeks?*

Your Own Personal Reflections

Chapter Twenty-Eight

....

Once Upon a Time—Fact or Fairy Tales

IF YOU PICK THE RIGHT SUMMER NIGHT to explore the woods of New York State, you may see the lunar moth in a large party. With a flashlight they can be seen fluttering their white wings against the black background of night, up and down the tree on whose leaves they lay their eggs. It appears that the tree is enchanted. Moths are some of the most beautiful of God's creations. They can be best appreciated in their natural habitat during their own waking hours. Perhaps these beautiful, quiet, peaceful, winged creatures were the inspiration of earlier peoples to insist upon the existence of forest fairies. Does the mention of fairies make you nervous? It did me, until I read Charlotte's defense of them.

Many Christian parents worry that reading fairy tales is harmful for children. What supports this apprehension? Two arguments: the fact that fairy tales are not true, and the knowledge that they can be frightening. Let's look at the last point. Which frightening or disturbing fairy tale characters remain in your memory? The wolf who swallowed Red Riding Hood's grandmother comes to my mind first. Then I picture the oppressive stepsisters of Cinderella, the giant at the top of Jack's beanstalk, the jealous fairy who made Sleeping Beauty prick her finger on the spindle and fall into a long, long sleep, and the jealous, murderous queen who gave Snow White the poison apple. Do they make you shudder? They are meant to.

Naturally we all wish our children to be spared the experience of suffering and terror in their early years, but even this immunity cannot be guaranteed. There are real, frightening characters who lurk around pleasant, well-trimmed neighborhoods. They are known by children as "strangers." "Don't talk to strangers," children are told. There are picture books that give more descriptive warnings, and show parents how to teach a child to recognize when he is being lured or abused (even possibly by an unsuspected relative).

Since the Bible and all teaching of absolute right and wrong has been removed from the public schools, crime of all kinds has risen. "Why not talk to strangers?" the children ask. "Because they might do very bad things to you," we reply. We barely get the words out before we cringe at the thought of such persons doing such evil things to our precious ones, worse evil than that personified in their fairy tales.

One of the strongest weapons we can provide our children is the opportunity to face and conquer in the abstract the frightening badness of the world, before they are compelled to grapple with such badness in reality. Fairy tales offer this opportunity. They are a buffer between what is scary but what won't happen and what is scary and could very well happen.

One day they will learn about the process of abortion—and other horrors of modern life—which surely is more terrible than the spine-chilling perils of the fairy tales. And it is the fairy tales that will provide the antidote to the fear and horror of these realities. They will rely on and wish to emulate the courage of Hansel and Gretel, or the Seven Dwarfs. They will learn that the good, the small, and the meek are not necessarily helpless or cowardly. Perhaps these story characters who faced evil and won will soften little worried faces who fear for what lurks under the bed or beyond the radius of the night light.

In works of fiction there is an underlying truth—like the tiny bit of sand that lies within a pearl. Truth is the grain of sand and the pearl the

tale it is based upon. Funny, I've heard of Christians who reject all fiction but who do approve of *Pilgrims Progress*—although the Slough of Despond is not found anywhere in Great Britain. Have you ever read John Bunyan's "apology" (his introduction to *Pilgrim's Progress*)? In the original text, he says in verse:

"But it is feigned." What of that? I trow
Some men, by feigned words, as dark as mine,
Make truth to spangle, and its rays to shine.
"But they want solidness . . ."
Solidity, indeed, becomes the pen
O him that writeth things divine to men;
But must I needs want solidness, because
By metaphors I speak? Were not God's laws,
His gospel laws, in olden time held forth
By types, shadows, and metaphors? Yet loth
Will any sober man be to find fault
With them, lest he be found for to assault
The highest wisdom![1]

He wrote his tale in a day when his fellow Puritans strictly avoided all fiction.

The escapades of fairy tale characters can awaken our eyes to intangible but essential truths of life, truths that are even more profound than two plus two equals four. From the splendid stories of Hans Christian Anderson, C.S. Lewis, or Oscar Wilde, for example, children become intimate with the spiritual laws that govern the universe and the concept of good and evil. And children—who are naturally faithful—know the fundamental truth of the famous last words, "And they all lived happily ever after." Jealous queens and stepsisters, wicked wolves and witches are outwitted by ordinary woodsman, dwarfs, or gallant princes; dragons are slain, enormous spiders are killed by hobbits; giants must set their captives free; princes and peasants alike wrestle with the powers of darkness and emerge victorious. Of course the courageous, righteous, generous, patient, the humble and hardworking, all lived happily ever after! Because . . . heaven is not a fantasy.

I am certainly not suggesting, here, that Fairy Lore take the place of the teaching of morality and essential truths of the Bible, or that all brave and generous persons go to Heaven. I am rather, asserting that the fictional characters of fairy tales have a way of profoundly demonstrating the contrast of good and evil without parading morals so obviously. For this quality they have won the right to be included in the memories of childhood.

Does this mean that all fantasy, all Fairy Lore is wholesome food for our children? The sensitive intelligence of parenthood will be able to discern. If the story is too frightening or grotesque, then it is not a fairy tale. It would be considered a horror story. I, personally, would not consider the Goosebumps books wholesome reading. By their very nature, horror stories are defective as literature, and cannot compare with the "tale as old as time, song as old as rhyme" of Fairy Lore. Just as we do not allow children the free use of the pantry or refrigerator, we also do not need to allow them to take out any book the public library has chosen to carry. Just as we stock wholesome food in the refrigerator, we need to keep a selection of tales on the home bookshelves we deem safe to read. And if we treat fairy tales like sweets to be divided out in small portions, we will not let our children be overcome or overfed.

Children first work and play at developing their powers of imagination. "Now imagination . . . grows by what it gets; and childhood, the age of faith, is the time for its nourishment. The children should have the joy of living in far lands, in other persons, in

other times . . . in their storybooks," said Charlotte. Imagination is a great ally needful in the mature intelligence of adulthood and we want our children to be able to call upon their powers of imagination throughout their lives. Therefore it is good that the imagination is fed and digestion stimulated in childhood. In childhood the imagination is so thoroughly and delightfully appreciated. But young children are weak in logic and reason. This is why we treat fairy stories like sweets. They are to be enjoyed once in a while and never as a main course, even when the skills of reason and logic have developed. And even though imagination requires feeding, its appetite must be curbed. In this way we are safely and carefully supplying our children with wholesome ideas. And you've heard me say before that ideas are what the mind feeds upon.

Charlotte Mason recommended Andrew Lang's collections of fairy tales. In an old review of *Lang's Violet Fairy Book,* G.K. Chesterton sums up his defense of fairy stories:

> Of all forms of literature, it seems to me, first and foremost that all doors fly open to courage and hope. We learn that the world is bound together in mysterious bonds of trust and compact precision, and that even green dragons keep their promises. We learn that nothing is wasted in the mills of the world, that a jewel thrown into the sea, a kindness to a stricken bird, and idle word to a ragged wayfarer have in them some terrible value and are here bound up with the destiny of men."[2]

Chapter Twenty-Nine

....

Approach to Poetry

THESE DAYS IT SEEMS the only verse the average person is exposed to on a daily basis is a popular jingle or an advertiser's catchy phrase. Certainly one merit of poetry is that it can often say more in fewer words than prose. But can a jingle really be called poetry?

In our fast-paced, hurried lives, too many of us only have time to "catch" a verse or phrase here and there. But the best poetry is not obviously displayed in society. We have to look for this hidden treasure in something not commonly found at the newsstand—a book of poetry. If reading the shortest poetry is all you have time for, then by all means begin with short poems. However, once you start, in some little time you may find you have developed a desire for a larger dose. When you have discovered the kind of poetry you like best, you will have gone even farther—you will have acquired a "taste" for poetry. I guess this is why an old phrase of folk wisdom says that "a good begun is half done."

The Golden Age of Greece was a time of peace. The average citizen of Athens was not only educated through poetry (among other things), but in his adulthood his leisure reading was poetry. The knowledge of the gods, of man, and of the world was gained through poetry. Compare this to the restless, artificial, luxurious existence of Rome. Like ancient Rome, our world today is a culture that places great value on building bigger and better everything—interstate highways, one-hundred-acre amusement parks, huge hotels, super supermarkets—and printing bigger and bigger magazines and tabloids.

Poetry is one of the things that can't be made bigger and better. It must remain quietly and unobtrusively and forever itself. Poetry was once an important part of the education of American children. More than that, it was read as literature—as we would read a novel today. Old school books included poetry that raised the students' consciousness of what goodness was, spoke of noble and worthy people, and depicted brave and altruistic actions. So many of the old poems were laced with an unabashedly Christian perspective that they are no longer allowed to show their faces in the public schools.

When an admired aunt of mine was bedridden with cancer, I wrote out into a card the short poem that follows and sent it to her. Because she loved God, and she loved the sea, I thought she would be especially comforted by it. It is by Emily Dickinson, one of America's most famous poets, and it is one of my favorites.

> I never saw a moor,
> I never saw the sea,
> Yet know I how the heather looks,
> And what a wave must be.
> I never spoke with God,
> Nor visited in heaven;
> Yet certain am I of the spot
> As if the chart were given.[1]

Emily Dickinson is still read today, at least a little. But sadly, quotable poems by Christians like John Donne, Edward Taylor, and George Herbert have dropped unnoticed out of the store of commonly known things, leaving us to our steel-girded world of material things with its greed for more luxury and prosperity. But despite the disappearance of noble poetry from our contemporary world, people still read and write poetry for pleasure today. I'd like my children to be among them.

The historian Macaulay said, "He who, in an enlightened and literary society, aspires to be a great poet, must first become like a child."[2] Children can easily believe the unseen—so can poets. While our adult senses have become dull, children are quite busy observing, in detail, the things that are going on around them. Poets also do this. When I was living under my mother's roof, she used to say, "You don't miss a trick, do you?" when I commented on some inconsistency or hypocrisy in the adult world. Poets don't miss a trick either.

Mothers—even though they know it is not possible or best for their children—secretly wish their young ones could remain forever ignorant of the sins of the world. That is why they try their best to create an Eden for them—in the home. But through carefully chosen poetry, mothers can teach their children to recognize sin, be inspired, and be filled with admiration of God's gifts to man. (And why it has to be carefully chosen is because poetry has suffered the same fate as art, music, literature, and dance: it has gotten into the hands of godless people who use it to describe and glorify a debauched world.) If a true poet is child-like, children will relate to his musical words, his emotion, his description, and his faith.

Poetry is Serious Business

Poetry is not just a means to moral instruction. It is part of the humanities. Poetry is one of those human things with which Charlotte Mason wished children to establish a relationship. It is a deep expression of thought and feeling of which certain exceptional minds are particularly capable. Poetry comments on all human experiences, it is comprised of everything from war poems and epics, to psalms of worship, to love sonnets, to delightful nonsense verse that trips off the tongue, to nursery rhymes. The subjects for poetry can be anything people think about or sing about. We can read it as though we ourselves shared in those thoughts and those emotions.

Poetry is for Everyone

Poetry has been helping men and women from all backgrounds and cultures throughout all recorded history share deep emotional experiences and insights. It was astounding for me to hear a translation of a remarkably beautiful poem written by King Tutankhamen to his wife! Chaucer, Milton, Homer, Shakespeare, and the author of Beowulf also wrote poetry that still speaks to us today on many different levels. The best poems in history weren't written for textbooks, so we may have to look elsewhere to find them.

Poetry for Poetry's Sake

A child would grow up lopsided if athletic prowess were his only ambition. We can take this idea further and say he'd receive a lopsided education if he could "make the grade" or come out "on top" without any love or respect for poetry. In the film *The Dead Poets Society,* a refreshingly different New England prep school teacher held strongly to this very opinion. His desire and goal was to put his young students in personal contact with poetry. "Open to the first page of the introduction of your text *How to Understand Poetry,*" he told them. They did so dutifully, but without any enthusiasm. One of the students was asked to read the first paragraph aloud. While the student read some academic-sounding things along with how to determine the perfection of a poem on a grid, the teacher frantically chalked the grid on the blackboard.

When both the reading and the grid were finished, the teacher surprised them by telling them plainly that it was all for naught—that a grid for judging poetry was good for nothing and so that whole first chapter was good for nothing. He instructed them to rip out that page of their textbooks. The boys looked up at him in disbelief.

"Rip it out!" he repeated. They looked at him speechless, their eyes round with incredulity. "That's right, you heard me: rip—not just that page, the whole introduction. I want to hear nothing but ripping!" he emphatically concluded. The boys were dumbfounded and hesitated to destroy their sacred textbooks.

"Rip!" he loudly commanded, so rip they did. "In my class," he said more quietly and in earnest, "you will learn to think for yourselves."

The goal of his class was to give the students an opportunity to develop their own opinion of poetry. It was essential they relate to it personally, unencumbered by any academic rating method. Charlotte Mason would agree, I am sure.

Making Introductions

How do we introduce our children to poetry? We can't force girls or boys to like a poem against their will. We can't bully them into it, or argue them into it. We can lead them to form a relation with it by indirect means. But like that of the prep school teacher in *The Dead Poets Society,* our own interest and gentle enthusiasm will be infectious. I began, years ago, picking out some poetry that appealed to me and simply reading it aloud to my children. When they learned to read, they started reading some on their own. My girls and I have similar tastes in poetry, but my boy has a preference a bit different from ours. It should be permissible to have a different taste for poetry than that of the teacher. Making a connection with poetry is the important thing.

If you do not like poetry, there is an obvious remedy: introduce the child and the poem and leave them to make friends for themselves.

Over the years I have received letters from mothers who shared their new-found excitement over things that Charlotte promoted in her writings, such as real books, the use of narration, art and music appreciation, and poetry. I am always happy to read these letters. I do enjoy reading about the delight these mothers experience in learning with their children those things they missed during their own school days.

A tip: In making introductions, it is generally a mistake to praise too highly the person whom you are introducing. In the same way, it is a mistake to talk about how wonderful a poem is before you read it aloud to the children. If you have suddenly "discovered" poetry after many years of living and learning without it, you could be over-zealous about sharing it with your children. A little restraint goes a long way. After all, the child is entitled to some of his own excitement. If we rob a child of the opportunity to relate to the poem himself, to make his own connection with it, the poem will lose some of those very qualities that make it precious. When you share a poem you can simply say, with tact, "I like this poem. Do you?"

In the case of younger children, we can create a mood of enjoyment, first by choosing the sort of poem they are likely to appreciate and then by throwing ourselves into reading it as beautifully as we can. I read nursery rhymes to my children when they were very young. They are the popular jingles of childhood. The first poems we committed to memory were those by Robert Louis Stevenson's, from *A Child's Garden of Verses*. His cadence, rhyme, and comments on life through the eyes of his childhood are a delight. If you introduce children to really good poetry, suitable for their age, as Charlotte advocated, children will do the appreciating of it for themselves. Below are some ways to take a poetry break.

Celebrate the Seasons

I enjoy and look forward to the passing of the seasons where we live. Each new season brings with it anticipation of that season's delights. The poets have made a contribution to my appreciation.

Look in the index of any large poetry anthology for anything that has to do with a particular time of year. Anthologies usually list poems by season in the subject index. Spring is a favorite subject with many poets. You are bound to find twice as many poems in praise of spring than the other seasons. I invite you to find out why. Whether it be winter, spring, summer, or fall, you are certain to find an array of poems to suit your season.

Read a few at a time to savor the season. In between new readings, any previously-read poems can be repeated as often as desired—a painless way to memorize poetry. Seasonal poems can be copied by the children into greeting cards or onto large paper, surrounded by their drawings.

Ask the Poets

Why not ask what the poets have to say about whatever you happen to be studying? If you are studying American or British history, you will find patriotic poems to put you in the spirit of your studies. The poets reveal to us that history does not exist without some emotion. It is this spirit that is most often left out of textbooks. Who can read poems such as Longfellow's "Paul Revere's Ride" and not be moved by the valor and determination of the patriots of our country? Do you remember how it starts?

Listen my children and you shall hear
Of the midnight ride of Paul Revere.
On the eighteenth of April, in Seventy-five;
Hardly a man is now alive
Who remembers that famous day and year.[3]

Welcome a child's comments on a poem. Ask him whether he thinks the mood is one of sorrow or joy, anger or entreaty, desire or regret. If the child is older, ask him to point out the word or phrases that explain the emotion.

Nature Poetry

Nature poetry abounds. I counted fifty short poems about birds in our poetry anthology! There are poems about the sea, trees, animals of various kinds, the wind, the moon. If nature is one of your child's favorite studies, he will find a kindred spirit when he reads the work of many poets. A child may find it interesting to discover how closely his observations resemble those of the poet. Poems of nature can be chosen to adorn a child's Nature Notebook.

There are poems about the early morning and the night; unusual people. There are heroic ballads; story poems. Poets write about honesty, fortitude, chivalry, loyalty, perseverance, hope, faith, and love. Their commentary on any subject, as well as their subtle or profound sentiments, are worthy to be woven into our homeschools.

A Poetry Party on Valentine's Day

A tea party is a good place to practice etiquette and perform a recitation. To commit a poem to memory and speak it with clear enunciation in front of a small audience is an excellent educational experience. As a child follows the directions of the composer of a piece of music to play either *forte* or *piano,* we can expect our children to do likewise with poetry. If a child has chosen for himself a poem for recitation, it is probably one to which he can instinctively relate on some level. Unlike music, there are no written notes or dynamics for the reader of poetry. But taking into account the child's level of understanding, he can be guided to show expression and speak his poem convincingly. The tone of the poem should determine his tone of voice. However, we shouldn't expect children to deeply understand the thoughts or the emotions of the poem. They will grow into a deeper understanding with time.

One Poet at a Time

Still another way to study poetry is to become familiar with one poet at a time. Here are a few favorites: A. A. Milne, William Blake, Samuel Coleridge, Eleanor Farjeon, Henry Wadsworth Longfellow, Walter de la Mare, Christina Rossetti, William Shakespeare, Robert Louis Stevenson, Lord Tennyson, John Greenleaf Whittier, Emily Dickinson, Ogden Nash, Carl Sandburg, and e.e. cummings.

This time look in the index under an author's name. Read in one week all of the poems of that poet that you can put your index finger on. We have several volumes with collections of one poet's work. This makes it convenient to have an "Emily Dickinson week" or a "Longfellow week." Biographical sketches serve to widen a child's knowledge and deepen his awareness of his cultural heritage.

Poetry is strewn with ideas. Saturate yourself in the words—they can have an intoxicating effect on the intellect. Ideas to the mind are what nutritious food is to the stomach. Remember, Charlotte encourages us to put children in contact with the minds of thinkers. Education is mind to mind, thought to thought, person to person. Notes, commentaries, lectures, long lists of questions, and other middlemen are not needed. Let the poets do the speaking and the children do the listening. Then you will have something to talk about.

Develop Your Inner Ear

A calm, stately voice echoes from the past, "Take your time." Poetry will speak wonderful things to those who give it time. As reading requires the inward eye of the imagination, poetry requires an inward ear. Unencumbered by modern media, our great-great-grandparents had both. They read poetry for pleasure and made a regular meal of their favorites.

Like replaying a favorite song, a really good poem is meant to be visited again and again. In so doing, we are renewing a friendship. The friendship of certain poems will increase over the years. This is the old-time method of "studying" poetry that deserves mention. Even today, the way people appreciate poetry most often is to read whatever poem they fancy whenever they fancy.

From Shorter to Longer Works

In the days before workbooks, young children in Charlotte's schools had copy books. Children were to choose some favorite verse and copy it neatly into these books. Thus the study of poetry also yielded better penmanship, spelling, and vocabulary.

After years of a relationship with poetry, built on shorter poems, children will be capable of enjoying and comprehending longer and more abstract works. High school students can become familiar with the longer classics of poetry just by checking out books of poetry from the local library. If your student has begun his relationship with the poets, it is time to offer him some background explanation in the form of critical commentaries.

Along with *Beowulf,* the works of Chaucer and the sonnets of Shakespeare are commonly studied in high school. They contain more adult themes, so use your discretion. These were included in Charlotte's curriculum. I am unfamiliar with more modern poetry, but the usual cautions apply.

Poetry For an Uncertain World

As an educator who was a follower of Charlotte Mason's philosophy reminds us:

Literature is the sum total of the courage and hope, the faith, delight, and despair of the past, and if we deny youth this, and give them instead a little pale skepticism of our own, a conscientious distrust of the ideals which have sustained other generations and other ages, a belief that the world began yesterday and if we are not careful will end tomorrow, because our own idealism is unequal to the problems it has to face, then we do them a poor service. All our aspirations for the young are likely to be defeated unless we hand on to them a certain moral stability, a belief in beauty, truth and goodness for their own sake; whereas if we give them these—and in giving them these, poetry will surely be included— we have at least the assurance that we have done our best to equip them adequately for the certain difficulties of this uncertain world.[4]

To do this we look to the Great Poet. Charlotte Mason said:

> We perceive that the Son of Man is a poet. Is there a poem in all the world that so fulfills all the functions of poetry, which is so full of sweetness, refreshment, rest, illuminations, expansion, as that poem which bids us 'consider the lilies of the field' and 'the fowls of the air'? All poets see and know, and inasmuch as He sees with an unbounded vision, sees all the past and all the future and all the issues of life, how could our Lord not be a poet?

Resources For the Young

Lavender's Blue is a book of nursery rhymes compiled by Kathleen Lines with pictures in soft pastel colors by Harold Jones.

We wore out a copy of *The Random House Book of Poetry for Children* compiled by Jack Prelutsky and illustrated by Arnold Lobel. It provides a cute and funny commentary on life. I suggest it as a "first" poetry book for kindergarten through second grade. The Halloween page can be "cut out."

A copy of *A Child's Garden of Verse* by Robert Louis Stevenson should be available in every public library. We have a copy illustrated by Jessie Willcox Smith and another illustrated by Tasha Tudor.

Favorite Poems Old and New, selected by Helen Ferris, is a handy anthology that has been around since 1957. I checked this book out of a library so many times that when I—happily—found it available at my first curriculum fair, I promptly bought a copy. The author had parents who not only read poetry to themselves for pleasure, but often read aloud to their children as a family pastime. This book is the result of the author's wish for all children to have the opportunity she had—to grow to love poetry.

The Book of 1,000 Poems is an inexpensive, hardcover, "no-frills" anthology of over 600 pages.

For Older Students

Treasury of Best Loved Poems, illustrated by Eleanor Fortescue Brickdale, is a good introduction to reading weightier works. I have used it to acquaint myself with poems by John Donne, Robert Burns, William Wordsworth, Lord Byron, Percy Bysshe Shelley, Elizabeth Barrett Browning, Walt Whitman, Emily Dickinson, Robert Frost, and others. It makes a beautiful gift for a high school student.

An old book still in print is *One Hundred and One Famous Poems,* compiled by Roy J. Cook. It has a black and white photograph or portrait of each poet. The poems do not seem to match the staunch Victorian faces, which leads me to believe that in some cases it may be better to read the poem without seeing the face. I guess we're more accustomed to the modern "cover girl/cover guy" look. Charlotte Mason would deem the poems in this book required reading for every high school student.

For the Serious Reader of Poetry

Five Hundred Years of English Poetry, edited by Barbara Lloyd-Evans, will satisfy any serious reader. It has 1200 pages of meaty, longer poetry, beginning with Geoffrey Chaucer (1343–1400) and ending with Matthew Arnold (1822–1888). It omits Shakespeare, as the editor assumes you already own his works and feels that including works from him would inconveniently lengthen the already lengthy book[5] ⇥

Chapter Thirty

....

Shakespeare—A Mother's Secret Resource

ONE SECRET RESOURCE at a mother's disposal for instructing a child's conscience with ideas of goodness, pity, generosity, courage, and love (distinguishing frivolous whispers of love from true love, which labors long) is the plays of William Shakespeare. In the lines of his plays he metes out morsels of proverbs spoken by his characters, who entertain us thoroughly. But Shakespeare was written for adults. This is one reason I thought it best to introduce my children to Shakespeare by reading simplified versions of his plays in story form. Very young students can easily keep track of the plot and associate names with characters in modern language before studying the original play written in Elizabethan English. But I do not like to use the word "study" when it comes to Shakespeare. If a child is brought up with an early appreciation of Shakespeare, if Shakespeare becomes a natural part of his educational life, he will not be apprehensive about Shakespeare in his high school years. He will not feel that he is studying, but rather that he is delving into the plays. And to delve into Shakespeare is to form a closer relationship with Shakespeare.

At the turn of the century, the children's writer E. Nesbit presented in story form twenty of Shakespeare's dramas in *Beautiful Stories from Shakespeare for Children*. It is intended for children as young as six years old. You may recognize her as the author of *The Railway Children*, now a classic of children's literature. Nesbit builds children a foot-bridge to cross over to Shakespeare's

Elizabethan English. The pen drawings in the book (the kind I like) depict all the characters in period dress, but oddly enough, instead of adult figures, all the characters are drawn as children.

When children reach the age of ten they might like to dip into *Tales from Shakespeare* by Charles and Mary Lamb. This book, written around the year 1800, was probably the first retelling of Shakespeare's plays written for children. Of their fourteen stories, Mary wrote the comedies and her brother Charles—the great essayist—wrote the tragedies. They use challenging vocabulary—often borrowing phrases from the original plays.

My eldest student and I are currently enjoying the more recent *Shakespeare Stories* published in 1985. One night it is left by my bedside, the next, by hers. The author, Leon Garfield, blends the flavor of Shakespeare's original verse into his narrative, which makes it a favorite with us.

Beginnings

We began our appreciation of Shakespeare when all my children were quite young. It all started one very hot summer evening when Dad brought home a video for the children. How fitting a time of year to watch the old black and white American production of *A Midsummer Night's Dream*—with James Cagney, Dick Powell, Olivia De Havilland, Mickey Rooney, Joe E. Brown and Victor Jory. The children were riveted and found it curiously amusing. The words were all Shakespeare's original ones. Yet, when it was over, little Sophia asked, "Please Dad, may we watch it just one more time before you have to take it back?" The children saw "shows" infrequently. However, the next day, a scorching hot southern Saturday, we allowed them to see it again. On Sunday afternoon, with windows tightly shut and the air conditioner running full blast, Sophia and her younger sister Yolanda danced—like little fairies—around the room to one of Dad's favorite classical music pieces—Felix Mendelssohn's *A Midsummer Night's Dream*. It's a pity Shakespeare never got to hear his play performed with Mendelssohn's beautiful composition.

From what I could tell, the girls were acting out the play, having pulled odd bits of clothing together for costumes. Nearly all of the energy they had stored up that morning, sitting docilely in church, was being used for their happy frolicking. How their napping brother stayed asleep during all this, I don't know!

An Early Appreciation of Shakespeare

"I want to try this!" I said excitedly, in the early years of my homeschooling adventures, when I read about how Charlotte Mason matter-of-factly included Shakespeare in the curriculum for (upper elementary) school children. I am so happy I trusted her about this. Charlotte described how certain young students from a poor Welsh mining community learned to love Shakespeare, although most had illiterate parents. After reading *Julius Caesar* in their PNEU school, some of the boys walked several miles into town to see a performance. When these students had saved up a few shillings, they bought their own copy of the play. Neither of these were school assignments. They were actions that had sprung out of a love of knowledge of things noble and worthy. Charlotte's fondness for Shakespeare had "rubbed off" on them, and this love of knowledge had spilled over into the boys' leisure. This was Charlotte's intention.

The only "testing" that was done in school, or shall I say "finding out what the children learned," was of their memorization and pronunciation of the lines assigned to them. A retelling of parts of the story in their own words was done not only with Shakespeare but with a number of literary subjects. Illustrations were drawn by the children, too, which revealed what they saw of the play in their imagination. How simple, how pertinent, how personal, how natural was this measuring of their understanding! If Shakespeare were alive today, he would probably be scratching his head at the many textbook discussions, commentaries, explications, and analyses of his work that abound today, as well as at the prevailing notion that only experts can really understand what he said. *The Christian Century,* January 1949, printed this gem:

> I dreamed that William Shakespeare's ghost
> Sat for a civil service post.
> The English paper for that year
> Was on the subject of "King Lear."
> William answered rather badly—
> You see he hadn't had his Bradley.

Substitute "Cliffs Notes" for "Bradley" and you get the idea. Should children cram for an English test using Cliffs Notes or anyone else's academic interpretation or commentary of a play? "Never!" proclaimed Charlotte. As we have discussed, her philosophy was that "education should be a science of relations." She believed, very strongly, that we should put children in touch with as many things and books as are suitable for them. And then, most importantly, we should allow them to relate to them. The Welsh boys were beginning a relationship with Shakespeare. They were being educated for life, not for getting a good grade or for coming out "on top." The PNEU schools, following Charlotte's curriculum, read three of Shakespeare's plays a year, starting at age nine, and at least one was performed by the children. Children at this age are language-sensitive.

Wow! A Full-Length Performance!

In practice, our family hasn't lived up to Charlotte's high goals for getting acquainted with Shakespeare. Her ideal of three plays a year, including one full-length performance, has been an ideal too high for our circumstances. However, I don't think I would have had the goals I do have if it weren't for Charlotte's influence. My children have had the opportunity to act in two plays, which I am very thankful for, although neither of them were Shakespeare plays. Nevertheless, our children have been growing up with Shakespeare's stories, have been listening to his original language on audio cassette, have seen several plays on video, and have attended a few performances over the past years. I sense a relationship with Shakespeare forming. With this I am content.

One Mother's Secret Plan

First, read aloud the story of one of the comedies. This might be one or two morning or casual bedtime readings.

Secondly, borrow or purchase a Shakespeare play on video. Discuss it. Our county library has a shelf of Shakespeare plays with some commentaries, but a very poor selection of Shakespeare on audio cassette or video. I guess we can assume it is the result of America falling into a kind of new dark ages.

Then, for grades one through eight—experience one play a year without notes or academic comments. Start with a one of the lighter plays, like the comedies. I found it interesting that when I recently asked the children which play they would like to study next, the younger ones asked to study again a previously experienced play. Their favorites so far are *Twelfth Night* and *Henry the Fifth*.

Next, listen to professional actors read the text of a play on cassette tape in the original language. At least one act a day or per lesson is recommended. This will probably take no more than a week of casual listening. My children have been caught choosing a Shakespeare cassette on cloudy winter afternoons from a pile of other cassettes so that they can listen to a play while they draw at the dining room table. The variety of voices and musical interludes stimulate their imaginations. A play on cassette can be heard again and again, any time

of the year. This is an advantage teachers did not have in Charlotte's day.

In high school, study two plays a year (more than are needed to meet high school requirements). Follow the sequence of activities above. Now is the time to be better acquainted with Shakespeare's histories and tragedies. A mature student will be able to recognize the consequences of the evil intentions of the villains, and place the historical characters on a timeline. Add to this the child's reading of the play in Shakespeare's original language. I've chosen The New Folger Library editions in paperback. Whenever the meaning of a word in the text is not readily accessible in a good dictionary, its meaning is noted on the left-hand pages. Also, if the word has acquired a very different meaning today than it had in Elizabethan English, a synonym is provided in the notes. The notes are there if you want them, but can be easily ignored.

Why Shakespeare?

I think Charlotte Mason had a high regard for Shakespeare because his plays can be understood by anyone whose eyes are focused on living the Christian life, anyone who recognizes his own propensity to sin and need for forgiveness. As the Bible tells us all we need to know about God, Shakespeare tells us some things we ought to know about man. Shakespeare's plays are performed everywhere in the English-speaking world. A fellow actor and friend wrote of him, "He was not of an age but for all time." Shakespeare observed man as he is, and from a moral perspective. His were not success stories but rather stories that displayed human weakness. He makes us hate sin but pity the sinner. His characters were the victims of their own choices:

"The fault, dear Brutus, is not in our stars, but in ourselves."

—Julius Caesar, Act I, Scene 2

How Can Children Be Expected to Understand it?

Like life itself, we don't understand Shakespeare's plays fully at first glance or upon first experience. That's OK. His characters have a way of growing on our understanding. And as we mature in life, we in turn learn more about life through Shakespeare. We are entertained, as he wishes us to be, but all the while we cannot be unaffected by his wisdom. We go back to his plays again and again because, as Charlotte said, "when we have read the best books once, we have only breakfasted."

When we introduce children to Shakespeare, we will be letting their curiosity do the teaching. By their attentiveness to each scene of the drama, they will be on their way to forming a relationship with Shakespeare. For those of us who follow Charlotte's principles of education—principles that have lasting value to our children's lives—this is our aim.

Our Second Play

Sophia was still in the lower grades when I read her *Twelfth Night* from Lambs' *Tales of Shakespeare*. I came across an advertisement for its performance that very month. How strange it was for me to spot it, as I rarely ever read the newspaper—bedtime stories being my top priority. I was excited to have the opportunity to see, for the first time in my life, the performance of a Shakespeare play, and thus I managed enough courage to drive into the city myself while Dad stayed home with the younger ones. You see, although I had a driver's license, I was out of practice. In those days, as I might have already mentioned, we shared one car in the family, which Dad needed to take to work. So it was, on that special Sunday afternoon after church, that we set off—Sophia in a gingham check dress hand sewn by Grandmother, and I in . . . I can't remember. We sat on the bleachers and observed a gathering of spectators slowly filing in—a large party of senior cit-

izens. How much of the comedy Sophia understood, that lazy afternoon, I don't know, but her giggles could be heard above the small chorus of some snoring senior citizens around us.

With Shakespeare We Must Be Discerning

Shakespeare's attitude toward the moral law shows us he was influenced by Christianity. He knew the Bible well, because we can trace hundreds of Shakespeare's passages back to biblical passages and thought. Behind many a passage, such as that on the characteristic of mercy, we can detect the passing of

> those blessed feet,
> Which fourteen hundred years ago were
> nail'd for our advantage to the bitter cross.
>
> —Henry IV

Beware: Shakespeare didn't point the moral. Instead, he painted it. We do not find good guys dressed in white and bad guys dressed in black as we do in American westerns. His characters—as in real life—are often a mix of virtue and sinfulness. Evil-doing changes personalities, just as repentance does. We watch for personality flaws and weaknesses as well as strengths. For example, in the comedies little deceptions are practiced by some good guys. It is an excellent exercise for any student to dig out the moral for himself, along with only a few needed questions from a mother or father, and therein lies the challenge. It is part of one delightful, secret plan to train our children to become discerning.

Not a Dead Classic

Can a person who has no knowledge of Shakespeare be considered well-educated? I'll let you decide after you become familiar with his plays. All in all, his plays provide the homeschool teacher and student alike with thoughtful entertainment, a look at human nature, the beauty of the English language, animated scenes from history, and even a good laugh.

High School Shakespeare

At the time of this writing, my first student is in her first year of high school. During the summer I was asked to lead a group of home educated high school students in an appreciation of Shakespeare's *Julius Caesar*. In return, one mother would give thirty hours of biology lab to the older students (a surprising answer to a prayer of mine) and another mother would do some activities around the book *The Bronze Bow* for our younger students. Sophia has been happy to have this opportunity to meet with other students her age for discussion and dialogue. Not ever having taught a "class" on Shakespeare before, and being unfamiliar with the play, I was somewhat apprehensive at first mention of this co-op plan, yet still interested. When I did agree, I explained to the other two mothers that I am not a scholar, but I am fond of Shakespeare, and that Shakespeare would have to do most of the teaching. With very little commentary, some background information and discussion questions from the book, *Brightest Heaven of Invention* by Peter J. Liethart (I like the author's Christian viewpoint), the students and I have been experiencing *Julius Caesar* together. And it has been a very enjoyable experience. I am so glad I accepted the challenge.

I familiarized myself with the play by reading the chapter on Caesar in Plutarch's *Lives* and by reading, viewing, and listening to all the material I expected the children to study. Before our first meeting together each student read a story version of the play at home. Lambs' *Tales* does not include

Julius Caesar, but I had another old book that included a story of the play and shared it with the other mothers. Each student received a paperback (original language) edition of the play and a set of audio cassettes. I assigned parts. The homework I gave was simple: Listen to one act a week on cassette and read one act a week to prepare for the reading (performing) of the act in class. A video film version of the play was circulated amongst the group. Before the play was read aloud entirely, the children thought about what "speech" they would like to memorize. They also practiced their memorized lines in class. We are nearing the end of the ten-week course, and at our next meeting we will read through the entire play—speaking certain lines from memory. Our families will soon be enjoying a dinner together where their memorized speeches (excerpts from *Julius Caesar)* will be given. Maybe some year I'll be up to directing a full production, but the speeches were a fun place to start.

Overall, my goal for each student was to sympathize with and be intrigued by the characters, attend to the voice inflections of emotion, sense the cadence of the words, and desire to perform in a Shakespeare play in future. Being so near the end of the course I think I can safely say (and very happily so) that this vibrant bunch of students has reached my objectives. "Well done, class! Bravo!"

Your Own Personal Reflections

Chapter Thirty-One

Charles Dickens From a Mother's Point of View

CHARLOTTE MASON lived during an age when people were avidly reading the novels of Charles Dickens. Their lifespans overlapped and it is likely that Charlotte attended a lecture room where Dickens read portions of his writing. These two Victorians in particular had something special in common. They both loved children and children loved them. Dickens, speaking through a character in his novel *The Old Curiosity Shop,* tells us: "I love these little people and it is not a slight thing when they who are fresh from God love us."

Both Charlotte and Dickens set out in their different ways to relieve the plight of children. Charlotte quietly changed the way people viewed and treated children. She began her appeal to fellow Christians whose hearts and minds were ready for reform in education. Dickens spoke out loudly through the characters of his novels. Both helped reshape society.

Charlotte Mason and Charles Dickens both came from poor families that bought books with their spare change. "Wear the old coat; buy the good book," must have been the old proverb their parents lived by. They were children who had a close and adoring relationship with books, even if those were few. There were few gifts given in Charlotte's family, but her eighth birthday brought her the gift of *Robinson Crusoe.* She was educated at home with a narrow assortment of school books, about which she comments, "I do not know that [they] did much for me beyond proving that Aesop's *Fables* were entirely congenial to a child's mind, a crumb of experience which I have since found useful."[1]

Little Charles Dickens was too small and weak to keep up with the outdoor games the other boys of his own age enjoyed. Most of his time was spent indoors reading in a very small room that nobody else cared to occupy. He would pretend to be the characters of the books he read, and fancied himself an actor. He went away to boarding school for a time, and at the age of nine he and his family moved to London. He was one of six children at this time and the family was too poor to pay for Charles to attend school any longer. He made himself useful around the house—polishing boots, and doing other such chores—and comforted himself with his books and make-believe. The poor family became poorer still, until Dickens' father was in debt. Bit by bit everything in the house had be sold. One by one his precious books were taken away from him.

Then the most miserable of things happened: his father was put in debtor's prison and Charles, still scrawny, was sent to work in a factory laboring for long hours for very little pay. His clothes were shabby, his stomach only half fed. He felt degraded and ashamed. All the week he worked, but on Sunday he visited his father in prison. It is not known how long this miserable situation lasted, but after his father was let out of prison, Dickens was able to attend school for a time. His spirit was renewed and he was able to put his misery behind him. He admits to learning very little in school. Yet because a love of reading was kindled in him as a young child, he set out to become self-educated. He visited the British Museum reading room and studied.[2]

Both Charlotte Mason and Dickens were mostly self-educated. Determination, patience, a lack of self-pity, and a concern for righteousness were chiseled into their characters. Dickens began his writing career as a reporter; Charlotte began her career in education as a governess. They started out affecting a few, but it wasn't long at all before they went on to influence many. Those who chose to read a Dickens novel were not unaffected by his opinion of Victorian British society and the sly lessons his stories unobtrusively teach. Charlotte Mason is far less popular a name than Charles Dickens, but through her ideas she is still affecting lives today. While Dickens had a part to play in England's social reforms by appealing to the heart of mankind through his stories, members of Charlotte's PNEU were doing their part to reform England's educational system.

Why Read Dickens?

In his own time, Dickens became famous—writing stories that highlighted the difference between right and wrong. His stories invite us to form an opinion and make decisions about a character's right or wrong actions. This practice enables us to more naturally make moral judgments in our own daily lives. As only an artist can, Dickens paints a moral picture of life.

When we read episodes from Dickens's stories aloud to the children, we get to know his characters more intimately than our own neighbors. We experience life along with his characters. We feel for them as they struggle in difficult situations.

To have sympathy for another human being, even one found in the pages of a realistic novel, is a virtue. We are happy when a child of ours identifies with a story character. Our eldest may say something like, "Mom, you tell the truth like Betsey Trotwood does," or "Nigel is as silly as Mr. Dick!"

"But he has the good common sense Mr. Dick has, too, doesn't he?" asks Mother.

When characters of whatever disposition are painted well, children can be caught acting them out. At our house we witnessed what seemed to be "The Further Adventures of Tiny Tim"—except with all the limping figures balancing on hand-made crutches, maybe it should have been called "Will The Real Tiny Tim Stand Up, Please?"

Terry Glaspey, in his *Great Books of the Christian Tradition* says of Dickens:

> Dickens could sometimes be faulted for being overlong and sentimental, but his novels seem to lodge in the memory long after they are read. His ability to create a multitude of memorable characters gave us the adjective "Dickensian." His staunch Victorian morality is a pleasant contrast to our modern sense of moral drift.[3]

And what wonderful characters they are! His heroes are people of everyday life who supply our children with a vision of goodness. When we read about Dickens' characters, we can imprint their beautiful kind acts upon our imagination and their goodness upon our hearts.

There was a time when Dickens was more widely read, when his wonderful characters would come up in lively conversation, spoken of as if they were people everybody knew. By contrast, in today's less cultured society, we often overhear idle gossip that focuses attention on idolatrous and adulterous "real people" from popular tabloids. How much more valuable and edifying it would be if we could still hear people talk about Dickens' "real people"!

Dickens Loved Children

Home educators may be interested to learn that Dickens took special interest in exposing the faults of the often tyrannical and regimented schools of his day. Some of Dickens' darkest villains are cruel schoolmasters. An old *Parents' Review* article said, "It may be that little Charlie Dickens, as a schoolboy, suffered many things at the hands of his teachers; if so, he certainly had the satisfaction, in after life, of what schoolboys called, 'getting his own back.'" Certain teachers today can still learn what not to do by reading Dickens!

Dickens loved children. He had ten of his own. And to sin against children was a thing Dickens could not forgive. It has been said that Dickens' description of the plight of the poor children of England was over-

drawn in Paul Dombey and Oliver Twist, but he speaks from experience. The work-house he was forced to work in is described as the establishment of Murdstone & Grinby in *David Copperfield*. Actually *David Copperfield* is nothing less than a pathetic and intensely human autobiography of Dickens himself, with certain fictitious additions. David Copperfield *is* Charles Dickens—notice the reversed initials. But aside from that, Dickens was a newspaper reporter of the debates in Parliament. And if you read the facts history has brought to light about children spending twelve to fifteen hours a day in coal mines, and the working conditions children endured in factories, you can't help feeling that the facts of history are more horrible than the pictures of it that Dickens gives us in his fiction.

Another reason for bringing Dickens into the homeschool is that his characters had a strong regard for home, as demonstrated by the following excerpts:

There's romance enough at home, without going half-a-mile for it; only people never think of it.

—Pickwick Papers

It is right to begin with the obligations of home, and, while these are overlooked and neglected, no other duties can possibly be substituted for them.

—Bleak House.

Big Words? Big Deal!

"But what about all his big words and long sentences?" you might ask. Anyone who reads Dickens should not be overly concerned with his big words. Sooner or later the word will pop up again. Each time you will understand it better. And about those long sentences: many of the best books ever written have long sentences. Why not dip into these great books—beginning with

Dickens? As reading his long sentences aloud may leave you out of breath, just inhale more deeply at commas! Then you can amaze yourself with your new ability to read aloud in true nineteenth century fashion.

You only need to start by reading aloud a single episode, not a whole chapter. A ten-year-old who is in the habit of narrating will find plenty to "tell back" in his own words. Remember, a child need not comprehend every jot and tittle. He will pick out and narrate the morsels of literary language that appeal to him.

Who was it that dictated the law that a child, or grown-up, must comprehend everything he reads? The best books deserve a second or even third reading. "When I pick up an old book I have read before," said a wise man, "I know what to expect; and the satisfaction is not lessened by being anticipated. I shake hands with and look the old tried and valued friend in the face, compare notes, and chat the hour away."

"It is not what people eat, but what they digest, that makes them strong. It is not what they gain, but what they save, that makes them rich. It is not what they read, but what they remember, that makes them learned," said H.W. Beecher. My eldest child, Sophia, at fifteen is just entering into her high school years. She recently picked up *Great Expectations* and read it in less than a week. I know I am speaking in a cliché but it's really true that she "couldn't put it down."

"Was it the best book you ever read?" I asked.

"How did you know?" she responded, face all aglow.

"Well, I heard the best book you ever read is the one you just finished, and you said that Jane Austen's *Pride and Prejudice* was the best when you read that a few months ago."

I am holding Sophia accountable for her reading, and she will receive high school credit for it. She is therefore doing a

book report—of sorts—on the book. She thinks up her own questions and answers them, makes a statement, and narrates the part that supports it. For her, it seems that this writing takes longer than the reading. But it is an important part of reading a good book.

How To Get Started with Dickens

An easy, popular, and readily available story to begin with is *A Christmas Carol.* Every library in the country should have a copy. The average ten-year-old should not have too difficult a time reading *A Christmas Carol.* Years ago, when I finished reading aloud the first chapter to ten-year-old Sophia—with its detailed description of Scrooge—she was drawn into the story enough to continue reading silently on her own. The same plan worked well with Yolanda when she turned age ten. (Note: Dickens trusts we have sense enough to understand that Scrooge's "ghosts" are his conscience and memories, girded with the Ten Commandments and threatening him with the imminent judgment of his sins.)

Although Dickens' stories are often long ones, (his publisher paid by the word)

don't be satisfied with reading the simplified watered-down editions—or worse, only seeing the motion-picture version. But I don't think it is a bad thing to read little stories taken from Dickens' larger works. This can be a good way to introduce the names of characters and become familiar with the main plots (he has several interwoven ones) of the story.

We strongly recommend Dickens to any homeschooling family. As the English say, his books tell "a ripping good yarn" to entertain us. Have more than a nodding acquaintance with this author. You will pick up his enthusiasm for life and hope for mankind.

A Warning

In story after story, Dickens's characters seek to either drown their cares or enhance their joy with alcohol. The "merry punchbowl" is present on many occasions. But Dickens doesn't mean to focus our attention on the drinks, but the predicament of the characters. And because of the overwhelming reasons we have for loving him, we can overlook this offense. ⇥

Questions for Personal Reflection or Support Group Discussion

1. *What did Charlotte Mason and Charles Dickens have in common? Give several examples.*

2. *How do Dickens's novels raise the conscience and develop the moral imagination?*

3. *How do his everyday heroes and villains correlate with true-to-life characters we will meet up with in present society?*

4. *Will we increase our moral will power, expand our vocabulary, and broaden our cultural literacy by reading Dickens? Explain.*

5. *Dickens's stories display an historically accurate picture of his times. Upon reading his stories have you a better insight into the need for the educational reforms for which Charlotte worked so hard? Give examples of specific reforms.*

Your Own Personal Reflections

It is right to begin with the obligations of home, and, while these are overlooked and neglected, no other duties can possibly be substituted for them.

Bleak House

Chapter Thirty-Two

History

ALL THROUGH THE EARLY YEARS of childhood, when parents follow Charlotte Mason's recommendation for stories and play for their children, a wonderful thing occurs. The children develop an imagination. It is well that we encourage children to develop their powers to imagine. Any child who spends the early years of his education with wonderful stories and bountiful play builds up fibrous brain tissue that children without these opportunities do not.

The ability to imagine is an amusement and a delight in one's childhood and remains a pleasure in adulthood. But it is also an important and necessary brain booster. The power to imagine is foundational to other thinking. Who would want his appendix removed by a doctor who couldn't imagine exactly what or where it was under the skin? Ridiculous example, I know.

"I can't imagine how she could feel that way," said one who lacked sympathy. This

one was not a true friend, because she lacked imagination: to sympathize is to imagine. Stories help us visualize morals. In them we learn what virtue looks like. Stories supply children with what Charlotte called the "moral imagination." Each time a child plays make-believe, he is stretching his imagination powers farther and farther.

Said the older child of six years to the younger by two years, "You be the lion caught in the net and I'll be the mouse who nibbles you out." He looked straight into the wide eyes of the younger: "OK? Are you ready?"

"Are you ready?" means a lot. It means: "Can you imagine yourself in the part, do you remember the sequence of events, can you feel as the character feels, can you remember the kinds of things the character

spoke?" If so, then the Aesop fable is ready to be played out. If the younger hesitates, does or says something "out of character," the older, who has been working on his powers of imagination a little longer, quickly corrects the less experienced member of the family.

This is why Charlotte Mason strongly believed in focusing on the story part of history while children are developing their powers of imagination. Myths and legends have a place, too. This appeal to the imagination in history gives emphasis to its literary side. According to Charlotte, no history should be read to young children unless it is in literary language. She dwelled on the pleasure derived from a study of former ages—the culture and refinement it affords, the enjoyment and mental profit that is gained through narrating it.

History should also provide lessons in the practical affairs of men—their philosophies, their politics, and all those sorts of things—but with regard to children, it is more important to secure interest, to train the imagination and reasoning powers. Imagination comes first. With age and experience—when social and political problems begin to occupy the mind—the more serious side of historical studies can be explored. What we can do now, by asking one or two narration questions, is encourage the younger student to draw out the moral in what he has read. As he narrates, the child is learning to notice some of the consequences of actions and their bearing upon their time as well as life today. Much of the politics and philosophies will be examined later, but young children can still learn to see the connections between events, and to trace the causes. Narration questions help to do this. Indeed, when a literary history is used, it makes a fine subject for Charlotte's method of narration.

Biography

Reading biographies is one of the most pleasing and useful ways to learn history. The life of a statesman is a history of the great events of a period; it is usually partisan in perspective, but it delineates the march of events with all the literary details that make a good story. And this is what Charlotte wished. She wrote in *Home Education* that it is a fatal mistake to think children must learn "outlines" or overviews of the whole of the history of Rome or England. Isn't this what many history books

do by including so many names, and dates, and events with little to no story aspect in between? Instead, Charlotte asserted,

> Let [the child] on the contrary, linger pleasantly over the history of a single man, a short period, until he thinks the thoughts of the man, is at home in the ways of that period. Though he is reading and thinking of the lifetime of a single man, he is really getting intimately acquainted with the history of a whole nation of a whole age. . . Let him know the great people and the common people, the ways of the court and of the crowd. Let him know what other nations were doing while we at home were doing thus and thus.

First published in 1941, Genevieve Foster's books are unique in providing this wider scope that Charlotte talks about. They are not as overtly Christian as some of us would like them to be, but her books do what textbooks do not: they tell a good story. Foster's books are biographical in nature, weaving the lives of diverse charac-

ters from around the world in and out of the time line of one specific age. Both *Augustus Caesar's World* and *George Washington's World* have been republished by Beautiful Feet Books.

In biographies we read of the great makers of history. Their lives afford perhaps the most instructive means of teaching young children both that the events of history and the lessons that men and women have power for good or evil, and that their actions live after them. Biographies provide examples for imitation as well as for warning. The deeds of heroes give us the opportunity to admire and form higher ideals. Biblical history abounds in such striking examples of good and evil, and they are the stock of material of many sermons. Similarly, the character sketches of a biography can be the pegs on which to hang the whole story of an age.

Like myself, many mothers are attracted to older history books—like those hundreds of out-of-print Landmark Books or the Ingri and Edgar d'Aulaire books, which were all written before we were born.

These books are not lacking in what Charlotte called the "dignity of history;" because, as she said,

> they purl along pleasantly as a forest brook, tell you "all about it," stir your heart with the story of a great event, amuse you with pageants and shows, make you intimate with the great people, and friendly with the lowly. They are just the right thing for the children whose eager souls want to get at the living people behind the words of the history book, caring nothing at all about progress, or statutes, or about anything but the persons, for whose action history is, to the child's mind, no more than a convenient stage. A child who has been carried through a single old chronicler in this way has a better foundation for an historical training than if he knew all the dates and names and facts that ever were crammed for examination.

Children Read and Play What They Read

When this kind of history is fed to children, they will be inspired to play at their history. In our house, which is sixty years old, there is a secret attic room off the master bedroom. It can be entered only through a munchkin-sized door, but when inside, an adult can stand up and look out the window (which has its own little dusty curtain). I have an old rolled-up carpet and some boxes of maternity clothes and Christmas gifts safely hidden there. Normally the room would be too hot to endure, but this very morning my girls asked if they could play in there since cool rain has brought a break in the summer heat. First they painted red marks on their arms to become Jews in hiding. Then they brought up tea things and chatted away. The stories *The Hiding Place* and *Twenty and Ten* must have had an influence on

them. My girls aren't *little* girls anymore, but they still like to act things out. Again and again I find Charlotte to be right.

She wrote that children

> will dress up, act scenes; or they have a stage and their dolls or puppets act, while they paint the background scenery and speak the speeches. It is a mistake to think that a child will have much of an imagination just because he is a child. An imagination must be fed for it to grow, develop and become a strong, useful part of his intellect . Twaddly stories will not do. Let a child have the meat he requires in his history readings, and in the literature which naturally gathers round this history, and imagination will bestir itself without any help of ours; the child will live out in detail a thousand scenes of which he only gets the merest hint.

Therefore, do not be afraid of a book because it is four hundred pages and looks too thick to ever get through. Some of the thickest books you and your child will ever read will be history books. If it is a good book, you could plan to read it over a period of time, allowing yourself several months—or even years. It could very well be that its thickness is the result of its dramatic intent or that it is copiously illustrated. Although Charlotte wished us to avoid outlines, one favorite outline of history, written by V. M. Hillyer and now sold separately by the Calvert School, is good for making connections. *A Child's History of the World,* is an introduction to history, but it is an anecdotal one, in which names and dates are introduced only sparsely. Hillyer says in his introduction that "it is necessary that the child do his part and put his own brain to work; and for this purpose he *should be required to retell each story after he has read it . . .*"[1] I find it very interesting that Charlotte's use of narration is intended to be such an integral part of learning his-

tory from his book. Both Hillyer and Charlotte Mason lived during the reign of Queen Victoria, although on opposite sides of the Atlantic. Do you think some of Charlotte's ideas might have reached Hillyer's desk?

Historical Fiction

Another kind of book frequents the catalogs of companies serving home educators: historical fiction. But why would home educators provide a wealth of fiction to children when history should teach knowledge of truth? Can fiction, such as the historical novel, be in any sense helpful in portraying truth? Yes, it can, when it is carefully selected and the children are guided.

After the age for fairy tales comes that for romance and adventure, and many of the best of these have been set in a particular historical period. Well-selected stories feed the imagination with what it craves.

The student reads them, not primarily as history, but as adventure. In the older student, there is little, if any, confusion about what is true and what is fiction. He is receiving historical impressions though the conversations, and minor episodes are all treated as fictitious.

There may be times, however, when a gentle reminder is necessary. Last year one of my children, who wishes here to be unnamed, was immersed in Sir Arthur Conan Doyle's *Adventures of Sherlock Holmes*. At the supper table one evening, with a gleam in her eye, she spoke of Mr.

Holmes' cleverness, bravery, and complete thoroughness at his task. "It's too bad such a man never existed," I jokingly reminded her with a smile and one raised eyebrow. She paused from eating, and with her fork swirled some mashed potato around her plate, then agreed. I was sorry to burst her bubble, but mothers are often called to do unpleasant tasks.

You've probably heard of the name of the Scottish writer Sir Walter Scott, though his novels today are rarely read by Americans. His most famous is *Ivanhoe*. There is an old movie based on this book. Scott was the first historical fiction writer. His novels were best sellers in Scotland and England—and in our country as well, especially in the Southern states. It wasn't long before other writers began fulfilling the public's desire for more stories of this type. It has been said, "How much do we all owe to Scott for his graphic illustrations of periods of chivalry and romance, with their pageantry and their squalor. If we ask what is left to us of the novels we once read with interest long ago, we shall find it is the characters and the pictorial vision of a period we never realized more fully than when we read his fascinating romances."[2] Scott's novels demonstrate the value of historical fiction for the understanding of history. In this country James Fenimore Cooper's works are examples of American historical fiction. The following list is a random selection of our family's collection of historical fiction:

- *Thee, Hannah* and *The Door in the Wall* by Marguerite De Angeli
- *The Buffalo Knife* and *The Perilous Road* by William O. Steele
- *My Name is Not Angelica* by Scott O'Dell
- *Caddie Woodlawn* and *Magical Melons* by Carol Ryrie Brink

- *Justin Morgan Had a Horse* by Marguerite Henry
- *Amos Fortune, Free Man* by Elizabeth Yates
- *Bartholomew Fair* by Mary Stolz
- *The Hawk and the Dove* by Penelope Wilcock
- *Otto of the Silver Hand* by Howard Pyle
- *Bold Journey; West with Lewis and Clark* by Charles Bohner
- *On To Oregon* by Honore Morrow
- *I Am Regina* by Sally M. Keehn
- *Snow Treasure* by Marie McSwigan
- *The Bronze Bow* by Elizabeth George Speare
- *Lorna Doone (edited)* by Richard Doddridge Blackmore
- *The Robe (unedited)* by Lloyd C. Douglas

Through these kinds of books a child gains knowledge of a time period in a way that makes the parade of historical facts more palatable. He establishes a relation with a time period and when he has finished a book, a historic sense of the time period remains. Historical fiction often serves as a spur to discovering more factual information about a time period.

It goes without saying that an accurate knowledge of history cannot be acquired exclusively by reading historical fiction. Such fiction can, however, be welcomed as a valued partner in the study of history. And I do agree with the assertion that it would be better for a person to know only the Julius Caesar, Richard III, Henry V, or Anthony and Cleopatra of Shakespeare's plays than know nothing at all of such persons.[2] ⟶

Questions for Personal Reflection
or Support Group Discussion

1. What does a child develop when he has stories read to him and he is given time and space to play? Why is practice in using the imagination called a brain booster? How is it foundational to other thinking?

2. Explain the term "moral imagination."

3. What does history in literary language provide the student?

4. How does Charlotte's use of narration draw out events in history?

5. A biography allows us to linger through history. Explain.

6. How does the Bible use biography?

7. Why do certain history books inspire children to play at their history, while others do not?

8. Can fiction, such as the historical novel, be in any sense helpful in portraying truth?

9. Would reading historical fiction alone give children an accurate knowledge of history?

10. Do you agree with the assertion that it would be better that a person should know only the Anthony and Cleopatra of Shakespeare's plays than to know nothing at all of such persons?

If we give our children regular opportunities to get in touch with God's creation, a habit is formed which will be a source of delight throughout their lives.

Chapter Thirty-Three

·····································

Nature Study

IF WE GIVE OUR CHILDREN regular opportunities to get in touch with God's creation, a habit is formed that will be a source of delight throughout their lives. Many people know little of the natural world because they never take time to observe it. Once our senses are on the alert, though, nature yields treasure after treasure. Children take especial joy in their little discoveries.

"Mom, look, I picked some flowers for you!" What mother could resist a generous nosegay of dandelions from her loving three-year-old? The dandelions are not new, but the children are, as they are seeing things for the first time.

A sneaky homeschool mom will take advantage of her children's "finds" by occasionally turning them into a lesson of sorts. To do this, you need a Nature Notebook. Any blank book will do. If your children are very young, you may wish to let them draw on loose paper. If they are happy with their drawing it can then be put into a binder. If they think it miserable they can crumble it up and start again.

Working alongside your children and filling out your own Notebook will provide your children with an inspiring example. Allow them to tell about their "finds." Then see how well you, and they, can draw a picture that resembles the real thing. When the drawing is complete, encourage the children to record their descriptions or "tellings" on the opposite page of the Notebook.

During the busy drawing time, I usually keep *The Handbook of Nature Study* and a field guide open on my lap under the table. I glance down at information and put it into my own words, casually sharing with the children as if I were an uncommonly knowledgeable mother!

Setting aside regular time for Nature Study is helpful. On these Nature Study afternoons, my children welcome what seems to be "free time" in between more bookish learning.

But special Nature Study lessons aren't always necessary. As you know, young children will discover toads, butterflies, beetles, earthworms, robins, thistles, squirrels, mushrooms, berries, and run into thorn bushes on their own, without any prodding from us. In summer, the screen door bangs shut as they enter the kitchen—bright red scratches and bee stings on their arms and legs, clothes covered with grass stains and stick-tight seeds—to show you their treasures.

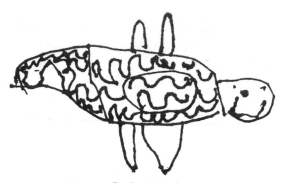

Dragonfly by Nigel, Age 4

Dragonfly by Nigel, Age 8

I can remember—when we lived in the hot South—chasing a blue-tailed western skink around our living room floor with a battered butterfly net. The children had such fun, laughing in the excitement of it all, but I wasn't laughing. To my great relief, this foot-long lizard was finally contained in a mop bucket and then drawn in our Nature Notebooks. It proved to be a colorful and impressive entry.

Keeping a Nature Notebook —A Welcome Pastime

Every student of Charlotte's was encouraged to keep a Nature Notebook or Nature Diary. Nature Notebooks were assiduously inscribed with fine prose and illustrated in delicate watercolors. This was a dramatic part of their education. Following Charlotte's example, I started a Nature Diary myself, and have led my children into doing the same.

According to Charlotte's recommendations, all illustrations should include captions: the Latin name of the specimen, if it's available, as well as its familiar name. A flower and bird list can be kept at the back of the Notebook, as well as other lists which may interest the individual child— fungi, insects, fossils, trees, sea weeds, etc. These lists are best kept in neat columns, with the name and date of the find all on one line. It's a pity to limit Nature Notebooks to any one subject, whether all flowers or all birds or all insects. There is simply too much to learn about and draw to confine oneself to such limits.

Although keeping a Notebook will be a school assignment, we can consider it part of living the educational life. Both mother and children can have a relationship with nature where a spirit of joy and praise are present as all admire God's work in creation. Try to avoid criticism, unless it is to give helpful suggestions. These Notebooks, as nineteenth century naturalist Anna Botsford Comstock said, "of whatever quality, are precious beyond price to their owners. And why not? For they represent what can

Flamingo by Yolanda, Age 11

not be bought or sold—personal experience in the happy world of out-of-doors."[1]

Being Outdoors

I was quite glad to discover how important nature study was in Charlotte's curriculum because I like to be outdoors with my children. I think Charlotte was very clever to encourage a child's further study into the things he naturally "takes to." Most children want to learn more about the world around them. The best way to do this is to give them opportunities for direct contact with nature where they live.

During most of our homeschooling years, and especially when my children were very young, I was home with them all day. My husband took the family car to work, so we were restricted to those activities that didn't require transportation. We rarely went anywhere—to shops, or to visit friends—except on weekends. But I think raising young children is much easier this way. Rather than staying indoors staring out of the windows, we spent as much time as we could outdoors. This diversion offered us refreshment for our mental health as much as for our physical well-being. Even though—through our many moves—we often ended up renting in the suburbs, there always seemed to be something in the outdoors to lure our interest. What my children could not learn from books, they learned from being outdoors. As Charlotte said,

There is no kind of knowledge to be had in these early years so valuable to children as that which they get for themselves, of the world they live in," said Charlotte. "Let them at once get into touch with nature, and a habit is formed with will be a source of delight through life. We are all meant to be naturalists, each to his own degree, and it is inexcusable to live in a world to full of marvels of plant and animal life and to care for none of these things.

In *Home Education,* Charlotte uses the childhood of John James Audubon, the famous American ornithologist, as an example of one who was lured by his parents to appreciate the nuances of nature at a very young age. He said,

When I had hardly learned to walk, and to articulate those first words always so endearing to parents, the productions of nature that lay spread all around were constantly pointed out to me. . . My father generally accompanied my steps, procured bird and flowers for me, and pointed out the elegant movements of the former, the beauty and softness of their plumage, the manifestations of their pleasure, or their sense of danger, and the always perfect forms and splendid attire of the latter. He would speak of the departure and return of the birds with the season, describe their haunts, and, more wonderful than all, their change of livery, thus exciting me to study them, and to raise my mind toward their Creator.

Mr. Audubon went on to make it his life's work to discover and record, by drawing, every bird in America.

The natural world is one way that God reveals himself to us. It is called natural or general revelation by the theologians. And this is why, as Mr. Downton, one of Charlotte's followers, has said: "Nature study should be approached

*Robin Redbreast
by Nigel, Age 6*

with reverence. For the natural world is the expression of God's personality in a form that is within reach of all of us to comprehend in some measure"[2]

God does not explain himself to us, He *reveals* Himself. In Job chapters 38 and 39, God points to nature for Job's understanding of Himself. Psalm 19 is a good outline of his revelation. The first verses speak of how he reveals Himself through nature (general revelation). The middle of the psalm speaks of His special revelation, because nature is not adequate for us to know God. We need further revelation. We need the Bible. To the psalmist, God's Word is more precious than gold, sweeter than honey. The last verses of the psalm are for our personal application. The psalmist's response may be familiar to you. It is one many choose to memorize:

> Let the words of my mouth, and the meditation of my heart, be acceptable in thy sight, O Lord, my strength, and my redeemer. (KJV)

Chick-a-dee
by Sophia, Age 13

A Sample of One Naturalist's Notebook

In 1990, not long after I had begun to take seriously Charlotte's emphasis on nature study, I found the book *A Country Diary of an Edwardian Lady,* by Edith Holden, on a sale table at a large book store. Upon opening its cover, I immediately recognized it as a perfect example of the Nature Notebook Charlotte required her students to make for themselves. What beautiful watercolor drawings it contained of the wildlife in the author's part of England! Her handwritten entries (in the facsimile edition I held) told of her walks—wherein she wandered a wood or cycled down a country lane to a place where she could sketch or set up her easel and paint. She was a teacher in a girl's day school and pursued nature study during her leisure. It was her mother who, years prior, had inspired her young children to take closer notice of nature and to draw it accurately. As a young lady she attended an art school in Birmingham. That's why her paintings are uncommonly beautiful. A few years ago I purchased a video based on *The Country Diary.* It beautifully captured the nature in her area, and used an actress to play Edith and narrate the notebook. I highly recommend it for those who desire to create nature diaries for themselves.

Nature Poetry

Just as Edith choose certain poems and mottoes to adorn her Nature Diary, Charlotte suggested that children pick poems to adorn their Notebooks, along with their pictures and written entries. Nature in verse is quite easy to find, and there are many suggestions in the poetry chapter.

Nature in the Hymns

Once I had begun learning to appreciate nature with my children, certain traditional hymns we sang at church suddenly began to stand out. The old hymn writers gave praise to God for His glorious works.

When I sang a verse about nature, a tear would surprisingly appear in an eye or two, as I was now more appreciative of these praises and felt I was really "joining in." Of course, the swelling of the music contributed to the emotion as well. I am still adding to my list of favorites.

At home I sometimes like to sing a hymn a cappella with the children at the start of our school day. We have learned verses by heart. Verses can be copied into Nature Notebooks. Let children choose the verses special to them. Periodically introduce new hymns. Eventually some phrase will ignite a spark and a child will show signs of wanting to make it his own possession.

"This is My Father's World" is the foreword of my Nature Notebook. "In the Garden" is a favorite of my eldest child. Perhaps you or your students would like to uncover nature in the following hymns or quote nature verses from any others:

> Morning Has Broken
> Like a River Glorious
> For the Beauty of the Earth
> Fairest Lord Jesus
> His Eye Is on the Sparrow
> All Things Bright and Beautiful
> Joyful, Joyful, We Adore Thee
> All Creatures of Our God and King

A Stroll Through a First Nature Notebook

As parents enjoy looking through early photo albums, I enjoy looking through the Nature Notebooks my children kept when they were young. I have one from 1991 on my lap as I type. The first picture drawn is of an Eastern bluebird, followed by a few other birds that were drawn but never colored. Next there is a drawing of our cat on her hind legs reaching for a butterfly. The description of this activity is written in very large letters. There is the poem "Queen Ann's Lace" with a drawing of some flowers in a vase beside it. What memories that drawing brings back!

Queen Anne's Lace

Toward the end of that summer, on a morning when the temperature was below 90 degrees, the children and I took a walk through our manicured subdivision. There was a vacant lot—that had been mysteriously left untouched for some time—where we reached out for wildflowers, trying not to fall forward into the entangling weeds. We gathered goldenrod in its fiery splendor and Queen Anne's lace in full bloom. One daughter picked the dried version of Queen Anne's lace, called "bird's nest," to entertain her little brother in his stroller.

The wildflower bouquet was placed in the center of the kitchen table. The girls began drawing in their Nature Notebooks while I held Anna Botsford Comstock's 600-page *Handbook of Nature Study* open on my lap. As they drew, I peeked down at my book and began casually talking about Queen Anne's lace. "It is told that Queen Anne of England fastened lace to her dress with pins made of precious gems. Do you think this flower looks like lace? Actually this isn't one flower, look closer. Can you guess how many tiny flowers there really are set together? Your brother's flower is dried up. Why do you think it is called bird's nest? What was made after the flowers finished blooming?"

The next morning I found the poem "Queen Anne's Lace." Ah, just what I was looking for. I wrote its three stanzas and posted it. It was copied one stanza a day into the girls' Nature Notebooks. We took turns reading it aloud at every meal. By the end of the week it was memorized effortlessly and the girls enjoyed reciting it to Dad.

Not every nature study lesson that autumn went so smoothly. When one of my children attempted to follow instructions for placing a few drops of sugar water into a container with Mr. Daddy Longlegs, she almost drowned him. But we did get to see him grooming his long legs, nibbling each leg to its hair-like end. I might mention too, that after one weedy nature walk one daughter broke out with poison ivy. We should have been aware of "Leaflet three, let it be."

Turning the Pages

As I continue to turn the pages of young Sophia's notebook, I see a picture of some deer we had touched at a petting zoo. An ant is drawn and has its three body parts labeled. On the adjacent page is the dotted line of a crazy path the ant made as it ventured from a fallen log toward our house. (Every spring brought ants into the kitchen.) As I slip several pages ahead, I come to her autumn entries. There are drawings of different leaves with an explanation about the varying lobes and the scent of the sassafras tree. There are some viney pumpkins and a drawing of a bewildered meadow vole, which I remember was brought to us by the cat. A few pages over, I am seeing snowflakes and a snowman beside a hemlock tree. Then spring arrives with its very first flower—the smallest weed in our grass is drawn. There is also a purple trillium—discovered in the woods—and some lily of the valley from the garden. A large orange oriental lily—with its parts

"Mom, these are the same things I have stuck to my shorts."

"Yes, these are the seeds . . ."

That evening, Dad was met at the front door by two small girls brimming over with suppressed excitement.

"Daddy, we picked flowers today!"

After some sneezes, Dad replied, "I spied that out."

"How did you, Daddy?"

"My nose knows."

labeled—takes up the whole of the next page. Above a crayon drawing of a robin is this poem by Emily Dickinson:

A bird came down the walk:
He did not know I saw;
He bit an angleworm in halves
And ate the fellow raw.
And then he drank the dew
From a convenient grass,
And then hopped sidewise to the wall
To let a beetle pass.

Associations Arrive Unannounced

Some educators make a great effort to correlate all subjects. Charlotte Mason said this is not necessary. When we include a wide curriculum, the so-called "subjects" will often overlap of their own accord. Children will naturally make associations themselves, and these will come unannounced. Here, with nature study, we can see how scientific observation, drawing, writing, poetry, and natural history come together. Knowledge in one "subject" helps us to understand another.

All the information your children are gathering in their nature study lessons, and the habits of observation they are acquiring, will form an excellent foundation for their future scientific education. In the meantime, let your children consider the lilies of the field and the fowls of the air.

Suggestions for Further Reading

I have found many helpful books for nature study in our homeschool. It would be impossible to list them all, but the titles below are ones that we found particularly valuable at different times.

The Handbook of Nature Study was written by Anna Botsford Comstock, a professor at Cornell University. This 600-page guide to teaching nature to children through observation was written at the turn of the century. From a biography of her life we learn that she was first introduced to nature by her parents. Enthusiasm and respect for nature is picked up by the teacher who reads her descriptions and observation suggestions.

Christian Liberty Press has some *Nature Readers* that are reprints of old books. They are an example of the kind of writing Charlotte spoke of—writing that provides information in literary form.

The Country Diary of an Edwardian Lady puts a replica of Edith Holden's private diary into our hands. Her experiences—beautifully handwritten—as well as her beautiful watercolor drawings, are preserved for us in this facsimile.

The Mystery Seed

In my memory is the experience of one particularly hot stressful weekend, which was spent chasing Saturday errands in our family car. It was parking lot after parking lot with the entire family pulled about. We all became cross. By late afternoon one child took on a fever, so Dean did the last errand with the two children while I stayed in the hot car with the docile one. The win-

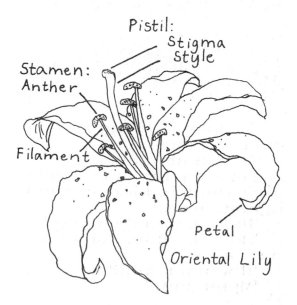

dows were rolled as far down as they would go and we had drinks to sip. Waves of heat rising from the hood of our car distorted my vision through the windshield, and I found myself reduced to searching the dark pockets of my purse for scraps of something—anything—to read. A gentle movement caught my eye, and I looked up. A fluffy dandelion seed had gracefully floated in through the car window. I didn't raise a hand to disturb it, but watched attentively as it sailed along, drifting nonchalantly past me; then out the opposite car window it sailed. It was carried by some rising current of hot air, up and away and out of sight above the traffic. It seemed to defy the pavement, the cars, the cement walls, the heat, and the noise of the city. After a

peaceful sigh, I closed my eyes to thank God for creation and His care. Nature is willing to share its peace with bumble bee watchers and those who stop and smell the roses or, in my case, follow a sailing seed.

Dean and the children returned and we were on our way home. I told the story of the mystery seed as we drove. None of us was cross anymore.

Not a Sparrow Falls

Corrie Ten Boom recalled a time when a skylark was sent by God into the Nazi prison camp to keep her from hating and rationalizing her hate. A cruel guard was in the habit of making the prisoners stand for a long, long time in the freezing early morning air for roll call. One morning, all the prisoners looked up at a skylark and listened to its song. For three weeks the skylark's song came exactly during roll call. It turned Corrie's eyes away from the cruelty of men to the immensity of God's love. The bird's daily visit helped remind her of the words of Psalm 103:11: "For as the heaven is high above the earth, so great is his mercy toward them that fear Him." She thanked God for turning her eyes in the right direction—unto Him.

Questions for Personal Reflection or Support Group Discussion

1. *Would you welcome the opportunity to observe the wonders of nature with your children?*

2. *Nature is not secretive, but she may not be showy either. She reveals her secrets to those who look for them. Is there a reserve or park near your town where you can take a nature hike? What nature do you meet up with when you spend time in the backyard? How can a sneaky mother turn a "find" into a lesson of sorts?*

3. *Nature study lays the groundwork for all the sciences your student will forever after study. And it also points to God. Read Job 38 and 39.*

4. *What verses of an old hymn would be suitable for a Nature Notebook?*

5. *Read Psalm 19. What do we learn about God in this Psalm? In what ways does God reveal Himself to us? What should be our response?*

6. *There are some helpful whole books in the non-fiction section of the library that can explain nature to children. Why is it also important to draw and write about personal experiences with nature?*

Chapter Thirty-Four

Nature for City Children

How does one go for a nature walk in the city?
Here is our story.

WHEN MY GIRLS WERE VERY SMALL, we lived on the busy London Road in Downham, England in a third-floor flat that was over a betting hall (horse races), a news-agent, and a used car dealer. During the day, my husband, Dean, volunteered his bookstore knowledge for a literature mission. Our flat was teeny-tiny, so to get "fresh air" my two little girls and I walked the streets and took buses.

We walked to shops for food, which we called "backpacking for our daily bread." The fish shop was of interest to my little ones because some of the fish were displayed on tables outside its doors along the pavement. Clams in the shell, prawns (shrimp), whole fish, and many other delicacies were at my little ones' eye and nose level. At the nearby greengrocer, they also learned the American and English names of the vegetables and fruits.

We were fortunate to have a football (soccer) field and park with swings two blocks away from our flat. After our shopping was finished, the park was our destination. It was hedged in by the backs of row housing, some with very small back gardens. If you swung high enough on a park swing, you could look over the fences into those green oases. Along the fences grew some wildflowers. But if we really wanted to see flowers, we would take one of the red double-decker buses to Churchill Theatre and Park. Its gardener always had something growing in the midst of the surrounding shops and bustling fast-paced people. Once in a while—when the sun shone—we'd meet Dad there for a picnic lunch. The girls would feed leftover sandwich crumbs to the birds. Mary Poppins' song "Feed the Birds" would come to mind as the pigeons and sparrows gathered round us. Despite popular opinion, city birds do not all look alike. Each pigeon seemed to have its own special effervescent markings. In the cracks of the pavement we would find insects, mostly ants. They seemed to be kept alive by the even smaller left-overs that broke away from the birds' rations. Wasps could be found alighting on the soda-pop bottles in the trash cans. These we watched at a distance.

Below us in the second floor flat lived a friendly neighbor we called Auntie Laura. She was an eighty-year-old widow who had survived the German occupation of the Isle of Jersey during the Second World War. Three of her six children had not, however, and although the story is too sad to be told here, suffice it to say that her loss had made of her not an embittered woman, but a deeply sympathetic and compassionate one. She befriended us, and clucked in sympathy over us—poor little chicks she considered us, so far away from home and friends and family. Many a gloomy, cloudy,

lonely day was made more cheery and warm by her kind sympathy and her home-made apple tarts or little round yellow cakes. She brought a good deal of sunshine into our lives—and many others as well. She loved nature as well as people: attached to the brick wall and out along the iron balcony that fronted her windows were pots of flowers. On Sunday her beau—dressed in a suit and tie—would come to "Sunday meal" bearing gifts from his back garden. One week it was lilacs; another, sweet peas; on others, roses or lilies. Auntie Laura always shared these flowers with us, and it was in this way that the children learned to recognize the different garden flowers and call them by name. These beautiful, living gems of nature never went unappreciated, and we still think of them as God's gifts to us during our city days. They were even more precious to us because they came to us from the loving hands of one of God's devoted servants.

In *Home Education* Charlotte Mason tells us what town children can do for outdoor life:

Town children may get a great deal of pleasure in watching the ways of sparrows—knowing little birds easily tamed by a dole of crumbs. Their days out will bring them in the way of new acquaintances. Much may be done with sparrows. A friend writes: "Have you seen the man in the gardens of the Tuileries feeding and talking to dozens of them? They sit on his hat, his hands, and feed from his fingers. When he raises his arms they all flutter up and then settle again on him and round him. I have watched him call a sparrow from a distance by name and refuse food to all others till petit chou, a tiny pied sparrow, came for his destined bite . . . Truly a St. Francis of the birds!

City children can have windowsill gardens. They will enjoy growing carrot tops, keeping their very own geraniums clipped and watered, starting dwarf marigolds from seed, and learning to recognize herbs by their scent while blind-folded.

Children living in a major city may have the advantage of living near a natural history museum that displays stuffed creatures, eggs, shells, fossils and rocks of various kinds. Planetarium shows are a treat that no one ever forgets, which brings me to the next point. In between the tall buildings of the big city, the sky—with its changing colors at dawn and dusk—is open to children. A night visit to a flat rooftop above the street lights will reveal the moon, stars, and the bright planet Venus, however faintly.

To fill in the gaps city children may have when it comes to nature observation, I recommend the Eyewitness books by Random House Publishers. The photographs are clear and vivid. Many of the short paragraphs are full of surprising facts. Most libraries should have these books. But for reading about—or telling the children about—nature, you know how I like *The Handbook of*

Nature Study. Also, Earnest Seton Thompson's animal observations in the form of stories are delightful. Sterling North is another American naturalist and writer. *Rascal,* his story about a boy and a raccoon, is currently in print, but we preferred one of his other books, entitled *Hurry Spring*—sadly, now out-of-print—which introduced us to a wide range of nature. We discovered *Hurry Spring* in a library, in the non-fiction section—a good place to find living books, if you are willing to hunt a little. During our first years of home education we used a book called *The Moon, Fact and Fancy* for one semester of science. Legends and superstitions once believed about the moon were interspersed with chapters that gave true explanations of the characteristics of the moon. Great book!

Most major cities have zoos. If you plan your trip so that you visit certain favorite creatures immediately upon your arrival, you will not end up spending long hours of weary wandering. Zoo trips can be tiring, but they are usually memorable, too. They give children such interesting subject matter to talk, read, and write about when you return home.

An apartment-size pet is a valuable friend for any child. In the chapter entitled "What Is Education?" it was noted that a home should provide children with something (or someone) to love, something to do, and something to think about. In the "something to love" category, we've gained experience in caring for teddy bear hamsters. They roll from room to room in their exercise balls and eat out of our hands. They are warm, fluffy, furry, and keep themselves very clean. All you need to do is change the bedding at least once a week. Since hamsters are nocturnal and keep their squeaky exercise wheels spinning all night, it is best not to keep their cages in bedrooms. We give our hamsters organic table scraps along with their usual diet of seeds. Vegetables from a supermarket produce department are laden with pesticides and can eventually make these little pets sick. Oh yes, males and females must have separate cages or you will be in the hamster business overnight.

More recently we've acquired two guinea pigs, three cats, goldfish, and a hermit crab—who doesn't seem to be able to make up his mind which shell to more permanently reside in. Dwarf rabbits and birds are also a suggestion, but I'm sure you hear plenty of suggestions from your own children. I hope this chapter has given those of you who live in the city some ideas. ➻

Your Own Personal Reflections

Chapter Thirty-Five

....

Neighborhood Nature Study

Dear Karen,

I love the whole idea of examining the outdoors with children. I don't know how to fit Charlotte's Nature Study field days in to our schedule and still have time to complete the rest of our studies. Can you give me some ideas?

Gratefully,

A devoted reader

I have received letters like the one above asking for ideas about how to incorporate nature study into the curriculum. My "devoted reader" speaks of nature study in terms of "field days." Let's think in terms of hours instead of whole days. There were reasons why in Charlotte's schools books were put away and the entire day was spent outdoors in the English countryside. The first reason is the familiar frequent drizzle of rain. The spring and summer I experienced in England did not seem to be two distinct seasons. It felt more like one longer season of drizzle with absolutely gorgeous, sunny, green, sweet flowery days in between. Since sunny days were infrequent, classrooms indulged in whole days of freedom and frolic.

The second reason for Charlotte's emphasis on whole days spent outdoors in nature is that it took time and organization for most classrooms to travel to the country, even if the country was a short train trip away. The majority of children lived in row housing (and still does). Pavement is plentiful and back gardens (yards) are fenced in, small, and very narrow. I remember staring out the window of a bus at the roses during the misty month of May. They were big, and abundantly crammed into every little crevice between cement walks—all the space the tiny front gardens had to offer.

My advice for those families with very small backyards like ours is to meekly ask some other friendly homeschooling family if you can visit their wooded lot or farmette for an hour of nature appreciation. Bring enough picnic luncheon for both families—in appreciation of their generosity—along with the Nature Notebooks.

A funny thing happened once when we had a fellow church family over for a Sunday meal. They live in Lancaster County, Pennsylvania on a farmette near woods and fields, but when their daughter took a walk in our tight neighborhood, she

returned to the house with a bag full of bits of nature she had never seen before. There is a parcel of ground (owned by the town) in the center of this old neighborhood that has a few big trees on it. Sadly, some of the trees originally planted in our neighborhood sixty years ago have had to be cut down. But there are still some grand old trees to observe. She found acorns with large frilly mossy cups. When we looked up the name of this oak tree in an old tree book of mine, we discovered that this moss cup oak, or burr oak, is rare east of the Allegheny Mountains, and is commonly found in marshy areas near the Mississippi. This may not be the "countryside," but even here in town we may find new things—if we look.

Just weeks after we moved into Stone Cottage, my children were much taken by a large crab apple tree in the same park circle. It is so big that it has become a shade tree with hundreds of miniature sour green apples that look and taste like little Granny Smith apples from the grocery store. At my children's urging, I inquired at a local nursery if they had any crab apple trees for sale. The man said, "Yes," but what he showed us was different than the grand old tree in our park circle. The crab apple tree I was looking for is no longer grown or sold, and a newer variety with much smaller apples has taken its place. People found the larger apples to be a nuisance. I guess one might say our neighborhood has at least two rare trees that most people don't realize or care much about (except the children of the neighborhood).

During our fall bike rides we stopped to pick a few wild flowers by the chain link fence and cracking pavement at the old whistle stop. A new flower for us was "butter and eggs," a difficult flower to draw because it looks like it has been turned inside out. Our bike rides usually take twenty minutes—and our walks less—but I feel we are getting the fresh air and the little bits of nature we need. If you can't fit in a hike at the local nature trail, at least take walks in your neighborhood or the neighborhood of a friend. Pushing the stroller and walking slowly with a two-year-old beside you is all some may be able to accomplish, but it is an approachable and legitimate goal I am sure Charlotte Mason would approve of.

A long-distance friend of mine has acreage with a winding, hilly, graveled front driveway that seems to go on and on. She gets her daily exercise by walking with her children to the mailbox at the end of it. Some afternoons they tarry along the way and get their nature time in, too.

Another way to experience more of nature is to expand the plant varieties in your own garden. Here are two examples.

Bleeding Hearts

Have you ever come across this advice concerning plants? "Plant shrubs and flowers that are thriving in your neighborhood. If they are doing well in your neighbor's yard, they will do well for you, too!" This safe advice appears in newspapers and garden nursery pamphlets every spring. Of course we need to grow what is indigenous, but if the selection of plants for our gardens depended solely on the neighborhood's selection of the token evergreen balled bushes and a few flower boxes, we would quickly run short of inspiration. We can successfully grow plants that we've never seen in anyone else's garden.

One spring, I took the chance of ordering a strange but beautifully delicate plant from a garden catalog. It was a bleeding heart, or as it is called by its Latin name, a *Dicentra spectabilis*. When the tiny box of two root pieces (or bulbs—I can't remember which; it's been some years since

we lived on that property) arrived, I set to work loosening a patch of ground on the north side of our house. I added peat moss to the soil and, with much anticipation, placed the two lifeless-looking root pieces into their fluffy bed. Then I waited.

I can't remember how many weeks it took, or whether it was April or May, but the sun's warmth did eventually reach that shady spot, and two fernlike stems arose. The stems arched over and each produced a row of dangling heart-shaped pendants. Each heart had dainty tear drop-shaped petals below.

Because of the memorable joy I experienced that year, I could not henceforth consider nature's beauty to be frivolous. Anna Botsford Comstock begins her lesson on bleeding hearts in her *Handbook of Nature Study* with a practical purpose for examining the

that garden some years ago. I wonder how those I planted are doing for the new residents? Have they developed into a little low billowing bush of bleeding hearts yet? This is what I like about perennials: they spread, multiply, climb, billow, brim, and last and last. One initial investment brings you a faithful friend. Some "dressing"—the Victorian lady's euphemism for manure tea—applied each growing season ensures vitality for a healthy plant that will need no pesticides.

By planting the bleeding heart, you will not only be beautifying your garden, but you will be providing a new flowering plant for your children's nature study. Do you have a shady spot for a bleeding heart?

A Seed is the Start of Miracles

Can you remember walking home from school, or riding the bus home from kindergarten, carrying a soggy red and white half-pint milk carton of soil? I can. I was a fascinated four-and-a-half-year-old who was proud to show her mother the little bean sprout standing in the center of that mud. I am remembering all the way back to a successful bean sprouting and photosynthesis experiment. Our sweet kindergarten teachers—there were two for our baby-boom crowd—allowed us to experience the fundamental miracle of growth.

Some of us—myself included—may not have thought of planting another seed as we grew up in New Jersey's suburbia. I say this because the next seed I was to plant was almost sixteen years later as a wife and homemaker. And since our marriage, Dean and I have lived in countless rental situations—leaving a trail of seeds, bulbs, and vegetable scrap heaps, in modest proportions, wherever we've gone. We still hold on to our dream of owning a house and living in it long enough to learn—along with Mistress Mary—just "how does a garden really grow?"

bleeding hearts of our gardens. One gets the impression that the bleeding heart was a more common flower in the neighborhood garden then, or that people grew a greater variety of flowers near their picket fences than we do today. She states: "For the intricate structure of this type of flower, the bleeding heart is much more easily studied than its smaller wild sisters, the Dutchman's breeches or squirrel corn; therefore it is well to study these flowers when we find them in profusion in our gardens, and the next spring we may study the wildwood species more understandingly."[1] She also tells us that "the two pink outer petals which make the heart, are really little pitchers with nectar at their bottoms, and although they hang mouth downward the nectar does not flow out."[2] Can you guess how the bees take nectar from these little heart pitchers?

I have seen very few bleeding heart plants since our family moved away from

A Dramatic Seed Experiment

Some springs ago, I wanted to do something dramatic with the children, so I purchased a seed packet containing the seeds of what I thought was the tallest sunflower. (Since that time I've learned that there is an even larger variety called the Gray Stripe sunflower, which can grow ten feet tall.) We started our sunflowers by giving the seeds a rousing wake-up bath. After a good soak, they were rinsed and given the night off in a loosely closed plastic bag. They had just one night to contemplate the acceleration of the life awaiting them. In the morning, I cut off the top of a cardboard egg carton and let the children fill the egg spaces with potting soil. Then they placed the seeds, then more soil, and finally, thoroughly watered the soil. Our egg carton became the soggy centerpiece of our kitchen table for a week before being promoted to a sunny window sill.

Sun, Soil, Rain, Let's Go!

I read that the little egg carton pots could be cut apart and planted outdoors "as is." The pots are supposed to disintegrate with numerous applications of spring rain. "Maybe it depends on the amount of acid rain," I thought. Being a worrier and unsure of the acid-rain content of our skies, we scooped our seedlings out of their comfortable snug homes and transplanted them where the sun rarely stopped shining.

Little needs to be done to prepare the soil for their arrival except pulling up any grass or weeds. Plant the tall varieties two to three feet apart, because they prefer not to compete for their precious sun. Sunflowers will flourish in poor soil where other flowering plants will stubbornly refuse to cooperate. This same rule applies to zinnias, which are also easy to grow in hot sun and poor soil—two commodities that have been in abundance wherever we have rented, it seems. The tall variety of zinnia is an attractive companion to the shorter, busier, sunflower. I may sound like a pro, but actually these two are the only seed-sprouted flowers with which I've had enough success to write about with confidence.

How pleasant it is to spot sunflowers in full bloom, in mid-summer, growing along fences and at the edge of barnyards during a drive out to the country. These tall varieties need stakes to support their top-heavy heads with their beautiful nodding faces. I have a photograph of my children standing shoulder to shoulder with their Goliath sunflowers—the sunflowers as tall as the tallest of them. They were planted at our front door. All you need is sun, water, a plot of poor soil, and you are ready to go.

jay, scrub jay. (I have placed an * preceding the birds that came to feed at our sunflower feeder when we lived in Nashville, TN) We also saw a junco and a wren near the feeder in late spring.

A recent study by the U. S. Fish and Wildlife Service showed that the small black oil sunflower is preferred by most seed-eating birds. Its shell is thinner than that of other varieties, making it easier for small birds, like the chickadee, to remove. Most importantly, it has a higher percentage of oil relative to its weight than do other sunflowers. This sunflower is grown on the Russian sunflower whose seeds are all black and do not have gray stripes like the tall varieties. Did you know that there are pink sunflowers, too?

Tuppence, Tuppence, Tuppence a Bag

To save seeds from your mature sunflowers, wait until the center florets have dried and cover the ripening seeds with a brown paper bag fastened with elastic. This will prevent birds and squirrels from sneaking an early snack of immature seeds. One homeschooling friend I know always leaves the flowers on the stalks for fall and winter feeding. You may harvest them by cutting the heads when the backs turn yellow. Keep the heads in their brown paper bags, and put them in a warm dry place until the seeds are thoroughly dry and can be shaken off. Voila! You now have bags of bird seed for tuppence a bag. Let your children plant a handful of these seeds next spring and they will experience the complete life cycle of a sunflower.

Nature Notebook Project

A sunflower is a good fast-growing plant that makes a convenient Nature Notebook project. Keep a group of pages free for recording the life span of this flower. Start by drawing the seed, giving the

Who Loves Sunflowers More Than the Birds?

According to *The Bird Feeder Book*, these are the birds that are attracted to sunflower seeds: *black-capped chickadee, Carolina chickadee, *tufted tit-mouse, white-breasted nuthatch, red-breasted nuthatch, *cardinal, *American goldfinch, *purple finch, house finch, pine siskin, *downy woodpecker, hairy woodpecker, red-bellied woodpecker, *red-headed woodpecker, *common flicker, evening grosbeak, *starling, *house sparrow, *blue-

common name of the variety. The Latin name *(Helianthus annus)* can be in parentheses. Quite soon, your students will be drawing the sprout, soon after, the first true leaves, transplanting day outdoors, then next a tall stem, and not long after, the first bud. The most fun is drawing and coloring the full bloom, of course. Date each consecutive drawing. A few observations can be recorded as well. In the fall, new birds may be added to the notebook's bird list, as they come to feed on your homegrown birdseed. ⇥

Chapter Thirty-Six

....

Magnanimity and Enthusiasm

"A soul occupied with great ideas best performs small duties."
—H. Martineau

Two words best reflect the high educational ideals of Charlotte Mason. The first word is *magnanimity*. Go ahead, pronounce the word again. I find it does get easier to roll off the tongue the more it's spoken. The second is *enthusiasm*.

What is "magnanimity," and what place can it have in your homeschool? Magnanimity is generosity or nobility of mind or greatness of spirit. This quality of mind and greatness of spirit comes about through a combination of "high thinking" and "lowly living." A magnanimous person thinks great thoughts but also is generous in overlooking injury or insult—for example, he or she rises above pettiness or animosity. His intellectual pursuits do not make him "too good" to do lowly chores.

"Do you wish to be great?" asks St. Augustine. "Then begin by being little. Do you desire to construct a vast lofty fabric? Think first about the foundations of humility. The higher your structure is to be, the deeper must be its foundation. Modest humility is beauty's crown."

Home school is the best place to raise children to be magnanimous. We can hold up Jesus Christ as the perfect example of magnanimity for our children. We can endeavor to be like Him. We can teach our children to share even when it is hard, to forgive when it doesn't seem fair, give them opportunities to absorb the principle of magnanimity, and eventually see them turn into magnanimous persons themselves.

Was there ever a time when magnanimous minds were more needed? Charlotte Mason bid us to "endow our children, not only with a multitude of ideas, but with the greatest ideas and most noble thoughts mankind has to offer, springing from great minds in every sphere of human relationships." A person who contemplates these noble and great thoughts in humility will not become "high-brow" or haughty, but magnanimous. It was Charlotte's hope and prayer that magnanimity would be a character trait common to all her students.

can develop a relationship with God and learn to desire righteousness. With the humanities, children learn to see as a painter sees, for example, by studying great art. They learn to feel as a poet feels by reading poetry aloud. They listen to great music and read the best literature (including heroic biographies) and plays. We lead them to observe closely the wonders God has made in nature. We encourage them to pick up noble ideas that contribute to the training of their consciences. We want them to add to their collection the ideas also owned by those who are chivalrous, noble-minded, large-hearted, altruistic, and unpretentious. All these great high ideas are wonderful, but they are not much good unless they are acted upon. Though a child's good, unselfish deeds be small ones, without some concept of and experience with servanthood he hasn't begun to become magnanimous. The words of George Elliot come to our aid:

If you sit down at set of sun
And count the acts that you have done,
And, counting find
One, self-denying deed,
one word
That eased the heart of him
who heard
One glance most kind
That fell like sunshine
where it went—
Then you may count that day well spent.
But if, through all the livelong day,
You've cheered no heart, by yea or nay—
If, through it all
You've nothing done that you can trace
That brought the sunshine to one's face—
No act most small
That helped some soul and nothing cost—
Then count that day as worse than lost.

Begin with a Regular Diet of Ideas

To become magnanimous is a high calling. But I believe our children will sense this calling when they experience the gentle art of learning found within Charlotte's educational principles. She wrote in her *Philosophy of Education* that "the work of education is greatly simplified when we realize that children, apparently all children, want to know all human knowledge." Children are born with all the curiosity they will ever need. It will last a lifetime if they are fed upon a daily diet of ideas. For finding ideas in "every sphere of human relationships," we can go to the Bible and to the humanities. With the Bible, children

An Ideal Goal

I invite you to make it an educational goal to raise magnanimous children. Magnanimity is one big reason for placing emphasis on ideas derived from the humanities. Through narration a child verbally expresses these ideas. Through servanthood he humbly lives for others. These three—ideas, narration, and servanthood—can work well with both young and old people. To Charlotte, every well-brought-up person is one who has become magnanimous. He is a large-hearted person who practices high thinking and lowly living.

Enthusiasm

The fresh to-morrow morn
Seems to give forth its light in very scorn
Of our dull, uninspired, snail-paced lives.

—Keats

I also believe that the high educational ideals of Charlotte Mason safeguard a child's enthusiasm for learning. Charlotte knew that the self-educated, self-made man is energetic, curious, and enthusiastic. Enthusiasm, more than any other quality, has powerfully and permanently influenced the shaping of mankind. Enthusiasm has swayed the hearts of nations and determined the lives and characters of many individuals. Therefore, Charlotte carefully considered enthusiasm in the scheme of education. Mr. Gibbon, the headmaster of a PNEU boy's school, said, "A nation whose teachers learn to conserve the ardor and curiosity of the seven-year-old for the twelve years that follow, unimpaired, would make itself well nigh invincible in the world."

Charlotte considered the value of enthusiasm at the start of her teaching career when she formulated her philosophy of "knowledge for the sake of knowledge." She was opposed to intellectual force-feeding and found it entirely unnecessary in her method. Grades were not given, though the children were expected to do their best. Real books were used and these—along with all the music, art, and nature study—were a major factor in the educating of the child as "a whole person." Charlotte believed enthusiasm for learning produced enthusiasm for life and culture. She did not believe a child could be spoiled by too much culture. Her ideal was that our Christian children would be the ones who would one day influence culture.

Some human beings express themselves best through painting. Some write poetry. Others put their heart into composing a symphony. Still others raise the spirit of mankind through a story or play. Charlotte wished all children, not just the well-to-do, to make contact with these different kinds of human expressions. A successfully self-educated person learns to pick up the enthusiasm of great thinkers and doers—he is cultured.

Nature

I heard some good common sense on the radio recently. The speaker offered what I thought was an excellent remedy for curtailing depression. She said to take a walk outdoors every day—no matter what the weather. Our elderly next-door neighbor can be seen through our dining room window taking his daily morning walk through all seasons. Although he is widower, he always has a smile and a kind word for us when we see him. Charlotte took her daily dose of fresh air in sunny or drizzly weather even in her old age. She knew that nature walks and first-hand scientific observation not only provide the groundwork for all the sciences, but that being outdoors—and for children, engaging in the huff and puff of play—provides the recreation that gives us rest so we can return to our indoor work with greater enthusiasm. As one poet says, "Students with ardor/Work harder." So it is also for the sake of enthusiasm in your homeschool that the chapters on nature appreciation and seasonal diversions were included in this book.

Entheos—God in Us

The word "enthusiasm," originally derived from the Greek word *entheos (en—*in, *theos*—god), literally means "full of God," or "inspired." We can, therefore, refer to an enthusiast as "one possessed by God."

Charlotte's philosophy mirrors that of John Calvin, who wrote:

> Whenever, therefore, we meet with heathen writers, let us learn from that light of truth which is admirably displayed in their works, that the human mind, fallen as it is, and corrupted from its integrity, is yet invested and adorned by God with excellent talents. If we believe that the Spirit of God is the only fountain of truth, we shall neither reject nor despise the truth itself, wherever it shall appear, unless we wish to insult the Spirit of God.

Enthusiasm is truly the "favorite virtue of heaven," said a poet. Charlotte would have agreed wholeheartedly. She wanted children to become acquainted with enthusiasts—heroes and heroines, the poets, the prophets, the warriors, the high-tempered spirits, the giants of human nature who through force of mind, courage, and perseverance, have won the day for nations and also for individuals, when all other hearts but their own were faint, and who against all hope believed in hope when others desponded. The enthusiast manifests a glowing splendor and gladness that leads him on to victory.

In Art

Only enthusiasm could have led to the creations of the great masters of art and music that I encourage you to explore in these chapters. For example, Beethoven, Handel, Schubert, and Bach, whom we widely regard as super-successful composers—not for their great financial suc-cesses (none of them died rich) but for their enduring contribution to the world of music—did not create their symphonies out of selfish ambition or desire for fame. They all felt an absorbing, passionate love for their art. Their enthusiasm gave full play to their emotions and led their inspired souls to give utterance to imprisoned thoughts and give the world a language without words. The beauty of their creations was within them and they were compelled to express it so that others could have an experience of it.

Michaelangelo, Raphael, Velasquez, and Rossetti were born with a love of form and color that led to their expression of it in their paintings. Because of their ideals of beauty the rest of the world has been enriched. None could have survived the laborious years of disappointment, failure, poverty, and discouragement had they been motivated by the vainglorious love of fame. The will of these great men was driven by desire born of a pure and true enthusiasm, that others might see in their God-given art and love what they themselves loved.

I hope the various topics covered in this book will give you ideas, as you consider a syllabus in your homeschool that safeguards enthusiasm in both teacher and student. True enthusiasm is far-seeing in hope and effort. Enthusiastic teachers press forward through difficulty and discouragement, knowing that the sovereign power of love will not fail in the end. For love—the greatest thing in the world—can never fail.

Charlotte encouraged enthusiasm and magnanimity in the young from their earliest days of school. She wanted to let them learn that without the *Entheos,* the Spirit of God in them, they would be nothing. She said, "Teach them how they must put their whole being into action at the fullness of their measure." Now that is success.

These are some little enthusiasms that have evidenced themselves in our home-school. My awareness of Charlotte's

emphasis on children living the educational life has given me the courage to provide my children with the childhood I've always wanted them to have. Children are naturally curious. They are always willing and wanting to learn something new about God, man, or the universe. And any school that snuffs out the flame of enthusiastic curiosity robs a child of his childhood and is not a fit school for children. "This little light of mine, I'm going to let it shine," is a wonderful thing all children ought to feel capable of expressing. Don't you agree? ➤

How to Tell Children Are Retaining Enthusiasm for Learning

1. *They voluntarily share new learning—"Dad, guess what?!"*

2. *They draw what they see, read about, or hear—"Look at my picture!"*

3. *They request Mozart during lunch or pick up their instruments outside the practice hour.*

4. *They get excited when a new flower blooms in the neighborhood or when they've uncovered a toad.*

5. *They play school the day you are too sick to get out of bed.*

6. *They act out historical characters in their "make believe."*

7. *They ask, "Dad, will you read me this, please?" (And not just because they wish to delay the bedtime hour.)*

8. *They exclaim, "Hey, Mom, that's Claude Monet's bridge!" when they see his painting at the dentist's office.*

9. *They dance about the living room without self-consciousness when hearing music by Rogers and Hammerstein, or George M. Cohan, or Irving Berlin.*

10. *They work at memorizing the words to their favorite hymn or poem without your suggestion.*

11. *They spontaneously count the floor tiles in the grocery store while you push the cart.*

Your Own Personal Reflections

Chapter Thirty-Seven

....

Picnics Any Time At All

Sweet recreation barred, what doth ensue but moody and dull melancholy, kinsman to grim and comfortless despair; and at their heels, a huge infectious troop of pale distemperatures and foes to life.

—SHAKESPEARE

ONE WAY TO ENDURE the good strenuousness of home study and home teaching is to alternate rest with labor, and to make time for seasonal diversions. I know many of you already know this, but some do give up on homeschooling because it is experienced as all work and no play. Although we must consistently be diligent laborers at home, teaching and nurturing character in ourselves and our children, we will not be kept from burn-out without what Shakespeare called, "sweet recreation." In these next pages I provide you with a few examples of the kinds of things you can do as an alternative to more bookish learning.

A British Picnic

At the time we were living south of London. It was a very special day for us: we took the children to a castle. The castle park and gardens allowed cars to use the adjoining field as a car park. When we had completed our tour of the castle we returned the grassy car park to see another fascinating sight. We watched a British family open up the boot (trunk) of their car, pull out a card table, folding chairs, and a picnic hamper. There were no fast-food places for miles. Their shiny car was parked next to our missionary bomb. (It may have looked like a bomb but it was the roomiest and most well-serviced car we ever had.) I tried not to stare at this British custom of "dining out," which I had only heard about but never before seen with my own eyes. As inconspicuously as possible, I gave side glances through our open car window while I was buckling our youngest into her car seat. I managed to see enough to satisfy my curiosity without openly invading their privacy. Yet how private can one expect to be in a parking lot!

The silverware and china were buckled securely onto the lid of the picnic hamper by leather straps. The husband removed elegant tall glasses from the hamper and poured red liquid into them. Next, he tossed a green salad that billowed over the bowl. In one more glance, I saw some French bread, a small wooden board with orange cheese, and a generous bunch of red grapes. Only the back of the wife's head was visible to me but, from inside our car, I heard her laugh quite clearly, so I imagined

a merry facial expression. The charm of their little picnic outing must have given her much pleasure that beautiful sunny summer day, even if it was spent in a crowded grass parking lot.

That's what is so magical about picnics. They seem to turn any ordinary setting into a special occasion—even if it is the simple enjoyment of a peanut-butter-and-jelly bag lunch under a backyard tree with the children.

P's & Q's of Tableware

Most of us will not be bringing grandmother's best silverware or Waterford crystal to our picnics (nor will there be a castle looming on the horizon.) Thick plastic spoons, knives, and forks are a wiser deci-

sion for our active (wiggly) families and can be just as special when they are reserved for "dining out." They are dishwasher-safe on the no-heat drying cycle, and are lighter to carry when walking across a meadow to a favorite shady spot.

Remember the Melmac dishes that were so popular in the fifties and sixties? They make great picnic plates. Some stores still sell them, but it is hard to find them apart from prepackaged place-settings, and you will probably never use the plastic tea cups. Along with sturdy plastic plates and tableware, plastic food storage containers are not only a convenient modern invention, they are a necessary picnic commodity.

I like to keep all the plastic items in my house carefully hidden from view. This is my attempt to create a decor resembling an earlier time period. My plastic tableware is kept inside Great-Aunt Miranda's antique picnic basket, which rests on top of my oak hutch. She gave me this old basket as a gift last Christmas. I love it! The poor basket collected dust all winter, dissatisfied at being used solely as a quaint dining room decoration. The children frequently asked me when we were going to have our first spring picnic. "When the snow melts and the ground is no longer muddy," I told them.

They started counting off the weeks.

Where Did You Get Those Napkins?

I found homespun cloth napkins in an Amish tourist shop this spring, for $3.65 each. (We now live just south of Lancaster County, PA.) The edges were not hemmed, but only serged. I didn't buy them, however. I was only window-shopping for ideas. Homemade napkins can be just as pretty, will cost much less per napkin, and can even be given a proper hem. Children who would delight in acquiring a new skill will welcome this simple sewing project. Calico, plaid check, or bandanna cotton print fabric can be cut into large squares measuring 18" square before the hems—allowing you to get two across if you have 36" material. The edges can be rolled (folded under twice) and sewn on a sewing machine. Hemming the edges by hand would also be good sewing practice for children. A contrasting color thread will make it easier for them to keep track of the size and placement of the little stitches.

A Neat and Tidy Bundle

Try this idea for set-ups using cloth napkins. Place one tableware set-up in the center of a napkin diamond. Fold the bottom corner up over the handles first, then wrap one side, the top, and the other side. Tie with ribbon. Children will welcome this "chore," because it is part of the picnic preparations. The ribbon, tableware, and cloth napkins will all be used again at your next picnic. Cloth napkins are a nice touch and have a practical use as well—they don't blow away like paper napkins do. The wrapped set-ups make for easy distribution. You can lay the cloth napkins on your lap with confidence. Bring extras to tuck into the collars of both adults and children.

Hooked on Blue and White

Great-Aunt Miranda's picnic basket is lined with a small blue and white check fabric. (Incidentally, I would never ask her to use a napkin that wasn't properly hemmed.) My favorite napkins are blue and white of a larger check and are hemmed. I would like to make a blue and white check table cloth to match. As I write, I happen to be wearing a blue and white check country dress, which makes the writing of this paragraph almost too corny to be true. Alas, it *is* true. (Perhaps there are some things that authors should not admit to their readers.)

Flowers

B.Y.O.F. stands for Bring Your Own Flowers. If the picnic gathering will be one for ladies, such as a backyard garden party, a vase of flowers will be the expected centerpiece. When each guest brings one type of flower from her garden, the result can be

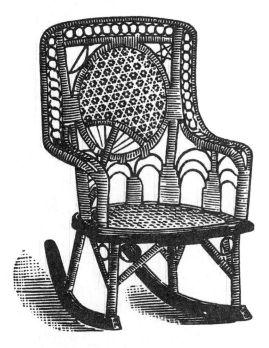

a beautiful bouquet. When each guest also brings a favorite tea sandwich, the group's assortment will make a festive table.

Cool Spring Grass

If you expect the spring grass to be moist on the day of your picnic, take along a large vinyl tablecloth. Place it under your picnic blanket or quilt for protection. I say this for two reasons. In the South, there are chiggers as well as fire ants. We've been bitten by both. I remember laying my first baby on the grass to change her wet diaper. I was about to put on the dry one, but within seconds her little bottom was covered with biting fire ants. The word "fire" gives you an idea of how much they sting. What a lot of bright red bumps there were, even after I wiped her down! The old cliché "ants in the pants" had to have been born of picnickers. Therefore, watch where you lay your blanket and take a first aid kit along for any kind of "boo-boo."

Pass the Gherkins, Please

A delicious scene in the children's classic, *Wind in the Willows,* stands clearly in my mind. It appears a few pages after Mole accepts Rat's invitation for a day out on the river. "There is simply nothing better than messing about in boats," says Rat. The passage reads:

> "Hold hard a minute, then!" said the Rat. He looped the painter through a ring in his landing-stage, climbed up into his hole above, and after a short interval reappeared staggering under a fat wicker luncheon basket. "Shove that under your feet," he observed to the Mole, as he passed it down into the boat . . .
> "What's inside it?" asked the Mole, wriggling with curiosity.
> "There is cold chicken inside it," replied the Rat briefly; "cold

tonguecold hamcold beefpickledgherkinssaladfrenchrollscress sandwichespottedmeatgingerbeer leamonadesodawater—" [This bit is spoken as smoothly as an auctioneer's litany—Author]

"O stop, stop!" cried the Mole in ecstasies. "This is too much!"

"Do you really think so?" inquired the Rat seriously. "It's only what I always take on these little excursions . . ."

A few pages later, after some conversation, and after they have reached their destination, we find the description of the laying-out of the picnic repast:

The Rat brought the boat alongside the bank, made her fast, helped the still awkward Mole safely ashore, and swung out the luncheon-basket. The Mole begged as a favor to be allowed to unpack it all by himself; and the Rat was very pleased to indulge him, and to sprawl at full length on the grass and rest, while his excited friend shook out

the tablecloth and spread it, took out all the mysterious packets one by one and arranged their contents in due order, still gasping, "O my! O my!" at each fresh revelation.

I love the descriptive writing in *Wind in the Willows*. While attending a literature club meeting once, I learned that Kenneth Grahame created the story for his blind son. The description was a thoughtful way of helping his son "see" the story—and, I should think, feel, smell, and taste as well. Perhaps you will come across a picnic scene in one of your favorite books.

We Laughed in the Sunshine

There is something special about sharing good food in the sunshine and fresh air with friends or family. It could be a lunch with an invited group of homeschool children in the backyard, a church barbecue, a knapsack of healthy treats on a hillside, or a frilly, lacy, ladies' garden party. Picnicking can have a holiday or birthday theme, an international menu theme, or it can simply be a way of celebrating a beautiful day. Breads, cheeses, fruit, cold meats and salads are among the favorite foods of picnickers.

Cheese

Cheese is a typical picnic food because it is simple, easy to eat, and is at its best when served at room temperature. As you most likely will be traveling in a hot car to get to your destination, it is best to keep food chilled in an insulated cooler. All food that goes into the cooler should be refrigerated beforehand and placed into the cooler while it is cold. Take along a small wooden cutting board for slicing cheese. Outdoors is the perfect place to serve children the most crusty kinds of breads—ones that complement the texture of cheese so well. Crumb clean-up is virtually non-existent.

Salad

Exercise your creativity with picnic salads. For instance, a simple tomato salad will take on a new dimension when you mix together several varieties of tomatoes. Golden, beefsteak, cherry—and don't forget those luscious backyard tomatoes—make an attractive array with a drizzle of vinaigrette dressing and a sprinkle of fresh chopped basil. Sliced, chopped, or grated vegetables (try grated fennel, mmmm) can be set to marinate in the refrigerator the day before the picnic. Prevent soggy lettuce salads. Bring rinsed, torn lettuce and garden greens to the picnic site in a separate container, then toss with marinated vegetables and serve. I like to add cubed avocado—soaked in lemon juice—to a cucumber and sweet onion salad. This is spooned into pocket bread at the site and topped with sprouts.

How to Handle Mayonnaise

It has been reported that warm mayonnaise is responsible for summer food poisoning. Bacteria finds it a perfect place to raise a family in haste. Deviled eggs, potato salad, macaroni salad, tuna salad, and coleslaw "sit around" at many picnics. For safety, remove food from coolers just at the time of eating. This is sometimes hard to do when large church groups must eat in shifts, waiting for the meat that is being grilled in batches. One remedy is to bring salads containing mayonnaise in smaller serving dishes, enabling you to put out only a portion of the salad at a time.

For a lighter mayonnaise dressing, replace a small portion of mayonnaise with plain yogurt, whisking it together before adding it to the salad. Potato and pasta salads can be made with a drizzle of Italian dressing instead of mayonnaise. Add lots of chopped raw or steamed vegetables to all your salads. Fresh herbs add a harmonious flavor to outdoor eating.

Ration the Salt and Sugar

Another picnic "no-no" is to bring great big bags of salty potato chips. If the weather is warm, active youngsters will naturally choose the salty foods and then seek after large amounts of beverage (at picnics usually the sweetest kinds are served). This fills stomachs with non-nutritious calories. Serve individual portions of chips in little paper cups or on each plate, then put the bag away. Our standard picnic beverage is watered-down juice punch. Lemonade with lots of ice is a special treat. Slices of lemon float about to add "visual flavor" without the extra tartness. We keep a jug of plain water on hand, too.

Desserts

For dessert, fruit kept fresh in its own skin is the most convenient and healthy choice. Children will enjoy making fruit salad a day ahead. Of course, this must be chilled. Fruit pies, a traditional American fare, add a certain Norman Rockwell atmosphere. Pies seem to be a favorite with the men (my husband's and dad's choice), and like cheese, are more flavorful at room temperature.

Homemade Ice-cream

Have you ever attended a backyard picnic gathering where everybody took a turn at cranking the old wooden ice-cream maker? Wow! That's ice-cream! My one and only experience at cranking was as a young girl at a party of mostly adults twenty years ago. It was at the house of a Mrs. Mustard (a real name and a real story) who lived in the woods and did things the hard way. Two barefoot maidens (my best friend and I) climbed around the slippery rocks of a hidden stream that flowed past Mrs. Mustard's house. When we made our way back to the party, we were introduced to the workings of the old barrel ice-cream maker. We were told it was our turn to do the cranking. My friend brought to my notice that no one else was taking a turn to crank. I responded that they must all have taken a turn while we were out exploring.

The sun rose higher in the sky and we wiped the perspiration from our brows. We yelled to keep the ice coming for the barrel. We cranked until our arms ached. After what seemed to be hours, the much-longed-for proclamation of "Ready!" was spoken by Mrs. Mustard. We stood side by side, our wide eyes watching the line of adult guests being served by Mrs. Mustard. With anxiety we wondered if there would be any left for us. Then our hostess discovered she was out of her fluted glass dessert cups. My friend and I glanced at each other, speechless.

Mrs. Mustard disappeared into her kitchen's deep, dark, walk-in pantry. She carried out two heavy crockery bowls, wiping off their cobwebs with the same limp tea towel that had been tucked into her apron all day. She filled each crock to the brim with all the remaining homemade peach ice-cream for her devoted crankers. Mmmm—what a perfect day! There are events in a person's life that will not escape memory—like picnics.

The Last Word

Have you read that hilarious true story *Cheaper by the Dozen,* by Frank B. Gilbreth, Jr., and Ernestine Gilbreth Carey? Before this large family left a picnic site, Dad—a motion study expert and the benev-

olent dictator of the story—insisted that all wrappings and trash of any kind must be stowed away and brought home. Often, the children would be expected to form a line—elbow to elbow—and march across the picnic grounds, picking up any trash in sight. Of course they would end up taking home more garbage than they brought. When the children brought empty whiskey bottles, copies of last year's magazines, and rusty tin cans to the picnic box, Dad voiced a complaining tease about the clutter his children created during just one picnic. They would try to tell him that it wasn't their mess. Dad would only grin as he stuffed it away. You know the moral of the story. Have a great picnic!

A Picture Book About Picnics

It was a happy coincidence that I found *Becky's Birthday,* by Tasha Tudor, in our local library when my daughter Yolanda was about to turn ten. As the story is about Becky's tenth birthday, Yolanda stole away to devour it silently in a corner of the house. Later, I asked her what she thought of Becky's birthday picnic, with the cake "floating down the river."

She smiled and said, "It's a sweet story but rather exciting. Things don't happen like that in real life."

Her eyes widened to learn that the story was a true one. The author and illustrator, Tasha Tudor, used her own children and country lifestyle as a model for her picture books.

Chapter Thirty-Eight

....

Summer Senses for Country Folk

MANY OF THE IMAGES in this chapter will remind us of kindlier, more gentle times, when the world wasn't in the bustle it is in today, and when many more families across the country ran small farms, or lived in the country or small towns. We may not be living in those gentler days, but I think we can pretend that we do, or at the very least, bring forward into our own times as much as we can of its kindliness, gentleness, and slower pace of life.

See how many of these suggestions you can take advantage of in your situation. Children might come up with some of their own, too. You are invited to read aloud one section a day or one section a week to give you a chance to experience what to see, hear, feel, taste, and smell this summer.

I like to think of rosy cheeked girls and freckled-faced boys in the country who will be free to work and play out of doors through the long, long, summer days. To help weed and mow in field or vegetable bed will give work enough, but there will probably be time to spend many hours with chipmunk or squirrel or robin redbreast, or in finding some new tree or wayside plant that has never seen before. In times of leisure we can add much to our knowledge of nature, and boys and girls should not neglect this.

The world needs "bumblebee watchers" who have knowledge of nature, because all agriculture is founded on this knowledge. There is always room for another successful farmer, and there is also a demand for the man in the city who is awake to his surroundings. This is why we want boys and girls to observe natural forces and objects for themselves. If one should become a farmer in the future, he will then have preparation to become a successful one. If they go to the city to live, they will nevertheless find that their training in the study of nature will help them in any line of work.

A boy or girl who wants to live well should train the senses. To see, to hear, to feel, to taste, to smell—all are important. Many persons have failed to make the most of one or more of these gifts. If any one of the senses is neglected in childhood, the use of its full power may never be realized. Children, therefore, ought to learn all that they can through sight, sound, touch, taste, and smell. The best time of year to do this is in the summer. There are hundreds of ways in which children can do this all by themselves. I am going to suggest some things to think about along the way.

Some Things to See

The dawn of the new day; what it reveals in the sky, in the fields, in the distant trees, in the life in and about the farm.

Sunset time. How many different colors will you see during the summer evenings? How does one sunset differ from another: Look out into the nights, some starry and some moonlit.

Note all the different greens that can be seen in a landscape: the greens of trees; the different crops; a far-away bit of water. Note the touches of rich color that brighten the landscape, all the reds and the yellows.

Try to see some bird that is smaller than a sparrow. Many boys and girls never see the very small birds. Watch a bird take a bath. What color is a robin's egg?

Look closely to find all the parts of some one flower—a tiger lily, a wild rose, or a marigold. Did you notice the tree blossoms this past spring? Often young persons do not realize that trees blossom.

What time of day do different flower blossoms open and close?

If you have red poppies growing in your garden, arrange some with ripened wheat and see what beautiful color you will have.

Notice the movement of a flag blowing in the wind or a kite soaring at the end of a string. Do Mother's white sheets on the clothes line resemble a ship's sails blown by the wind at sea?

Notice the best-kept grounds in your neighborhood, and notice the most attractive house inside and out.

Look in villages near, or in your own community, for the most attractive garden.

Learn to see at a glance when mother or father needs you. When you truly see this your heart will answer the need.

Some Things to Hear

Listen to the early morning sounds. Sound gives to some persons as much joy as does sight.

Try to distinguish the different bird notes.

Make wind chimes with shells or bamboo sticks and fishing line.

Listen to the music of the crickets and katydids, and to the sounds of other insects by day and night.

Learn to recognize the sounds made by the pines, and the rain on the roof, the hail near the close of the summer shower.

Listen for the sound of the church bell that may come to you from the village near. Can you hear the difference between a freight train and a passenger train traveling by?

Listen for the wind in the trees and the distant thunder of an approaching thunder shower.

Notice how restful and pleasant it is to hear persons speak in low, soft tones at the close of an active day. Try to speak in this way when talking to others on summer evenings.

Some Things to Feel

The warm, sweet breezes of summer.

The touch of a gentle rain on your face.

A mud puddle under your bare feet.

The cool soft moss in the deep wood.

The joy that all clean and tidy things give: cleanliness of person; of clothing; of everything in the house or barn.

The confidence of your dog when he puts his nose into your hand.

The response of the farm animals to your affection.

Find the feeling of a well-prepared, happily eaten meal by helping Mother with supper.

The difference between the shiny smooth skin of a plum and a fuzzy peach on your lips before you bite into it.

A cool, soft pillow after a day of work and play.

Charlotte Mason told us that mothers have so kind a touch that their hands seem to smooth away our troubles. This sort of touch is only learned by loving.

How do you feel after reading a chapter of a good book, or reading aloud a bedtime story to a younger brother or sister?

Some Things to Taste

Homemade bread and butter. Some persons do not know what bread from the home oven tastes like. Learn to make bread and do not be satisfied until you know you can make it.

Learn to distinguish the tastes of different apples.

....

A homegrown tomato ripened on the vine.

....

Learn the value of cool, refreshing, pure water.

....

How do you get a drop of honeydew from the honeysuckle flower?

....

Some boys and girls like to chew on fennel seeds, caraway seeds, pumpkin or sunflower seeds on the day Mother does baking.

....

Some Things to Smell

As you approach the ocean, notice when you can first smell the sea air.

....

The pine woods. The distant buckwheat field. The lilac hedge. Garden flowers at night. Cut grass. The ground after a rain. The herb garden when you weed it.

....

A clean barn.

....

Clean rooms at home. Do not let the air in the house become stale, mildewed, or stuffy. Open the windows wide after a heavy rain.

....

Good cooking.

....

Make a sweet-smelling gift for someone with lavender or rose petals from the garden, cinnamon, or anise seed.

....

To what would you compare the fragrance of the leaves of a sassafras tree? If you can find one of these trees "with mittens," rub one leaf or "mitten" on your hand and find out.[1]

Your Own Personal Reflections

....

....

....

....

....

....

....

Chapter Thirty-Nine

Ready, Set, Go!

Recreation is not being idle; it is easing the wearied part by change of occupation. To re-create strength, rest. To create mind, repose. To re-create cheerfulness, hope in God, or change the object of one's attention to some more elevated and worthy of thought.

—SIMMONS

I REMEMBER PLAYING a lot of Hopscotch in years gone by. Three neighborhood friends and myself executed our skipping, scuffing, and balancing carefully from square to square, each with the same dogged seriousness. We wore out the bottoms of our Keds, but became proficient at the game by summer's end. By that time we were going barefoot anyway and were looking forward to our usual new pair of back-to-school shoes (and tin lunch box).

My young son enjoys playing the game of Hopscotch with his sisters. I join in, at times, to encourage them along, but I cannot balance as I once could. Therefore, I had opportunity to teach them, early on, that if they touch the pavement with the hand that is not being used to retrieve their stone, in an effort to steady themselves, they must remember to call out, "Butterfingers!" or their turn ends prematurely.

Did you know that Hopscotch used to be a grown-up's game? According to the book, *Something to Do, Girls!* written in 1916, it is a very old game. On the pavement of the Roman Forum were found several Hopscotch figures, such as you might see on sidewalks today, which the children have drawn in with chalk. The book also says that the early Christians played Hopscotch and they made seven spaces in their figures, because seven was a number with a religious meaning and the space marked seven was called "Heaven." The object of the game was to overcome all difficulties and get safely into "Heaven." In Germany and some other countries one of the spaces was named Paradise, and the name of the game meant "Paradise Hopping."

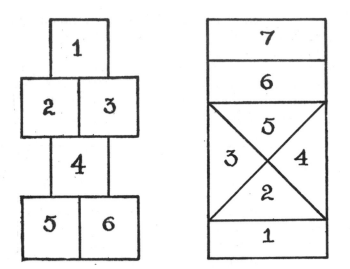

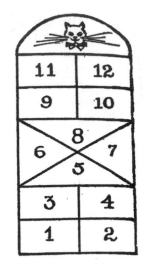

To determine place, you first "pink" or pitch the stone you play with. The one who pitches the stone nearest the first figure has first play. We always played a simple version of the game. The stone is left at each space in turn, the player hopping through the figure and returning to the stone each time. But a much more difficult version of the game was once played. Stones were kicked or scuffed onto various spaces during the hopping. And the stone was carried by balancing it on a shoulder, the back of the hand, or on the head. Hopscotch is really a wonderful game that requires much bodily control and skill.

Can you remember playing Hopscotch, Jump Rope, Cat's Cradle, Green Light-Red Light, Simon Says, and Charades? Will all these personal face-to-face games be replaced entirely with impersonal computer games by the 21st century?

Whether you are in need of some less competitive summer games for Vacation Bible School, a birthday party, family reunion, field day, or just plain neighborhood outdoor frolicking, here is a supply brought to you from the days before the invention of the television. We may recognize some of these games, but have our children ever played them? Will they be lost in this generation?

The Snake Game

According to a 1919 edition of *The Young Folks Treasury*, Chinese boys—thirteen years old and under—played a snake game that was quite exciting. This is how it's played: A dozen boys form a line, each fellow with his hands on the shoulders of the boy in front of him. One of the fellows is the "Wolf." The boy at the head of the line is the "head" of the snake, and the last is the "tail." The Wolf stands near the head of the serpent until the signal is given.

At the signal, the Wolf tries to catch the "tail" without touching any other part of the snake. The boys who form the body of the serpent protect the "tail" by wreathing about in all sorts of twists, to prevent the Wolf from catching the "tail." This must be done without breaking the line. When the "tail" is caught, the Wolf becomes the "head" and the "tail" becomes the Wolf. The game can be continued until every boy has been the Wolf. This game can also be played with all the boys wearing roller skates.

I should expect, in this late part of the 20th century, girls would be welcome to join in.

The Cat Tiggy

As soon as the players have agreed to play this game, they cry: "The last perched is Cat," at which every player tries to get a perch, that is, to get his feet off the ground. The players may stand on a piece of wood, sit on a gate, or in fact do anything so long as their feet are not on the ground. The last to find a perched position is the Cat.

The other players beckon to one another, changing places by signal, or going to new perches, and the Cat has to touch them before they have perched themselves. If the Cat should succeed in touching anyone who is off his perch, the player touched becomes Cat.

"Dicky, Show a Light!"

This is a splendid game for a dark night. It is a kind of Hare and Hounds, in which the hare, called "Dicky," shows a light to guide his hunters. Girls may be called "Donna."

The player who takes the part of "Dicky" or "Donna" is provided with a dim flashlight, and is allowed a few minutes' start. The hunters then go after him, and they also carry flashlights, the light of which they must show the whole time, while "Dicky" need only show his light about once every two minutes. If the hunters get quite astray, and "Dicky" is too long showing his whereabouts, they cry, "Dicky, show a light!" He must then flash the light in their direction.

A good "Dicky" or "Donna" never keeps the hunters too long without a light, but dodges round the party like a will-o-the-wisp—first here, then there—making the most of his two minutes to get to the other side of a hedge or fence, or round the

party in an opposite direction. It is a good idea to fix upon some boundary beyond which "Dicky" may not go, as he has such advantages over the other players that if he can wander wherever he likes, there is little chance of his being caught.

Follow My Leader

Even if you've never heard of the above-mentioned "old fashioned" games, you are sure to recognize the title of this one. I'm including it here to let you know how useful it was with my kindergarteners Sunday school. After one round of "Follow My Leader," allowing each child to be leader for two minutes, the children were ready to settle themselves down onto the Bible story rug.

One of the players is chosen as leader, and the rest range themselves in a long row behind him. The leader begins to advance

and those behind must follow wherever he goes and copy his every action. This is a good time to let animal noises, clapping, or stamping of feet be heard. Children are more frequently reminded to be quiet.

When a certain time has elapsed, it falls to the part of the next player in the row to become leader, and the previous leader goes to the rear. The game is over when each player has had a turn to be leader.

Dunking for Peaches

This game is played the same way one would play "Dunking For Apples" in the fall. If you don't happen to have one of those shiny round wash tubs, a smaller rubber tub will do fine.

With arms behind their backs, children must use only their teeth to grab hold of a peach and lift it out of the water. You may think securing this smaller, softer fruit would be easier, but remember, peaches are not usually found with those reliable stems the apple often has.

Blind Man's Bluff

In ancient times this game was known by the name of "Hoodman Blind," as in those days a hood that was fastened at the back of the neck was placed over the head of the child chosen to be "Blind Man."

By the year 1919, the game was called "Blind Man's Bluff," and very popular it was among young folk.

If you are not playing this game out-doors, before beginning to play, the middle of the room should be cleared of the coffee table, the chairs placed against the wall, and all toys and footstools put out of the way. The child who has been selected who is to be "Blind Man," or "Bluff," is blind-folded. He is then asked the question: "How many horses does your father have?" The answer is "Three," and to the question: "What color are they?" he replies: "Black white, and gray." All the players then cry: "Turn round three times and catch whom you may!" "Bluff" accordingly spins round and then the fun commences. He tries to catch the players, while they in their turn do their utmost to escape him, all the time making little sounds to attract him. This goes on until one of the players is caught, and when "Bluff," without having the bandage removed from his eyes, has to guess the name of the person he has secured. If the guess is a correct one, the player who has been caught takes the part of "Bluff," and the former "Bluff" joins the ranks of the players.

Marbles

The best method of shooting a marble is as follows: Bend the thumb at the first joint and grasp it firmly with the middle finger. Place the marble in front of the thumb and hold it in position with the first finger, then suddenly, taking good aim, let fly the thumb and the marble will be shot forward with considerable force. If you think I am about

to describe how to play marbles here, you are mistaken. None can do it better than those who once played for hours on end in the dust and hot sun. Let's allow the grandfathers a chance to reminisce and reveal the secrets of a good game of marbles.

And no gambling for marbles!

Ring o' Roses

Have you played this game lately with any two- or three-year-olds? This game has been played for no one knows how many generations. I read somewhere that children began to sing this rhyme in Europe during the time of the Black Plague. But you don't have to tell the children this may be a song about death. I sometimes wonder how people dealt with so much death. Even at the turn of the century, the child mortality rate was fifty percent. But it's because the little children enjoy it so much that the game has endured. You may sing the verse differently in your part of the country. Here is what I found in *The Young Folks Treasury*. The children form a circle holding hands, and walk round singing the following verse:

Ring-a-ring o' roses,
A pocket full of posies,
Hush-a, hush-a
We'll all tumble down.

When they sing, "We'll all tumble down," over they go, roly poly on the grass. They get up again, and the game begins afresh.

Here is how we sang it in my old neighborhood:

Ring around the roses,
Pocket full of posies,
Ashes, ashes,
We all fall down.

How was it sung in yours?

Leap Frog

This is the simplest and at the same time one of the best of the "over-back" games. The players stand behind each other, forming a long line. The first player in the line "makes a back," the second leaps over, and makes a back a few feet farther on, the first one still remaining down. The third player goes over first one then the other, forming another back in the same manner as the second, and so on until all in the line are down. Then the boy who made the first back starts again, and leaps each of the backs and makes another back at the end, the next player does the same, and thus a continually advancing line of backs is formed.

If the players are anxious to get over the ground quickly, they can run a dozen yards or so before "going down." The whole fun of the game lies in its being played smartly and with spirit.

Join in with the fun, Mom and Dad. Have we forgotten how? ⇥

Chapter Forty

·······································

Old-Fashioned Sand Play

Sand is an indestructible toy. It can't be worn out, broken, lost, or stolen. If sunlight reaches it now and then it is perfectly sanitary (though a sand box should be covered when not in use to protect it from wandering cats). Sand is perfectly agreeable to children's use because they can play in it with their legs crossed. To kneel in the sand and sink the knees into it while the hands are free to shape or create is another way to really get completely involved. We chair inhabitants (grown-ups) might not realize how uncomfortable it is to a child to use his legs as hanging fringe to a chair and to do most of his occupations thus. One exception is Beatrix Potter's tailor of Gloucester, who accomplished his tasks cross-legged.

A manifestation of having fun is getting messy, dirty, or wet. But grown-ups are mistaken when they say that the reason children love to play in the sand is because "they like making messes." While children have no special aversion to a mess when it occurs naturally, it is not the messiness of sand that they like, but the fact that it is something they can work with (and in). It is said, "The hands are the heart's live wire." So the child rejoices in a substance so light, so pliable, and so "open-minded."

The first use of sand that seems to delight a toddler, after he learns not to put it into his mouth, is to hide something in it. The mystery of being unable to see his buried hand or leg gives him an inexplicable delight. A participating grown-up can make his hand a hibernating rabbit or other shy pet that likes to play hide-'n-seek. To put sand in brown bags or plastic cups is a similar pleasure—the sense of controlling it being an added accomplishment. Why a child will continue to fill and empty a pail for an entire morning with placid joy is something an adult can't fathom. It seems to be restful to the nerves, even though he doesn't make progress. Toddlers are not anxious to "get ahead." Their attention is fully occupied on the present.

When a small child empties the sand onto his hair or throws it at playmates, he needs a little guidance.

A sand sieve, strainer, or funnel seems to add an entirely new aspect to the situation. A few dollars buys a sand-mill, a wheel turned by the action of the falling sand. My best memory of sand is sitting on the New Jersey shore making my sand-mill spin. The sand on the New Jersey shore is remarkably clean, white, and dust free—which is surprising as it is so close to New York City where there once was extensive off-

shore dumping. A law prohibits removing sand from the beach for personal use. Walking over the dunes and picking the hand-sown dune grasses is now prohibited as well. I can remember wandering for hours up and down the dunes in the cool of the evenings long before these laws were in effect. My grandmother had a house that overlooked the ocean and the rolling dunes. We caught the fattest, ugliest toads in the dune grass and used the tallest dunes as slides. Every year I would fill a small bag of this pure sand and lay it carefully in my suitcase before we said good-bye to the sea gulls and headed inland for home.

An old-fashioned sandbox or even just a shallow rubber sink bucket can be a mini-vacation for both mother and child. Pull up a chair, Mom. Put your feet up for a while, you've been on them all morning. Take out a magazine or book and read a few pages while the sand complies with your child's wishes.

Older children may gather 'round the sand-box, too. Mine have, when occasionally drawn to the idea of shaping something. At one time the entire sandbox was formed into a miniature medieval city—complete with sand-castle, of course—and its surrounding walls. This summer when we visited my parents at their shore house there was a sand modeling contest on the beach. We ventured out to the contest spot that evening, hours after the contest had ended. I was surprised to see how close the sand designs were to the water's edge and approaching tide. We carefully walked circles around the large sculptures, saying things like, "Ooo, look at this one!" Mounds of sand were molded into mermaids—one with brown strings of seaweed as hair—a hammerhead shark, an octopus, a starfish, a lighthouse, a sea turtle, and sand castles. Since the once hot afternoon summer sun was soon to set, the air cool, the wind mild, and the sand moist, Dean and I sat and waited while our children, ages fifteen, twelve, and eight, immediately began to mold their own sand sculptures. It was pure inspiration and creative energy at work.

I can remember, though, that the first modeling experiments of my children with sand were simplicity itself. They just dug holes and built smooth mounds, with a peaceful, sweeping back-and-forth motion—accompanied by quiet content sounds of melodious humming. The holes were sometimes filled with water. The mounds were what the hand shaped as a consequence of moving lovingly over the sand.

The second stage for children is usually to make tunnels, especially under the mound or between two neighboring ones. Bridges, limited in duration, are constructed next.

Ordinary household objects become extraordinary when played with in the sand. Any size or shape scoop with a handle—whether it be from an old box of laundry soap or a can of coffee—makes a fine shovel. I like the sugar scoops. The handles are much easier

to hold and the sand doesn't slide out over the sides. And what about those magnificent toy steam shovels and dump trucks? How about your daughter's plastic tea service, or the picnic plates and spoons? Marbles can roll down slopes and into pits. Add your own ideas and the list goes on. ⊷

Chapter Forty-One

Autumn Diversions

E VERY AUTUMN I reach for the picture book *The Oxcart Man* by Donald Hall to read aloud to my children. Even the eldest child doesn't mind hearing it again. There is something about autumn and *The Oxcart Man* that evokes an instinct in me to start little projects to celebrate the season.

Autumn Is Mittens in the Making

I've adopted my mother's tradition of knitting mittens every autumn. During my childhood our home seemed to offer up an endless supply of mittens of all sizes and colors—with or without stripes. My brother, sister, and I would go in and out the side door, exchanging soggy mittens for dry ones. On very cold days we would wear them double. My mother would use any leftover yarn from sweaters she had knitted. One day I hope to knit a project as large as a sweater, but for now I have been very happy to knit hats and mittens for my own children.

Since I asked my mother to share her pattern with me and guide me in my first pair, I have come across simpler patterns that are seamless and claim to require no counting, but I've stuck with her familiar method. Last autumn I discovered a sewing pattern with instructions to cut mitten shapes out of hopelessly stained or worn sweaters, cleverly converting the cuffs of the sweater's sleeves into mitten cuffs. I might try this project, since I have at least one hopeless sweater wanting to be transformed.

I would publish my mother's mitten pattern here, except that there are so many ways of knitting mittens that I will leave you to meet up with an obtainable pattern that appeals to you. Once you get started, you too may find yourself driven by instinct, digging out the knitting needles every autumn—signaled by the first bright orange maple leaf.

In *The Oxcart Man* it is the little daughter of the story who knits five pairs "from yarn spun at the spinning wheel from sheep—sheared in April." My eldest daughter has caught the spirit and has begun her first pair this autumn. Perhaps soon her younger sister will as well.

Autumn is Acorns

Padded by our thick sweaters, we relaxed on a quilt near the oak tree, soaking up the last available autumn afternoon sun—all of us, that is, except for a small boy of four years who had his hands busy in the grass. After a few relaxing moments he declared, "Mom, look what I have!" A brimming brown handful of acorns spilled onto the quilt and he rolled on his stomach lacksidaisily about the lawn to gather more. When he came upon an acorn patch, he ceased his rolling and, lying on the grass on his stomach—raised up by one elbow—with his free hand he slowly built a pile of acorns.

"Mom, look, a mountain!" he exclaimed.

Children at that age have an interesting sense of proportion. His sister ran inside the house to get a bucket. Before we were ready to fold up the quilt there was a bucketful of acorns for us to admire.

"What should we do with these, Mom?"

"How about a wreath for the door?" I ventured.

A Wreath for the Door

Here is how it is done: Cut a wreath shape out of cardboard. Thin cardboard is much easier to cut and will do fine. Wreaths no bigger than the size of dinner plates can be completed in one craft-time. First, glue on a scant layer of dry autumn leaves.

Then, begin to apply the acorns. Dried wild flowers, small pine cones, or any other interesting dried natural objects from your yard or park can be stuck in between the acorns, if acorns are scarce. Before displaying, let dry overnight—or longer—to allow the acorns to set. I found that placing our wreaths on top of our refrigerator worked well because the outside coils behind the refrigerator create a gentle rising warmth for any glue-drying project.

The following poem, I think, reflects one "Charlotte Mason How-to." The idea is based on an acorn.

Little by Little

"Little by little," an acorn said,
As it slowly sank in its mossy bed;
"I am improving day by day,
Hidden deep in the earth away."
Little by little each day it grew;
Little by little it sipped the dew;
Downward it sent out a thread-like root;
Up in the air sprung a tiny shoot.
Day after day, and year after year,
Little by little the leaves appear;
And the slender branches spread far and wide,
Till the mighty oak is the forest's pride.
"Little by little," said a thoughtful boy,
"moment by moment I'll well employ,
Learning a little every day,
And not spending all my time in play;
And still this rule in my mind shall dwell,
'Whatever I do, I will do it well.'
Little by little I'll learn to know
The treasured wisdom of long ago;
And one of these days perhaps we'll see
That the world will be the better for me."
And do you not think that this simple plan
Made him a wise and useful man?

—Author unknown

Autumn is Marigold Seeds

Some people don't care for the fragrance of marigolds—some people and some creatures. Marigolds, we are told, are a natural deterrent for certain pests that desire to devour a vegetable garden, and so they have become a humble easy-to-grow back garden variety of flower. I am particularly fond of marigolds and I like their fragrance. I spend my summer nipping off any wilting flowers and am rewarded with more and more flowers. By autumn, we have a little bush of blossoms arrayed in precise autumn colors, but in late October, I let our marigold flowers dry up and form seeds. Vertically splitting open the base of a dry flower fills the air with that unusual fragrance. I let the children see if they can spot the black seeds inside, separate them, and spread them out to dry.

"How about making our own seed packets for gifts?" I asked the children the year that marigolds were in abundance. I let the children solve the problem of making tiny envelopes by working out their own personal paper-folding techniques. It took several tries before they were content.

"Let's draw and color a picture of a marigold on the front and write the name on the packet before we fill them," I instructed.

I suppose these seeds could be sold or traded for a neighbor's portion of saved seed, but they do make lovely gifts that can be conveniently and inexpensively sent by mail inside a greeting card. You are free to design your own packet. If you have very young children, you may wish to use a regular-size white envelope and just decorate it. Making your own seed packets with any saved seed can be a good project for bored or book-weary children on a rainy autumn afternoon.

Autumn is Apples, Carrots, Raisins, and Marshmallows

I do try to limit my children's intake of sugar. Sometimes I am even militant about it, especially when flu season approaches. Here is one autumn treat that is a healthy compromise. I cut up pieces of an apple in little dice-sized cubes. There is no need to peel the skin. Pesticide-free fruits and vegetables are used whenever possible in our home. Two thin carrots are washed with a vegetable brush and sliced into thick "pennies" with a crinkle cutter. I take out some tooth picks, a handful of raisins, and a handful of mini-marshmallows. The children eagerly make their own treats by pushing onto the toothpick, in sequence, a carrot slice, a raisin, a marshmallow, an apple cube, and another marshmallow or raisin. When the treats are made, place them in a seal-tight container with one tablespoon (or less) of brown sugar and 1/4 teaspoon (or less) of cinnamon. Shake until coated. This camouflages any browning of the apple. This quantity serves six children. Double or triple the recipe as needed. Use as a treat for Brownies, birthdays, or any autumn party. Be careful to keep toddlers from swallowing or sucking on any tooth picks. Designate an obvious and easy-to-reach place for the used toothpicks to be deposited. A small lunch bag—with the sides rolled down a bit—works well on any table where the children are gathered. Our children enjoy making these colorful treats as much as eating them.

Wind and the Leaves

"Come, little Leaves," said the Wind one day,
"Come o'er the meadows with me, and play;
Put on your dresses of red and gold;
Summer is gone, and the days grow cold."
Soon as the Leaves heard the Wind's loud call,
Down they came fluttering, one and all;
Over the fields they danced and flew,
Singing the soft little songs they knew . . .
Dancing and whirling the little leaves went;
Winter had called them, and they were content.
Soon, fast asleep in their earthy beds,
The snow laid a coverlet over their heads.

— George Cooper

Narration Idea

With so much action and color in this poem, "The Wind and the Leaves," it is easy to form a picture of it in our imaginations. It longs to be drawn. Older children may use it as a subject for watercolors or color pencils. Younger children may enjoy bold felt pens or crayons. It can be copied into a copy book, or made into an autumn greeting card.

Bumblebees are Free

Collect on nature walks: tiny pine or fir cones—like alder or hemlock cones—and maple seeds (we call them helicopters). If there are few maple trees where you live, search for other winged seeds. Maple trees are not the only seeds with wings. You will also need some string, a pair of scissors and glue.

With scissors, cut the "wings" off the maple seeds. Lay a tiny pine cone on its side. The wide end is the face of the bumblebee. Tuck a pair of wings into the pine cone at an upward angle—riding the upper sides of the cone. Are all the maple wings exactly alike? Are all your bumblebees exactly alike? Attach string with a squeeze of glue, or tie round a bit of cone. Hang several outside a window or on a tree branch and watch them buzz. You might press a thin twig under the bumblebee and press it onto a fall moss bowl or terrarium.

Autumn Spider Webs

Spiders and insects have grown to a mature size by the beginning of autumn, when they are considerably large enough to become conspicuous. Their size makes them easier to identify with a field guide and to draw into Nature Notebooks. The praying mantises (hundreds) we hatched indoors in a jar in the spring and distributed throughout the yard are so many times larger than they once were. Early autumn is also a good time to draw insects because the cooler weather slows them down. They don't wander off when they are asked to sit for a drawing—well, except for the woolly bears, who walk the streets looking for a place to hibernate. On a rainy, windy day,

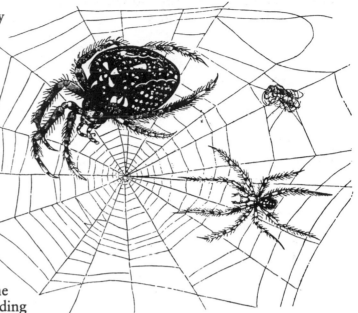

when an insect-spotting afternoon is canceled, children may like to make a model spider and web.

You will need:

- cotton twine (The cotton is absorbent. I found it at the grocery store.)
- wax paper
- glue
- throw away containers like yogurt cups
- paper plates or cardboard

This is a sticky project that will excite young students who like getting their hands messy. We did this craft during our early years of homeschooling—when it seemed my little ones were always using their hands to do something. Come to think of it, they are still restless to put their hands to use. Start out with your table protected. All busy crafters should wear bibs or aprons.

Tear off one square of wax paper per child. Lay it flat over some cardboard or a paper plate. Give each child six pieces of approximately four-inch pieces of twine.

Place twine pieces into the container and squeeze in some glue. Knead with fingers until completely coated. Straighten out each piece of twine. Lay one end pointing toward a corner of the wax paper. The other end should point toward the center of the paper. The arrangement should resemble the spokes of a wheel. In the center of the wheel should be a little space where the spider will dangle. Now cut a long piece of twine and coat it completely with glue also. Keep wet paper towels or damp rags handy for those children who fret about sticky fingers. (Some will giggle at the sticky mess. Boys may instantly say, "Ah, cool!") Spiral this long piece of twine. Start near the center and spiral around and around toward the edges of the wax paper. Press firmly over the places where this twine meets with the twine spokes. Can you see the web forming? These must remain flat until the next day, when they should be dry and stiff.

Next day: Gently turn web over and peel away wax paper. Tape to a window or a corner wall. Draw and cut out on black paper a spider. There may be some hefty living models outdoors to copy.

Thumbelina or Floating Baby

For this project, you will need the following items:

- empty walnut shell halves
- cotton fabric swatches
- wooden beads or tiny acorns
- unspun wool or cotton balls
- glue

Tear off with your fingers a bit of unspun wool or use a cotton ball. Squeeze a dot of glue into the walnut shell half. Press the wool inside. Cut a one inch square or oval piece of cotton fabric and tuck your baby's blanket in place over the wool into the edges of the shell. Use glue if necessary. It should be a little mound. Draw a few marks on a small wooden bead or tiny acorn to make a sleeping baby face. Place the bead at one end of the blanket inside the shell. Very carefully set your baby afloat in a puddle or bowl. Last fall my daughter Sophia attached a loop to one end and saved it to hang on the Christmas tree. Her illustrations are provided below.

Autumn Leaf Window Decorations

Autumn wax-paper window decorations are a family tradition in our house. About the middle of October we look forward to our stroll through the yard and neighborhood to select leaves that catch our eye. When we return, the leaves are fanned out across the kitchen table where they are admired, while Mom sets up the iron and ironing board. Any wet leaves are gently dabbed with a tea towel.

A rectangular piece of wax paper is torn off and placed wax side up on the ironing board. (To test for wax side, scratch with finger nail.) The youngest participating child has the first turn to arrange a few of his leaves on the wax paper, keeping a little space between the leaves and at the borders. Some leaves may overlap slightly. Another piece of wax-paper is placed—wax side down—over the arrangement. A dry

A Lighter Pumpkin Pie

Have on hand a pre-baked pie shell or a Graham cracker crust. I always double this recipe to make two pumpkin chiffon pies.

- Soak: 1 tablespoon gelatin in 1/4 cup cold water. I use those little orange envelopes of gelatin.

- Beat slightly: 3 egg yolks. Refrigerate the whites. They will be used later.

- Add: ½ cup white or brown sugar, 1¼ cup canned or cooked pumpkin, ½ cup milk, ½ teaspoon salt, ¼ teaspoon each of cinnamon, nutmeg, and ginger.

Cook and stir these ingredients in a double boiler, or you may do what I do and float a smaller pot in a larger pot of boiling water. A double recipe takes more time to thicken. The mixture may become less thick than you might expect. Nevertheless, stir in the soaked gelatin until dissolved.

Let cool a bit, then cover and refrigerate until mixture begins to set.

Whip until stiff, but not dry: 3 egg whites.

Stir in gradually: ½ cup sugar. I've used a little less sugar and it has come out fine. Fold into the pumpkin mixture.

Fill the pie shell with the pumpkin mixture.

Refrigerate several hours to set. Garnish with a dab of whipped cream and a sprinkle of cinnamon.

An Indian Corn Necklace

In her *Handbook of Nature Study,* Anna Botsford Comstock says,

Had Columbus found the Indies with their wealth of fabrics and spices, he would have found there nothing so valuable to the world as has proved this golden treasure of ripened corn. . . So long had maize been cultivated by the American Indians that it was thoroughly domesticated when America was first discovered. In those early days of American colonization, it is doubtful,

cloth napkin or thin tea towel is laid on top. With a guiding hand from Mom, the child smoothes the napkin with the medium hot iron. Steam is not necessary. Mom keeps one eye on the hot iron at all times, especially with anxious brothers and sisters gathered round awaiting their turn.

All wish to see younger brother's creation as the napkin is lifted. Mom carefully slides the warm wax-paper decoration over to the edge of the ironing board to cool and set before it is picked up. A new piece of wax-paper is immediately torn for the next child, who eagerly arranges her leaves.

When the decorations are cooled, the rough border is rounded with scissors. The beautiful leaf decorations are now taped to a window. The autumn glow of sunlight reveals the colors to be as bright as they were on the tree. Their colors will linger even after the fallen leaves outdoors turn brown.

Our October wax projects were saved until November and mailed to far-off grandparents and pen pals, along with an autumn poem to celebrate Thanksgiving. They stay fresh at least until Christmas.

says Professor John Fiske, if our forefathers could have remained here had it not been for Indian corn. No plowing, or even clearing, was necessary for the successful raising of this grain. The trees were girdled, thus killing their tops to let in the sunlight, the rich earth was scratched a little with a primitive tool, and the seed put in and covered; and the plants that grew therefrom took care of themselves. If the pioneers had been obliged to depend alone upon the wheat and rye of Europe, which only grows under good tillage, they might have starved before they gained a foothold on our forest-covered shores.[1]

Indian corn necklaces are made with the same colored corn that is displayed on door-fronts in October and November. The cheapest place to purchase this decorative corn is at a rural farm market. Perhaps if a special little trip is taken along the country roads—to view

the changing leaves *en route* to the pumpkin patch—you may pick up some dried Indian corn, too.

To make an Indian corn necklace, you will need:

- dried colored corn
- needle
- thread

Soaking the pieces of corn first softens them for stringing. A spool of clear nylon thread is especially durable and just a bit more tangle-proof, but regular thread will work, too. With a not-too-small sewing needle children simply string on the kernels in any color combination. A collection of acorns and other dried seeds gathered on nature walks may be strung together with the corn and worn at any festive fall celebration.

Country Corn Husk Dolls
by Sophia Andreola

Five years ago I was seated at a rough table in a spacious old barn with about twenty other children. The place was called Traveler's Rest, an historical museum and park in Tennes-see. It was here that I was taught how to make my first old-fashioned corn husk doll— an experience I hoped I'd get the chance to have again. Soon after my first corn husk doll experience, my father had a job change and we transferred first to New Jersey, then to Oregon. That summer seemed to crawl by (as we had no air conditioning), but finally fall arrived. The season reminded me of my previous year's experience at Traveler's Rest. When I asked my mother if we could make another doll like the ones my sister and I had made the year before, she said, "If you peel and dry the corn husks I'll help you." She knew how much I like to make things. Those dolls were a bit silly looking, with wobbly necks, odd-shaped heads and crooked skirts. But we were proud of them anyway. My mother must have been proud, too, for they were her conversation piece with every visitor.

A few years later we found ourselves renting a house in Maryland. The subdivision was surrounded by corn fields. That fall my sister and I took our bikes and cycled to the end of a side street that ended where the corn field began. The corn had already been harvested, but on the ground was a bountiful supply of dry husks and stalks. For about an hour we picked through the husks, gathering the choicest ones. We piled our husks in the rusty basket of my squeaky old bike—the same bike and basket that had caused me some embarrassment in the neighborhood, but which I was at that moment happy to have. We invited a neighboring homeschooling family to make the dolls with us and join in our family's tradition. This year we invite you to make some dolls with us, too.

Instructions and Illustrations for Making Basic Corn Husk Dolls

You will need:

- whole dried corn husks
- white thread
- scissors
- dried corn silk (optional).
- calico fabric (optional)

Dry Husks

Save corn husks and silk when peeling corn-on-the-cob. Dry husks in the sun or atop the refrigerator for two weeks or more. You will know they are dried completely when they are a yellowish-tan color and feel like paper.

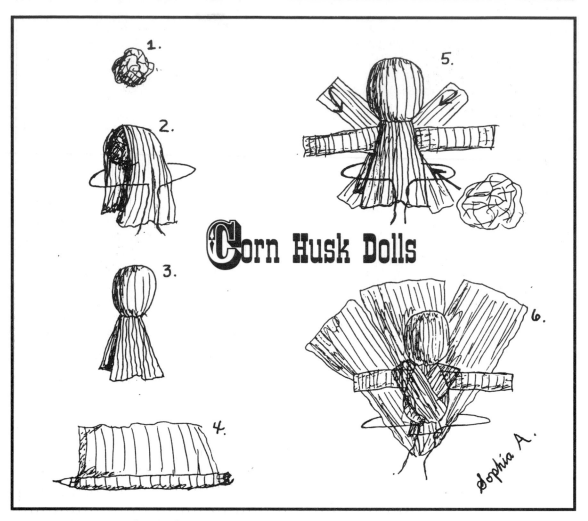

1.

2.

5.

3.

Corn Husk Dolls

6.

4.

Sophia A.

Soak Husks

On the day of doll-making, soak the husks gently in warm water for five to ten minutes.

Strain husks and lay on a plate. Have tea towels handy. Now you are ready.

Head First

To make a head: crumple a husk into a tight ball about the size of a large marble. Fold a husk over the ball like a large hood. The smoothest side will be the face. Tuck the side flaps into each other. Gather husk snugly just below the ball and tie tightly with thread. It is important that some husk extends several inches or more below the tie.

Arms, Shoulders, Chest

To make the arms, place a long piece of husk horizontally on the table. Using a pencil, roll it over the husk, wrapping the pencil up in it. Slip the pencil out, but keep the rolled husk wound up like a drinking straw. Like the cross of the letter "T", this roll forms both arms when centered below the head. Tuck it up inside the husks that extend below the tied head. A crumpled piece of husk will make the chest when stuffed just below the arm roll inside the extending husk pieces. Tie husk pieces together under the stuffing to make a waist. Your doll should not have a visible neck. The head will look more like a ball on shoulders. This prevents wobbling. To complete the chest, take two husks and fold at either side of the head (over the arms) to make shoulders. The husk strips should criss-cross in the front and in back like sashes. Tie these over at the same place you tied the waist.

Skirt

The skirt of the doll is attached upside down. First make the back: take three or four large, smooth husks and spread them on the table like a fan. (They will overlap.) Place the doll (face up) over the point (apex) of the fan. Can you see how the skirt appears to be upside down behind her? Leave some husk to overlap at the waist and tie the skirt (or fan) tightly at the waist. Do the same for the front. Carefully bend the moist pliable husks down over the ties and—voila!—a skirt.

The Finishing Touches

To finish, trim the ends of the arms and skirt with scissors. If the skirt is trimmed straight across and arranged in a bell shape to dry, the doll may stand up. Decorate with cloth if you like. An apron can easily be made by gluing some cotton calico at the waist. A long piece of corn silk will make cascading locks when glued over the head. Cut a calico triangle just the right size to make a kerchief that hides the glue and keeps the hair in place.

To make a gentleman doll, divide skirt in two and loosely tie husks at the end of the trousers. A bit of corn silk can be used to make a mustache. Corn husk dolls are traditionally faceless, like Amish dolls. You might decide to draw a face on yours with a fine felt pen. I hope you will enjoy creating all kinds of country corn husk people to decorate your fall table. ⤞

> Had Columbus found the Indies with their wealth of fabrics and spices, he would have found there nothing so valuable to the world as has proved this golden treasure of ripened corn.
>
> —Anna Botsford Comstock, *Handbook of Nature Study*

Chapter Forty-Two

Snowflakes and Black Velvet

MOTHER DIDN'T GO UP INTO THE ATTIC OFTEN—at least that is what the children believed—so it was a curious place for the growing boy. It smelled of cedar and was the quietest place he had ever been. Mother's opinion was that time didn't exist up here, only the things that marked time. She mostly made trips to the attic when all her little ones were asleep, for she never wished them to be tempted to climb the narrow steps themselves, or ever consider it an optional place to hide during winter's indoor hide-and-seek rampages. She needed to have one out-of-way place to arrange the cluttery sorts of things and thoughts that women are always lovingly planning and secretly preparing. Her eldest child was now allowed to accompany her into the attic while the others napped, as he was becoming such a help to her.

They finished carrying up the last of the boxed Christmas decorations. Mother opened a large trunk to remove heavy cold-weather draperies. She should have replaced the light summer draperies with these months ago, but autumn had been so sunny and pleasant she had had no wish to shroud an extra inch of it from view with the winterizing. As she gathered the heavy bundle in her arms, a jet black swatch of material came loose from the surrounding folds of drapery and caught the boy's eye. It caused his eyes to sparkle for, to him, it represented winter's first snowfall. He anticipated the pleasant feel of its luxurious softness and flashed an outstretched arm to catch it before it tumbled onto the floor.

"Has winter come?" he asked. He already knew what her answer would be, but he found joy in the confirmation. "How soon do you think it will snow, Mother?" he asked absentmindedly. Then with a growing excitement, he said, "Do you think it will snow today? It didn't snow on Christmas."

"I'm sure it will snow quite soon," she reassured him. "I know how anxious you are to use our old scrap of velvet."

Catch a Fallen Snowflake. . .

When was the last time you looked closely at a snowflake? If you live in the Southern states, the answer may be "never." If you live up North, you probably have had many—too many—opportunities, but still may not be able to answer the question. Here is your chance to begin a simple and inexpensive family tradition and follow through with the unfinished story above.

You can celebrate the first fluffy cold snowfall with a black swatch of fabric. Keep it hidden until the big event. It doesn't have to be velvet—any inexpensive black fabric can become your traditional swatch. You may want to have several on hand if there are many enthusiastic children in your family. Black construction paper has a tendency to absorb the moistness of the snowflake when the temperature outdoors is not quite cold enough and the snowflakes will disappear before you get the chance to look closely at them. This is one reason to re-use a special swatch of fabric each winter, apart

from the obvious sentimental reason.

Keep the fabric outdoors in a plastic bag long enough for it to become as cold as its surroundings. Then remove it from the plastic and use as a snow-catcher. Snowflakes will stay frozen and retain their shape as they gently land on the cloth. With a magnifying glass—or even the unaided eye, if you have good eyesight—you'll be able to get a clear look at the beautiful crystals.

Paper Snowflakes

When my little boy was four years old he liked to fold construction paper and snip pieces from it with blunt scissors—something his big sister taught him when I wasn't looking. He enjoyed opening up the colored construction paper to see the design he had made. I remember saying, "What a pretty (green) snowflake you've made, Nigel."

"It's not a snowflake," he said plainly.

Whatever it was, it kept him happy for what seemed to be just the right amount of time while his older sisters read aloud or narrated, and so I didn't interfere with his concentration. I can also remember standing at the edge of the old gold shag wall-to-wall carpet in the living room of our rented house gazing over the sunken family room with my hands on my hips and declaring, "I thought I just vacuumed this place." And during the period of his boyhood that he enjoyed this snipping activity, it seemed I never had an uncluttered scrap-free carpet. But how could I complain, since he was quietly occupied during the most crucial moments of our homeschool lessons?

After the Christmas decorations are put away and the anti-climatic month of January is upon us, we make paper snowflakes. I made them in college, although my worldly roommates thought it was overly quaint and had something to do

with my recent conversion to Christianity. (Christian people do odd and corny things, I suppose.) I made them when our girls were babies in Florida—just before the orange trees bloomed. I made them when we wintered in New Jersey, Pennsylvania, England, Tennessee, and Oregon. This January, in Maryland, we will have snowflakes on our windows again.

Paper snowflakes can chase away the grayness of a gloomy winter day. They are another inexpensive way to celebrate nature's beauty. Simply fold a square of thin white paper in half and in half again. Then cut and snip in between the two open sides, and as you unfold your paper a snowflake will appear. For older children let the goal be to figure out how to create six spokes (a January math project). It is not such a necessary goal for the younger ones. A modified square with varying holes in the middle will be an object of fanciful interest to them. For the perfectionist-prone, iron the snowflakes under a tea towel, then add opaque glitter to create a touch of frost on each unique design.

When you find a hexagon pattern you like, make a cardboard template. The children can trace the shape onto paper, then fold to form six overlapping triangles. The triangle can be cut on all three sides in whatever way the child designer decides.

For those who are challenged to acquire the old-fashioned skill of more sophisticated designs, there are patterns and instructions for folding and cutting over sixty paper snowflakes in the craft book, *Easy-to-Make Decorative Paper Snowflakes,* by Brenda Lee Reed.

Another good snowflake resource is a lovely book called *Snow Crystals.* This book has over two thousand photographs of actual snowflakes. You will be amazed at God's creativity. ❧

Chapter Forty-Three

....

Victorian Lace or
Favorite Lace Edging

I CAME ACROSS A PATTERN to knit lace from an old *Parents' Review* magazine dated 1898. Until then, I hadn't known lace could be made by knitting. Since Queen Victoria lived until January 1901, this lace is truly from the Victorian era. It was actually a home education project for girls aged twelve or so.

Discovering this project brought back memories. When I was very young, I lived three houses down from my grandmother and her mother, my great-grandmother. After school I'd run over for a chat with my great-grandmother. She was a young girl during the Victorian era and had probably learned how to make lace at that time. She still wore her white hair in a bun and of course always wore dresses. While we talked she sat crocheting fine, colorful, lace edging on white pillow cases and handkerchiefs. Her sunny bedroom was painted violet, and had lots of white lace accents. The fragrance of the room was lavender—perhaps from the powder she used daily from her powder puff box. We played our usual round of Chinese checkers before I ran home, my stomach growling for supper. When she passed away, I had sadly lost a confidante. Her bedroom was unused for at least a decade but remained her choice of color—violet. It was furnished, but it seemed so empty—and never as sunny as I had once remembered it to be.

The directions for "Favorite Lace Edging" appeared on the pages of the old *Parents' Review* in long paragraphs. I kept losing my place, knitting wrong stitches, having to unravel my work and start over. I never got as far as the second set of patterned rows. This happened exactly nine times. Perhaps it was the sweet memory of my great-grandmother that rooted my determination. By the following week of evenings it occurred to me to put the directions in shorthand. They could be read at a glance, and I could keep most of my attention on the stitches, counting out loud as I went along. My usually talkative husband sat beside me in silence until I finally accomplished one set of rows. It took quite a bit of concentration; therefore, after finishing one set of rows (one scallop), I laid the work aside for the following evening.

 One week later, five scalloped edges had appeared, and then I began to whiz along. In the midst of the hustle and bustle of late 20th century life, I can claim to knit true Victorian lace. I know, some people get their thrills climbing mountains, but why go through all that trouble when a similar feeling of accomplishment can be experienced in a little time, with a little domestic thing?

To do this project all you really need to know is:

- how to cast on
- how to go from knitting to purling and back to knitting again
- how to slip stitch
- how to cast off

I used narrow needles, size three, along with embroidery floss to make a lace collar for my younger daughter's Easter dress. A disadvantage of the floss is that it is not twisted, and strands can separate while knitting. Cotton crochet thread costs less and can also be knitted using several strands at once. Young girls can begin by using thin yarn to make an edging on pillows or fabric mats.

Abbreviations:

K   ...knit
B.for ...bring thread forward
K2g   ...knit two together
( )x2   ...do this twice
( )x3   ...do this thrice
@ce   ...wrap thread around needle twice

Particulars

To knit ribbing you must bring the thread forward before you purl and then bring it back again before knitting. Remember to do the same here when needed. Sliding a bookmark or index card over the rows to mark your place is a must. Each purl stitch will seem loose. Be careful not to drop this stitch. The purling makes a twist that adds to the lacy aspect of the pattern. The numbers of the stitches increase as you follow the rows until five stitches are cast off for the scalloped edge. Eventually the pattern will become more automatic. If you have never knitted lace before, this will be a bit of a challenge. Here is your opportunity to enjoy a little diversion in true Victorian lace making style!

A Final Word

For your peace of mind I re-examined these directions to eliminate any errors. I even referred to it while knitting my own lace so that you'll be certain that if you hit a messy spot in your knitting, these directions cannot be blamed.

A First Knitting Project

A very easy knitting project is that of making a triangular shawl. I made one out of home-spun wool for Felicity, my younger daughter's American girl doll. A plastic cameo brooch (which amazingly looks like ivory) pins the points under the neck. Using a set of long needles, simply cast on two stitches. Knit the first row. Increase by one or two stitches at beginning of every row. (Tight knitters should increase by two stitches). Cast off when the desired size is reached. More experienced knitters can hand-sew Favorite Lace Edging of the same color yarn or a white yarn to the lower two edges of the shawl. ✦

Instructions for

Victorian Lace

....

Cast on eleven stitches.

1st Row - Knit

2nd Row - Slip 1 K1, (B.for K2g)x3 @ce K2g, K1

3rd Row - K3 purl 1, K5, B.for K2g, K1

4th Row - Slip 1 K1, B.for K2g K1, (B.for K2g)x2 @ce K2g, K1

5th Row - K3 purl 1, K6, B.for K2g, K1

6th Row - Slip 1 K1, B.for k2g K2, (B.for K2g)x2 @ce K2g, K1

7th Row - K3 purl 1, K7, B.for K2g, K1

8th Row - Slip 1 K1, B.for K2g K3, (B.for K2g)x2 @ce K2g, K1

9th Row - K3 purl 1, K8, B.for K2g, K1

10th Row - Slip 1 K1, B.for K2g K4 (B.for K2g)x2 @ce K2g, K1

11th Row - K3 Purl 1, K9 B.for K2g, K1

12th Row - Slip 1 K1, B.for K2g K12

13th Row - Cast off 5, K7 B.for K2g, K1

Repeat from Second Row

Chapter Forty-Four

···

School Motto

IN 1891, A SCHOOL WAS STARTED WITH NO BUILDING to mark its site. Instead of a building it consisted of the "blessed company" of children all over the world who used Charlotte Mason's home education program. All the children read the same books, took the same examinations, wore the same badge, thought about and acted upon the same motto. The picture on the badge was a skylark which represented the ideas in Wordsworth's poem, "To a Sky-lark." The motto read, "I AM. . ,I CAN. . . ,I OUGHT. . . , I WILL." The idea is one of soaring high, ascending in heart and mind in prayer and with high and heavenly ideals ("glorious light"). But we also descend like the skylark to its nest to do all the lowly simple deeds that are our daily duty to home ("who soar but never roam").

When I first read the poem I read it eagerly, yet as impatiently as I read prose. I admit, not being steeped in Wordsworth as Charlotte was, I wasn't able to pick up its fine meaning at once. Then I read it again more slowly and discovered the meaning wasn't as cumbersome to pick up as I originally thought. Today, as I type out the words of the poem into this chapter, I realize the best pace at which to read a poem is as fast as one can type.

To a Sky-lark

Ethereal minstrel! pilgrim of the sky!

Dost thou despise the earth where cares abound?

Or, while the wings aspire, are heart and eye

Both with thy nest upon the dewy ground?

Thy nest which thou canst drop into at will,

Those quivering wings composed, that music still!

Leave to the nightingale her shady wood;

A privacy of glorious light is thine,

Whence thou dost pour upon the world a flood

Of harmony, with instinct more divine;

Type of the wise who soar, but never roam;

True to the kindred points of Heaven and Home!

I am

Our heavenly Father, and Christ the Son have declared themselves to be the great I Am. This is something on which to meditate.

Every child, can say, "I am, because I am a child of God and I am His gift to my parents. Charlotte teaches children to recognize what they are as persons created in the image of God.

I can

A child experiences confidence by first trying to do his best at little things. "Look, Mom, I made a tower!" says the three-year-old who has balanced his blocks in a pile as high as he is. Oh no, here come the tears as the tower tumbles to the floor.

"You *can* build it again, says Mother.

"Mom, watch what I *can* do," says the six-year-old a day after his training wheels are removed. This time it is the child himself who may fall to the ground. Gradually, he learns through experience that he is able to do amazing things, even if he stumbles toward his goal.

Can any of us say we have never fallen? Is there any who has never sinned? Confession is necessary everyday as is Christ's forgiveness. We can do things through Him even though we stumble because He alone is our strength and our song. Even a page of one hundred multiplication problems can be done without tears eventually, if the student has started out small, been "faithful in the little things," like daily drill. Consequently, when "much is given" he will think and say, "I can."

I ought

"Why bother?" says the unmotivated person who has not learned that he ought. At one time children were trained in public school in the righteousness of the Christian faith. This was just a few generations ago, before all godliness was removed from the classroom. My next-door neighbor became a widow this year. She is in her eighties and has lived in her house since the first years of her marriage. She remembers watching the construction of our house in 1929. I pay her little visits when I can. I love to hear her talk of the past. She was never able to have children of her own but taught many of them in the public school system. Every morning she and the children would pray the Lord's Prayer aloud together. One day a student stood up and said, "I don't have to say this, you know."

"Fine," she said, "you may stand outside the door until we are finished." Our children needn't be fools. When we teach them to fear God, to reverence Him, to respect the authority He has given us, they will gain wisdom along the way. We do things because they are right. I asked my child, after we prayed together, "How do you know God is real and that he hears our prayers?" Her eyes became wide with surprise, not expecting to hear such a question.

"Because you say He is."
"How do you know I am right?"
"Because the Bible tells me so."

I will

It is not enough to know what is right. We must choose to do what is right. This is the function of the will—to decide. Joshua said to the Hebrews, "Choose ye this day whom you will serve. . . as for me and my house, we will serve the Lord."

A book was published some time ago with the title *Love is a Choice*. The title is a good one. It reminds us that love, generosity, servitude, kindness, courage, patience, etc. are all things we do not fall into. They are things which we, by choice, labor to make part of our character. Our daily walk in Christ is a choice. Charlotte tells us, "The one achievement possible and necessary for every man is character; and character is as finely wrought metal beaten into shape and beauty by the repeated and accustomed action of will . . . We who teach should make it clear to ourselves

that our aim in education is less conduct than character; conduct may be arrived at, as we have seen, by indirect routes, but it is of value to the world only as it has its source in character." With every choice we make we grow in character and our will to choose is strengthened. Training the conscience is a prerequisite. Right thinking prepares us to do right choosing and right acting. "Right thought flows upon the stimulus of an idea, and ideas are stored . . . in books and pictures and the lives of men and nations; these instruct the conscience and stimulate the will, and the man or child 'chooses' . . . To fortify the will is one of the great purposes of education," said Charlotte.

Whene'er a noble deed is wrought,
Whene'er is spoken a noble thought,
Our hearts, in glad surprise,
To higher levels rise.

—Longfellow

Summer break began several weeks ago. Each morning the children were to accomplish a series of small assignments—a math drill page, some writing, light chores, practice of their musical instruments, etc.— while Mother's back was turned for a couple of hours writing this book. After a week of stumbling, there came unpleasant penalties, Biblical admonishment, "pep talks" and prayer. I told them we would not go cherry picking, or to the pool, or shopping for fabric to make dresses, as we had planned, because they chose not to do each thing thoroughly and with promptness. Their conduct was adequate as far as obeying the letter of the law. Obedience in the spirit of the law was what I wanted, and this is the result of character. We would do the fun things if they chose to do their assignments in the spirit in which I had instructed them. Well, I have been amazed at how well they have picked up after themselves and how the older children have gone beyond what was expected of them. I congratulate them. "Wow, the winning over of the will works wonders!"—my tongue twister sentiment for the day.

I invite you to adopt a motto for your school. You are welcome to claim Charlotte's cherished one. I have found it a convenient check list to keep in the back of my mind. It is very easy even for the youngest student to understand and remember. Its guidance has effectively inspired us.

May the seeds of an inspiring motto find fertile soil in your life as well as the life of your children.[1]

Your Own Personal Reflections

....

....

....

....

....

....

....

....

Chapter Forty-Five

··

A New Grading Method: Motivation by Admiration, Hope, and Love

Dogs, dolphins, chimpanzees, and killer whales have this in common: they can be trained (motivated to perform) with edible treats and a little physical affection. But what about children? Should we use the same method in teaching children? Charlotte Mason begins her educational philosophy with the thought that "the child is a person, a human being with a spiritual origin." Yet most schools govern by a system of treats: grades, prizes, and competitive placing. Even Sunday schools give out balloons, happy face stickers, candy, and plastic trinkets as rewards for a children paying attention to the Word of God! Charlotte Mason believed this type of motivation to be harmful for learning and dangerous for a child's character. Grades were not a part of her program. She recognized that in many schools statistics, prizes, and grades were more important than the child's genuine attainment of knowledge. Her students either understood or they didn't, but each was expected to do his best.

In order to grade, one must have a grading system: a certain number of completed questions to arrive at a grade percentage. To accommodate these numbers, the curriculum becomes more factual: terminology is highlighted, memorization over-emphasized, and real thinking left behind. The desire for knowledge is crushed by the heavy weight of this system. Curiosity, with which every normal child is born, becomes "schooled out," and the child's soul is forced into a "good grades" straight-jacket. Today, when children become weary of this means to an end, teachers remind them that the grade is what's important. "You want to get a good grade, don't you?" asks the teacher.

Charlotte didn't see the advantage of grades, but she did see that a love of knowledge was the best motivation for learning. "The race is to the swift," said Mr. Gibbon, headmaster of a PNEU boy's school, "so why not let it be known from the start? Only let some of the reward go to those whose effort has been greater than their actual achievement. What kind of students are these, the ones who want to know?"

This is a different way to look at it, isn't it?

Charlotte's Motto of Education

According to Charlotte, teachers possess three legitimate educational instruments—three ways to motivate children to learn: **the atmosphere of environment, the discipline of habit, and the presentation of ideas.** Thus her motto: Education is an atmosphere, a discipline, a life.

I would like you to consider some new "grades" (or reasons for living and learning) that need to come out of the shadows and into the light. As William Wordsworth said:

We live by Admiration, Hope and Love!
And even as these are well and wisely fixed,
In dignity of Being we ascend.

Admiration: The New Grade "A"

May all children know the light of grade "A"! Children should be taught to recognize and *admire* the righteous, the pure, the heroic, the beautiful, the truthful, and the loyal in their educational life.

Charlotte Mason tells us,

Admiration, reverent pleasure, delight, praise, adoration, worship; we know how the soul takes wings to herself when she admires and how veritably she scales the heavens when she adores. We know, too, how the provincial attitude of mind, *nil admirari,* paralyses imagination and relaxes effort. We have all cried, "Woe is me that I am constrained to dwell in the tents of Mesech," the Mesech of the commonplace, where people do not think great thoughts or do noble acts, and where beauty is not. Our dull days drag themselves through, but we can hardly be said to live; wherefore all praise to the poet who perceived the vital character of admiration.

We can rely upon living books and experiences to put children in touch with other minds and persons. Charlotte sought to give children books written by single authors who are writing about their favorite subjects rather than textbooks for the classroom compiled by committees. Living books touch the emotions as enthusiasm seeps through the information, but nothing inspiring can be read between the pure facts and information of dry textbooks. Reading inspiring biographies, diaries, historical novels, allegorical fiction, nature journals, and sweeping poems gives larger margin for admiration among the necessary drills and skills of education. Why? Because the authors of these books are themselves admirers and they have chosen to put us in touch with the inspiring lives of people. They can lead the way for our awe of God, wonder of nature, interest in history, and the finer, simpler or noble things of life. It would be a pity if this part of education were missed.

Admiration by Experience

One day, our family drove north to visit Daniel Boone's Homestead. Seeing the buildings and objects once used by actual settlers evoked a certain awe, and brought home to us the amazing reality of the pioneer people, whom we may admire for different reasons. The way in which the history was personally related made the trip even more of a special event.

Our young tour guide obviously shared an intimacy with history. I don't know how many times he gave the same speech, but it seemed directed exclusively to us and the small group of onlookers—as fresh as if it were spoken for the first time. The way he described each scene, we couldn't help but sense his admiration for these more simple, self-sufficient, hard working, determined, courageous, God-fearing, and skillful people. He invited questions and gave answers accurately with pleasure, even the questions asked by my attentive young son—whose older sisters, by the way, although a bit too self-conscious to ask questions of the handsome young man, were similarly impressed by the day.

My husband, Dean, and I talked about the visit during our drive home. "There was an important question I forgot to ask the tour guide," I said to him as I leafed through my new purchase (the thickest book the Homestead sold on domestic colonial life).

"What was that? Should we turn back?" he replied teasingly, taking his foot off the accelerator.

I lowered my brow and said with false anxiety, "I should have asked him which bit we had to know for the test!"

Hope: Grade "H"

What in the world is grade "H"? What good is hope in education? Some people might connect it with daydreams of vacationing in Hawaii as they are shoveling snow. This is an example of a false hope. Yet we cannot live without the benefits of this grade "H."

How sad it is to think of so many children, poor of soul, who show up to the classroom without any hope of really learning anything or aspiring toward anything. And as if the child hasn't suffered enough, insult is added to injury when some dreadful adult utters the ultimate condemnation: "He'll never amount to anything." Then I think of Charlotte's words:

> If we [want to] know how far we live by hope, how far it is our bread of life to us, we must go where hope is not. Dante understood. He found written upon the gates of hell: "Abandon hope all ye who enter here." The prisoner who has no hope of release, the man with the mortal sickness who has no hope of recovery, the family which has had to abandon hope for its dearest. These know, by the loss of hope, that it is by hope that we live. Our God is

described as "the God of Hope," and we might get through many a dark day if we realize this. Hope is a real if not tangible possession, like all the best things we can ask for and have. Let us try to conceive the possibility of going through a single day without any hope for this life or the next, and a sudden deadness falls upon our spirits, because we live by hope.

I Can

Students of Charlotte were taught, encouraged, guided, and disciplined in the light of their school motto: "I am, I can, I ought, I will." Their love of knowledge helped to develop their characters rather than achieve a grade.

Let us be faithful teachers. No matter what the pace, children need to know they can accomplish the tasks set before them. Meeting grade-level requirements in the early years is not as important as steadfast effort. So-called "late bloomers" are only flowers that bloom at a different time, and we all know that the beautiful varieties of flowers in God's world do not all bloom in the same season. Yet, no matter when the buds open or the fruit forms, all children also need to be nourished daily on ideas from experience, culture, and a wide curriculum.

Children will be motivated by the happiness and hopefulness of their own brands of accomplishments. Two equally intelligent siblings may be good at altogether different tasks. The homeschool is sensitive to the different learning styles and the way children express their differing intelligences. Acknowledging a child's strength and giving him opportunity for development, as well as showing patience with any skills that are slow in developing, will give him hope. He is reassured that he will amount to something.

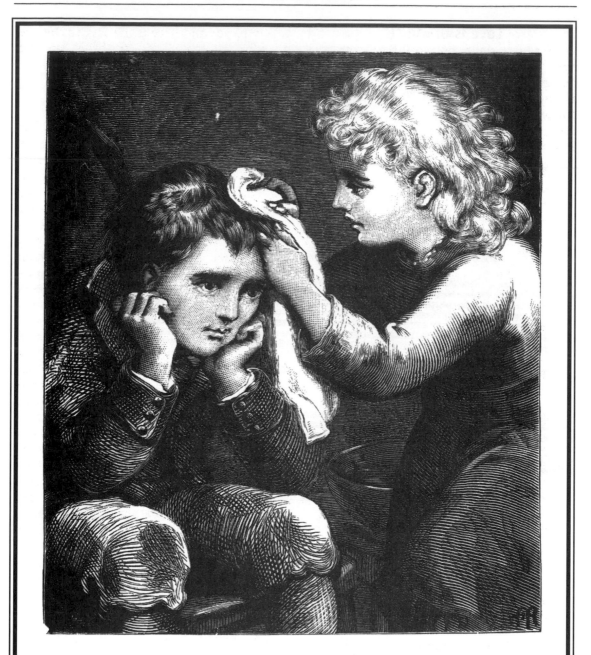

We live by love and the love we give and the love we receive, by the countless tendernesses that go out from us and the countless kindnesses that come to us . . .

Love is Grade "L"

Set your sights on working toward the new grade "L." No one can progress through life without this grade. The scholar and preacher John Wesley said, "An ounce of love is worth a pound of knowledge." Charlotte tells us not to ignore the greatness of love in the atmosphere of the homeschool. She says,

We live by love and the love we give and the love we receive, by the countless tendernesses that go out from us and the countless kindnesses that come to us; by the love of our neighbor and the love of our God. As all love implies a giving and a receiving, it is not necessary to separate the waters of love that flow. We do not ask what makes us happy, but we are happy, abounding in life, until some single channel of love and goodwill is obstructed, someone has given us offense or received offense at our hands and at once life runs low within us. We go languid and devoid of pleasure, we are no longer fully alive, because we live by love. Not by a consuming and unreasonable affection for any individual, but by the outgoing of love from us in all directions and the intaking of love from all sources. And this is not a state of intense and excited feeling, but is calm and continuous as the act of breathing. Thus we receive into us the love of God, and thus our own hearts go out in answering love.

Charlotte taught that we live by admiration, hope, and love, and without these three we do not live. And what is the consummation of our admiring, our hoping, and our loving? According to Wordsworth, a "gradual ascent in dignity of being." Charlotte said, "We see it, now and then, in beautiful old age, serene, wise, sweet, quick to admire, ready to hope against hope, and always to love. These three, which are identical with the three of which St. Paul says, 'Now abideth these three,' must be well and wisely fixed; and here is the task set before us who are appointed to bring up the young."

Obedience in Love

And what is an educated person but someone who is "well brought up?" I've read that "life is the first gift, love is the second, and understanding the third." Part of the educational life is an atmosphere of love and understanding. On the other hand, that doesn't mean there should be a lax atmosphere. Parents are in authority, and children in obedience. There is much that goes into a pleasant working atmosphere of the homeschool. The ideal educational syllabus would be one of strenuous effort alternating with wisely employed leisure. Character traits such as patience, long-suffering, kindness, and forgetfulness of past wrongs are no longer vague abstractions but very real qualities given substance by the actions of love. Because knowledge without virtue is nothing to God, when students strive to obtain grade "L," they will learn respect, courtesy, discipline, responsibility, honest effort, forgiveness, acceptance of natural consequences, restitution, careful service and allegiance. These new grades apply toward all three areas of education: education for character (moral), education for serviceableness in life (technical), and education for the understanding and appreciation of life (culture). Education is threefold. We can use the new grades without ignoring any of the three in favor of the other two. ⭑

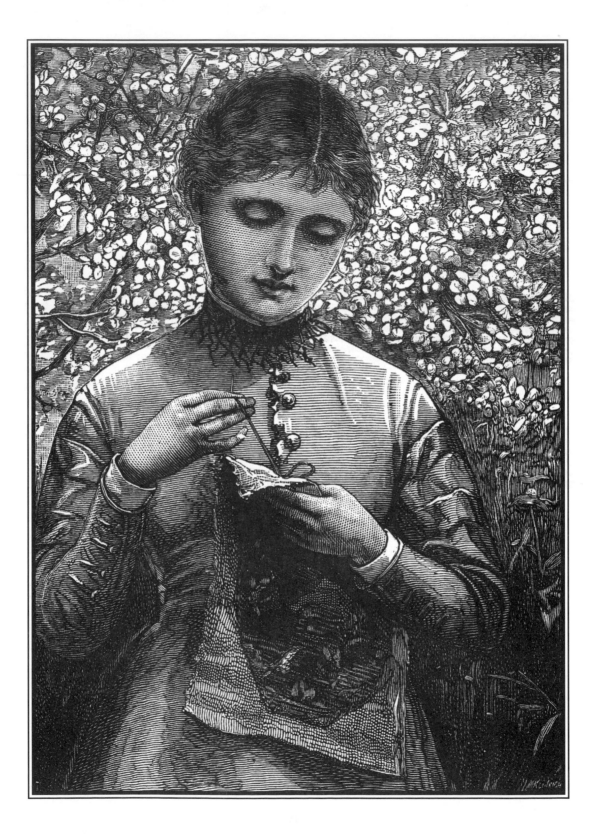

Chapter Forty-Six

....

Mother Culture

Make yourselves nests of pleasant thoughts, bright fancies,
faithful sayings; treasure-houses of precious and restful thoughts,
which care cannot disturb nor poverty take away from you,
houses built without hands for your souls to live in.

—JOHN RUSKIN

This chapter holds my words of good wishes to you who are hard-working mothers, who do lowly chores, and who have high ideals—what Charlotte Mason thought a felicitous combination.

Somewhere it is written that "A mother is only a woman, but she needs the love of Jacob, the patience of Job, the wisdom of Moses, the foresight of Joseph, and the firmness of Daniel." But a mother not only has to have all these things, she must have them all at once, often when she is quite young, and too often when she has had no previous training of any kind for the marvelously varied duties she has to perform. Before she marries, a young lady does not imagine herself facing the difficulties of managing the complicated workings of a household. Untried responsibilities come upon her as soon as she does marry. And, perhaps, just as she is grasping the situation, her first child is born and fills her whole heart. Then, not only her own health but that of another's depends on how she manages her life. The question of child training and how to "bring up" children becomes a new study and practical concern.

Another child is born, who eventually becomes a sunny companion for the first. But it seems that with each passing year, a mother's job description is revised. The desire for her husband's love and friendship is still strong, but a careful division of her attention is given up to the various aspects of maintaining a happy, well-managed home. Time alone with her husband now seems to have to be either previously planned moments or stolen ones. There are holiday celebrations to arrange, extended family parties and visits, church functions, occasions for neighborly hospitality, etc. In the center of it all is one little woman—wife, mother, mistress all in one! As the children approach their years of more formal education, there is the organization of the home schoolroom, and thus she walks over new ground again.

Is it a wonder she feels overspent? She wears herself out. In her efforts to be dietitian, laundress, nurse, hostess, teacher, taxi driver, wife, mother, and mistress, she forgets that she needs a little time for herself. And it is then that she stops growing spiritually and mentally. Physically she feels ragged and drags through the day until, without being able to mark the hour it began, she lives with depression. Her mind is in a drifting fog when she wants it to think clearly and efficiently. With the distractions of her multi-faceted duties she is unable to follow a train of thought. She considers herself hopelessly behind in everything. Her feet are in the quagmire. It takes an incredible amount of effort to keep up appearances,

to wear a winsome countenance. The last straw is the guilt she feels that she is "lukewarm" in the Lord. If I hadn't experienced these symptoms myself I wouldn't be writing this chapter. Therefore I can validate the need for Mother Culture.

And you, my dears, will no longer grow
If you rest contented with what you know,—
But a pitiful object you will dwell,
Shut up inside your hickory shell.

—from *Little Wide Awake*

Revival

A fresh wind of change will revive you when you participate in Mother Culture. Some may say, "I simply have no time for myself." Others, "I don't think it is right to think of myself." Such mothers are stuck in a rut of self-sacrifice to the extent that they are starving themselves spiritually, mentally, and, consequently, emotionally. Their children will grow up with that "Oh it's only mother," tone in their voice. Some children will eventually carry the attitude that they know more than Mother on all points.

But all this can be altered. Each mother must settle this for herself. The only way to do it is to be so deeply impressed herself with the necessity of growing that she makes it an aim in life. We hear people pray and ask God for strength to get through trying circumstances. This is good. But how does God's strength come to us? He blesses us with His strength if we are in His Word renewing our minds, if we pray, and if we follow the fourth commandment. Strength can only be acquired by building *stamina*. Just as a muscle needs both scrupulous exercise and rest to build stamina and to become strong, we must also exercise our minds and give ourselves some healthy leisure and diversion in order to be strong. Jesus, God's own Son, left the crowd to find solitude to pray and strengthen His spirit. He is our example. It is very right to find time for yourself, especially when so many others depend on you.

The resolute planting of Miss Three-year-old in her high chair at the end of the table with a ball of play dough, of Mr. Five-year-old at the other with his occupations, and of Mr. Baby on the rug with his fascinating ring of beads—with the decided announcement, "Now Mother is going to be busy"—will do these young ones a world of good. Though some of their charms will be missed, they will gain respect for mother's time, and some self-reliance into the bargain, while mother's tired back gets a rest—if only for a short time—either on the sofa or flat on the floor. Then she can listen to her children with one ear, and perhaps do a little thinking, or reading.

I found it easy to catch some light reading whenever the sandbox, puddle pool, or tricycle occupied my little ones. I'd pull up a lawn chair or blanket and do a little thinking, read an article, turn the leaves of a catalog or "how to" book. I have also enjoyed and benefited from learning along with my children what I missed during my childhood, from reading aloud everything from *Winnie the Pooh* to *The Robe*. This is something . . . but it is not enough.

Mother must have time to herself. We must experience the daily wholesomeness of Mother Culture. And we must not say, "I cannot." We need persistence to find time for ourselves, especially if our lives are hectic, hurried, and we have learned how to live on adrenaline in place of that highly practical virtue, fortitude. I like this quote by William Penn: "In the rush and noise of life, as you have intervals, be still. Wait upon God and feel his good presence;

this will carry you evenly through your day's business."

First we must find ways to simplify our lives. Only then can arrangements be made for a quiet time. It may be a time early in the morning, before children have awoken. It could be during the early afternoon when baby is sleeping and the other children stay in their quiet places until the kitchen timer buzzes.

Organize your time so that between ten and thirty minutes can be spent in an uninterrupted quiet time to focus on prayer, reading, etc. Ten minutes is substantially more worthwhile than no time at all. It *will* make a difference. After a week or two the children will become accustomed to Mother's quiet minutes. Settle them down with an afternoon "read-aloud" story or poem. Suggest a quiet activity while the younger ones nap. When the time is over, ring the little bell and reward them with time spent outdoors together, or preparing a meal together, giving them attention and kind words. They will come to appreciate you more after the separation and the wait.

Keep Three Books Going

The habit of grown-ups reading "living" books and retaining the power to digest them will be lost if we refuse to give a little time to Mother Culture. A wise woman—an admired mother and wife—when asked how, with her weak physical health and many demands upon her time, she managed to read so much, said, "Besides my Bible, I always keep three books going that are just for me—a stiff book, a moderately easy book, and a novel, and I always take up the one I feel fit for." That is the secret: always have something "going" to grow by.

A stiff book is a challenging one. It may be one of Christian doctrine or a collection of meaty sermons. I find reading C. S. Lewis requires concentration and though I do not understand everything of his that I read, I am enriched by what I do understand. Many feel the same about Charlotte Mason's books.

An easy book may be biographical. It lets us into the life of another struggling person, a person with integrity, determination, and the ability to surrender to God, perhaps. An inspiring book I read last summer was *An Ordinary Woman's Extraordinary Faith*. It is the autobiography of Patricia St. John, a British author of children's stories. You may be familiar with her book *Treasures of the Snow*. I read Edith Schaeffer's *L'Abri* years ago and also found it inspiring. *Drawn From New England* is a refreshing and easy-to-read biography about Tasha Tudor, the children's illustrator, written with fondness by her daughter. Though she isn't a Christian, she is a woman dedicated to giving her children a memorable childhood through a simple life in the country. *Stepping Heavenward* by Elizabeth Prentiss was written over a century ago in the style of a personal diary. The compatibility I felt with the author amazed me. It had to be a result of her honesty in dealing with the feelings and struggles we women experience while trying to live righteously. If you are a mother of a large family, you will laugh as you turn the pages of *Cheaper by the Dozen,* and you will be sure to find *The Story of The Trapp Family* Singers inspiring also. These are just a few suggestions.

For novels I recommend you read good ones. My small cast of venerable novelists includes Jane Austen, Charlotte Brontë, Nathaniel Hawthorne, George Eliot, and Charles Dickens.

Charlotte Mason advised the teacher to replenish her soul with a continual supply of ideas. "Never be without a good book on hand," she said. "If you will read and ponder your *Parents' Review* you will find that it stimulates your educational thought in many directions and keeps you from drifting into mere routine . . . Do not think this is a selfish thing to do, because the advantage does not end with yourself."[1]

"Whatever is down in the well is going to come up in the bucket," said a country man. Let's not let the water in our well become stagnant or freeze over. We mothers will make trouble for ourselves later in life by shutting up our minds in the present. What we need is to make Mother Culture a habit. We should continually take our minds out of the "laundry bag" of domestic perplexities, and give it a fragrant soaping, a rainwater rinsing, and a sunny airing in that which keeps it growing. Mother Culture is living the educational life *with* our children by learning alongside of them. But it is also learning and contemplating off to the side.

I like to explore poetry on my own. From time to time I borrow the same old book from our local library—*One Thousand Quotable Poems* compiled by Thomas Curtis Clark. It is filled with sentiments of valor, chivalry, virtuosity, courage, contentment, gratitude, vision, and other high ideals.

An Occasional New Plant

Every other year or so, even if we are renting our property, I like to plant something new. An occasional new plant has a way of lifting my spirits. It may be a garden flower I've rarely seen in anyone else's garden. This year I spotted a lone fox glove plant at a nursery and purchased it without hesitation—though some may consider that a frivolous purchase. For a hard-working mother this is not a frivolous thing, especially when she is known to buy her skirts at the Goodwill store. This purple fox glove will stay in its pot

in case we move again. Yolanda drew "Mommy's new plant" in her Nature Notebook, and I've included it on this page for your enjoyment. Just a few days later the "gloves" of the flower stem faded away and fell off. It was a fleeting bloom, but nevertheless it was enjoyed in its time and should greet us again next year. Why not start your *own*

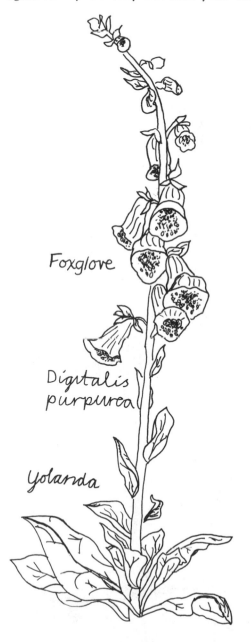

Foxglove

Digitalis purpurea

Yolanda

shell, butterfly, or decorative egg collection displayed on "Mommy's Shelf" next to the shelf of "Mommy's Books"? Let the family listen to "Mommy's Music" occasionally, or watch Mom and Dad play "Mommy's Game" of badminton!

Stimulating Conversation

Modern research has revealed that women use an average of seven thousand words per day while men use an average of two thousand. This is a significant difference. When Dad comes home from work he may have already reached the two thousand mark (especially if he works in administration) but Mother is still raring to go.

Thousands of brain scans have also revealed that when men talk, one particular area of the brain is used. When women talk, however, two separate areas light up bright green on the viewing screen (double trouble). The tests showed no exceptions. (Scientists were actually researching an entirely different subject and discovered the information about

the "talking area" accidentally.) Clearly a mother likes, or shall I say *needs,* some adult conversation. I felt isolated in suburbia for years. Wherever we moved there seemed to be a lack of community. Just a few generations ago, mothers used to talk over the fence while they hung up clothes or weeded their back gardens. People used to walk to the corner grocery and pass neighbors along the way. Now everyone drives into large parking lots and shops in malls.

How does one love his neighbor as himself if he never sees or bumps into him anywhere and everyone seems to have a full-time job outside the home? One of the ways I found to make friends was to invite people into our home. How about starting a monthly literature discussion group? I find conversations made comfortable by a shared love of good books and the relaxing intimacy of a home atmosphere stimulating, and the fellowship that results from such good conversations encouraging.

Another way I've satisfied the need to express myself has been to talk on paper. I enjoy writing letters to long distance friends. A blank book for writing prayers helps take the frazzle out of life. Open and truthful communication with God the Father can occur in moments all throughout the day, but a prayer journal keeps a record of what we are learning about the Christian life and how God is leading us and answering our prayers. I also have a Nature Diary. It is not used on a daily, or even weekly, basis, but when something about nature strikes me, I like to record it. Knowing I would probably be too busy to fill it with very many lovely paintings, I didn't let that stop me from writing about how I've cared for our suburban garden.

My Nature Diary holds many pleasant memories. One afternoon I heard the rattle of the red wagon and my attention was drawn to my children giving each other rides near our plum tree. Just at the moment that they passed under the tree, a breeze rocked the branches and the tree began snowing pink blossoms. The children stopped in their tracks and with raised arms and upward gazes did a joyful jig as the blossoms fell gently upon them. I wanted to remember the scene, so I wrote about it in my Nature Diary. I only make an occasional entry, but when I do, the children have a way of being included in its pages, because a lot of our time outdoors is spent together.

A Field Trip for Mother

When my husband, Dean, and I and the children took a walk along the New Jersey shore in May, I carried a shore bird field guide with me. I wanted to finally learn the accurate names for the sandpipers, sanderlings, and seagulls with whom I have been sharing the beach since I was a child. The excitement of spotting a pair of nesting oyster catchers made the long walk worthwhile. Just as we were inching our way closer to the nest—binoculars trained on the pair—the town's sanitation truck emp-

tied a drum of garbage and headed straight for us. I waved my arms at the drivers, mouthing the word "birds" and pointing to protect the brooding female, but they whizzed by within a foot of the brooder anyway. I watched them drive away, their heads thrown back with laughter. Because the male and female oyster catchers were frightened away a short distance, their nest was left exposed, allowing us to see a little gray chick that otherwise would have been hidden from us. Although this was a nature walk for Mommy, the children were curious. I didn't tell them to look out for the birds or give them an assignment. They were voluntarily sharing in *my* experience. Funny, my usual activity is to share in theirs.

Museum Moments for Mother

Dean and I visited the Delaware Art Museum when I heard that a collection of Pre-Raphaelite paintings on loan from England would be on display. Taking only one hour (for the sake of the children) we moved at a slow but steady pace from painting to painting. The rooms were dark and there was a quiet hush about the place. Each painting was lighted with its own lamp, like the jewels in a shop window display. But if you are familiar with the Pre-Raphaelite's style of using light, you will know they are illuminated with their own brilliance. It was so quiet that the only noticeable sound came from the corduroy of my husband's and son's trousers as we walked over the plush carpeting. We lingered, slowly admiring the vivid beauty of the paintings. The girls trailed behind us and did the same. We left with that feeling of refreshment that beauty— and the admiration of it—gives a person. The activity was mainly for my husband and myself, but we knew it would be a benefit to the children as well. John Ruskin, the great champion of the Pre-Raphaelite painters said, "Make yourselves nests of pleasant thoughts, bright fancies, faithful sayings; treasure-houses of precious restful thoughts, which care cannot disturb nor poverty take away from you, houses built without hands for your souls to live in."

I think it is a definite gain to the whole family when mother is able to take a little time to pursue her own interests, whether they be crafts, painting, sewing, gourmet cooking, a literature group, gardening, nature study, going to plays or ballets with her husband, bicycling, or ice skating. "I have no time for these simple pleasures," is the mournful cry. Yes, there isn't time for *all* of them. Think seasonally. One interest per season, coupled with thirty minutes of reading a day, may be all that is needed to keep up the Mother Culture and regain any lost enthusiasm for living. Billy Graham said, "Mothers should cultivate their souls, that in turn they may cultivate the souls of their children." If we would do our best for our children, grow we must. On our growth depends, not only our future happiness, but our future usefulness.[2] ⇥

A mother who wears many hats must find time for Mother Culture.

Questions for personal reflection or support group discussion

1. *A mother is a very important person to the family and to society. She takes pains to educate herself through "on-the-job" training. So much is expected of her. Why is it right to make time for herself? Why must she not say she cannot?*

2. *Explain how a mother can "cultivate her soul."*

3. *How can a mother simplify her life? Which are the less important aspects of her day? Is a gourmet three-course meal with homemade dessert necessary each evening? Does each child need to take several kinds of lessons outside the home each week? Must a busy homeschooling mother also be the leader of "Women in the Church?"*

4. *Think about what circumstances or what activity has refreshed and revitalized you.*

5. *Which time or times of the day is best for you to make room for yourself?*

Your Own Personal Reflections

Chapter Forty-Seven

....

Charlotte Mason Support Groups, Then and Now

When I first started reading Charlotte's writings, I was so excited about what I was learning, that with my husband's help I started my own evening group meetings. As I was relatively new to the state, didn't have a car or participate in field trips or lessons outside the home, I knew few home educating parents at all. It was in the year that *The Original Homeschooling Series* was published by Tyndale House and was first being purchased by curious parents that I wrote up a small message and sent it into the state homeschool newsletter. The note read something like this:

> All those who have read Susan Macaulay's *For the Children's Sake* and are interested in discussing Charlotte Mason's philosophy and method of education, or wish to learn more, call Karen Andreola for the time, date, and directions. Bring nursing children only, please.

A handful of interested mothers called, none of whom I had ever met. I was nervous and bashful about speaking in front of a living room full of sweet people, so my husband helped lead the talk for the first meetings. These were the first of many group meetings that were to follow. We have moved in and out of different states across the country since those first meetings; therefore, during the shuffle, I have not always had my own meetings, but have been invited to give little "talks" to other groups. Friendships were formed at those meetings that I still hold dear, although they are now carried on long distance.

In Turn-of-the-Century Lecture Halls

When I started my support group, I was carrying on a tradition that had begun many years before. Once upon a time Charlotte's views were expounded in lectures all over England and in her book *Home Education*, which was first published in 1886. Concerned people gathered to hear different aspects of educational reform addressed.

Who attended the gatherings? Parents with children of all ages, grandparents, teachers, headmasters of schools, and professors of universities. Some people did the speaking, others did the listening and learning. The many members of this group founded an organization in 1888 called The Parents' National Education Union. The PNEU information meetings were open to the public. These meetings upheld the educational ideas of the PNEU and continued propagating these sensible and helpful ideas to people who longed for a better education for children. Local chapters throughout the United Kingdom voluntarily helped to start schools that used Charlotte Mason's method. Charlotte's magazine, *Parents' Review,* tied the members together. For the first time, there was help for parents teaching their children at home. Today, too much responsibility for children's education has been pre-empted by the government, and the majority of parents seem to have a low opinion of education.

The teachers who worked in these schools were trained at Charlotte's House of Education. This training college was nicknamed "The House of the Holy Spirit," as its purpose was to train young women not only to teach their own future children, but to become teachers and governesses of other people's children, using Charlotte's sound Christian philosophy and method.

Some of the articles that have been published in my magazine are reprints of lectures that were read aloud many years ago at PNEU gatherings and later published in Charlotte's *Parents' Review.* The topics in Charlotte's writings were elaborated in many of these articles. My research into the old PNEU lectures has helped me with this book, although it has taken me many long hours to sift through this old material. Most of it is outdated and not applicable to us today, but oh, how useful the sifted bits of gold have been in helping me to understand Charlotte's ideas.

Home Meetings at the New Turn-of-the-Century

Since I am a veteran Charlotte Mason support group leader, I'd like to share what takes place in the meetings, and how I go about preparing for those I lead. I first choose a topic, such as Nature Study, Picture Study, or Education Is a Science of Relations. Then I read relevant passages from Charlotte's books several times and look over back issues of my *Parents' Review.*

For my presentation, several note cards keep me on track. I read aloud quotations from Charlotte's books that I have underlined and paraphrase other passages. My own collection of living books that support the topic of the evening is often passed around for "show and tell." Many times, however, I display examples of living books that can be found at the local library.

After fifteen minutes of presentation on my part, the actual discussion will last from forty-five minutes to an hour, as mothers naturally enjoy participating—sharing what they are doing with their own children, and

asking questions. Sympathy springs forth in the discussion as mothers in the group volunteer helpful advice and answer questions.

One mother may be particularly anxious about a particular problem ("My son can't do division"). Such problems can, if allowed to, dominate the whole evening's discussion. If the discussion strays too far from the scheduled topic, the leader should get the group back on track. In fairness to the group, the leader should be free to carry on with the material she has carefully prepared for the meeting. But in mercy, the leader, seeing that the problem cannot possibly be solved in ten minutes of discussion, may ask a question, such as, "Mrs. B., would you like to telephone one of us, or meet later this week to discuss your question in more detail?" *Homeschooling is so personal that sometimes the questions of an inexperienced home educator cannot be answered fully in a group setting.* Supporting this mother with prayer will also give her hope and lift her spirits. "Worry often gives a small thing a big shadow," as the Swedish folk saying goes. We don't wish to belittle a mother's problems, but there is a point at which the anxious mother will have to—in faith—wait on the Lord, do some of her own reading, and take courage to work out her problem within her home routine. The Lord is her ever-present help in trouble. (Psalm 46:1)

Handy Topics for Conversation

May I suggest you use *A Charlotte Mason Companion* as a handy guide to major themes for discussion in a Charlotte Mason meeting? If the members of the group are especially keen, they may wish to read the appropriate chapter before the day of the gathering, but this is not imperative. I welcome ladies to my home group who haven't read anything about Charlotte Mason. After hearing my little talk, they may be inspired enough to read on their own, but I do not hold anyone accountable.

If you feel inclined to start a group yourself, to surround yourself with kindred sprits, you may decide what, if any, preparations will be required by those who attend. After some months it would be helpful if another experienced mother could take turns giving the little talk and leading the discussion. The questions appended to many of the chapters of this book have been designed to be useful in getting the discussion under way.

Since publishing my own version of Charlotte's *Parents' Review,* I have received letters from subscribers from across the nation who have started Charlotte Mason support groups. In one area in Michigan the original group became so large—because of such interest in Charlotte's ideas—that it was split into three! A group in Dallas, Texas, has split into several subgroups. Some groups are currently composed of just two enthusiastic members. I have also received letters from isolated home teachers who live in an area of the country (or overseas) where none other shares their interest and enthusiasm for Charlotte's ideas—no kindred spirit has yet

been found. For these ladies, may this book be one form of fellowship for you.

It is well that a support group leader only take on what her energy will allow. There have been periods in my life as long as two years when I was unable to attend or hold meetings—times when I have had more pressing family needs to attend to, such as our household relocations. Presently, I hold a home meeting about every other month.

For me, a necessary aspect of hosting a support group is providing a warm, friendly, home atmosphere, and that includes refreshments, fine china, flowers, and lighted candles. Most of us live very busy lives, with little time for the amenities that are a comfort to so many women. An evening spent with kindred spirits—away from the duties and cares of teaching and household management, discussing matters dear to one's soul over a cup of tea—can be both a respite and a healing balm to many a busy mother.

A Pot of Herb Tea

First, my grandmother's blue and white cross-stitched tablecloth is gaily flung over the dining room table. Pouring cups of herb tea is a pleasure of mine, so I remove my collection of old and odd tea cups from their place of safe-keeping when ladies are expected to fill my dining room. It is gratifying when I can gather flowers from my own garden for the table, but if they aren't in bloom, supermarket carnations will do nicely. A few scented candles are lit. Light refreshments are served. Blueberry muffins, a bowl of fresh fruit salad, apple or pumpkin pie, chocolate biscuits, scones, cinnamon buns, or lemon cake with apricot filling are some of the treats my feminine guests have tasted. If a mother has been to a meeting more than once and asks if she can bring some refreshment, I say, "Yes, thank you very much." If it's her first visit, I say, "No, just come as you are, but maybe you could bring something for the next meeting."

Before the guests leave, I point out the basket of back issues of *Parents' Review* for borrowing. Before nine o'clock, I ring a little bell that rests on my buffet and thank everyone for coming. Although I've never read this in any book of etiquette, this is the signal that the evening has drawn to a close. With the last wave, I close the door, let the tea cups soak, hidden in a mound of bubbles, and get upstairs to bed before my bedtime.

I remind you that there is nothing so potent or powerful as a good idea. It is my intention for each mother to leave the meeting strengthened with an idea of Charlotte's clutched under her arm. A good homeschool can only run well on good ideas. ━┥

Your Own Personal Reflections

Chapter Forty-Eight

....

Two Testimonies — Mrs. Brown and Mrs. White Tell Their Stories

WHAT FOLLOWS ARE TESTIMONIES OF TWO LADIES who began homeschooling in midstream so to speak. In the 1930's Mrs. Brown used the curriculum provided by the Parents' Union School (P.U.S.), a correspondence school established by the Parents' National Education Union (P.N.E.U.) according to Charlotte Mason's principles. Mrs. White used the P.U.S. in another part of the world in the 1950's. May you find their testimonies an encouragement and inspiration as they share the advantages of following Charlotte's teaching methods.

Although we are separated from them by space and time, I consider Mrs. Brown and Mrs. White homeschooling neighbors, ones that I have come to know and appreciate over the years. Such is the wonder of the written word: it allows us to cross the boundaries of time, country, and culture and learn about people we would otherwise have no opportunity to meet.

Mrs. Brown's and Mrs. White's stories demonstrate that homeschools are just as unique as individual personalities. I think this is what Charlotte anticipated. I am certain she purposely made room for it in her curriculum plan. Our homeschools do not have to be just like Mrs. Brown's or Mrs. White's, but it is a pleasure—and one that is full of insights—to read about kindred spirits.[1]

Mrs. W. J. Brown's Experience

For four years now in my house we have had a Parents' Union School, and I look forward to at least another two years. We have followed the whole programme of the Parents' Union School up as far as Form IV—in which the average age is fourteen—from almost the lowest form. The reason that we did not begin at the very beginning was because I was unfortunate enough never to have heard of the Parents' National Educational Union (P.N.E.U.) and its correspondence school until my eldest girl was ten years of age. My adventures may be of interest because I started as a person absolutely unqualified for the work I was setting out to do. I use the word "adven-

tures" advisedly: I really was, to start with, quite as much at sea as any merchant adventurer of Elizabethan times; my ideas as to my actual route very vague indeed. My aim was to hunt for treasure. My reward has been great gain. As my experiences have been limited to my own schoolroom, will you please excuse what may seem a very egotistical use of the pronoun I? Fortunately the first person singular soon changes to the plural as I realize more and more that it was not I who was to teach but rather the children who were to learn.

What To Do with My Girls?

Four years ago I found myself faced with the question of "What to do with our girls," aged ten-and-a-half, nine, and six. We live in the country far from adequate schools. Until this time we had shared a governess with friends, but the elder ones had outgrown that stage—then came the problem of what to do next. On inquiry I found that a well qualified governess was beyond my means, and although I had always thought and said that I would do any bit of work under the sun rather than teach—well, we never know what we may come to, do we? When it became a choice of giving up a life in the country and going

to live in a town near a school, or staying in the country and teaching them myself, I chose what was in one way the greater of two evils and decided to teach them myself. I've been thankful ever since that I did—though, in the early days, there were times when my courage nearly failed. We "carried on" alone and unaided for a term with moderate success; then came salvation in the form of a letter from an old school friend of my own. Hearing of my difficulties, she wrote: "Why don't you do as I did? Join the P.N.E.U. and their Parents' Union School. If you can't afford it have a P.U.S. governess, teach the children yourself with the P.U.S." I wrote to headquarters at once and obtained all particulars, then spent the holidays reading three of Miss Mason's books which I had sent to me from the lending-library.

With Increasing Enthusiasm

The beginning of the new term came and with it the programme of work. When I read our programme for the few weeks ahead of us, my heart sank. Little did I think then that the day would come when I should seize each new programme with avidity. However, we set to work on this terrifying programme, following our instructions to the letter and, as far as it was possible for new disciples to do so, in the spirit. We did our work that term not too badly, the examination results were moderately good, and the children had come to the conclusion that they liked this school—the books were so interesting. From that day we have never looked back (though we have gone through some strenuous times). We have, for four years, done all the work set every term with increasing enthusiasm and better results. The day came at last when I was able to send the two elder girls to their [private] schools where they have taken places which compare, I am told, quite favourably with those taken by girls educated under much better qualified instruction. Any success we have attained is due to the fact that the Time Table and the Programme were strictly adhered to. Nothing short of real catastrophe must be allowed to interfere with the work. That is, I think, the one essential, but it is essential. It is absolutely necessary that the whole of the work set should be done—in fairness to the children. As one subject helps another, it is easier in the long run to attempt it all rather than to try leaving out bits of the work here and there as being either apparently unnecessary, or too difficult, or rather a bother to do.

Teacher and Taught—Fellow Students

We found that most of the subjects can be attempted in spite of the fact that the teacher may be almost as ignorant of the subject as the pupil! The secret of this method of attack is for the teacher and taught to work together as fellow-students. I never, from the beginning, took up the attitude of pedagogue. The whole of our enjoyment and success depended on the fact that we did the work together as friends and fellow-labourers. There is no need to fear that this attitude lowers the dignity of the teacher—it doesn't. When

the teacher really knows—the fact is obvious and the pupil accepts his decision as final, and when the teacher doesn't know, the method we adopted leads to endless interesting discussions and to strenuous effort to arrive at the solution of whatever problem may have arisen.

Let us take arithmetic as an example of a subject with which we were likely to have some difficulty. At school I was decidedly poor at arithmetic. I'm not brilliant now, but I have spent many interesting hours working at problems with my children—problems which baffled us, sometimes for days, but we were never beaten, we always solved them in the end—occasionally, it must be admitted, with some assistance from relatives and friends. It may be an unconventional way of doing arithmetic, but a child who has taken the trouble to walk half a mile with a problem, or written a letter to an aunt in the North of England to ask her to explain some knotty point, is not likely to forget the working out that she carefully follows on receiving the answer to her S.O.S. Our method, if unconventional, acted well. It kept us keen and interested in our work—and is the average child in the average school really interested in arithmetic, apart from the mark-gaining [grades] point of view? I don't think so. At school I hated mathematics, although there were marks to be gained. None of my children dislike mathematics, though they have no marks to gain. They are none of them mathematically minded, yet they do enjoy doing their work. The school standard for arithmetic in these days is high, but in spite of our unconventional methods we managed to keep up to it.

Find It Out

With an unqualified teacher, such as myself, in charge, the children develop a very useful habit of learning to find out things for themselves. After having met, several times, in answer to a question, with the reply, "I don't know, go and get an atlas", or "You'll find it in the dictionary," or whatever book of reference may be necessary, they soon begin to hunt out things for themselves without help or suggestion. They learn to use their tools for themselves to dig out bits of the treasure of knowledge—and it is these little bits of hard-won knowledge that stay with us and become permanent parts of our equipment. The facts that are poured out to us in lectures and in oral lessons and even in oral replies to questions, as we know, run through our head like water through a sieve; but the facts that we have taken trouble to find out we usually take the trouble to remember.

Eventually it became so that I was referred to not so much on matters of fact as on matters of opinion. As for matters of fact it is so simple to make a habit, during a history lesson, of having an atlas handy, and so with other lessons, we soon learned what books of reference were likely to be needed, and this was one of the ways in which we learned from experience that what the P.U.S. says is quite true. The children must have books—they are absolutely essential if the work is to be properly done. I think I have proved from experience that lack of knowledge is no bar to undertaking the work. Let the children do the work and educate themselves. I work alongside my children and enjoy it—getting at the same time a good education without much effort.

Some Music To Love

Another subject which we might take as a similar example is music. Now I am not very musical. I had, of course, piano lessons in my youth and, fortunately for me, was taken to concerts and brought up to enjoy music, but on the other hand, once I had left school I never played again, and certainly no one had ever shown any signs of pleasure when I had played formerly. Also I cannot sing a note—not a very promising beginning. Knowing that one road to happiness is closed to anyone who does not love and appreciate music, I decided that in spite of everything the children should have the opportunity of getting to know and love some music. Also music and musical appreciation lessons were on the programme and therefore the subject had to be attacked. Now I have always felt that many a child's early liking for music, if not exceedingly well-developed, must have been strangled in infancy by that dreadful half-hour of piano practice on a dark, shiny and forbidding-looking instrument usually kept in a room quite apart from the ordinary homely part of the house inhabited by the younger members of the family. For my children I bought what is known as a school room piano. These pianos have only five octaves; they are encased in unpolished oak—no French polish, nothing cold or forbidding about them, more friendly-looking altogether than the ordinary adult instrument in the eyes of the small folk. Ours lives in the schoolroom as one of the family. It belongs to the children and they use it. Of course we have a gramophone, a good one, and the remainder of our outfit consists of tin whistles at sixpence each—not to be despised. Have you ever heard how really recognizable the Rosamund Ballet Music or Wagner's Motifs can be on a tin whistle?

Then a music library of books and gramophone records began to grow—our great stand-by being Mr. Scholes' two books which are given in our programmes as books for study and reference—affectionately known in our schoolroom as "fat Scholes" and "thin Scholes." I think that a book with a nick-name must have proved itself many a time a real friend. Most of the gramophone records recommended each term for study we bought. With this outfit and by doing the work set for us each term in the programme we have learnt a tremendous amount and have had an indescribable amount of pleasure.

The proof of the pudding is in the eating. Has it been worth while? Have we had any repayment for the time, trouble and money spent? We have. Out of three children I must admit that there is only one who can produce real music from a musical instrument. But that is not our standard of success. That is the standard of the old days when visiting relations sat in state while Jane played her piece and Tommy recited his. No. A better proof of the success of the work is this. Last winter the children all bought their own tickets for the children's concerts at the Central Hall, Westminster, out of money which they themselves had earned. I had taken them to one concert as an experiment, and after that they insisted on going to the others as being the greatest possible treat they could have. Our experience with this subject may give, I hope, encouragement to someone who may be diffident about undertaking such a specialized subject as music.

Century Books—A History Notebook

There is a note on each programme saying that the children cannot do their work completely unless they keep Nature Note Books and Century Books. We have found the Century Books invaluable. In connection with our music they are a great help. Each musician as he is studied in his turn (one each term) is entered in the Century Book in his own century among his contemporaries, with the artists, scientists, writers, historical characters and events of his own period. This gives us the proper perspective which is necessary to the understanding and enjoyment of his music. The children who have this historical perspective do not, when listening to an air by Purcell, expect the sort of music they would hear if they were listening to Wagner. Thanks to the Century Books they put the

music against its proper background. To a child with a training like that, Purcell and Arne do not sound thin. They expect to hear a clear melody and know that these men had not the means of producing the vast effects achieved by Beethoven or Wagner.

You will see from what I have said that there is nothing here but what may be attempted by the veriest amateur. Of course if any instrument is to be studied a proficient teacher must be engaged, but as regards the training of the child as a music-lover, I think I may claim that our efforts succeeded. When I can hear my children whistling about the fields and garden the themes from the works of the great musicians, or hear them fingering out on their piano a tune that they have heard at a concert—and sometimes even working away at a tune they have made up themselves—then I am satisfied. The Time Table we have always kept most conscientiously, the number of hours spent in school varying, of course, according to the forms in which the children are working.

Wednesday Afternoons are for Nature

I have to admit that anyone who undertakes the education of her own children is taking on a whole-time job—it cannot be run as a side-line. When we started, our schoolroom hours were from nine o'clock to noon. Later on, as the children went into the higher forms, we were in school until 12:45. Now that there is only a lower form child left at home we are back to the shorter hours. In the afternoons we do handwork, reading, music, nature notes and drawing, and in the evenings we do a certain amount of reading also. I hope the hours do not seem discouragingly long. I have often wished them longer. There is so much to do and the work is so extraordinarily interesting that the time literally flies. Every

Wednesday we go for a nature walk and spend the whole of the afternoon in the woods and fields searching for treasures of very various kinds—all to be recorded later in our Nature Note Books. A frosty evening, too, will take us out for a sharp walk when we are working on star maps. Saturday afternoons are often employed in undertaking more distant excursions, usually with some special object in view, such as a visit to a museum in connection with our history lessons, or to see some building of historic interest.

Dickens in a Tree House

Occasionally our visit will be to some site made familiar to the children by their reading of a story book. In our family *The Pickwick Papers* can only be properly read in a little wooden house up an oak tree, by the light of a stable lantern and as the accompaniment to a feast of roasted chestnuts. I remember that those readings led us to undertake an expedition to see Mr. Pickwick's bedroom at "The White Horse," at Ipswich, where he had his adventure with the lady in curl papers. For the benefit of the youngest member of the party we carefully explained that Mr. Pickwick was an entirely imaginary character (she had a short time before that expressed both astonishment and disappointment on finding out that Julius Caesar was dead). After duly admiring the early Victorian furnishings of Mr. Pickwick's room, with its two great four poster beds, as we wandered through the maze of narrow passages in the old inn, a small voice asked, "But was Mr. Pickwick a real person?" I suppose to a small child of seven he must have seemed quite as real, in spite of our explanations, as the Romans whose actual dishes, spoons and brooches we had been to see on a previous Saturday. In the three years which have intervened since then she has gradually disentangled the real from the imaginary world enough to know that Julius Caesar's visit to Britain really happened, while the visit of the Pickwickians to Dingly Dell is the effort of a vivid imagination.

Please do not suppose that these excursions, designed to combine instruction with amusement, are a penance to the parent—I mean parents. They can be great fun. History and picnics, geology and swimming, go very well together. The instruction and the amusement often become so intermingled that it is difficult to tell where one ends and the other begins.

Home Education Away From Home

One of the advantages of a home-schoolroom is its adaptability as regards space if not as regards time. We spent the middle of the summer term many miles from home, but lessons continued as usual. At short notice we had packed a few clothes, a good many books, and transported ourselves to a cottage in the downs, near the sea. During our stay the mornings were spent dutifully over our books, and the afternoons devoted to outdoor studies. In long explorations on the shore and in the hills during a glorious June we did indeed find "earth crammed with heaven." Innumerable finds rewarded our search for treasures—birds, and butterflies new to us, lots of new insects of many kinds, and very many new flowers. Providence was very kind to us on this occasion—we had rain nearly every morning and glorious weather in the afternoons. Virtue was rewarded very promptly in this case.

The term we had whooping-cough we remember, as we lost so little time by being ill—another of the advantages of our home schoolroom. Whooping-cough ordinarily means many weeks' absence from lessons. One advantage a home schoolroom mother has over the mother who does not teach her own children is that she sees more sides of the child's mind and nature. So many mothers see their children in out-of-school hours only, and school hours take up a good part of the days.

Parent/Child Discussions

On the subject of the numerous points of contact which the teacher-mother can have with her child's mind, I have found that, working as we do through a very wide curriculum, it is inevitable that a vast number of subjects must come up for discussion. Many of these are subjects which are more easily discussed between parent and child than between class and teacher. It is often specially important that they should be discussed as soon as they occur to the child, otherwise the opportunity is lost and they may never

come up for discussion again—in the case of a child in class I can imagine that many of them may never be asked at all, either from shyness or possibly from discouragement.

The Bible and Shakespeare are in every school. These classics cannot be read without innumerable questions entering the child's mind. I think it must be much easier for a mother to explain and discuss questions which are naturally difficult of discussion between people of different generations and who have not had the same amount of experience of life. The children, I may say, never showed the slightest hesitation about asking any question that occurred to them on any subject whatever. The mother knows, or ought to know, what stage the child's mental development has reached—she can

enter just as deeply as may be necessary into the question according to the stage of the child's development. A mother who has taught her own children, or rather, who has read the same books and discussed problems and difficulties of various sorts, has an intellectual tie with her child's mind which strengthens as time passes. Some of the earlier ties are inevitably weakened—the tie of dependency disappears, but the ties of common interests increase.

An Extraordinarily Interesting Occupation

From the parent's point of view, in teaching one's own children there is much to be gained—more time spent in company with the children, an extraordinarily interesting occupation, a widening of one's own intellectual outlook as one is kept in constant contact with all the best thought of all time, and, in short, a thoroughly happy existence.

I suppose I ought to mention the difficulties we have met with. Well, I found that they were, in most cases, like the apparent hills one often meets in driving along a straight road—the nearer one comes to them the more they tend to flatten out, and the steep hills turn out to be after all easy gradients. Probably some people might consider that one difficulty would be that the child taught at home would suffer from lack of companionship. My experience is that, until the age of thirteen or fourteen, the family, with their immediate friends and neighbours, and their pets, fill their minds and provide plenty of companionship for out-of-school hours. In school they do not need companionship as each child works alone—my three were usually working in three separate forms—and of course in a P.U.S. schoolroom there is no room for the companionship which is sometimes considered necessary in order to provide competition in the work. We all know that in the P.U.S. there is no such word as competition, and, personally, I did not find that we ever needed it. The children enjoy their work and need no spur.

A real difficulty and a danger to be avoided in a home schoolroom is this: each home has a mental atmosphere of its own. This atmosphere surrounding the child influences its mind unconsciously. The mother who teaches is in danger of taking that atmosphere into the schoolroom with her and the children run the risk of becoming narrow-minded. The school child who leaves home every day leaves this atmosphere behind him: he hears questions discussed from many points of view and soon learns that there may be more than one opinion on most subjects. Once the danger I have spoken of is realized it can be avoided. The home atmosphere, the family tendency towards conservatism or enterprise, as the case may be, has its chance in out-of-school hours. In school hours a habit can be formed of approaching all questions in an absolutely open-minded way. All arguments for and against ought to be welcomed. It is only fair to let the children know that though one can and indeed ought to have an opinion of one's own, that opinion is not either necessarily correct or shared by the whole of mankind. It is a temptation to be avoided—that of pushing one's own pet theories on to the young expanding mind, however dear they may be to oneself. The child in a P.U.S. schoolroom has in the wonderful supply of nourishment provided for its mind—if left alone to choose its impressions and opinions—a real chance of developing an individuality of its own. It is, of course, far more of a temptation to a mother than to a teacher to interfere unduly and to aim at producing a replica of herself instead of giving the child a chance of becoming something different and, possibly, better.

A Tidy House

A minor difficulty is to keep track of the books we use. A rule which has to be more and more strictly enforced, we found, as time goes on and we reach higher forms and the books become more interesting, is this: "All books borrowed by adult members of the household must be returned before breakfast time. This rule applies particularly to those books borrowed surrepti-tiously after the owners have gone to bed." It is not conducive to an atmosphere of school discipline to hear a low-toned voice mutter to a hot and bothered sister, vainly searching her shelves for a missing book, "Try the table by daddy's bed." And that reminds me about the importance of each child having its own library. In our case we each had a plain oak book-case with several shelves, and, what I found an admirable plan, the lowest space turned into a cupboard by the addition of two little doors—this is most useful for all odd, untidy forms of books such as pamphlets, loose maps, etc. The possession of this book-case, where all the books can be kept by their owner in order, does encourage the child to love and care for its books.

Perhaps it occurs to someone that it is difficult to be, at the same time, both school-mistress and house-mistress. Most mothers are housekeepers. I am one myself, but please do not imagine that because I go into the schoolroom every morning at nine o'clock, I rival Mrs. Jellaby in my housekeeping methods. I have tried and find it quite possible to live comfortably with the minimum of outside assistance and yet to leave time available for a more intellectual occupation than the usual round of housekeeping duties.

May I suggest that in establishments where there is not a large staff the children can help very considerably. Work which is classed as dull and uninteresting by adults is often quite interesting to them. And of course household, like any other work, is, to some extent, interesting and enjoyable according to the spirit in which it is undertaken. At the worst it can be looked upon as means of making money. My children have always been paid wages for their work! This is a good plan. Their interest in the work is kept up and it gives them money to spend which they themselves have earned, and they have therefore a proper appreciation of its value.

Thanks to the P.U.S., our family has spent four very happy years. We can never feel grateful enough to the P.U.S. or to Miss Kitching for her kind help, and we do hope that other home schoolrooms may be encouraged to embark on a similar voyage of discovery. 🌿

An Adventure in a PNEU Correspondence Course, by Mrs. White

"What will you do about schools?" asked various friends and relations. The children were tiny, so I replied that we would cross that bridge when we came to it. We arrived at the bridge far sooner, of course, than we expected. And what, indeed, were we to do, living on a mountainside, 5000 feet up in the French Alps, with the village school far down the valley? Transport was erratic and, anyway, there was no road near our isolated chalet, which was embedded in snow six months of the year. It seemed we had the choice of a governess or a do-it yourself plan.

Even had a governess agreed to share our life, we did not relish the thought, nor would it have been financially possible. Yet I felt I could never take over teaching them myself. My own education had been very sketchy and the more I thought about it the more certain I was that I would not know where to begin, let alone continue.

We had almost decided on the unsatisfactory but seemingly sole solution of an *au pair* when, out of the blue, arrived a thick letter from one of my daughters' godmothers. Well aware of our plight, she had sent me the brochure of the P.N.E.U. (Parents' National Education Union). I had heard of the name but I had not known that there was a correspondence school (Parents' Union School). Their brochure told me that, through them, I really could teach my children. At last I saw the solution to our desperate problem and I was thrilled, though not quite confident in my own capabilities in such an important venture. However the P.N.E.U. motto is: "I am, I can, I ought, I will." I took this to heart and went ahead.

First, I had to fill up a simple questionnaire regarding my eldest child, then just five. When returning this form I sent the absurdly small school fee. Actually it was only later, when I understood the inestimable value of this school, that I realized just how small was the fee! In return I was sent the programme for five-year-olds in which were the titles of recommended books. Some books are obligatory for the programme, others are optional and can be chosen out of quite a selection. Charlotte Mason's *Home Education* is recommended as a guide to teaching. But I'm afraid that my first anxious glance at *Home Education* put me way back into a state of despair. Miss Mason's standards are saintly and her erudition is such that I began to feel myself quake as I used to when hauled up before the ancient, purple-gowned headmistress of a boarding school I once attended in England.

However, I remembered the motto and tried reading the book again. I saw that the archaic style was a large part of the stumbling block and perseverance really was rewarding. I wonder though if I am not one of many ordinary and busy mothers who might be put off entirely after their first attempt to read *Home Education*. I sincerely hope it will be rewritten one of these days. Well, there we were with all the tools—books and pencils, chalk and counters—and we started school.

Adjusting the Schedule

We had the right books, we did the right lessons but, oh dear—I did not seem to have the right approach. My big mistake was that, although I took the whole idea awfully seriously, I said to myself that as we were all so busy—my husband's office was in our chalet too—I would fit in the lessons some time during the day. For how could I keep rigorous hours? Anyway I was a little scared of becoming schoolmarmy.

In our first week we never once managed to complete the programme of the day. Obviously this was no good, yet I knew I couldn't keep to the P.N.E.U. programme hours. So I made our own which contained all the subjects but allowed the necessary breaks for looking after the baby, preparing lunch, and so on.

Although this may sound fairly easy, it was not! Our life was one of many interruptions and it was terribly difficult to achieve strict hours. It was essential that school came first. I was careful to allow enough breaks to cope with unforeseen events, but sometimes it needed a lot of willpower to keep to them. Perhaps that was our first good lesson learnt.

An important part was played by my husband, even though he was so busy and often away. He considered the children's education as all important and was extremely patient and understanding. Nearly all my time was taken up by the children and the household chores. Even my evening reading was in preparation of the next morning's lessons—I had to keep at least a day ahead! Later, my husband was our invaluable help over many geographical or historical questions and over Latin pronunciation.

Short Lessons to Start

A big mistake of mine was keeping lessons on too long. My eldest child loved number (the P.N.E.U. name for arithmetic) and wanted to go on and on with it. I love number too and would often continue the lesson for twenty minutes—that is to say double its time. The P.N.E.U. told me that ten minutes is enough for number, for writing, and for reading at the age of six or seven, but fifteen minutes for story lessons. It seems incredibly short but I learnt that longer lessons may cause inattention and dawdling, bad habits hard to banish. As the children mature and progress, I learned, the length of their lessons can increase.

Once a member of the P.N.E.U., I could write to them for help and advice. This is freely and expertly given by one of the staff and saves many a sinking into the Slough of Despond.

Move About A Bit

Yet another early mistake quickly corrected was that we were too immobile during lessons. Healthy small children are full of energy and it is important that they can move frequently. It is the child that should put away the paraphernalia of one lesson and set out the next. This makes for nice tidy habits too. A fidgety child is often helped by being asked to move: "Put this in the basket, please," or, "Would you lend me your eraser a minute?" This sounds rather silly and perhaps a waste of time, but it seems to repay in concentration. For my youngest, a boy with endless energy who found sitting still most irksome, we had a change of place for each lesson. During the early story lessons he used to walk about but his learning never suffered from this activity, quite the opposite. Little by little as the weeks went by he quieted down until, by the time he was seven and a half, he sat by my side quite still while I read out *Pilgrim's Progress* or *Tanglewood Tales*—admittedly his favorite books.

It is important to realize that children are learning from the moment they are born and therefore school lessons must come as a gradual change from play. Important, too, to keep the light touch. We had fun in our reading lessons with fat Mrs. Bun and her little B's with their round tummies. It was one of the P.N.E.U. books that were invaluable for the tricky job of teaching to read. Each child writing the five vowels on five fingernails works marvelously. Maybe a bit messy but an important lesson for mothers to learn is that, quite often, mess mustn't matter.

The French method, practiced in all schools, of enveloping both girls and boys in long-sleeved smocks greatly reduces fuss over mess.

Math

Next to reading I suppose number might be the most puzzling subject to teach, unless the child is keen on it. It was always one of my favorite lessons with the children—the eldest and the youngest having marked facility with figures—but the middle one had no comprehension at all. It took me ages to explain that the place of the figure was what mattered most—even longer to show that a zero was not necessarily nothing. It was by means of huge sheets of paper, colored chalks and counters and the "Street Game"—Unit Street, Ten Street, Hundred Street, etc.—that she eventually got the idea. From then on we went slowly through the excellent text books and, having firmly understood from the somewhat laborious beginning, she never looked back even though the progress was not rapid.

She sailed happily, at a slow but even speed, through fractions, decimals and the English monetary system. To stop my fingers from itching to help her through the sums, I took up knitting. Not in the P.N.E.U. programme perhaps, but some

occupation for my hands seemed essential. This knitting helped me to keep from interfering in certain other lessons, too. How right the P.N.E.U. is to tell us to let the child learn with his own faculties and not to intrude one's own personality between him and the subject. The importance of this becomes apparent in literature and art, particularly with older children.

Nature Drawing

With young children it can be a strain to watch them attempting to paint wild flowers, for example, and not to show them how a lifelike flower can be achieved in no time at all, thereby reducing their interest to boredom. At first I thought that this Nature Note Book that should be kept by the children was going to be rather a trial. I was perplexed as to how small children could either paint or write their own notes. They soon showed me that they could paint anything, from a bird to a fungus, in its true colors. Even if I couldn't quite recognize the subject they knew all about it, which was what mattered. To start with I wrote in names and places and any other information told me by them.

These nature paintings, the early blotches included, are the result of hours of fascinated study by the children. The marks of a hare or a fox in the snow, the flowers or vegetables in their gardens and every kind of insect caused interest and admiration. Much control was necessary for me to show the desired admiration and not disgust for some of the creepy-crawlies until one day, much to my surprise, I, too, let a spider walk over my hand.

Music and Art a Must

I feel about the picture study and the music lessons as I do about the Nature Note Books. They are sources of immeasurable riches to which a child must only be guided, being allowed to discover the treasures for himself. Each subject is associated with each other subject just as everything is connected with everything. Perhaps the best part of the adventure of learning is in finding that all one touches with one's thoughts, eyes, ears, fingers, or any part of oneself is a part of a whole—that we are all parts of a whole yet each a whole in ourselves.

I suppose I am one of the few mothers who had difficulty over Bible lessons, yet here, for me, was a tremendously exciting adventure. Having a mere scraping of knowledge of the Bible, as it had hardly come into my early life, I found it most bewildering. Each lesson took ages to prepare with the authorized version of the Bible, *The Little Bible,* and, for help with the Old Testament, two excellent books suggested by the P.N.E.U. For help with the New Testament, William Barclay's commentaries on the Gospels were invaluable, and we love a beautifully illustrated book called *The Life of Jesus of Nazareth.*

The fact of my learning together with the children almost from the first lesson had advantages, surprisingly enough. I was thrilled, it was a complete revelation to me and the lessons, which we took entirely naturally without the ring of the "clergyman's voice," were awaited eagerly. We reveled in the meatier Old Testament stories; we felt deeply and laughed, or cried, and always wanted to read just a bit more. The New Testament provoked entirely different feelings. I truly believe my children have learnt what is meant by "Love thy neighbor."

It seems to me that the most important of Charlotte Mason's beliefs is that children are people—they are themselves. Ever since my first child was born I have felt strongly that every child arrives in this world with every possibility in him. That we, the parents, are his guardians, the house he is sent to for help and guidance. I believe that we do not own our children in any measure at all and it is our sacred trust to do our best for them always.

Heroes and Antagonists

As much of a child's character is developed and behavior formed by environment, surely not only should children find as good a pattern as possible in those they live with, but also have great lives to read and think about. During their first terms the P.N.E.U. children meet many courageous, valiant, and good people in their story lessons. They meet wicked people too, but I learnt not to shelter them from the evil step-mothers of life. The desire to protect them is terribly strong but it is best they get to know the evils early, in fantasy, rather than only later in shocked reality.

Duty to Mankind

The P.N.E.U. takes the children further into the wealth of knowledge by nine years old when they extend their studies in a subject called Citizenship, which has a strong appeal to the children as it treats them as intelligent observers of character and situation. It is interesting to watch how each child, by about this age, starts to concentrate upon one particular aspect of man's development, whether it be literature, science, music or gardening! By nine the children are also ready for the complex and fascinating characters in Shakespeare's plays. The stories of the plays, however, are greatly enjoyed much younger.

Food for Thought

Charlotte Mason tells us that children are hungry creatures. Not only wholesome food for their bodies is required: their minds demand and digest an incredibly large amount and variety of knowledge. So what happens if good food for the mind is not available? Surely they absorb whatever there is, unwholesome as it may be: wretchedly-written books, comic strips, unsuitable television programmes, newspaper headlines, backdoor gossip, etc. Isn't this an explanation of the aimlessness and the wrongly-directed activities of some of our brave new young?

How sad it is to find people who cannot read. Not that they are illiterate, but that they are incapable of sustaining interest in any literature above the level of the glossy magazines, "grown-up" equivalents to Enid Blyton. I doubt that any child brought up on the P.N.E.U. system could fail to love books and to grow up as a discriminating reader. To begin with, the textbooks chosen for the school work are first class. They not only present the subject with clarity essential in the case of the teacher being untrained—they are often so attractive that they become the children's companions out of school hours.

I wonder how many mothers can recall those gray geography books, very compact with tiny print and stuffed full with facts and figures. Oh! What joy to meet the human stories of the little boy that lives in the Congo and the Eskimo child on Baffin Island and to learn about other people and places far more happily, and certainly, than by trying to memorize those eternal gray lists.

One of the advantages of being a member of the P.N.E.U. is receiving a copy of their magazine, the *Parents' Review,* every month. This is full of interest for all parents and anyone whose life is in contact with children.

Library by Mail

Another advantage is the Lending Library, where we found the nicest friend in the librarian, Miss Wareham. She finds the titles the children particularly want or chooses their books for them, and with her perception and experience, helps all round as far as books are concerned. It was amazing how she chose books to the taste of each of my children. It seemed as if she had known them for years. What excitement the day the library books arrive, how carefully they're scrutinized from cover to illustrations. Even the occasional grubby mark of a former reader has its attractions, a link between one isolated child and another.

Physical Exercise

A child that enjoys reading is never bored and my husband and I are delighted with our children's good taste in books, largely given them by the P.N.E.U. But the physical side of their education is important too. Children miss companions more outdoors where games are far gayer with several together. A substitute that appeals to nearly all lonely children is the friendship of a dog. Perhaps it is essential for an only child to have a pet of some kind that belongs entirely to him. In our home we are exceptionally fortunate in having superb skiing at our door and, for the rest of the year, mountains and valleys, forests and streams of great natural beauty of an endless variety of activities.

Crafts

Our handwork is often done outdoors. Things like bird tables and sort-of-wheelbarrows or chairs for bears are fun to make. We took great pains over our models. Those that transported water were the most successful. How important, here again, that the children should do the work as much on their own as possible. That the limited space indoors will become cluttered up with the examples of the children's talent is unavoidable and most desirable. One of our largest hanging exhibits is a "Time Line." We had a piece of plaster board measuring seven feet by nine inches which we covered with thick white paper. We drew a black line right along the top, marked out into equal divisions, one and a quarter inches representing one hundred years. Our dates were from 4200 B.C. to A.D. 2000. Under the Time Line itself we drew several parallel horizontal lines, which we marked off and colored in to show the length of the various civilizations and empires. From the horizontal lines we drew vertical lines of different lengths and colors to show the dates of kings, musicians, inventions, religious leaders, etc. We placed no personality or event on the Time Line unless we had learned about it. Again I found it difficult not to interfere and rush ahead with this fascinating picture of time. It is a great source of interest and gives correct perspective as nothing else could.

Narration

So many other excellent ideas are to be found in P.N.E.U. Narration for example, where the child tells back, in his own words, the story he has heard once. I am sure this is why the exams are no difficulty. In many small ways old problems are overcome. For instance, in dictation, those unhappily married pairs of words so often stuck in the mind forever are banned from the start. As soon as a misspelt word appears, the teacher obliterates it, replacing it with the correction. In this way one spelling only is seen and remembered.

Reference Books

Whether the "Look-it-up" system was brought into our schoolroom by the P.N.E.U. or by myself I cannot recall. I established it in the first week after my eldest child with her inquiring mind had asked me five tricky questions in as many minutes. The look-it-up system entails owning at least three reference books—a good dictionary, a child's encyclopedia and an atlas—as well as the textbooks. Obviously the answer sticks more firmly in the child's mind if the time and trouble are taken to look up the question, but I must admit that

that was not my original reason for incorporating this system into our school room.

You Can Do It!

The first attempts to teach in a home schoolroom may present difficulties that appear insurmountable. However, after a methodical system has been practiced for a bit, the obstacles appear less formidable. By the time a second child reaches school age the teacher is one of experience! Of course, a certain amount of extra organization is necessary with two or more separate programmes to follow, but it is wonderful how the older child cooperates. I feel sure that any determined and energetic mother who loves her children, putting their guidance as the most important task of her life, could undertake their education by following Charlotte Mason's principles. ✐

Afterword

In 1990, my husband Dean wrote and made overseas phone calls to inquire about the curriculum used in the old P.U.S. Forms—the original home study course started by Charlotte Mason—and it seems to have gone out of record. The reason, in part, is due to the fact that the books used in the curriculum changed each year. This was Charlotte's policy. It kept the teachers challenged and supplied them with a fresh outlook.

The P.N.E.U. curriculum is incorporated in the W.E.S.—the British Worldwide Education Service and the Bell Educational Trust. We have not been in touch with anyone who has used the curriculum in recent years. At one time, the W.E.S. mailed out a brochure with a picture of Charlotte on the cover and a little story about her as their founder. It does not anymore. The Charlotte Mason College has in recent years changed its name to St. Martin's College.

The Calvert School program is similar to that of the P.N.E.U., one W.E.S. board member told us. Due to the exchange rates, for Americans the P.N.E.U. curriculum would cost almost twice as much as the Calvert program. We are unable to give you an account of the merits of the W.E.S. and I have no current address for you.

I believe that presently there is no accurate form of a Charlotte Mason home-education-in-a-kit for sale anywhere. We can, however, gather from Charlotte's books and the old *Parents' Review* articles an outline of subjects studied, the kinds of books used, and the method of learning. This is what we have to go on. And it is quite a lot. With this knowledge, if you do choose a full-curriculum course, you will have more confidence to modify it to suit any particular ideas you'd like to implement.

In *A Charlotte Mason Companion,* I've tried to give you something to go on. I've given you a look into Nature Study, and History, and how to incorporate Narration, Art and Music Appreciation, Dickens and Shakespeare into your home studies. I've stressed the use of shorter lessons for the little ones, whole books, narration, as well as the acquisition of good habits and the training of the will. Aspects of education—as an atmosphere, a discipline, a life—have been discussed. Though I offer you no kit, I hope you have benefited from my research and have gained better insight into Charlotte's philosophy and method.

If you venture to implement Charlotte's ideas in mid-stream, expect a period of transition. Take patience. You will start to recognize little accomplishments, and then bigger ones. Home teaching is work—a labor of love. "What we sow in tears we will reap with joy," says the Psalmist (in Psalm 126). Praise be to Providence who has made it the kind of work that reaps such satisfying rewards. Believe in God, believe in your children, believe in Charlotte's principle for a gentle art of learning, and you will find joy. ➤

Your Own Personal Reflections

Chapter Forty-Nine

....

Parting Words

I HOPE THAT YOUR READING of my book has been a pleasant experience and that it has added encouragement and enlightenment to your endeavors to teach your children at home. I want your educational goals to be met and your dreams to come true within your precious family. When three important aspects of a Charlotte Mason education are attended to and worked out, I believe her vision of education can be realized. These three are discipline, a love of knowledge, and magnanimity of character. My purpose has been to make these three ideals accessible to you. My prayer has been that God will show you the way. May He increase your faith and give you courage to set out to do what is in your heart to do.

I find no adjectives adequate to describe my admiration for Charlotte Mason. Therefore I will tell you that I consider her as an adopted grandmother or great aunt. I don't know what I would have done in my homeschool without her. Here, with these parting words, I leave you with a quick overview of some of the main points brought forth in this book.

Profile

Charlotte's teaching approach aims at reaching the heart of the child, quickening his curiosity, vitalizing his mind and imagination, satisfying his need for play and physical activity, and providing him with opportunities for character development and good deeds.

Without apology she eliminated from the schoolroom those things that were detrimental to her educational goals: 1) dry textbooks (which dull the mind); 2) lecturing (which produces lazy learners); 3) prizes and grades (which encourage students to perform for superficial rewards); and 4) homework and long school days (which leave no time for outdoor activity).

She replaced these with intellectually nourishing, "living books" by the best authors, narration (oral and written), short lessons, and short school days for the younger students.

Students learned good habits (to pay attention, to concentrate, to do their best) and their curiosity was encouraged and in time grew into a love of learning. Through disci-

pline (provided by the good habits that became second nature) and knowledge (gleaned from the writings of the world's best writers and thinkers), they gained wisdom and developed magnanimity of character.

A young child learns the habit of attention by listening while his mother reads a good story. He develops concentration by narrating the story he has just heard. As he grows, and the habit of attention is established, more is required. He reads on his own, narrates from longer selections, and chooses special passages for his copybook. Always he is expected to do his best work. Through narration he acquires the ability to concentrate, recall, reason, analyze, and finally evaluate what he has read, what he has experienced, what he has heard and what he has observed. These narration

skills naturally carry over to his writing.

Charlotte was careful to choose the very best books. Among them were classic children's stories, good histories and biographies, plays, poems, nature stories and observations, and novels for mature readers. Textbooks were used sparingly and readers full of excerpts were eschewed.

What will be the result of using Charlotte Mason's principles? Our children will acquire a taste for the best works our civilization (culture) has to offer, and they will have the discipline and will–power to rise to the moral and intellectual challenge the modern age presents to them. They will be well brought up and well educated, and, if we have done our jobs well, they will continue to pursue their own education for the rest of their lives. ⇥

Keep in Touch

If this book has whet your appetite for a more in-depth study of Charlotte's philosophy and method of education, perhaps you may wish to own her original writings, which have been re-titled *The Original Homeschooling Series.* Because there has been a resurgence of interest in her princi-ples, my husband and I have endeavored to keep this first-hand source material in print for this generation.

To share your comments and/or to keep up to date on future publications, write:

Charlotte Mason
Research & Supply Co.
P. O. Box 1142
Rockland, ME 04841

Visit our web site:
charlotte-mason.com

It is well we should recognize that the business of education is with us all our lives, that we must always go on increasing our knowledge.

—Charlotte Mason

Endnotes

....

One of the shortcomings of this book is that all the many quotations (long or short ones) by Charlotte Mason have not been footnoted with their appropriate book and page numbers. Also, I beg your pardon for the inadequacy of my task at keeping accurate records in general of the source of many of the quotations which I have collected over the years. Unless otherwise footnoted all of Charlotte Mason's quotations come from *The Original Homeschooling Series*.

Chapter Three (What is Education?)

1. This chapter is my revision of an article appearing in the original *Parents' Review* in 1925 by Essex Cholmondeley.

Chapter Six (The Atmosphere of Home)

1. H. Clay Trumbull, *Hints on Child Training* (Eugene. OR: Great Expectations, p. 152.
2. This chapter is my revision and expansion of an article by M.F. Jerrold from the original *Parents' Review*.

Chapter Eleven (Inconstant Kitty)

1. The source of this chapter is found in *Formation of Character*, the fifth volume of *The Original Home Schooling Series* by Charlotte Mason. It has been abridged and revised for use in this book.

Chapter Twelve (Living Books)

1. Brewster, The First Book of Indians, Franklin Watts, Inc., 1950.
2. Holling, *Pagoo*, Houghton Mifflin Co., 1957.
3. Cody, Sherman, *The Art of Writing and Speaking the English Language*, The Old Greek Press, 1905.

Chapter Fourteen (Narration, the Art of Knowing)

1. Quoted in Trumbull's *Teachers and Teaching*.

Chapter Eighteen (Kernels of Wisdom)

1. Criticism Lessons: *Some Personal Memories of Charlotte Mason* by Essex Cholmondeley. Published in the original *Parents' Review*.

Chapter Twenty-One (Vocabulary)

1. Edward Blishen, from the *Parents' Review* article, "Very Remarkable Words."
2. Ibid.

Chapter Twenty-Four (Hero Admiration as a Factor in Education)

1. A large part of this chapter is based on a paper read by Lady Aberedeen in 1901 at the Fifth Annual PNEU Conference. Passages have been freely adapted.

Chapter Twenty-Five (Picture Study)

1. Parts of this article are freely adapted from an article written by E. C. Plumptre about sixty years ago for the original *Parents' Review*.

Chapter Twenty-Seven (Greek Myth)

1. Charles Kingsley, *The Heroes,* Robert M. McBride & Co., 1930. The preface was revised for this chapter.

Chapter Twenty-Eight (Once upon a Time—Fact or Fairy Tales)

1. John Bunyan, from the introduction to *Pilgrim's Progress*
2. G. K. Chesterton, *Parents' Review.*

Chapter Twenty-Nine (Approach to Poetry)

1. Emily Dickinson, "I never saw a moor . . ."
2. Tryon Edwards, *The New Dictionary of Thoughts; A Cyclopedia of Quotations.* (New York: Standard Book Co.), 1955.
3. Henry Wadsworth, Longfellow, "Paul Revere's Ride"
4. Monk Gibbon, the original *Parents' Review,* 1936 from which parts of this chapter is also based.

Chapter Thirty-One (Dickens From a Mother's Point of View)

1. Essex Cholmodneley, *The Story of Charlotte Mason,* P.N.E.U., 1960, page 4.
2. H.E. Marshall, *English Literature for Boys and Girls,* T.C. & E.C. Jack, Ltd., 1909, pages 656-658.
3. Terry Glaspey, *Great Books of the Christian Tradition,* Harvest House Publishers, 1996, page 158.

Chapter Thirty-Two (History)

1. Hillyer, *A Child's History of the World,* Calvert School, 1924, page xviii.
2. Armitage-Smith, Esq., *Parents' Review* from which much of this chapter is also based.

Chapter Thirty-Three (Nature Study)

1. Anna Botsford Comstock, *Handbook of Nature Study,* Cornel University Press, 1967, page 15.
2. G. Downton, from the original *Parents' Review.*

Chapter Thirty-Five (Neighborhood Nature Study)

1. Anna Botsford Comstock, *Handbook of Nature Study,* Cornell University Press, 1967, p. 558.
2. Ibid, page 559.

Chapter Thirty-Eight (Summer Senses for Country Folk)

1. The ideas in this chapter are based on "Senses in Summer," from *The Young Folks Treasury,* The University Society, Inc., 1919

Chapter Forty-One (Autumn Diversions)

1. Anna Botsford Comstock, *The Handbook of Nature Study,* Cornell University Press., 1967, pages 598-599.

Chapter Forty-Four (School Motto)

1. Information for this chapter was taken from an article in the 1935 *Parents' Review* by E. Kitching.

Chapter Forty-Six (Mother Culture)

1. Passages in this chapter are borrowed from an article published in Charlotte Mason's *Parents' Review* 1892, author unknown.

Chapter Forty-Eight (Two Testimonies: Mrs. Brown and Mrs. White Tell Their Stories)

1. These testimonies were first published in the original *Parents' Review.* They have been abridged for this chapter.